ANTIMODERNISM AND ARTISTIC EXPERIENCE:
Policing the Boundaries of Modernity

Edited by Lynda Jessup

Antimodernism is a term used to describe the international reaction to the onslaught of the modern world that swept across industrialized Western Europe, North America, and Japan in the decades around the turn of the twentieth century. In *Antimodernism and Artistic Experience,* scholars in art history, anthropology, political science, history, and feminist media studies explore antimodernism as an artistic response to a perceived sense of loss – in particular, the loss of 'authentic' experience.

Embracing the 'authentic' as a redemptive antidote to the threat of unheralded economic and social change, antimodernism sought out experience supposedly embodied in pre-industrialized societies – in medieval communities or 'oriental cultures,' in the Primitive, the Traditional, or Folk. In describing the ways in which modern artists used antimodern constructs in formulating their work, the contributors examine the involvement of artists and intellectuals in the reproduction and diffusion of these concepts. In doing so they reveal the interrelation of fine art, decorative art, souvenir or tourist art, and craft, questioning the ways in which these categories of artistic expression reformulate and naturalize social relations in the field of cultural production.

LYNDA JESSUP is an assistant professor in the Art Department at Queen's University.

Antimodernism and Artistic Experience

Policing the Boundaries of Modernity

EDITED BY LYNDA JESSUP

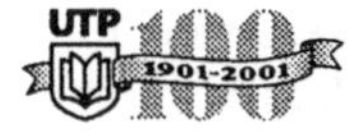

UNIVERSITY OF TORONTO PRESS
Toronto Buffalo London

Toronto Buffalo London

Reprinted in paperback 2014

ISBN 978-0-8020-4821-9 (cloth)
ISBN 978-0-8020-8354-8 (paper)

Printed on acid-free paper

Canadian Cataloguing in Publication Data

Main entry under title:

Antimodernism and artistic experience : policing the boundaries of modernity

Includes bibliographical references.

ISBN 978-0-8020-4821-9 (bound) ISBN 978-0-8020-8354-8 (pbk.)

1. Primitivism in art. 2. Modernism (Art). 3. Art, Modern – 19th century.
4. Art, Modern – 20th century. I. Jessup, Lynda, 1956–

N6494.P7A47 2001 709′.04 C00-931946-8

University of Toronto Press acknowledges the financial assistance to its publishing program of the Canada Council for the Arts and the Ontario Arts Council.

University of Toronto Press acknowledges the financial support for its publishing activities of the Government of Canada through the Book Publishing Industry Development Program (BPIDP).

Contents

Illustrations

Chapter 2: Performing the Native Woman

Chapter 3: The Colonial Lens

Foreword

This book has grown from papers presented at a weekend symposium held at the Art Gallery of Ontario, Toronto, in April 1996 as part of the OH!CANADA Project. This Project constituted a complex and controversial 'framing' through ancillary programming (including performances and fora for discussion as well as a range of small exhibitions) of 'The Group of Seven: Art for a Nation,' a major exhibition circulated by the National Gallery of Canada to celebrate the seventy-fifth anniversary of the first exhibition of that well-known group of Canadian nationalist artists. The National Gallery exhibition, organized by Charles Hill, Curator of Canadian Art, presented a representative selection of works by the Group of Seven and their adherents drawn from the sequence of exhibitions from 1920 through 1931 in which they pursued their nationalist vision of a uniquely Canadian art. In the accompanying catalogue Hill effectively chronicles the various ways in which the Group and their supporters positioned their case within the developing English-speaking Canadian cultural matrix. The ancillary exhibitions that were presented as part of the OH!CANADA Project questioned the breadth of the Group's vision and presented a forum for discussion of their current relevance, specifically within the multicultural context of present-day Toronto. The scholarly symposium, 'Policing the Boundaries of Modernity/Anti-Modernism and Artistic Experience' (organized by Lynda Jessup of Queen's University, Kingston) provided the forum that generated many of the essays that follow in this publication, and explored the international context of ambiguity around the concept of modernity within which the Group of Seven evolved.

It was an intense, exhilarating weekend. For me, the most pleasurable aspect of the proceedings was to experience the countless congruences arising from seemingly disparate subjects, points of view, and methods, all seeking a new understanding of received history, national myths, and too-rigidly defined structures of understanding. The sweeping questioning and restructuring of our institutions, which for various economic, practical, ideological reasons we have been undertaking over the past decade or more, has touched many of us where we work and live: in universities, in museums, and in the reading, thinking, writing, showing, that is the métier of both academic and curator. The experience can be painful but it is inevitable, for we are in the midst, I believe, of a great sea change in the way humankind understands and orders itself. Previously monolithic-seeming cultural entities are deconstructing all around us as entire nations and cultures convulse with change. In Europe and areas of Asia and Africa, this change is partially the result of mass migrations as old colonial chickens come home to roost. It is also partially due to the rise of powerful settler societies that were at first part of the colonial structures (and to that degree participating in their sense of homogeneity) but now share in the diversity of post-colonial migration. Canada is one of these societies. (The United States, the most prominent example, skews the model because of its historically powerful drive to create a homogenous, 'blended' culture of its own on the old-world model.) These societies are now striving to create a new basis for individual and community (and perhaps even 'national') identity, as the old order slumps and begins to crumble. The debate almost always implicit in this – concerning the relationship of race to culture to nationality – has also pulled aboriginal cultural history dramatically to the foreground. These are exciting times, and during that weekend I was pleased to realize that as scholars – as academics and curators – we are right in the middle of it.

One commentator remarked that to explore issues around modernity (modernism) and primitivism is to connect two of the most turbulent streams of contemporary cultural debate. To add the Group of Seven and issues of national identity to this debate is to create a veritable Lachine Rapids of discourse. The essays collected in this volume, the reflective, considered results of specific areas of research, offer a remarkable range of skilled pilots for the journey.

DENNIS REID
Chief Curator
Art Gallery of Ontario

Acknowledgments

The beginnings of this book lie at the Art Gallery of Ontario in the 1996 symposium 'Policing the Boundaries of Modernity/Antimodernism and Artistic Experience,' and many of its chapters have grown out of papers presented on that occasion. My sincere thanks go to my fellow committee members, Lora Carney, Dennis Reid, and Jim Shedden, all of whom were instrumental in making the event a success, and whose sustaining support of the project has made this book possible. I am grateful as well to Jennifer Andrews, Michelle Dupuis, Wendy Eberle, Cynthia Klaassen, and Nicola Spasoff for organizing the graduate student workshop at the symposium and for the countless tasks they undertook to make things run smoothly. For their generous support of the project, I also thank the Office of the Principal, the Office of Research Services, the Faculty of Arts and Science, the School of Graduate Studies, and the Department of Art at Queen's University. At the University of Toronto, I thank the Office of the Dean, Faculty of Arts and Science; the Office of the Vice-President, Research and International Relations; the Canadian Studies Program, University College; and the Department of Fine Art, as well as the Office of the Principal and Dean, and the Division of the Humanities at the University of Toronto at Scarborough. In addition to providing the venue, the Art Gallery of Ontario also provided funding, for which I am grateful. My thanks also go to the Social Sciences and Humanities Research Council of Canada for its support of the project. Annabel Hanson and Charles Prior provided valuable editorial assistance in the preparation of this collection and have my gratitude. Finally, of course, I would like to thank all the participants in the symposium and contributors to this volume for their interest and engagement in the project.

LYNDA JESSUP

ANTIMODERNISM AND ARTISTIC EXPERIENCE

Antimodernism and Artistic Experience: An Introduction

Lynda Jessup

This volume is a collection of essays that considers artistic production in the light of a response to modern social existence now described by the term antimodernism. A broad, international reaction to the onslaught of the modern world that swept industrialized Western Europe, North America, and Japan in the decades around the turn of the century, antimodernism has been defined by historian Jackson Lears as 'the recoil from an "overcivilised" modern existence to more intense forms of physical or spiritual existence.'[1] Critically explored many years ago by Raymond Williams in *The Country and the City* as a form of consciousness – a structure of feeling – that gave rise to a 'sentimental ... unlocalised "Old England"' among the alienated urban population of industrializing Britain, what has come to be known as antimodernism is still more familiar today perhaps to cultural historians than to historians of art.[2] In the field of cultural history, the term antimodernism is used to refer to the pervasive sense of loss that often coexisted in the decades around the turn of the century along with an enthusiasm for modernization and material progress. Thus, antimodernism was often ambivalent and Janus-faced, smacking of accommodation as well as protest. It describes what was in effect a critique of the modern, a perceived lack in the present manifesting itself not only in a sense of alienation, but also in a longing for the types of physical or spiritual experience embodied in utopian futures and imagined pasts. As such, it embraces what was then a desire for the type of 'authentic,' immediate experience supposedly embodied in pre-industrial societies – in medieval communities or 'Oriental' cultures, in the Primitive, the Traditional, or the Folk.

Of course, we now recognise that such rubrics as folk, primitive, authentic, and traditional are concepts. More than this, Robin Kelley explains in his article, 'Notes on Deconstructing "The Folk,"'

> terms like 'folk,' 'authentic,' and 'traditional' are socially constructed categories that have something to do with the reproduction of race, class, and gender hierarchies and the policing of the boundaries of modernism. 'Folk' and 'modern' are both mutually dependent concepts embedded in unstable historically and socially

> constituted systems of classification. In other words, 'folk' has no meaning without 'modern.' Unless we deconstruct the terms 'folk' and 'authentic' ... and see 'modern' and 'traditional' as mutually constitutive and constituting, we will miss the dynamic process by which culture is created as well as its relationship to constantly shifting experiences, changes in technologies, and commodification.[3]

The essays in this collection critically address the ways in which 'modern' artists used such antimodern constructs in formulating work they saw as responding to, or expressing, modernity. They examine the involvement of artists and intellectuals in the reproduction and diffusion of these concepts as ways of thinking about modernity in Europe and North America, and they assess the impact on those people implicated in the construction of such social and cultural categories as Folk, Primitive, Authentic, and Traditional. In doing so, they also address the interrelation of fine art, decorative art, souvenir or tourist art, and craft, interrogating the ways in which these categories of artistic expression reformulate and naturalize social relations in the field of cultural production. In other words, the essays in this collection bring to bear perspectives developed in social and cultural theory to the study of artistic production, giving shape to an approach to work of the period nascent in the discipline of art history.

This approach effectively situates the collection within the broader critique of representation and discourse undertaken most rigorously to date in disciplines other than art history. Anthropology, history, sociology, and cultural studies are perhaps most active in this respect, building on such formative works as Hayden White's *Tropics of Discourse* and *Metahistory*, Stephen Bann's *The Clothing of Clio*, Edward Said's *Orientalism*, and James Clifford and George Marcus's *Writing Culture*.[4] Art history has responded on 'a more subdued scale.'[5] At a time when other disciplines were already actively involved in the critique of authoritative knowledge, ethnographer George Marcus noted the intransigence of its dominant practitioners.

> Art history is by reputation and, I think, by conviction ... the most conservative of the disciplines that unapologetically constructs its authority in terms of a canon, but it is a visual canon, rather than a print one, as ultimate object. The critical canon that grows up around this tends to be more mystified and potentially dogmatic. Good and tireless historic scholarship participates in an aura of taste and connoisseurship – the scholar takes on something of the ethos of the collector. Value judgements go hand-in-hand with scholarly ones in a way that is much more explicit than in other humanities disciplines.[6]

It is perhaps appropriate to this discussion to note that Marcus's comments were made in response to a senior scholars' seminar at the Getty Center in 1989 that dealt specifically – and derisively – with an early internal critique of art history, Hans Belting's *The End of the History of Art?*[7] Since that time, however, critical contributions to the discipline – among them notably Griselda Pollock's *Vision and Difference*, Sally Price's *Primitive Art in Civilized Places*, and

Donald Preziozi's *Rethinking Art History* – have begun to foster larger debate, especially the reflexive critique of disciplinary authority implicit in the study of representation.[8]

So it can now be said that, despite its late arrival, such a critique is underway in art history, effectively advancing the belief expressed by Hayden White that the body of thought and writing that is 'history,' 'anthropology,' and 'art history,' in other words, 'discourse' itself, '*constitutes* the objects which it pretends only to describe realistically and to analyse objectively.'[9] Art history has registered a growing sensitivity on the part of its practitioners to issues of power and difference, to the relation of representation to social contexts, and to the formative role of institutions in the field of cultural production.[10] 'Critical historiographic accounts of the discipline,' as Preziosi calls them, have increased as well, making their way – often from the margins of the discipline – to mainstream scholarly audiences.[11] For example, many of the key works in the most recent generation of writings on the politics of the object are feminist critiques of art historical narratives,[12] while issues of race, ethnicity, and class have been hotly debated in studies coming from the well-established, though recently invigorated domain of museums, exhibiting, and collecting. In this area, traditionally focused studies, offering biographies of patrons, histories of institutions, and narratives of collecting, have been supplemented by the more overtly self-critical contributions made by art historians, alongside scholars from other fields.[13] Discussion has been advanced noticeably as well by those working at the boundaries of anthropology and art history; James Clifford's *The Predicament of Culture*, George Marcus and Fred Myers's *The Traffic in Culture*, and most recently, Ruth Phillips and Christopher Steiner's *Unpacking Culture* mark significant moments in the anthropological assessment of art history and its institutions.[14]

Antimodernism and Artistic Experience is designed to stimulate debate further by focusing explicitly on the making and maintenance of boundaries. In itself, such boundary work is not new to art history. Fred Myers points out in his contribution to this collection that the discipline's ongoing critique of Modernism is closely tied to notions of primitivism and the perceived boundaries between Western and non-Western expression. The only problem, he argues, is that the critique operates solely within existing disciplinary boundaries, feeding the Western notion of art as autonomous from other spheres of activity – the very notion that premised the development in the late nineteenth century of art history's now admittedly Eurocentric methodology. Thus, both the discipline and such critiques ultimately reproduce boundaries between art and non-art, Western and non-Western, while 'the promise of such debates,' Myers suggests, 'is ... to question the supposed isolation (autonomy) of art from other spheres of activity [and] to place modern art and aesthetic activities more complexly within the specific historical nexus of modernity.' Ruth Phillips advances a provocative example of the result, using evidence drawn from family albums and oral history. She argues the importance of such a seemingly commercial form of entertainment as performance (rather than plastic or graphic art) as the site of Native artistic production during the modernist century (1860 to 1960), one within which Native performers negotiated the dominant culture's representations of Indians as degenerate, premodern, and vanishing.

Her paper also suggests the interdisciplinary nature of the project as a whole. Reflecting Phillips's background in anthropology and art history, her essay is interdisciplinary in itself and, like the work of a number of contributors, addresses a range of audiences. As part of this collection, it contributes to a gathering of papers from a variety of disciplines, including anthropology, history, political studies, communications, and art history, that is suggestive of the broader context within which this study takes place. So, while the individual essays in this volume remain situated in the respective fields, debates, disciplinary or interdisciplinary spaces from which they have come (and within which they can still be read in isolation from other papers in the collection), they also provide, by their juxtaposition with the other papers, the provocative areas of intersection, tension and interest suggested by their common focus on antimodernism. The essays that introduce each of the three sections (by Fred Myers, dealing with modernism and primitivism; by Benedict Anderson, dealing with state formation, identity construction, and commoditization; and by Kim Sawchuk, dealing with modernist nostalgia and conceptualizations of time) are intended to expand this field of discussion further. They not only offer the reader a unifying perspective from which to approach each section, but also open the essays to perspectives generated by fields other than art history, and develop ideas and issues raised by the intersection and juxtaposition of the essays in each part.

Myers's essay appears first because it offers an introductory discussion of modernism and primitivism that can be used as an approach throughout the book, although it need not be applied throughout. In fact, the essays by Anderson and Sawchuk are intended on another level to disrupt such unidimensional reading and to further complicate the notion of antimodernism underpinning the collection as a whole. Benedict Anderson does this by drawing on the notion of 'antimodern modernism' – the idea that antimodern sentiment was usually a compromised expression that was rarely seen in its purest form as a rejection of the modern world. His remarks are based on a recognition that, in practice, antimodernist thought, action, and rhetoric represented an attempt to come to terms with modernity, not by rejecting it wholesale, but by moderating it through the inclusion of pre-modern physical and psychological zones of retreat. In its dominant form, this reflected a deep-seated ambivalence to modernity, which had seemingly overwhelmed traditional values and notions of community and replaced them with something akin to a civic religion based on individualism, material progress, technical rationality, and science. The antimodern response constituted a great variety of personal and collective quests for innocence, for authenticity, and for simpler, safer premodern spaces within the broader borders of the modern world. With the concurrent rise of the nation state, Anderson observes, 'on one side, the hunt was on for "authenticity," "roots," "originality," and "history," as nationalism's historically new consciousness created a radical break with the past. On the other side,' he notes, to underscore the essential ambivalence of the project, 'nations were everywhere understood as "gliding into a limitless future," developing in perfect synchrony with the breakneck speed of Progress.'

Constructing a Canadian case study from the papers in his section to situate his analysis historically within a larger discussion of the issues raised by the essays, Anderson then considers the implications of his observation: the involvement of settler nation states in advancing antimodern constructs as guarantors of what he calls 'national originality,' whether through support of nationalist schools of art that advanced their own myths of origination in folk and Native art forms, or by involvement in the revival or creation of folk art forms that aestheticized marginalized cultures for consumption by nationalist colonials and growing tourist markets, while maintaining the political and economic subjugation of those cultures by intellectual elites and their local collaborators. In doing so, he broadens the discussion to include other related areas of interest, whether political, geographical, or disciplinary, that enrich the essays in this collection and enlarge the possibilities for further investigation.

In keeping with this desire to be provocative rather than conclusive, the three introductory essays – whether taken individually or together – are not intended to be comprehensive, nor are the other essays in each section intended to be considered in isolation from other sections of the book. Thus, Elizabeth Childs's exploration of Paul Gauguin's modernist nostalgia appears in the same section as Ruth Phillips's essay. Childs's paper shares points of reference in existing debates about modernist primitivism with Gerta Moray's discussion of Emily Carr's work. At the same time, Childs's sensitive treatment of nostalgia resonates with other papers in the collection, including Matt Matsuda's analysis of the avant-garde revival of shadow theatre in fin-de-siècle France, Amy Ogata's exploration of the artisanal in Belgian art nouveau, and Vojtěch Jirat-Wasiutyński's treatment of Van Gogh's retreat to Arles. In other words, Childs's paper demonstrates the degree to which the sections of this book are only provisionally distinct. One of the advantages of such overlapping lies in the fact that Childs's paper can also be read in the light of Kim Sawchuk's introductory comments to the other three papers.

In her opening remarks, Sawchuk points out that the antimodernist's longing for another place and time was not only a desire for the simplicity of premodern pasts, the serenity of paradisial places, or the innocence of childhood; it also embraces what Childs describes as Gauguin's 'escape from Paris' and his subsequent effort to construct a place for himself in the margins between the Parisian métropole and modern colonial Tahiti of the 1890s. Sawchuk describes this longing as the search for an alternative space-time relation to that being inaugurated in the name of Progress. Fixed on an other-time, most often marked by nature's seasons and cycles and the social and cultural practices based upon them, it arose at least in part, she argues, in reaction to modernity's standardization of time, and (through the imperialistic imposition of standardized time from Greenwich out) of time-space relations around the globe. As 'sentiment –

and aesthetic practice' she argues, it 'expresses a complex critique of modernity from within modernity, a critique found within the politics of the day.' Finding support for her argument implicit in the papers in her section, Sawchuk then uses her discussion to contextualize them, offering at once insight into the final selection of essays for this book and space for thoughtful consideration of those preceding it. As she demonstrates, the relationships established or suggested among the contributions mitigate against easy categorization of the papers into distinct areas of concern. Her comments inform Ian McKay's discussion of the commercialization of nostalgia in interwar Nova Scotia. In turn, McKay's paper acts both as a touchstone for Benedict Anderson's introductory remarks on antimodernism in the age of high capitalist nationalism and as an illuminating counterpoint to those essays – particularly Michelle Facos's, Lora Carney's and my own – that look at identity construction in the realm of elite culture and fine art. McKay's discussion of the creation and commoditization of Nova Scotia folk art also stands on the Other side of art history, where, like Phillips's contribution, it serves to illuminate the discipline. The result, I hope, is as stimulating as it is rewarding: although case studies originating in the domain of art history still constitute the majority of the essays in this collection, by expanding discussion further than would normally be possible within the disciplinary boundaries of art history, the boundaries themselves open to critique.

NOTES

1 T.J. Jackson Lears, *No Place of Grace: Antimodernism and the Transformation of American Culture, 1880–1920* (New York: Pantheon, 1981), xv.

2 Raymond Williams, *The Country and the City* (Frogmore, St Albans: Paladin, 1975), 20.

3 Robin Kelley, 'Notes on Deconstructing "The Folk,"' *American Historical Review* 97 (December 1992), 1402.

4 Hayden White, *Tropics of Discourse* (Baltimore: Johns Hopkins University Press, 1978); Hayden White, *Metahistory* (Baltimore: Johns Hopkins University Press, 1973); Stephen Bann, *The Clothing of Clio* (Cambridge: Cambridge University Press, 1984); Edward Said, *Orientalism* (New York: Pantheon, 1978); James Clifford and George Marcus, *Writing Culture* (Berkeley: University of California Press, 1986).

5 Zeynep Çelik uses this phrase to characterize the response of art historians to the challenges posed by Said's work. See his 'Colonialism, Orientalism, and the Canon,' *Art Bulletin* 78 (June 1996), 202. Çelik's phrase is appropriate here as well. Robert Nelson makes a similar evaluation of the response of art historians to critical theory in 'At the Place of a Foreword: Someone Looking, Reading, and Writing,' in *Critical Terms for Art History*, ed. Robert Nelson and Richard Shiff (Chicago: University of Chicago Press, 1996), ix–xvi.

6 George Marcus, 'A Broad(er)side to the Canon: Being a Partial Account of a Year of Travel Among Textual Communities in the Realm of Humanities Centers, and

Including a Collection of Artifactual Curiosities,' in George Marcus, ed., *Rereading Cultural Anthropology* (Durham, N.C.: Duke University Press, 1989), 118.

7 Hans Belting, *The End of the History of Art?* (Chicago: University of Chicago Press, 1987). See Marcus, 'A Broad(er)side to the Canon,' 117–119.

8 Griselda Pollock, *Vision and Difference: Femininity, Feminism and Histories of Art* (New York: Routledge, 1988); Sally Price, *Primitive Art in Civilized Places* (Chicago: University of Chicago Press, 1989); and Donald Preziozi, *Rethinking Art History: Mediations on a Coy Science* (New Haven: Yale University Press, 1989).

9 White, *Tropics of Discourse*, 2.

10 The term 'cultural production' is taken from Pierre Bourdieu, *Distinction: A Social Critique of the Judgement of Taste*, trans. Richard Nice (Cambridge, MA: Harvard University Press, 1984).

11 Donald Preziosi, ed., *The Art of Art History: A Critical Anthology* (Oxford: Oxford University Press, 1998), 15.

12 In addition to Pollock's *Vision and Difference* see, for example, Norma Broude and Mary Gerrard, eds., *The Expanding Discourse: Feminism and Art History* (New York: Icon Editions, 1992); Katy Deepwell, ed., *New Feminist Art Criticism: Critical Strategies* (Manchester: Manchester University Press, 1995); Griselda Pollock, ed., *Generations and Geographies in the Visual Arts: Feminist Readings* (London: Routledge, 1996) and *Differencing the Canon: Feminist Desire and the Writing of Art's Histories* (London: Routledge, 1999).

13 The increasingly rich body of literature on museum representation is perhaps best suggested by such collections as Ivan Karp and Stephen Lavine, eds., *Exhibiting Cultures: The Poetics and Politics of Museum Display* (Washington: Smithsonian Institution, 1991); Marcia Pointon, ed., *Art Apart: Art Institutions and Ideology across England and North America* (Manchester: Manchester University Press, 1994); Daniel Sherman and Irit Rogoff, eds., *Museum Culture: Histories, Discourses, Spectacles* (Minneapolis: University of Minnesota Press, 1994); Sharon McDonald and Gordon Fyfe, eds., *Theorizing Museums* (Oxford: Blackwell Publishers, 1996); Reesa Greenberg, Bruce Ferguson, and Sandy Nairne, eds., *Thinking About Exhibitions* (London: Routledge, 1996).

14 James Clifford, *The Predicament of Culture: Twentieth-Century Ethnography, Literature and Art* (Cambridge: Harvard University Press, 1988); George Marcus and Fred Myers, *The Traffic in Culture: Refiguring Art and Anthropology* (Berkeley: University of California Press, 1995); Ruth Phillips and Christopher Steiner, *Unpacking Culture: Art and Commodity in Colonial and Postcolonial Worlds* (Berkeley: University of California Press, 1999).

PART ONE

CHAPTER ONE

Introduction to Part One: Around and About Modernity: Some Comments on Themes of Primitivism and Modernism

Fred R. Myers

The ensemble of these tropes – however miscellaneous and contradictory – forms the basic grammar and vocabulary of what I call primitivist discourse, a discourse fundamental to the Western sense of self and Other.

Marianne Torgovnick, *Gone Primitive*[1]

There is probably no topic in contemporary cultural study that is more rehearsed than that of primitivism. A virtual torrent of publications was unleashed in the wake of the Museum of Modern Art (MOMA) 1984 exhibition '"Primitivism" in 20th Century Art: Affinity of the Tribal and Modern.'[2] The articles (and books) are no doubt familiar to most readers: Clifford's 'Histories of the Tribal and the Modern,' Foster's 'The "Primitive" Unconscious of Modern Art, or White Skin Black Masks,' Manning's 'Primitive Art and Modern Times,' McEvilley's 'Doctor, Lawyer, Indian Chief,' and subsequently books such as Torgovnick's *Gone Primitive.*[3] In anthropology, Sally Price's *Primitive Art in Civilized Places* attends in a different way to the exclusionary practices of Western modern art's frames of evaluation. Recently, Colin Rhodes surveyed this burgeoning area in a book entitled *Primitivism and Modern Art.*[4]

The focus of the critical discussions – some might call them a controversy – has been to detail a linkage between the ideological structure of an aesthetic doctrine of Modernism and notions of the Primitive. It has been within these debates that some of the central features of the ideological functioning of art have been set forth. The promise of such debates is not merely to question the supposed isolation (autonomy) of art from other spheres of activity but to place modern art and aesthetic activities more complexly within the specific historical nexus of modernity. In this section of the present book we are exploring whether the figures of the Primitive and their deployments can illuminate the larger movement of 'anti-modernism' – 'the recoil from an "overcivilized" modern experience to more intense forms of physical or spiritual experience' to which this book as a whole is devoted.[5]

A brief review of the currents of the primitivism debate may help to clarify what could be potentially confusing about a set of terms that includes modernity, anti-modernism, modern art, and Modernism. I take it as given that Jackson Lears's use of the term 'anti-modernism' refers not to any aesthetic doctrine in particular but to movements of social and cultural protest against the processes of modernity and modernization. These processes have a significant linkage to developments in the arts, and the historically prevailing ideologies of artistic practice are born in precisely this context. The linkage between 'modern' art and modernization crystallized in mid-nineteenth-century France, where Haussmann's project of transforming Paris – the exemplary moment of modernization – is the subject of Baudelaire's ruminations about the role of art in managing what he recognizes as the contradictory dislocations of these processes of social planning, rationalization, and so on. Neither Baudelaire's call for a 'modern' art, while it addresses the contradictory conditions of 'modern life' and therefore could take the form of 'anti-modernism' in the sense proposed by Lears, nor the advent of various doctrines of modern art should be confused with the particular aesthetic doctrine of Modernism. For analytic purposes, I suggest we understand the lower case 'modernism' to embrace a range of artistic doctrines and practices that address the contradictory qualities of modernity; upper case 'Modernism' in art should refer to the specific doctrine of an autonomous art domain in which the appropriate problem for each art form is the investigation of the formal properties of its own medium. Blake and Frascina have written:

> By 'modernism' we refer to those new social practices in both 'high art' and 'mass culture' which engage with the experiences of modern life, with modernity, by means of a self-conscious use of experiment and innovation. Their engagements are sometimes critical, sometimes celebratory, sometimes ironic. The term 'modernism' should not be confused with Modernism which represents one particular, much contested account of modernist art practices, which stresses 'art for art's sake,' artistic autonomy, aesthetic disinterestedness and the formal and technical characteristics of works of modern art.[6]

Thus, Lears's anti-modernism is not anti-Modernism, as Gerta Moray (and others) point out. Much Modernism is critical of modernity, albeit complexly related to the latter's processes. The contribution of the primitivism debates to theorizing modernity has been the recognition of the role of the Primitive (external or internal) to constituting the modern.

The Primitivism Debate

The primitivism debate as it developed in the art world, however, must be understood initially as manifesting criticism about MOMA and its ideological construction of Modernism – by which, following Blake and Frascina, I mean a particular aesthetic doctrine rather than the whole of what I should call modern art.[7] In the recent attention to primitivism, one can discern two strands. The first strand is a Foucauldian critique of ideological incorporation of the non-West as

Other(s) – as in Orientalism.[8] This critique emphasizes how such representation traps or subjectifies Others and has defining power (as dominant knowledge) over their identities. The second strand is a postmodern attack on Modernism itself, its structures, and its codes, as subordinating or managing a threatening 'difference.'[9] This primitivism, as Foster argues, is an instrumentality of modernist cultural formation in the 'fetishising' service of sustaining and producing a Western identity.[10] This identity is confirmed in the articulation of what Clifford calls the 'Modernist Family of Art' (following Barthes's famous essay on the ideology of MOMA's 'Family of Man' photographic exhibition).[11] The 'Family of Art' allegorized in the 'Primitivism' exhibition at MOMA, he argues, emphasizes creativity and formal innovation as the gist of 'art' everywhere.[12] Thus, so-called primitive artists have the same formal motivations and interests as those artists said to be central to the modern avant-garde, making art in this sense a human universal. The focus of suspicion about this use of primitivism is aimed at the critique of the transcendent, autonomous aesthetic domain postulated by Modernism. Following such critiques, we might recognize that the emergence of doctrines of art as autonomous from other domains of social life is linked organically to the same processes of modernization that associate primitivism with the sort of anti-modernism that Jackson Lears identified as protesting modernity. This is the Janus-faced quality of modernity.

Thus, critics approached the MOMA show on grounds of the inapplicability of the Modernist concept of 'art' itself as a universal interpretive/evaluative category. The dominant notion of 'art' that came under criticism was the notion of an aesthetic experience constituted through the *disinterested* contemplation of objects as art objects removed from instrumental associations. This was a view entirely compatible with the formalist emphasis of prevailing art discourses at the time, but one whose hierarchies of value have been the subject of challenge.[13] In his influential review, for instance, James Clifford writes that:

> the MOMA exhibition documents a *taxonomic* moment: the status of non-Western objects and 'high' art are importantly redefined, but there is nothing permanent or transcendent about the categories at stake. The appreciation and interpretation of tribal objects takes place within a modern 'system of objects' which confers value on certain things and withholds it from others. Modernist primitivism, with its claims to deeper humanist sympathies and a wider aesthetic sense, goes hand in hand with a developed market in tribal art and with definitions of artistic and cultural authenticity that are now widely contested.[14]

With a different slant, Thomas McEvilley criticized the show for its effort to demonstrate the universality of aesthetic values in the service of formalist modernism as the highest criteria of evaluation. Such an effort took place through a censorship of the meaning, context, and intention of the exotic objects:

> In their native contexts these objects were invested with feelings of awe and dread, not of esthetic ennoblement. They were seen usually in motion, at night, in closed

> dark spaces, by flickering torchlight. Their viewers were under the influence of ritual, communal identification feelings, and often alcohol or drugs; above all, they were activated by the presence within or among the objects themselves of the shaman, acting out the usually terrifying power represented by the mask or icon. What was at stake for the viewer was not esthetic appreciation but loss of self in identification with and support of the shamanic performance ...
>
> By repressing the aspect of content, the Other is tamed into mere pretty stuff to dress us up ... In depressing starkness, 'Primitivism' lays bare the way our cultural institutions relate to foreign cultures, revealing it as an ethnocentric subjectivity inflated to co-opt such cultures and their objects into itself.[15]

The critique, then, is of Modernism's claim to universality and its suppression of 'difference' in constructing itself. What is selected is that which sustains Modernism's insistent identification of art with formal, artistic invention; difference is acknowledged only insofar as it conforms to this hegemony.

The conceit underlying the primitivism skirmishes has been the complex relation between a fascination with an exotic Primitive and so-called modernist developments in Western art. More deeply, however, the appropriation of the constructed Primitive Other has been seen as a theme not simply of something so ethereal (in many Western discursive formations, of course) as 'art,' but as a theme in the very ideological constitution of the 'modern.' The modern, after all, is not just the present; it came to exist as a category in opposition to the 'traditional,' and as such, the lure of modernization or modernity – of directed, progressive, rationalized social change – has been one of the most widely dispersed cultural formations. If the Primitive (kinship-based, traditional, customary, superstitious, religious, unchanging, group-oriented) must be overcome by modernization (rational, directed, individualist, functionalist, progressive, secular) then, ironically, this very modernity must be redeemed or critically evaluated by the Primitive. Modernism in the very broad sense – within the arts, then, varied as it is – may be seen as addressing the contradictory qualities of modernity. Primitives and avant-gardes, separately and conjoined, occupy this discursive space. Whether we are speaking of Baudelaire's artist as the hero of modern life (1964), or the figure of primitivity in Gauguin, or even Greenberg's (1939) construction of 'Modernist' art as progressively claiming its own autonomy (in avant-gardist critique of mass-produced kitsch),[16] I stress (however superficially and dilettantishly) we should take care not to lose sight of a connection between the opposition of 'modernity' and 'primitivity' on the one hand, and on the other, the special function of art to comment on the qualitative transformation of everyday life.[17]

Modernism and Modernization

'Modernity is a discourse in drag; it is always cross-dressed.' In other words, it must always reach out to appropriate what is alien in order to perform itself, to establish its difference. In this attempted appropriation, dislocation occurs and points of weakness emerge.[18]

What is particularly difficult to manage is the deeply contradictory quality of artistic discourses of modernism as an ideological formulation of modernization. A well-known use of the Primitive – Gauguin's Primitive, for example – has been in imagining an alternative to fragmented modes of being where art and aesthetics are divided from life defined by rationality, mass production, capitalism, and the commodity. One must acknowledge that historians disagree in how they understand the emergence of such a set of discursive practices – with art as healing and the artist as heroic individual. Baudelaire's concern with the 'heroism of modern life' and its lack of comfortable certainties is conventionally regarded as a turning point that coincides roughly with Courbet's development, after the revolution of 1848, of an oppositional art that questioned art's own status in society.[19] Others regard the development of alternative technologies of representation (for example, photography) either as freeing painting from its historical limits or as forcing it to find a new mission in its placement(s) vis-à-vis the social world.[20]

A common view is that high art takes transcendence of the fragmented, dislocated nature of contemporary life in the industrial era as a central concern.[21] In this analysis, primitivism is essential to the contemporary category of 'art.' The Primitive Other – as evidence of the existence of forms of humanity that are integral and cohesive, that work as a totality – functions not merely as the critical opposite to such an experienced world. Such a figure and its represented reality also permit the very characterization of the 'modern' as fragmented, and a sense of contemporary mass culture as 'spurious' and somehow 'inauthentic.'[22]

The trope of the Primitive continues to exercise considerable rhetorical power in the present, and not simply in New Age frameworks, as is demonstrated by the much publicized Parisian exhibition 'Les Magiciens de la Terre,' by the continuing boom in the sale of 'genuine' African art (that has not been in touch with the contaminating hand of the West or the market), and by the critical responses to Aboriginal acrylic painting.[23] Thus, while figures such as the Primitive, the 'exotic,' or the 'tribal' have offered a basis for challenging Western categories by defining 'difference,' they have done so principally, it would appear, within the ideological function of Western cultural systems. The 'different' as invoked in much of modern art history is supposed to be on an evolutionary line where the Other is Primitive – as before the Fall or before the Rise – and not just 'difference.' This is 'difference' managed in a particular ideological structure, as Clifford and Foster insist in invoking postmodernism's interest in pure difference.

Performing Primitivism

My own sense of the larger frame for grasping primitivism is that of intercultural exchange and transaction – a frame that can include the sort of appropriations that have concerned critics, but one that is anyway a charged social field. As one can see both from Ruth Phillips's paper and from much other work with Aboriginal Australian and First Nations people, the construction of primitivism has a particular salience for the production and circulation of political and cultural identities. Clifford has made this point eloquently, particularly with reference to museums.[24] However, much of the recognition and criticism of these constructions follows from the emerging indigenous political project that involves critiques of the binding doctrines of authenticity and cultural purity: 'We are not dead, nor less "Indian."'[25] By and large, critics of the varieties of what they see as the 'primitivist fantasies' paradigm have drawn on the Foucauldian association of power/knowledge to give theoretical shape to their efforts to discern the imposition of meaning and values on Native peoples.

The exemplary case for such formulations is the display of cultures in museums or exhibitions, a situation where Native voices, if not entirely absent, are more muted. Phillips points to what was surely a more widespread occurrence, namely the situation of *performance*: Wild West shows and the like. Here, she suggests, it is easier to see what we ought to have expected – that is, a more creative, self-conscious deployment of available categories in the actions and projects of historical actors. Phillips's paper certainly takes off from the recognition of this problem to show how some First Nations performers at the turn of the century were more than the shroud of primitivism would have suggested: these Native performers embraced primitivist representations of their cultural identities as allowing them a space of recognition. Her analysis shows that, indeed, the discourse of the Primitive as valuable could be re-deployed or, as the Situationists say, *dé tourné* towards other ends. I think this is a salutary move beyond the now-conventional gloomy fin de siècle overestimation of the power of colonial projects and classification, although here again it is also possible to be too celebratory of 'resistance' and 'agency.'[26]

These themes seem to be popular in the world of art criticism and art history, where they sprang up beyond the shadow of anthropology. Indeed, I wonder if the very figuration of subjectification and resistance, a figuration that is highly evaluative, hasn't a suspicious family resemblance to art's nineteenth-century arrogation of responsibility for the human spirit in the face of the oppression of modernization, capitalism, and industrialization.

Most analyses of intercultural performance do not address these events as forms of social action. Instead, the prevailing discourse about such performances, emerging from the discussion by many analysts, revolves around a view that indigenous people (Natives) should present *themselves*. This position, which grew out of an opposition to previous representational frames that ignored the exhibitionary gaze as defining, still tends to dismiss intercultural productions of identity as complicitous, as Phillips maintains. However, the case she presents of the Native performers and their willingness to participate has many correspondences elsewhere. Critics seem ambivalent about just practices, reflecting a continuing view of colonialism as absolutely determinative and Native peoples as merely victims or passive recipients of the actions of others. This corresponds to Clifford's discussion of the valorization of cultural 'purity' as an essential prerequisite for authenticity.[27] Thus, one response to Aboriginal Australian acrylic paintings among predominantly Euro-Australian art critics in Sydney and New York (about which I have written elsewhere) has been to dismiss the painting as an inauthentic commodification of Aboriginal culture.[28] As Phillips argues here, such judgment erases from our sight the ways in which aboriginal peoples use these discourses and opportunities to define and gain value from the circumstances that confront them: a double erasure.

It may be that a structure of domination will ultimately determine the outcome of individual initiatives. It does not follow, however, that one should accept such an *outcome* as representing the actions of the participants themselves. In contrast to the extremes of romantic resistance and devastating domination, other recent work in cultural studies and anthropology has recognized the intersecting interests involved in the production and reception of such events. It is particularly interesting to see the traces of a deeper primitivism both in the events Phillips discusses and in Martha Graham's construction of modern dance in opposition to classical ballet. The two figures – the Native American and the African American – stand for the 'natural'; they are closer to the earth, and more expressive of the primitive, emotional 'self.' This apparent appropriation is not necessarily unwelcome to Native performers as part of a Joycean 'modern' reinvention of themselves.

If one dispenses temporarily with the wish to evaluate (good/bad, authentic/inauthentic), one can recognise powerful forces of culture-making. What Phillips shows is particularly important, I believe, and is a pattern of more than minor significance in the histories of colonial relations. I do not mean by this to refer to the relationship articulated by Fanon in *Black Skin, White Masks*.[29] Colonized peoples – or, I should say, segments of colonized peoples – have drawn on Western portrayals of themselves in formulating their own responses, embracing a notion of themselves as 'spiritual,' as did the Indians of South Asia in complex relationships to the British Spiritualist (and Theosophist) representations of Indian religiosity as a counter to a corrupt Britain.[30] Such interrelation led Homi Bhabha to notions of hybridity to overcome radicalized notions of separateness and authenticity.[31] Often these responses are also part of the processes of state-formation, but that is a topic I should leave for others.

Primitivism's Particular Contexts

Elizabeth Childs's main consideration seems to be the dialogue, as she puts it, between photographic stimulus and artistic response in Gauguin's work. She sees Gauguin's relationship to colonial photography as one of disdain and dependence, a fitting match for the complex situation of colonial photography – 'one that simultaneously looked back mournfully to a mysterious idyllic world, never fully knowable by Europe, and one that saw in the present Tahiti the final moments of inevitable cultural decay.' These contradictory sentiments evoked by modernity are sensitively articulated by Childs's account.

In this respect, Gauguin is seen – as in Clifford's criticism of MOMA[32] – to be engaged in a denial of history. The result, as critics have noted elsewhere, is a denigration of the Polynesian present, a devaluation of it as contaminated or corrupt, and a derogation of those less 'pure,' less authentic Natives. The fetishising of purity and pure Otherness that Childs notes is clearly rooted in a critique of what modernity has brought. Her work helps us begin to trace the specificities of the institutions and circuits through which images of the Primitive move and are recuperated, although she doesn't ask (or answer) where these attitudes come from and why or how they are located in art.

For Gauguin, Tahiti appears as a fragment of an unknown world, an exotic paradise. It was a place in which – through contact with primitive Others – he could regenerate his art. These Others, it would seem, represented the vanishing origins of both 'them' and 'us,' origins that Gauguin imagined he could recuperate in his art. Appropriately and interestingly, Childs gives much attention to how colonial photographs of Tahiti 'managed' the coeval presence of colonial and native subjects and how Gauguin used and resituated these images.

Accordingly, her paper shows how the photograph – as much as any Tahitian 'reality' – offered Gauguin a space for fantasy and desire, a space in which the fetishization that is primitivism (according to Foster[33]) could be accomplished. Here modernity's ravages – in the form of an increasingly rationalized world – are at least partly met by nostalgia for a lost earthly paradise, a paradise allowed through the mediation of photographic imagery. These photographs are signifieds becoming signifiers, as in Roland Barthes's famous notion of myth.[34] They provide mastery combined with reveries. They are seemingly objective complements to private visions.

Childs's mention of mastery carries another trace of what can be understood about primitivism and the space for fantasy. In looking at the images Childs presented (both those Gauguin made and those he appreciated) in combination with Gerta Moray's discussion of Emily Carr, another dimension of the modernist (male) artist becomes unavoidable. This dimension is the gendering of modernism. Surely an abundance of critical writing about the male gaze and the prominence of the female nude should make us attentive to the gendered and sexualized positioning of the Primitive. The anxiety of the modern artist is also arguably an anxiety of sexuality; fragmentation of being is confronted with difference within as well as from without. As Marianne Torgovnick argued forcefully, the connection between primitivism and sexuality is difficult to ignore,[35] especially if the most salient Modernist painting is *Les Demoiselles d'Avignon*, with Picasso facing the threatening spectre of female sexuality. It is no accident that the figure of the Primitive that Gauguin seeks to inhabit and recuperate is principally the female.

The National and the Native

> Concern with otherness and its metonymic objects occurs in specific historical contexts, contexts that may be obscured by analysis of a more global nature and by such broad terms as Primitivism and Orientalism.[36]

Gerta Moray's paper on Emily Carr breaks down the generalized notion of the Primitive that is often deployed in analytic considerations. Instead, she suggests the value of tracking the figure of the Primitive through the distinctive circuits of artistic, regional, and national institutions and identity. The reception of Emily Carr's work is illuminating in this regard. As Moray writes, Carr's earlier paintings that deployed historically specific images of native villages were 'not welcomed by the settler society of British Columbia in 1913. Her work was neither supported nor purchased, as she requested that it be, by the provincial government for the museum that was being installed in the newly built Legislative Buildings in Victoria.'

The specificity of the contemporary, contingent scene of villages as historically present was not at all attractive within the region, because it signified the continued survival and adaptability of Native people. With land and land claims a burning issue between aboriginal and settler populations in the province at this time, one is hardly surprised. Instead, the Native presence Carr depicted is more successfully appropriated in a general form, as part of the rendering of a Canadian nation. Within this discursive space, the Native villages and totem poles are part of a timeless ethnographic present, a feature of the landscape, rather than a population whose presence is a barrier to development. Their romanticized images are then, as Moray suggests, annexed to the dominant settler group in the guise of a national heritage.

In turning to Moray's paper on Emily Carr, I am struck by the importance of the First World War – in Canada, the United States, and Australia – in leading these settler nations to pursue more actively an identity distinct from that of Europe. Often, this effort to escape the anxiety of European influence and to express a unique experience has resulted in an appropriation of the 'native,' the 'indigene,' as a component of an authentic national culture. To some extent, critical receptions of Carr's portrayal of Northwest Coast Native villages understood her work to have made this contribution. The workings here seem to differ from the ideological function of primitivism in the MOMA exhibition of 1984, which was concerned with making the Other legitimate the Western construction of 'art' in its most essential form, as formal and creative, as a basic human impulse. The appropriation of Carr by nationalist culture represents different temporal and spatial juxtapositions.

Moray characterizes Carr's work as participating in the antimodernism identified by Lears – that is, as critical of the modern ethnic of instrumental rationality that desanctified the outer world of nature and the inner world of self.[37] Carr's antimaterialism is said to have drawn on a nostalgia for her childhood days in a more pioneer-like British Columbia. Moray argues persuasively that Carr saw her project of documenting the Indian presence of her youth as 'an assertion of the value of Native achievements, skills and traditional culture.' Carr's work can be seen as an effort to re-educate the settler community in its attitudes, but it accomplishes this in ways defined by the dominant culture – that is, in terms of a hegemony that does not really accept 'difference.' These significations, which seem to have been resisted within British Columbia, have a different meaning when they are 're-placed' in the context of emerging Canadian nationalism in central Canada that, through the work of the Group of Seven, was laying claim to a landscape and asserting a passionately emotional and mystic communion with the land. Indians are stripped of their historical specificity and co-presence in this shift of region, and their images – like Gauguin's photographs – are converted from signifieds to signifiers in a Canadian myth. What is interesting is that, as Moray points out, Carr's Indian images and stories that had a strong edge of protest against race relations in the province ironically secured her recognition and fame in a more remote context, through the national cultural institutions developing under the domination of central Canada where they helped to revitalise elite cultural domination.

In processes of nation-building, a central activity of modernization, distinctive values may be conveyed to the 'native.' This occurs both by regional transposition and by class and gendered positionings – since the emerging hegemony is one articulated within the particular class/gender fraction of wealthy, white, central-Canadian men. At this point, Moray argues, when Carr's work is hailed within that hegemony, her own points of difference begin to assert themselves, to be discovered by her. Carr is not only 'appropriating the cultural production of aboriginal populations residing within the borders of the modern nation [state]; she is also from the region and she is female. Thus, Carr herself was figured by the Group of Seven as someone who had 'gone native,' someone who was in communion with animals and Indians, and with Nature herself. Apparently, it is not only the contemporary analyst who can see the gendered component of this primitivism. As we have come to expect with hegemony, this imagery is not without critical content. Carr's distinctive artistic identity is formulated and articulated in a series of paintings of great carved female figures. Moray suggests that Carr's continued painting of female figures in the guise of Native carvings represents an attempt to confront and assert her feelings about femininity, and to assert her sense of difference from the broader configuration – a site where Carr could construct an alternative identity for herself as a woman and as a Westerner. Here, Native imagery becomes her own, a forging of intercultural appropriation at a level of culture-making far more intimate than we usually imagine.

NOTES

1 Marianne Torgovnick, *Gone Primitive: Savage Intellects, Modern Lives* (Chicago: University of Chicago Press, 1990), 8.

2 See William Rubin, ed., *'Primitivism' in 20th Century Art: Affinity of the Tribal and Modern*, 2 vols. (New York: Museum of Modern Art, 1984).

3 James Clifford, 'Histories of the Tribal and the Modern,' *Art in America* 73 (April, 1985), 164–77; Hal Foster, 'The "Primitive" Unconscious of Modern Art, or White Skin Black Masks,' in *Recodings: Art, Spectacle, Cultural Politics* (Port Townsend,

Wash.: Bay Press, 1985); Patrick Manning, 'Primitive Art and Modern Times,' *Radical History Review* 33 (1985), 165–81; Thomas McEvilley, 'Doctor, Lawyer, Indian Chief,' *Art Forum* 23 (November, 1984), 54–61.

4 Sally Price, *Primitive Art in Civilized Places* (Chicago: University of Chicago Press, 1989); Colin Rhodes, *Primitivism and Modern Art* (New York: Thames & Hudson, 1994).

5 T.J. Jackson Lears, *No Place of Grace: Antimodernism and the Transformation of American Culture, 1880–1920* (New York: Pantheon Books, 1981), xv.

6 Nigel Blake and Francis Frascina, 'Modern Practices of Art and Modernity,' in *Modernity and Modernism: French Painting in the Nineteenth Century*, ed. Francis Frascina et al. (New Haven and London: Yale University Press in Association with the Open University, 1993), 127.

7 Blake and Frascina, 'Modern Practices.' This aesthetic is frequently identified with the doctrine of Modernism that, in Clement Greenberg's famous formulation, strips away everything nonessential to an artistic medium.

8 Edward Said, *Orientalism* (New York: Pantheon Press, 1978).

9 See James Clifford, *The Predicament of Culture: Twentieth-Century Ethnography, Literature, and Art* (Cambridge, Mass.: Harvard University Press, 1988); and Foster, 'The "Primitive" Unconscious.'

10 The sense of hierarchy and exclusion as defensive strategies underlies much of the critical work and gives weight to the notion of fetishism. One significant insight of postmodern criticism has been that formalist definitions are projected and circulated partly as *defensive* responses to a surrounding context – to responses, for example theatricality, entertainment, kitsch, and mass culture as threats to 'art.' Such threats are specifically addressed in the formulations offered by Clement Greenberg. See Clement Greenberg, 'Avant-Garde and Kitsch' (1939), reprinted in *Art and Culture: Critical Essays* (Boston: Beacon Press, 1961); Michael Fried, 'Art and Objecthood,' *Artforum* 5 (Summer 1967): 12–23; and Theodor Adorno, *Aesthetic Theory* (London: Routledge and Kegan Paul, 1983). Critically oriented postmodern theorists such as Rosalind Krauss, Hal Foster, Craig Owens, and others of the October group, as well as more straightforward sociological critics such as Pierre Bourdieu; see art's defensive strategy of self-definition not as a neutral fact, but as a form of cultural production itself, an exclusionary, boundary-maintaining activity, a hegemonic exercise of power through knowledge; see Pierre Bordieu, *Distinction: A Social Critique of the Judgement of Taste* (Cambridge, Mass.: Harvard University Press, 1984.

11 James Clifford, 'Histories of the Tribal and the Modern,' 166; Roland Barthes, *Mythologies* (Paris: Éditions de Seuil, 1957).

12 Ideological critiques have long been suspicious of such naturalizing and regard it as an attempt to provide legitimacy for current formations of power.

13 While not necessarily involved with primitivism, one of the main perspectives relevant to the criticism of this universalist theory of art comes from Pierre Bourdieu's work, especially *Distinction*, in which he emphasizes the extent to which disinterested aesthetic contemplation is a bourgeois class position or habitus that is exclusive of other classes. In *The Field of Cultural Production: Essays on Art and*

Literature (ed. and intro. Randal Johnson [New York: Columbia University Press, 1993]) Bourdieu made a significant attempt to understand the social and historical conditions that made possible the autonomy of different fields of cultural production, 'where what happens in the field is more and more dependent on the specific history of the field, and more and more independent of external history' (188).

14 Clifford, 'Histories of the Tribal and the Modern,' 170.

15 McEvilley, 'Doctor, Lawyer, Indian Chief,' 59–60.

16 Charles Baudelaire, *The Painter of Modern Life and Other Essays,* trans. J. Mayne (New York: Phaidon Press, 1964); Clement Greenberg, 'Avant-Garde and Kitsch.'

17 It is difficult to ignore the way in which High Modernism of the Clement Greenberg sort mimes or replicates the principal features of modernization: specialization of function and autonomy of one technique as forms of rationalization that free the self of historical residues.

18 Timothy Mitchell and Lila Abu-Lughod, 'Questions of Modernity,' *Items* (Journal of the Social Science Research Council) 47, no. 4, 83.

19 See T.J. Clark, *Image of the People: Gustave Courbet and the 1848 Revolution* (London: Thames and Hudson, 1973).

20 Arthur Danto, *The Philosophical Disenfranchisement of Art* (New York: Columbia University Press, 1986).

21 See Daniel Miller, 'The Necessity of Primitive in Modern Art,' in *The Myth of Primitivism: Perspectives on Art,* ed. Susan Hiller (London and New York: Routledge, 1991), 52.

22 The signifying locations of the Primitive obviously vary with the particular narrative of 'loss' presumed to have occurred with modern life. In a certain sense, Primitive supposed traditionalism – which violates avant-garde requirements for originality and self-creation – has had to be repressed to capture the organic opposite for modern fragmentation.

23 Benjamin Buchloh, 'The Whole Earth Show: An Interview with Jean-Hubert Martin,' *Art in America* 77 (May 1989), 150–9, 211, 213; Christopher Steiner, *African Art in Transit* (Cambridge, Mass.: Harvard University Press, 1994), Fred Myers, 'Representing Culture: The Production of Discourse(s) for Aboriginal Acrylic Paintings,' *Cultural Anthropology* 6 (1991), 26–62.

24 Clifford, *Predicament of Culture,* 189–214.

25 Some of the strongest interventions of this sort have been in Canada, as exemplified in Bruce Ziff and Pratima Rao, eds., *Borrowed Power: Essays on Cultural Appropriation* (New Brunswick, New Jersey: Rutgers University Press, 1997).

26 Lila Abu-Lughod, 'The Romance of Resistance: Tracing Transformations of Power through Bedouin Women,' *American Anthropologist* 17 (1990), 41–55.

27 See Clifford, *Predicament of Culture,* 189–214.

28 Arguments of this sort may be found in Tony Fry and Anne-Marie Willis, 'Aboriginal Art: Symptom or Success?' *Art in America* 77 (July 1989), 108–17, 159–60, 163; Paul Taylor, 'Primitive Dreams Are Hitting the Big Time,' *New York Times* 21 May 1989. However, there are many other examples. For a discussion, see Myers, 'Representing Culture.'

29 Frantz Fanon, *Black Skin, White Masks* (New York: Grove Press, 1967).

30 For insight into these matters, I am indebted to Peter van der Veer's work in progress.

31 Homi Bhabha, 'The Other Question: Difference, Discrimination and the Discourse of Colonialism,' in *Literature, Politics and Theory*, ed. F. Barker et al. (New York, Methuen, 1986).

32 Clifford, 'Histories of the Tribal and the Modern.'

33 Foster, 'The Primitive Unconscious of Modern Art.'

34 Barthes, *Mythologies.*

35 Torgovnick, *Gone Primitive*, 1–18.

36 Molly Mullin, 'The Patronage of Difference,' in *The Traffic in Culture: Reconfiguring Art and Anthropology*, ed. G. Marcus and F. Myers (Berkeley: University of California Press, 1995), 167.

37 T.J. Jackson Lears, *No Place of Grace.*

CHAPTER TWO

Performing the Native Woman: Primitivism and Mimicry in Early Twentieth-Century Visual Culture

Ruth B. Phillips

The more I dance, the more I want to interpret my emotions without limitation, to create a freedom of primitiveness and abandon. If only one could dance solely for art!

Molly Spotted Elk, New York, 1929[1]

I'm just an injun in the flesh parade.

Molly Spotted Elk, New York, 1930[2]

The desire of colonial mimicry – an interdictory desire – may not have an object, but it has strategic objectives which I shall call the metonymy of presence.

Homi Bhabha, 'Of Mimicry and Man'[3]

Prologue – A Penobscot in Paris, 1931

Picture this. It is May 1931 in Paris. At the Gare St Lazare a train from Le Havre pulls in and disgorges a jazz ensemble, the United States Indian Band. Striking up a 'lively tune' and wearing 'feathered head-dresses and costumes of American Indians,' as the Paris newspapers will report the next day, the members march to a bus which takes them to their performance venue at the International Colonial and Overseas Exposition.[4] A quintessential modernist scene, one would say, complete with internationalism, new music, embedded primitives, layered appropriations, and a subtext of colonial domination.

The official government photograph that records this event (fig. 2.1), taken in front of the replica of Mount Vernon built for the Exposition, does not let us halt the deconstruction there. It also testifies to other kinds of historical energies – of resistance, of hybridity, of contestation, and of 'travelling cultures,' in James Clifford's sense.[5] The punning double entendre of the word 'band' in the group's name, for example, is ironic and self-reflexive in a manner we think of as post-modern, but which characterised a range of modernist performance forms during the inter-war years. In 1931 this doubleness was manipulated to satisfy two potentially conflicting sets of desires: those of the aboriginal actors for employment, travel, and the affirmation of identity, and those of the exhibition commissioners to demonstrate the success of assimilationist policies and to appropriate the Native to a modern nationalist construct. Both, of course, also wanted to draw in the crowds. The two classic stereotypes of Indianness that were used as the hook – the Indian princess and the feathered warrior – created the requisite exotic spectacle. As many scholars have shown, these fictive images are projections of European desire with a genealogy as old as contact.[6] The transformation of Native performances into spectacles mounted for the pleasure of a white audience is nearly as old.

This paper argues that during the modernist century that lasted from the 1860s to the 1960s,[7] performance, not graphic or plastic art, was the available space for Native artistic production, and further, that performance offered the most favourable site for Native negotiations of the dominant culture's images of Indians as pre-modern, degenerate, and vanishing.[8] While commodity culture and new technologies of travel and reproduction tended toward the further hardening and broader diffusion of old stereotypes and new assimilationist dogmas about Indians, these same aspects of modernity also enhanced the mobility of the Native actor and therefore of his or her ability to intervene in racist discourses. In the early twentieth century, when visual fine arts were confined to static plastic and graphic forms, the added dimensions of performance – temporal, spatial, and vocal – offered better tools for Native intervention. The directness and immediacy of live performance confronted audiences with the fact of the Native performers' contemporaneity and bodily co-presence.

A notion of ambivalence runs through the literature both on fin de siècle culture and on the manipulation of stereotypes of the other. T.J. Jackson Lears has argued that ambivalence towards the social and material effects of modernity characterises the dominant White Anglo-Saxon Protestant culture of the United States. In Lears's formulation, this ambivalence expressed itself in an obsessive search for 'authentic' experience, a search that produced the Primitivist movement of the early twentieth century. Groups that were defined as tribal or pre-modern were mined for their expressive forms as part of what Lears has termed 'the artistic avant-garde's recovery of primal irrationality.'[9] As Robert Goldwater's classic study of Primitivism showed,[10] this 'recovery' unfolded as a series of progressively more radical anti-Academic revolts that sought to include medieval, folk, naïve, children's, and – finally – non-Western 'tribal' objects within the realm of 'Art.' Thus, although the roots of the appreciation of Primitive Art lie in an *anti*modernist reaction, Primitivism rapidly became the hallmark of *modernism* in early twentieth-century art. The promotion first of African and Oceanic arts and later of indigenous American arts during the first three decades of the twentieth century represents so sharp a turn in the path of antimodernist taste that the vector of modernism seems almost to double back upon itself. These conflicting impulses could only be reconciled by emptying the recovered or appropriated forms of their Native significations and filling them with Western ones.

A notion of ambivalence is also central to Homi Bhabha's discussion of colonialist discourses (including, of course, Primitivism). The stereotype, Bhabha writes, is 'the major discursive strategy' of these discourses, and 'ambivalence' describes the process by which the stereotype produces meaning as 'a form of knowledge and identification that vacillates between what is always "in place," already known, and something that must be anxiously repeated.'[11] 'Vacillation' and 'anxious repetition,' the hallmarks of ambivalence, signal the imperfect registration of stereotypical images with their objects. We *know* that the feather-bonneted figure is a saxophone player rather than an 'Indian warrior,' and the pleasure we take in the image is uneasy. As Bhabha explains, his theory leads away from analyses that seek to expose contradictions in order to dismiss them. Rather, it encourages a focus on the spaces and the slippages between images and their objects that allow subversion and negotiation.

The more detailed argument I want to make in this paper concerns the ways in which Native performers exploited the twists and ambivalences of anti-modernist sensibility through reverse appropriations of the stereotype, a process that falls within Bhabha's discussion of colonial mimicry. During the first three decades of the twentieth century white attitudes towards Indians were characterised by radical contradictions: social progress (for Indians) was defined as assimilation to modernity, while artistic progress (for everybody) was identified with the lost authenticity of the past. For many Native people, 'playing Indian' – which involved a surface denial of their own modernity – was one of the few readily marketable commodities. It was also one of the few ways in which they could express pride in distinctive Native culture that the dominant society would tolerate. Unmediated, these conflicting impulses had the potential to paralyse Native peoples' economic and expressive energies. The necessary mediation took the form of mimicry of the white man's Indian.

As we will see, in choosing to play the fictive or negative roles pre-scripted for them, performers also subverted these roles by revealing their shallowness and the arbitrary nature of the signs of Indianness. As exemplified by the United States Indian Band, the resulting amalgam was active and mobile, destabilising Victorian hierarchies of race and gender. In the last section of this paper I will examine two case studies that reveal ways in which successful Native performers of the 1920s and 1930s (one of them the woman who went to Paris with the United States Indian Band) used artistic Primitivism to negotiate stereotypes of Indian women. It will be useful to frame this analysis first with a brief discussion of the methodological issues it raises, and second with an equally brief account of the earlier history of Native performance and white spectatorship that lies behind Primitivist inventions.

Native Art in Art History: The Necessity of 'Visual Culture'

My decision to talk about Indian entertainers in the context of discussions about modernist and antimodernist art arises from considerations both of principle and of practice. I work, first of all, from an assumption that historians of twentieth-century art, like other academic practitioners, need to seek more pluralist understandings of their objects of study, and that these understandings need to incorporate the responses of aboriginal people to the representations of their cultures that were featured in this art. It is necessary to interrogate standard representations that depict Native populations as silent and passive victims of colonization, not only by locating the sites of Native action and participation, but also by problematizing Native peoples' apparent complicity in aspects of Primitivist discourse.

It is impossible, however, to recover a sense of the Native presence in early twentieth-century art history if we limit ourselves to the fine arts. An empty space gapes in accounts of the history of Native art during most of the modernist century; in standard accounts, the production of 'authentic' and 'traditional' art is perceived to end in the reservation period, while a contemporary art employing Western fine art media did not begin until the early 1960s. The traditional Native arts promoted by the Primitivists were defined as belonging to a tribal past, available for appropriation as a means of restoring authenticity to modernist Western art. As a corollary, contemporary makers of 'traditional' art were regarded as inauthentic if they were guilty of innovative incorporations of 'modern' Euro–North-American genres and styles.

Native participation in mainstream fine art was impossible because of economic and racial barriers that prevented attendance at professional art schools. The few self-taught Native artists who worked in Western genres and media and gained a limited acceptance (for example Ernest Smith and Frederick Alexi)[12] were classified as naïve painters whose work possessed largely ethnographic or curiosity value. As a result art museum collections hold almost no examples of painting or sculpture made by aboriginal people during the first half of the twentieth century. If the old linear and progressivist meta-narratives excluded Native art on evolutionist and racist grounds, the more recent, pluralist accounts must exclude it by default unless they renegotiate the terms of the discourse. It makes no difference, in this sense, whether the story being told is of the triumph of modernism or of the antimodernist resistance to that triumph – of Jackson Pollock or of Emily Carr. The Native artist has been written out in either case.

A partial solution to this dilemma lies in the recent movement in art history towards a redefinition of its field of study as 'visual culture.' In an essay on the interdisciplinary emphasis in recent art-historical work, W.J.T. Mitchell asks whether, 'art history [should] expand its horizon, not just beyond the sphere of the "work of art," but also beyond images and visual objects to the visual practices, the ways of seeing and being seen, that make up the world of human visuality?'[13] As we have seen, in the case at hand the question is more basic still: How can we understand Native people either as subjects or as objects within modernist/anti-modernist debates if we *don't* address these more generalised 'ways of seeing and being seen?' Working across disciplines in this way, as feminist art historians point out, acts as a strategy of defamiliarization that fosters the interrogation of long-standing assumptions about art.[14]

Visual culture encompasses the full range of visual representations that shape both social and artistic worlds. It includes not only the 'minor' applied arts, but also folk and popular arts, photography, film, television, and theatre. It can include advertizing and documentary imagery, cartoons, commercial lithography, and all forms of spectacle – expositions, parades, and circuses. Art, as a category, is located within visual culture according to a continuum of expressive forms in which aesthetic expression is more or less concentrated. There are a number of reasons why a visual culture approach is not only helpful but necessary to the study of images of the other (whether created by Native or non-Native) within Primitivism and modernism. As Bhabha has argued, the stereotypes that are the common coin of all such discourses are characterized by a fixity and a clarity that are closely associated with processes of visualization; the object of colonialist discourses, he writes, is to produce 'the colonised as a social reality which is at once an "other" and yet entirely knowable and visible.' Following Said, Bhabha identifies this visibility with forms of realist representation: a colonial discourse 'employs a system of representation, a regime of truth, that is structurally similar to realism.'[15]

The expanded field of visual culture has been addressed for some time by scholars in other disciplines. In her important 1973 dissertation on the American Indian in vernacular culture, for example, Cherokee scholar Rayna Green examined the iconography of the Indian not only in paintings, prints, and drawings, but also in cigar-store Indians, figureheads of ships, weathervanes, carousel figures, dolls, firedogs, advertizing, commercial packaging, textiles, pottery, and Wild West shows.[16] She argued not only that these popular and commercial arts reflected constructs of aboriginal people developed within elite academic and artistic cultures, but also that elite writers and artists were influenced by vernacular arts. According to her analysis, 'ideas about the Indian are conveyed by whites who insist on certain aspects of Indian personality, culture, and behavior and on certain aspects of Indian-White relations as (1) whites act them out; (2) Indians re-enact them for whites, and (3) they are projected into objects, verbal utterances, and actions associated with the Indian and with his image.'[17]

Green's choice of verbs ('act out' and 'project') indicates the performative aspect of this – and other – iconographic traditions. A number of recent studies by theatre and film scholars have further illuminated the nature of exchanges of images of Indianness among expressive genres during the nineteenth and twentieth centuries. For example, Rosemarie Bank documents several exemplary conjunctions of theatre, Native oratory, and fine art production during the 1830s, all of which prefigure the similar conjunctions that I will document for the 1930s. During the first half of the nineteenth century it was common to bring Native leaders visiting Eastern cities (whether by choice or under duress) to theatrical performances to witness the acting out of fictions of Indianness. They, in their turn, regularly used theatrical spaces to stage their resistance to the politics of the dominant culture (and the politics of representation). They delivered orations, sometimes in conjunction with a non-Native play, a panorama, or some other spectacle. The portraits painted of these visiting Indian leaders by Catlin, King, and other noted artists of the day are, in fact, artefacts of complex processes of visualisation and exchange.[18] The tradition of oratory linked to spectacle is at one end of a spectrum of performance forms, and it continued throughout the century. During the 1850s, for example, when Ojibwa historian George Copway was engaged to speak at showings of the 'Seven Mile Mirror' panorama, he fed the audience's desire to see a real Indian, but used the opportunity to speak against racism and for Native land rights. Iroquois poet E. Pauline Johnson, one of the most celebrated of the Native women performer/orators active around the turn of the twentieth century, exploited popular stereotypes of Indianness through dress and stage props as a strategy for affirming a positive Native identity. The Indian performer as artist's model was also a long-lived tradition. Esther Deer and Molly Spotted Elk, the dancers whose careers will be discussed later in this paper, both modelled for noted sculptors of the day.

Until the late nineteenth century Native characters in plays were played by white actors, but during the 1870s Buffalo Bill Cody, who was acting in semi-autobiographical plays about his years as an Indian fighter, introduced the notion of having Native people perform themselves.[19] Cody's more famous invention of the Wild West show in 1882 built directly on these theatrical experiments, moving them outdoors, expanding their scope, and heightening the effect of the play as simulacrum. The popularity of the Wild West show was paralleled in the theatre by the regular inclusion of Native acts in the vaudeville shows that had their origin in the last quarter of the nineteenth century.[20] With the development of moving pictures at the beginning of the twentieth century these same dramatizations and re-enactments were transferred to celluloid.

All these new performance forms are, of course, aspects of the expansion of mass culture that is central to modernity. They constitute a new phase in old traditions of imagery in which the stereotypes of Indiannness came to be inscribed with unprecedented vividness and to reach unparalleled numbers of people. 'No other single form of popular entertainment or expression which included the Indian had more effect on a particular set of Indian images than the Wild West show,' Green writes, 'It was, like the later movies modelled after it, a culmination of images in circulation for a long time before its inception. The Wild West show ... provided a dramatic visual dimension for those images.'[21] Furthermore, the Wild West show and related phenomena, were, as Green notes, accompanied by a mass dissemination of graphic representations that lingered on in the visual environment. All these examples suggest both the extreme permeability of the boundaries between graphic and performative representations, and the extensiveness of their inscription, made possible by the conditions of technological modernity, in the late nineteenth century.

Methodological questions of 'interdisciplinarity' and 'visual culture' are, of course, rarefied academic concerns. It is equally important to ask how a visual culture approach aligns itself with aboriginal concepts and practices. How, in other words, might performers themselves have regarded the space offered by performance for aesthetic creativity and expressive behaviour? The detailed examples to be presented in the last sections of this paper will suggest some answers to this question, but it is important also to make the more general point that visual culture is merely a new term with which to describe an already existing integration of modes of aesthetic expression in traditional Native life. In aboriginal societies, performance was and is a complex mode in which dance, song, instrumentation, body decoration, and dress combine to express spiritual and social beliefs and values. Lakota artist and historian Arthur Amiotte defines the role of aesthetic elements in the Plains Sun Dance, for example, as 'sacred acts':

> music, dance, visual-arts compositions, and projection of one's will into the heart of the experience of relationship ... Through the use of these forms in ritual, tribal people interact: they express, celebrate, and reaffirm their relationship to the originating powers of their very being and their particular roles in the great cyclical potency that governs all dimensions of the environment that sustains them.[22]

Native dances, understood in these terms as complex performances, have for centuries been (and remain today in the modern powwow) the most important modes for the expression of identity. There is a sense in which the individual becomes fully known only through his or her dance.

A Brief History of Native Dance as Performance

From the time of Jacques Cartier to Queen Elizabeth II, Europeans have been greeted by Native people with dance performances. During the initial centuries of contact in eastern North America, the region from which my examples will be drawn, the structures of interrelationship were governed by military alliances and the fur trade. Both because of the occasions which drew Native and European together, and because of their own cultural predisposition to privilege military display, visitors to North America became far more familiar with war dances than with the many other kinds of Native ritual and social dance. During campaigns, and at the annual distributions of treaty gifts, soldiers regularly watched dances performed in preparation for and in celebration of military engagements. The Italian explorer Gian Costantino Beltrami reported that Great Lakes Ojibwa in the 1820s were accustomed to perform war dances for the Indian agent whenever they paid him a formal visit.[23] And in 1820, Henry Schoolcraft described a visit from a group of Ojibwa who came 'to show their skill in dancing, upon which they all pride themselves, and spent some time in this amusement, which is also done as a mark of respect.'[24]

As late as the 1820s warriors from Kahnawake continued the custom of coming into Montreal to acknowledge the receipt of their annual gifts. One observer, a Colonel Leslie, described the event in detail:

> This afforded us an opportunity of witnessing the extraordinary sight of the savage exhibition of an Indian dance in the public streets – wearing paint ... agreeable to

their wonted usage previous to preparing to attack their enemies in battle ... they proceeded to the house of the General Superintendent, in front of which they commenced their fantastic exhibition, by dancing and capering through fanciful evolutions in an odd style. Their principal movement consisted of a kind of measured stamping with both feet, and at the same time turning their bodies to and from, to right and left, and all brandishing their weapons and flourishing their sabres in the air ...[25]

The responses of the English traveller and art critic Anna Jameson to Anishnabek dances were similar. While she was visiting Mackinac Island, Michigan, in 1838, a dance was arranged, 'for [her] particular amusement.' In her travel book she demonized the Native dancers by transposing the scene into the conventional metaphorical language of Eden and the Fall:

We had taken our place on an elevated platform behind the house ... The dazzling blue lake and its islands [were] at our feet. Soft and elysian in its beauty was all around. And when these wild and more than half naked figures came up, painted, and flourishing clubs, tomahawks, javelines, it was like a masque of fiends breaking into paradise ... The whole exhibition was that of barbarism, that it was at least complete in its way, and for a time I looked on with curiosity and interest ...[26]

Throughout the nineteenth century, Euro-North American 'looking on' usually conformed to this pattern of reception. Like Mrs Jameson, other visitors sought out the spectacle of Native dances and arranged for special performances, but responded with 'curiosity and interest' rather than admiration. A similar aura of detached inspection informs several early nineteenth-century paintings that depict European spectators viewing Native dances. The earliest such scenes are those painted about 1805 by George Heriot at Lorette (Wendake) outside Quebec. He depicts the Huron performing 'their several dances, descriptive of their manner of going to war'[27] for the entertainment of British officers and their wives. William Berczy's *Indian Dance at Amherstburg* (fig. 2.2) of about 1825 depicts a war dance performed near modern day Windsor by a group of Anishnabek. In the compositions of Heriot and Berczy, the European spectators, interpolated between the real space of the viewer and the pictorial space occupied by the Native dancers, become the dominant, activating presence. The inscription of the paintings is that of the objectifying power of the European gaze.

In most paintings of Indian dances, however, no spectators are shown (as, for example, in Rudolf von Steiger's 1815 painting of an Ojibwa deputation visiting the British commander in Upper Canada).[28] After the 1820s, as white settlement rapidly altered the demographics of eastern North America, indications of the staged contexts of Indian performance were systematically removed from the pictorial space in order to assert the authenticity of the represented scenes. Artists such as George Catlin and Paul Kane, convinced of the inevitable disappearance of Native people, systematically eliminated references to non-Native spectators in order to capture the illusion of primordial, pre-contact Native life. The origins of the antimodernist romanticization of Native peoples lie in such images, and it is therefore all the more important, in establishing the utility of a visual culture model to the understanding of purely pictorial representation, to remember when we look at them that these images are records of staged or recreated performances, and that the non-Native spectators were, in fact, just outside the frame.

As long as Native–European relations were based on mutual recognitions of sovereignty, Native dance performances for white spectators functioned as ritualized gestures of respect and/or self-presentation (fig. 2.3). However, as the pace of colonial settlement and economic dispossession increased, and as Native economies deteriorated, dancing was increasingly undertaken for pay as one of a number of strategies for survival. The commodification of performance occurred in some areas with a startling suddenness that matched the rapidity with which Native people were dispossessed of land and way of life during the nineteenth century. In 1828, for example, two Onondaga Iroquois chiefs spoke and performed at Peale's Museum in New York City – an event that would have been hard to imagine before the traumatic defeat and demoralization of the Iroquois nations following the American Revolution.[29] Economic need, it is clear, lay behind such early performances. Thomas McKenney, travelling in the central Great Lakes in 1827, commented sardonically that he had viewed a Chippewa 'pipe dance, a dance of ceremony, or rather, as it ought to be called, *a begging dance*. Their object was to get money. We put out a mocock filled with tobacco, and some whisky.'[30]

During the second half of the nineteenth century the nature of performance was further affected by the development of a modern tourist industry along the St Lawrence–Great Lakes corridor. The rapid growth of tourism, as Patricia Jasen has shown, was directly tied to the growth of cities and to a nostalgic desire for lost experiences of nature.[31] We know that modernity has arrived when we find that an 1863 article in the Toronto *Globe* recommended steamboat excursions to the Thousand Islands to its readers as a way 'to separate themselves from the many cares which environ the accustomed walks of life.'[32] Indians were, from the first, identified as prime embodiments of the naturalness the tourists sought, and consequently, sites of Indianness were written into the touristic landscape of the Northeast.[33] Guidebooks such as *Hunter's Panoramic Guide* created not just individual troupes or performers but whole communities as objects of the Euro-North American gaze, encouraging tourists to journey to villages such as St Regis (Akwesasne) or Lorette (Wendake) to gaze upon the 'remnants' of the great Native nations of old and to meditate sentimentally on history and the transitory nature of worldly power. These representations inscribed Native communities as fixed locations, bounded and contained spaces where the inhabitants met tourists' desires by performing their Indianness in dance and dress and by selling souvenirs.[34] The touristic sensibility is also, of course, a quintessential expression of the antimodernist search for authenticity identified by Lears. The enormous popularity of mid-nineteenth-century panoramas such as 'The Seven-Mile Mirror' is due to the success with which they fulfilled their expressed purpose of simulating touristic experiences for urban audiences.

As I have argued elsewhere, in order for the Victorian tourist to construct herself as mobile and modern it was necessary to construct the Native as immobile and pre-modern.[35] In reality, by the late nineteenth century many Native people travelled more widely and were more cosmopolitan than their white neighbours. To the continuing displeasure of Indian agents, the inhabitants of reserve communities in the Northeast regularly left their communities to seek audiences and markets, foreshadowing later out-migrations of high-steel workers and other specialized work forces. During the second half of the nineteenth century travelling troupes of entertainers criss-crossed the continent, sometimes joining forces with a medicine show or with a larger and more professional troupe. Both the 1894 photograph taken in Kansas of a band of Mohawk entertainers from Akwesasne (fig. 2.4), and the numerous early twentieth-century postcards that show Abenaki, Mohawk, and other eastern Indian performers at Earl's Court, London, capture long-distance journeying that was continuous with age-old patterns of Native travel.

In addition to the need to negotiate modernist desires for progress and assimilation and antimodernist desires for authentic experience and 'nature,' Native performers of the late nineteenth century also had to meet new expectations that all Indians should look like Plains Indians – the only 'real' Indians left in North America according to most people. The primacy of the Plains cultures had a profound effect on the clothing Native people wore in performance situations. In the east, as elsewhere, performers replaced their traditional dress with feather bonnets and fringed hide clothing. Sherry Brydon, who documented the Hiawatha pageants staged by Native entertainers at Great Lakes resorts around 1900, has argued that the pan-Indian clothing worn by participants was an effective means for affirming distinctive Native identity and for articulating political unity with other Native nations.[36] In examining the visualization of identity through dress, however, it is important to look at small details as well as the overall ensemble. The dress worn by the standing woman in the travelling Mohawk entertainment troupe photographed in Kansas (fig. 2.4) is embroidered with the great tree of peace, the key symbol of traditional Iroquois cosmology. Though masked by a folkish hybridity, the references to sacred oral traditions would have been clear to Iroquois viewers.

This location of authentic Indianness in the Plains was, of course, the reason for the success of the Wild West shows that became popular in the 1880s. In the re-enactments of the Indian wars that were the centrepieces of these shows, Indian actors were called upon to act out fictions of their own 'savagery' and subsequent humiliation. Indian leaders such as Sioux Chief Chauncey Yellow Robe saw clearly the negative effects of the standard forms of performance. In a 1913 speech to the Society of the American Indians he asked:

What benefit has the Indian derived from these Wild West Shows? None, but what

> are degrading, demoralizing and degenerating ... Tribal habits and customs are apt to be degraded for show purposes ... All these Wild West Shows are exhibiting the Indian worse than he ever was and deprive him of his high manhood and individuality.[37]

Yet, as Chief Yellow Robe himself acknowledged, these shows provided urgently needed employment for Native actors;[38] as we will see, they also allowed some of the participants to become established in the entertainment industry. As postcolonial writers have argued, it is important to scrutinize the doubleness of all such forms of colonial mimicry, in which Native actors appear to inhabit the stereotypes constructed within colonial systems of domination. Complicity is not necessarily complacency. Norman Bryson has commented on this phenomenon in the broader context of the 'logic of the gaze': 'Participation in the regime of the stereotype does not entail a surrender by the viewing subject to the content of the exhortation,' he writes. 'Neither submission nor hypnosis, the process is rather one of a consensual agreement to accept such-and-such a stereotype as a fiction of legitimation advantageous both to the "dominating" and the "dominated" groups.'[39]

Esther Deer and Molly Nelson: Performing the Indian/Woman

How, then, were stereotypes of Indianness used to advantage by Native performers as 'fictions of legitimation'? The lives and careers of the two women I want to discuss in the final section of this paper, Esther Deer and Molly Nelson, offer textbook examples of the working out of processes of mimicry and negotiation. Both women were born in the late nineteenth century and participated in the full range of possibilities that the field of Indian performance by then offered; both accepted the need to meet the highly specific expectations that early twentieth-century audiences had of Indian performance. Both women also got their start with bands of travelling Indian entertainers, joined up with famous Wild West shows of the day, and used these popular entertainment forms as springboards to mainstream theatre and dance. They were members of the first generation of Indian performers to succeed in this milieu, they travelled widely, and they became stars in New York and Paris.

At present, the life of Kahnawake Mohawk dancer Esther Deer can be known only by reconstructing it from the scrapbooks and memorabilia she left to her great-niece, Mrs Sylvia Trudeau.[40] More is known about Molly Nelson, a Penobscot from Old Town, Maine, thanks to a recent biography by Bunny McBride[41] based on the diaries and letters the dancer wrote throughout much of her life. These more intimate records offer rare insight into the ways that female Native performers experienced and were able to negotiate the dominant stereotypes of Native women in the first three decades of this century.

Esther Deer was born about 1891, and, at the age of eleven began to perform as Princess White Deer with the act founded by her father and uncle, 'The Famous Deer Brothers, Champion Indian Trick Riders of the World,' which performed both on its own and with larger Wild West shows.[42] In the years leading up to the First World War she travelled to Europe and South Africa, probably singing and dancing in dramatic performances such as 'Daniel Boone,' and 'Deer Family, Indians of the Past.' During a lengthy stay in Russia she met a Russian prince whom she subsequently married, only to lose him six months later when he was killed at the beginning of the Great War.

Esther Deer returned to New York as the United States was preparing to enter the war, and her participation in war bond rallies, where she was billed as 'White Deer, a bright example of genuine Americanism,' helped bring her to the attention of Florenz Ziegfeld. She joined his famous Follies and soon became one of the principal artists (fig. 2.5). In addition to participating in such acts as the 'Nine-O'Clock Frolic' and the 'Midnight Frolic,' she also performed dances that were built around specific constructs of ethnicity. One reviewer noted that 'Princess White Deer exhibited a Dance to the Great Spirit that is bound to be imitated. She also showed that an Indian can copy from the Black race as well as the White by executing a difficult Buck and Wing Dance.'[43] In another review, titled 'Hitchi Koo,' she was praised for her 'particularly clever Indian dance number, followed by a jazz selection as an encore.'[44] The visualization and commodification of ethnicities evidenced by these dances was rampant throughout popular and visual culture during the early twentieth century; images inserted into spaces ranging from orange crate labels to sheet music covers reflected the tides of immigration and imperialism that were shaping North American societies.

Despite the absence of more personal narratives, it is possible to draw certain conclusions about the nature of Esther Deer's performances from the memorabilia she left. The title of a highly successful 1925 production she created and performed, 'From Wigwam to White Lights,' for example, argues for an ironic sensibility – shared by actor and audience – of the inadequacy of common stereotypes of the Indian as rural, primitive, and confined by the reservation. Laurence Senelick's work suggests that the play of irony revealed in this title paralleled that employed by the avant-garde theatrical creators who regularly wrote and performed cabaret acts in the inter-war period. 'Irony,' Senelick notes, 'is essentially an oblique weapon, and the fin de siècle "artistic" cabaret had to exploit its many facets, predominantly parody, in its sorties on social and aesthetic flanks.'[45]

The clothing worn by Esther Deer in publicity photos and newspaper clippings testifies to another type of doubleness. For her musical review Indian dances, Princess White Deer wore the clothing of the 'temptress,' one of the two main images of the Indian woman as identified by Terry Goldie.[46] Throughout her performing career, however, Esther Deer also appeared as a representative of American Indians at charity events organized by both Native and non-Native groups. For example, she performed at annual balls given by Native lobby organizations such as the American Indian Defense Association, whose goals were 'to secure for all Indians the right to land, to legal protection, health protection, modern education and liberty of conscience.' On such occasions she wore modest pan-Indian beaded and hide clothing, the costume of the pure and noble Native maiden, the 'virgin' in Goldie's schema (fig. 2.6). Princess White Deer appeared in a testimonial performance organized by the American Legion to honour General Pershing; the letter of invitation stressed that her presence was particularly desired because she was a 'REAL American.'[47] She performed a Dance of the Great Spirit, a Pocahontas Dance, and a Waltz, together with 'Divertissements of the Revolutionary, Civil War, and World War Periods' – a program carefully calibrated to ally both Native authenticity and Native difference with American patriotism. She wore the same pan-Indian dress in 1937 when she went to Washington and personally presented an invitation to attend a meeting of the Grand Council of Chiefs of the Six Nations of the Iroquois to President Roosevelt and Canadian embassy officials.

The centuries-old duality of the temptress and the virgin was, of course, an imposition of a Western fiction of femininity. This imposition was especially repressive when applied to Native women because the general associations of Western women with the 'natural' and the domestic (rather than the industrial or the technologically progressive) doubled the natural and pre-modern significations of Indianness.[48] In the early twentieth century, performers such as Esther Deer successfully resisted these constructs by juxtaposing them with blatantly up-to-date, modern acts. Alongside her roles of seductive temptress and demure virgin, Esther Deer also performed as a contemporary Western woman. She teamed up with a partner known as the Sheik of Brazil to dance the tango and the waltz wearing the chic evening dress of a 1920s flapper, but she also added to the standard ballroom dances a number called the 'Deer Stalk' that was described by one journalist as 'an invention of the Princess ... descriptive of the spirit of the field and wood.' In 1928 Esther Deer went to Paris to perform her Indian dances. She seems to have been well received, though not on the order achieved soon after by Josephine Baker. She retired at the beginning of the Second World War and when she died in 1992 she had lived more than a century.

Scrapbooks and mementoes can only take us so far, and they yield little understanding of Esther Deer's interior life. They evidence, however, a strategy of role playing that allowed the dancer not only to manipulate contemporary tropes of Indianness but also to reframe them within a larger discourse of Primitivism. Her rapid changes of costume and persona are transformative – a kind of destabilizing tricksterish play that renders transparent the standard icons. In a photograph taken in 1921 (fig. 2.7) Esther Deer holds a False Face mask next to her face. It is a provocative juxtaposition. Her own face appears as white and flapper-modern; the mask, in contrast, is an icon of the 'tribal,' an object by then clearly defined within Primitivist discourse as a powerfully expressive form, but also, in the specific case of False Face masks, as a grotesque.[49] In this image Esther Deer plays herself as Native-woman-object-of-desire and opposes her own image to that of Native-as-object-of-fear; she inverts two colonialist tropes of the European and the Other, the trope of colonialist mimicry later expressed by Fanon in *Black Skin, White Masks*, and the Primitivist trope of appropriation that Man Ray would express in his famous 1926 photograph *Noire et Blanche* (fig. 2.8). The restless alternation and rearrangement of the signs of Indianness, of blackness, and of femininity, dislodges them from their accustomed textual locations and inscribes instead the modernist reality of the fragmented subject.[50] The standard publicity shot of Princess White Deer expresses in its utter banality the vacillation enacted by the performance of the stereotype, which produces a text, as Bhabha writes, 'rich in the traditions of *trompe l'oeil*, irony, mimicry and repetition'; in it, 'mimicry emerges as one of the most elusive and effective strategies of colonial power and knowledge.'[51] Esther Deer's performances would have made it impossible for her audiences not to know that the Indian stereotypes were as much (dis)guises as were the other, more patently fictional images she adopted.

Molly Nelson was born in 1903, more than ten years after Esther Deer. She formed, while still a schoolgirl in Maine, the determination to become a writer and to record the oral traditions of her people. Her initial entry into entertainment, as a member of a small travelling troupe, was motivated by a desire to earn money for her education. Performing as an Indian entertainer was also, in some ways, a natural extension of childhood experiences of dressing up as an 'Indian' to sell baskets and to perform in pageants for summer tourists. Encouraged by the noted anthropologist Frank Speck, Molly Nelson spent two years at the University of Pennsylvania. When her funds ran out she joined the Miller Brothers 101 Ranch Wild West Show, a large and famous show based in Kansas, in order to earn the money to go back to school. Here she acquired the name Molly Spotted Elk from a Plains Indian colleague. Over the next few years she went on to work in musical reviews and nightclubs in the Southwest, accomplishing a transition to mainstream theatre with an ease that seems to have been typical of the era. When she returned to the theatrical Mecca of New York in the mid-1920s she had a new artistic goal – to perfect herself as a serious dancer in order to acquire the means to express authentic Indian themes.

The path to this goal was marked by many detours, necessitated by the endless, grinding need to support herself and to help her family. She regularly held down two or three jobs at a time, and her mainstay remained nightclub acts that featured eroticized and exploitative versions of Indian dance. She regularly had to perform in costumes that she considered both inauthentic and embarrassingly scanty, and she wrote of her discomfort and resentment in her diary: 'My costume made me embarrassed,' one entry reads, 'Looked like a loin cloth affair of satin and beads instead of leather and fringe. Not natural for my Indian dance ...' In another place she commented, 'Something new once in a while ... but mostly nude parades. I am an injun in the flesh parade. Feel terrible about being bare and walking around, but I must work ...'[52]

These experiences were exacerbated, of course, by the racist attitudes toward Native women she had learned to anticipate from childhood. As a high school girl in Maine, Molly Nelson had complained bitterly of the lack of respect:

> The white boys and men shun the ... Indian girl like poison, each afraid to be seen

> even saying 'how do you do,' tipping their hats or treating an Indian girl as a 'girl' ... that is why we admire and welcome as a friend the one who is not ashamed to be seen with us and who is bred in the real American democratic spirit of manhood to respect any lady, whether of the black, yellow, red or white race, of any class, creed or tongue – if she is a LADY or TRIES to be one.[53]

During the 1920s, in addition to her night-club dancing, Molly Spotted Elk also took up all opportunities that came her way for more artistically challenging roles in theatre or dance. As she wrote in her diary, 'How I wish I could always have the proper atmosphere to do my work as it should be ... The more I dance, the more I want to interpret my emotions without limitation, to create a freedom of primitiveness and abandon. If only one could dance solely for art! Maybe someday I will have that chance, if not in America, then in Europe.'[54] In 1929 she was given the female lead in the classic silent film *The Silent Enemy*, which was shot in northern Ontario over the winter of 1929. She found this artistically satisfying because of its serious attempt to authentically recreate the lives of pre-contact woodlands Indians. This role won Molly Spotted Elk a modest fame, and led to the chance for her to go to Paris with the United States Indian Band.

It is not surprising, in light of her association of Europe not only with greater artistic freedom but also with freedom from racial prejudice, that Molly Spotted Elk decided to remain in Paris when the rest of the band returned home. Paris opened up a whole range of new opportunities for the pursuit of her artistic and intellectual interests. Here, despite the fact that the deepening Depression made subsistence ever more difficult, she was able to manage without resorting to the exploitative flesh trade.

During the mid-1930s Molly Spotted Elk became a habitué of the Parisian artistic and intellectual circles which are most identified with early twentieth-century modernist Primitivism and surrealism, those of the anthropologists Marcel Griaule, Michel Leiris, and Paul Rivet. She attended lectures given by Marcel Mauss at the Sorbonne and returned to the writing projects to which she had never given up her commitment. (The publication of two manuscripts – a semi-autobiographical novel and a collection of Penobscot stories – was cancelled by the outbreak of the Second World War.)[55] In Paris, too, Molly Spotted Elk's dancing style seems to have developed into a more fully realized and expressive modernist style, stimulated both by the cosmopolitanism of that city in the 1930s and by contacts with other avant-garde dancers.

From the moment of her arrival, the foreignness and cosmopolitanism of Paris had a liberating effect, a freedom she expressed through a recognisably Primitivist vocabulary. In an article Molly Spotted Elk wrote on the Colonial Exposition for a hometown Maine newspaper, she provided a vivid description in which this language is used to subvert the recognized cultural hierarchies:

> Against the white of the African villages, the mellowed yellows of the distant Oriental buildings, the verdant green of spring and the brilliant flowers, color rolls

> up like the tones of a symphony barbaric in its splendor. It glints from the sabres and tips of bayonets, from gay robes and gowns, from black inscrutable men from North Africa, from little yellow men from the Orient, the brown faces of the desert, and the copperish tints of the American Indians. Besides such people, the pale faced man and woman seem colorless.[56]

Exposure to the strange customs of other peoples, including those of the French, had a levelling effect, suddenly making nonsense of the labels of racial inferiority that had been attached to her as an aboriginal woman since birth. Molly Spotted Elk wrote in her diary: 'Each race of people has as many different customs as even us Injuns.'[57] She became close friends with dancers from India, Indonesia, and Malaysia who had also remained in Paris after the Exposition. The four women taught each other their dances and sometimes performed in each others' costumes – a kind of role swapping that, though reminiscent of Esther Deer's ethnic role playing, was quite different because it was produced through acts of collaboration and exchange that refused the extreme objectification of the stereotype.

Molly's dances were well received by audiences drawn from the Paris artistic elite. Another article in a Maine newspaper reported both her own and her audience's discriminating appreciation of authenticity: 'I have found already that [Europeans] appreciate real expression and Indian art.' The writer continues, 'The princess is emphatic, in her desire for nothing but genuineness ... and she tells of the struggle she had in the States for a true appreciation of Indian dances. The average American, the princess declares, "is satisfied with a dancer bedecked in feathers, making war-whoops and leaping aimlessly about with savage gestures to the beat of a tom tom."'[58]

During her Paris years, too, Molly Spotted Elk fell in love with and eventually married a French journalist named Jean Archambaud. Her marriage to a European, like that of Esther Deer, was an escape from the prejudice she had experienced in her homeland, a prejudice born of the fear of miscegenation, hybridity, and impurity. And, also like Esther Deer, Molly Nelson's brief marriage was ended prematurely by the violent outbreak of a world war. When the Germans invaded France, she was forced to flee with their daughter over the mountains to Lisbon. Her husband, denied a visa, was forced to remain behind and died soon after. Molly Spotted Elk returned to America, but never completely recovered either mentally or physically from this loss or from the years of struggle and physical deprivation that had preceded it. She lived out the remainder of her long life in the relative seclusion of Indian Island.

It is not accidental that the decades during which both Molly Spotted Elk and Esther Deer experienced their greatest success and their greatest artistic freedom, the 1920s and 1930s, were those during which Primitivism enjoyed its greatest intellectual and artistic vogue. This period also witnessed a radical reversal of American policy towards its aboriginal peoples, a change that had been prepared in part by the antimodernist interest in tribal cultures of a segment of the dominant class that was also politically liberal and nationalist.

The shift from the trope of the Vanishing Indian to that of the Changing Indian (in Rayna Green's phrase), with its attendant legal and institutional reforms, has been chronicled by numerous historians.[59] It culminated in the appointment of prominent Indian reformer John Collier as Commissioner of Indian Affairs in 1930, a year before Molly Spotted Elk's arrival in Paris. Although the Primitivism of Collier and his associates continued to employ a currency of stereotypes, the disenchantment with the superiority of European culture that lay at its heart could also be used as a tool with which to erode the evolutionist theories of racial hierarchy that had produced assimilationist doctrines. The context in which stereotypes were played out during the 1920s and 1930s was thus radically changed from that of earlier decades. As Bryson has commented:

> In such cases as these one is dealing not only with the transformative power of context and of the work of interpretation in context, but with the actual reversibility of power-relations: volatility is the key word. When the image takes upon itself to act on behalf of another power, yet continues to speak in its own name, the combined spectacle of delegation with the self-confessedly inferior rank of the delegate introduces a dangerous instability into the field of forces.[60]

Native artists accepted the essentialist constructs of Primitivism as the price of their own avant-garde modernism, but it was also the fee payable for the power to assert their own collaboration in modernity *as* Indians. The art that articulated these re-positionings is suggested by the very fragmentary information we have about the specific dance movements used by Esther Deer and Molly Spotted Elk. One newspaper described Esther Deer, for example, as 'whirling every night in the delirious savagery of her Native dance.' Around the same time Molly Spotted Elk, also in New York, noted in her diary that she had helped the well-known modern dancer Chester Dale choreograph his Indian ballet: 'Chester used some of my dance movements in groups and they looked lovely – the head shake, the rigid arm and body bend, and the bell stamp.'[61] Later, in Paris, she choreographed her own dances. Her diary entries describing performances at the prestigious Salons du Cercle internationale des arts note that she performed 'the corn dance, variation of step dances and warrior' on one occasion and, on another occasion, 'the corn, fat man, variations and my warriors ...'[62] We can perhaps recapture something of the way in which Primitivist principles informed the modern dance theory that lay behind the Native dancers' creative work in a statement written by Martha Graham:

> America's great gift to the arts is rhythm: rich, full, unabashed, virile. Our two forms of indigenous dance,. the Negro and the Indian, are as dramatically contrasted rhythmically as the land in which they root. The Negro dance is a dance toward freedom, a dance to forgetfulness ... The Indian dance, however, is not for freedom, or forgetfulness, or escape, but for awareness of life, complete relationship with that world in which he finds himself: it is a dance for power, a rhythm of integration.[63]

In these lines the logic that links the performance of the United States Indian Band with the jazz dances of Esther Deer at the Ziegfield Follies and with the Primitivist agenda is made clear. Graham's modernist appropriation of the Indian and the Negro, like the contemporary appropriations of Native American and African visual arts by Western modernist artists, was admiring, even worshipful. Although many contemporary aboriginal and non-aboriginal people have come to regard such appropriations as forms of theft when they are performed today, this judgment is historically specific. For Molly Spotted Elk and Esther Deer in the 1930s the opposite appears to have been true. For both, Primitivism opened a space for the negotiation of more oppressive discourses. Molly, like the avant-garde thinkers and artists she mingled with in New York and Paris, understood the Primitive as a positive core of cultural identity that allowed her to reformulate her personal identity, to recover elements of authenticity from her heritage, and to add dimensionality to the cardboard popular-culture images of Indianness.

It is common for writers to rather simplistically condemn early twentieth-century Native performances of Indianness as sell-outs expressive of complicity with the repressive structures of both sexist and colonialist domination. This judgment must be reconsidered in discussing the work of Native women performers and artists. Feminist scholars have led the way in tying these debates to individual biographies and specific works of art. Elliott and Wallace have used the term 'modernist (im)positionings' to 'evoke the interpellation *but also* the agency of these [women] artists.'[64] I have argued that performances by Native artists, were, similarly, intended as highly nuanced interventions in Primitivist discourses, rather than uncomplicated or even mercenary collaborations in the dominant culture's fictions of Indianness as Daniel Francis and others have recognized. The critical work on colonialism, hybridity, and the politics of identity of Said, Bhabha, Clifford, Wright, and others offers powerful theoretical tools of explanation that can be introduced into the more detailed examinations of specific historical examples. As I have suggested, Bhabha's discussion of mimicry is particularly useful in understanding the agency of performers like Esther Deer and Molly Spotted Elk in the destabilization of stereotypes. When Molly Spotted Elk referred to herself as an 'injun' in her diaries (in the 'flesh parade,' in relation to the multitude of other 'others' she encountered in Paris) she was pointing to the provisional nature of her acceptance of the cardboard template of her identity. Primitivism changed 'injun' to 'Indian'; it sought, as she did, a greater 'genuineness,' and thus offered her a space of ambivalence in which to act. Her choice of modern dance as her medium of expression was, on one level, a matter of individual predisposition, but the success of this choice was also predicated on the long history of Indian dance and white spectatorship. In the first decades of this century the distance from basketry or bead embroidery to modernist easel painting or marble sculpture was harder to travel, yet all these forms were deployed within a visual environment whose common terrain it is important to recognise if we are to appreciate the resonances of mimicry as they echo across the distances and down the years.

NOTES

1 Quoted in Bunny McBride, *Molly Spotted Elk: A Penobscot in Paris* (Norman, Oklahoma: University of Oklahoma Press, 1995), 128.

2 McBride, *Molly Spotted Elk*, 136.

3 Homi Bhabha, *The Location of Culture* (London: Routledge, 1994), 89.

4 McBride, *Molly Spotted Elk*, 150.

5 James Clifford, 'Travelling Cultures,' in *Cultural Studies*, ed. Lawrence Grossberg, Cary Nelson, Paula Treichler (New York: Routledge, 1992), 97–112.

6 Among the classic studies of Native stereotypes in literature are Robert F. Berkhofer Jr., *The White Man's Indian: Images of the American Indian from Columbus to the Present* (New York: Alfred A. Knopf, 1978); Roy Harvey Pearce, *Savagism and Civilization: A Study of the Indian and the American Mind*, rev. ed. (Berkeley: University of California Press, 1988). Studies of stereotypes in popular visual culture include Deborah Doxtator, *Fluffs and Feathers: An Exhibit on the Symbols of Indianness, A Resource Guide* (Brantford, Ont.: Woodland Cultural Centre, 1988); Daniel Francis, *The Imaginary Indian: The Image of the Indian in Canadian Culture* (Vancouver: Arsenal Pulp Press, 1992); Raymond Stedman, *Shadows of the Indian: Stereotypes in American Culture* (Norman, Oklahoma: University of Oklahoma Press, 1982); and Rayna Diane Green, 'The Only Good Indian: The Image of the Indian in American Vernacular Culture,' (PhD diss., Indiana University, 1973).

7 By modernist century I intend an era characterized both by modernity in socio-economic forms and by modernism in artistic forms. Although periodizations are always somewhat arbitrary, the 1860s mark the beginning of a period of particularly rapid industrial and urban growth and of intellectual cultures attendant on this growth. This decade was also marked by clear changes in Native–white relations. In the United States westward expansion and the end of the Civil War created an urgent sense of a need to resolve the 'Indian problem' and forced clearer formulations of ideology and policy. See Frederick E. Hoxie, *A Final Promise: The Campaign to Assimilate the Indians, 1880–1920* (Cambridge: Cambridge University Press, 1984) and Brian W. Dippie, *The Vanishing American: White Attitudes and U.S. Indian Policy* (Middletown, Conn.: Wesleyan University Press, 1982). In Canada there was a parallel situation. In 1867, Confederation removed the management of Indian Affairs from Great Britain, while the subsequent creation of western provinces stimulated the passage in the 1880s of legislation that was based on the same assimilationist assumptions that dominated American policy. See J.R. Miller, *Skyscrapers Hide the Heavens: A History of Indian-White Relations in Canada* (Toronto: University of Toronto Press, 1989); and E. Brian Titley, *A Narrow Vision: Duncan Campbell Scott and the Administration of Indian Affairs in Canada* (Vancouver: University of British Columbia Press, 1986). Modernism in art is conventionally traced to Manet's work of the 1860s, which set in motion a chain of artistic developments centred on an avant-garde leading through impressionism and post-impressionism to the invention of abstraction in the early twentieth century and the high formalism of the 1960s.

8 For a thorough documentation of the trope of the vanishing Indian during the late nineteenth and early twentieth centuries see Dippie, *The Vanishing American*.

9 T.J. Jackson Lears, *No Place of Grace: Antimodernism and the Transformation of American Culture, 1880–1920* (New York: Pantheon Books, 1981), xiv.

10 Robert Goldwater, *Primitivism in Modern Art*, rev. ed. (New York: Vintage Books, 1967).

11 Bhabha, *Location of Culture*, 66.

12 Ernest Smith (1907–75), a Seneca painter from New York State, is best known for a series of paintings he made during the 1930s as part of a program sponsored by the Works Project Administration to revive traditional Iroquois arts. Frederick Alexi (1853–ca. 1940) was a self-taught artist of Tsimshian and Iroquois descent who painted scenes of Northwest Coast villages and traditional ceremonies (see Dierdre Simmons, 'Frederick Alexi, Indian Artist (ca. 1857 to ca. 1944),' *Journal of Canadian Art History* 14 [1991]: 83–93. Other artists who achieved success and recognition during the first part of the twentieth century include the Blood painter Gerald Tailfeathers (1925–75) and the large group of Southwestern and Plains artists associated with The Studio School in Santa Fe and its first director, Dorothy Dunn. For an introduction to these painters, see Margaret Archuleta and Rennard Strickland, *Shared Visions: Native American Painters and Sculptors in the Twentieth Century* (Phoenix, Arizona: The Heard Museum, 1991); Bruce Bernstein and W. Jackson Rushing, *Modern by Tradition: Native American Painting in the Studio Style* (Santa Fe: Museum of New Mexico Press, 1995); and Janet Catherine Berlo and Ruth B. Phillips, *Native North American Art* (New York: Oxford University Press, 1998), 209–39. Although patrons sought to promote these painters as fine artists, their work has remained in a curatorial grey area of regional and para-ethnographic collecting and display and has not yet found broad acceptance in the venues of high art.

13 W.J.T. Mitchell, 'Interdisciplinarity and Visual Culture,' *Art Bulletin* 77 (1995), 542.

14 Bridget Elliott and Jo-Ann Wallace, *Women Artists and Writers: Modernist (im)positionings* (London: Routledge, 1994), 7.

15 Bhabha, *Location of Culture*, 70–1.

16 Green's 'The Only Good Indian' was a dissertation in Folklore and American Studies.

17 Green, 'The Only Good Indian,' 318.

18 Rosemarie K. Bank, 'Staging the "Native": Making History in American Theatre Culture, 1828–1838,' *Theatre Journal* 45 (1993), 461–86.

19 Eugene H. Jones, *Native Americans as Shown on the Stage, 1763–1916* (Metuchen, N.J.: The Scarecrow Press, 1988), 110–14.

20 Jones writes, 'Indians continued to appear occasionally as they had done in variety shows since the eighteenth century ... some appeared in circus-like surroundings and their acts partook more of sports events than of theatre.' *Native Americans*, 121.

21 Green, 'The Only Good Indian,' 331. Green notes (p. 332) that, in 1893 alone, the Buffalo Bill Wild West show was seen by six million people, and that there are thousands of extant posters in archival collections. When one considers that these must represent only a fraction of the posters that were used to publicise the shows, it is evident that the Wild West show image of Indianness was diffused throughout the visual environment of the late nineteenth century.

22 Arthur Amiotte, 'The Sun Dance,' in *Native American Dance: Ceremonies and Social*

Traditions, ed. Charlotte Heth (Washington, D.C.: National Museum of the American Indian, Smithsonian Institution with Starwood Publishing, 1992), 135–7.

23 Gian Costantino Beltrami, *A Pilgrimage in Europe and America, Leading to the Discovery of the Sources of the Mississippi and Bloody River*, 2 vols. (London: Hunt and Clarke, 1828), II, 241–2.

24 Henry Schoolcraft, *Travels through the Northwestern Regions of the United States* (1821; reprint, Ann Arbor, Michigan: University Microfilms, 1966), 155.

25 Charles Joseph Leslie, *Military Journal of Colonel Leslie, K.H. of Balquhain, whilst Serving with the 29th Regt. in the Peninsula, and the 60th Rifles in Canada, etc. 1807–1831* (Aberdeen, Scotland: Aberdeen University Press, 1887), 311–12.

26 Anna Brownell Jameson, *Winter Studies and Summer Rambles in Canada* (1838; reprint, Toronto: McClelland & Stewart, 1990), 435.

27 George Heriot, *Travels through the Canadas* (London: Phillips, Heron, Addie E., 1807).

28 For a reproduction of Steiger's painting, see Ruth B. Phillips, *Patterns of Power: The Jasper Grant Collection and Great Lakes Indian Art of the Early Nineteenth Century* (Kleinburg, Ont.: The McMichael Canadian Collection, 1984), 86. This painting is now held by the National Gallery of Canada.

29 Banks, 'Staging the "Native,"' 473. The giving of a speech at Peale's Museum was indicative of an interesting conceptual overlap, during the early nineteenth century, between the spaces of the museum and the theatre. A museum in Albany, in operation as early as 1798 as a venue for the display of curiosities, soon added wax figures and a lecture hall in which, 'occasionally appeared an actor in a monologue, or a comic singer or dancer.' During the nineteenth century, performance came to be the primary activity of this venue, which continued to be known as The Museum. See H.P. Phelps, *Players of a Century: A Record of the Albany Stage* (1880; reprint, New York: Benjamin Blom Inc., 1972), 127.

30 Thomas McKenney, *Sketches of a Tour to the Lakes, of the Character and Customs of the Chippeway Indians and of Incidents Connected with the Treaty of Fond du Lac* (Baltimore: Fielding Lucas, Jun'r, 1827), 286.

31 Patricia Jasen, *Wild Things: Nature, Culture, and Tourism in Ontario 1790–1914* (Toronto: University of Toronto Press, 1995). See also Ruth B. Phillips, *Trading Identities: Souvenir Arts in Northeastern North America, 1700–1900* (Seattle: University of Washington Press, 1998).

32 Quoted in Patricia Jasen, 'From Nature to Culture: The St Lawrence River Panorama in Nineteenth-Century Ontario Tourism,' *Ontario History* 85 (1993), 52.

33 Joseph Earl Arrington, 'William Burr's Moving Panorama of the Great Lakes, the Niagara, St Lawrence and Saguenay Rivers,' *Ontario History* 51 (1959), 141–62.

34 Jasen also notes: 'When the steamer docked at St. Regis, the guidebooks claim that it was customary for tourists to toss coins to the children who dived in the water for them. Like the Tuscarora village near Niagara Falls, St. Regis also presented tourists with the opportunity to ponder and pass judgement on the Native people's level of civilization' ('From Nature to Culture,' 54–5).

35 See Ruth B. Phillips, 'Why Not Tourist Art? Significant Silences in Native American Museum Representation,' in *After Colonialism: Imperial Histories and Postcolonial Displacements*, ed. Gyan Prakash (Princeton: Princeton University Press, 1995), 98–

125. Tourism also provided a market for commoditized souvenir art such as baskets and beadwork – major sources of subsistence throughout the Northeast. To enhance the authenticity of the goods offered for sale, vendors often staged small performances wearing special costumes that played to the common stereotypes, an early example of what MacCannell has termed 'staged ethnicity.' See Dean MacCannell, 'Staged Authenticity: Arrangements of Social Space in Tourist Settings,' *American Journal of Sociology* 79 (1973), 589–603.

36 Sherry Brydon, 'Hiawatha Meets the Gitchee Goomee Indians: The Visualization of Indianness in the Nineteenth Century,' (MA thesis, School for Studies in Art and Culture: Art History, Carleton University, 1993). Such dress was also worn by travelling vendors of souvenir goods. The sale of these objects remained as important a source of income as the revenues of performance, and no travelling troupe of entertainers left home without trunkloads of souvenir art to sell. In reading the many mentions of such activities in the travel literature or when looking at stereoscopic cards and early postcards it is often difficult to say whether 'dressing up Indian' and performing were supports for the sale of souvenirs or whether the souvenir sales were an adjunct to the performances.

37 Quoted in McBride, *Molly Spotted Elk*, 68.

38 In 1889, as a result of effective lobbying by reformist groups, the Commissioner of Indian Affairs authorized new regulations for those contracting Native people for Wild West shows, including a provision for fair salaries. The highest salaries were equivalent to two-thirds the average salary of an Indian agent. See, L.G. Moses, 'Wild West Shows, Reformers, and the Image of the American Indian, 1887–1914,' *South Dakota History* 14 (1984), 201–2.

39 Norman Bryson, *Vision and Painting: The Logic of the Gaze* (New Haven, Conn.: Yale University Press, 1983), 158.

40 This reconstruction was recently undertaken by myself and Trudy Nicks, with Kanatakta, Anna Mae Rice (niece of Sylvia Trudeau), and Martin Loft of the Kanien'kehaka Raotitiohkwa Cultural Centre at Kahnawake. The details of Esther Deer's career cited in the following pages have been drawn from copies of the unindexed papers that are on deposit at the Cultural Centre. A preliminary discussion of Esther Deer's life and career was presented in a paper by Ruth B. Phillips and Trudy C. Nicks, '"From Wigwam to White Lights": Princess White Deer's Indian Acts,' that was presented to the American Indian Workshop, Oporto, Portugal, April 1995.

41 McBride, *Molly Spotted Elk*.

42 On the history of entertainers from Kahnawake see David Blanchard, 'For Your Entertainment Pleasure – Princess White Deer and Chief Running Deer – Last "Hereditary" Chief of the Mohawk: Northern Mohawk Rodeos and Showmanship,' *Journal of Canadian Culture* 1 (1984), 99–116; and Johnny Beauvais, *Kahnawake: A Mohawk Look at Canada and Adventures of Big John Canadian, 1840–1919* (Kahnawake, Quebec: Khanata Industries Reg'd, 1985), 136–48. Blanchard traces Mohawk involvement in the entertainment industry to the displays staged for the Prince of Wales on his visit to Canada in 1860, which was followed by an invitation to the Mohawk performers to visit England.

43 Ethnic acts in vaudeville belonged to the realm of spectacle rather than drama, and they relied on the easy identification of popular stereotypes. Alfred Hitchcock was quoted as saying, 'If one can fathom the plot, one is a person of superior intellect.'

44 Even within these rigid parameters, Esther Deer worked to assert authenticity and to gain economic advantage. Preparing for the Indian role in 'Hitchi Koo,' she returned to Kahnawake to 'secure two full-blooded Indian maidens to appear with her, Miss Bauveis [*sic*] and Miss Skye.'

45 Laurence Senelick, ed. and trans., *Cabaret Performance: Volume II: Europe 1920–1940, Sketches, Songs, Monologues, Memoirs* (Baltimore: The Johns Hopkins University Press, 1993), xi.

46 Terry Goldie, *Fear and Temptation: The Image of the Indigene in Canadian, Australian, and New Zealand Literatures* (Kingston and Montreal: McGill-Queen's University Press, 1989).

47 Letter from Robert Redmond for the Committee for the National Tribute to General John J. Pershing, 26 March 1925.

48 The dramatic impact of many of her Indian acts was intensified by intentional juxtapositions of the modalities of the Princess with other 'commodities' of Indianness identified by Goldie – in particular Indian Spirituality and the Indian Warrior. See *Fear and Temptation*, 15.

49 I have discussed in detail the display of False Face masks during this period and the construction of grotesquerie commonly placed upon them in books of the 1920s and 1930s in 'Disappearing Acts: Traditions of Exposure, Traditions of Enclosure, and Iroquois Masks,' in *Questions of Tradition*, ed. Mark Salber Phillips and Gordon Schochet (Toronto: University of Toronto Press, forthcoming). The Hotel Astor in New York City had a large display of these masks in its Hall of the Americas during the early years of this century. A hotel publication described them thus: 'The most peculiar objects are two hideous masks beset with hair and smeared with red and black paint. They belong to the outfit of medicine men, who, up to the present day, prey upon their kinsmen by pretending to have power over the many demons and witches which threaten the life of the Iroquois. Opposite the moose head, hanging on the balcony, are several other masks, one of which is fearfully distorted.' (Cited from a copy of the publication in the Bayley Art Museum, University of Virginia, which now owns the mask. I am grateful to Mary Jo Ayers for making this known to me.)

50 Green has traced the figuration of the Indian princess trope of the Native woman as 'Caucasian and classical in features, bearing, trappings, and behaviour' back to the early years of contact and has analysed the structural oppositions of this figure with her 'dark twin' the 'dumpy, drunken, lazy, prostituted squaw' ('The Only Good Indian,' 374, 377).

51 Bhabha, *Location of Culture*, 85.

52 McBride, *Molly Spotted Elk*, 136.

53 Ibid., 50.

54 Ibid., 128.

55 Esther Deer also had aspirations as a writer. During her year in Paris in 1928 a newspaper reported that she was 'finishing a history of the Mohawk people, on

which she has been working for two years.' The manuscript does not seem to have survived.

56 McBride, *Molly Spotted Elk*, 157.

57 Ibid., 154.

58 *Portland Sunday Telegram*, 14 June 1931, quoted in McBride, *Molly Spotted Elk*, 167.

59 Dippie's *The Vanishing American* has already been cited. For a discussion of the same period in Canada, where the policy shift was not so dramatic or sudden, see also Miller, *Skyscrapers*.

60 Bryson, *Vision and Painting*, 155.

61 McBride, *Molly Spotted Elk*, 135.

62 Ibid., 202–3.

63 Quoted in Rosalie Jones, 'Modern Native Dance: Beyond Tribe and Tradition,' in *Native American Dance: Ceremonies and Social Traditions*, ed. Charlotte Heth (Washington, D.C.: National Museum of the American Indian, Smithsonian Institution with Starwood Publishing, 1982), 170.

64 Elliott and Wallace, *Women Artists*, 16.

CHAPTER THREE

The Colonial Lens: Gauguin, Primitivism, and Photography in the Fin de siècle

Elizabeth C. Childs

Paul Gauguin's escape from Paris to the South Seas is the most notorious and mythologized episode of modernist primitivism. Abandoning conventional bourgeois norms, Gauguin sailed to Polynesia in 1891 to seek rejuvenation in a confrontation with the 'primitive.' The story of his rejection of modernity, civilization, and the métropole to pursue what he termed the life of a 'savage' in the tropics seems, at first glance, to be an uncomplicated tale of fin de siècle anti-modernism – the ultimate individualist quest to recuperate the self in a rejection of a modern urban world perceived as overly industrialised, bureaucratic, and rational.[1] Yet the Tahitian capital of Papeete that Gauguin found in 1891 was modern in its own right, the product of a century of contact with Europe. Following its annexation as a French colony in 1880, Tahiti had become a hybrid of the Parisian and the Polynesian. By the 1890s, over a century of contact with Europe had transformed the island: many Tahitians spoke some French or English as well as Tahitian; they bought imported European fabrics printed with tropical designs; they wore missionary-style clothes while dancing modified versions of prohibited dances; and they sang native songs that were syncretic variations of Christian hymns. Most Europeans of the fin de siècle arrived expecting a 'pure' or 'authentic' paradise, frozen in a mythic past. What they encountered was the dynamic culture of modern colonial Tahiti.

But Gauguin's self-proclaimed mission was primitivist retreat, and the terms of his retreat escalated throughout his Polynesian career: following a brief return to France, and another six years in Tahiti, he moved yet again to the less Europeanized Marquesas Islands. It is tempting to romanticize Gauguin's final days in Hiva Oa, spent in his native-style home he called 'The House of Pleasure,' as his most 'primitive' of all – wearing a *pareu*, mixing with native friends, taking up the cause of the Tahitians against a local magistrate, and railing out against the hegemony of the Catholic church and the colonial government.[2] By 1903, Gauguin was clearly more integrated into native life than he had been during his first trip to Tahiti in 1891–3. But 'going native' never made him a native. The colonizer, even if he rejects colonialism, never fully escapes to the other side. He or she lives, as post-colonial theory proposes, in a state of cultural reciprocity, touched and changed by a new culture, yet unable to completely disassociate from Europe and its fundamental legacies of social and psychological conditioning.[3] The result is ambiguous and impossible to characterize adequately by the structuralist polarizations of primitivism (old/new; primitive/civilised; slow/fast; natural/cultural; native/European). Gauguin's identity in Polynesia was a cultural hybrid – part French (both bohemian artist and sailor) and indeed part Polynesian. In spite of the primitivist rhetoric,[4] there was no going back in time or escaping modernity for the fin-de-siècle exoticist – just a departure for the new and unfamiliar and a need to negotiate a relationship to the heterogeneous culture of colonial Tahiti. Much of Gauguin's negotiation took place in the controlled environment of the studio, where his fertile imagination and incisive command of the language of colour and pattern could give expression to his recently acquired vocabulary of exotic motifs. Some of his subjects were specifically Tahitian, some were more broadly derived from Oceanic cultures, and some were unique exoticist pastiches of the sensual, the aesthetic, and the mythic. Both Gauguin's life and his work are inflected by his conscious efforts to craft an idiosyncratic, avant-garde identity in the margins between the worlds of the Parisian métropole and the Tahitian village. For Gauguin, that liminal position in the colonial world was a stimulating and creative space, if not always a happy one.

Although the biographical narrative of Gauguin in Tahiti is rich, thanks largely to the historical work of the anthropologist Bengt Danielsson, there is more to be said about Gauguin's relationship to the context of fin-de-siècle colonial culture in Tahiti.[5] Several recent studies have considered the important connections between colonialism, racism, and gender, examining Gauguin's representation of Tahitian men and women in terms of the power relations between the colonizer and the colonized, and considering Polynesian culture as the mediating force in Gauguin's formulation of his critique of bourgeois European values.[6] The present essay examines the impact of colonial experience on Gauguin's primitivism by focusing on a specific aspect of the artist's working process – the unfolding role that the photographic image played in his exoticism after he determined to live in a French colony.

Photography emerged in the nineteenth century as a distinctly modern, and at least initially Western, medium, and its rich history is deeply associated with the history of French art and technology. From the beginning, the powers of photographic mimesis and representation provoked artistic controversy over its aesthetic agency. Champions of artistic imagination such as Baudelaire valued photography only as a modern tool of science and documentation – nothing more than an *aide-mémoire* for the artist.[7] Yet within a decade of its invention, a vanguard of photographers forcefully claimed the artistic potential of photography. No other medium in the nineteenth century generated so strong a challenge to the traditional domain of the painter, and most key artists of Gauguin's symbolist generation experimented with the medium. While these painters were seldom neutral about the importance of photography to modern art and visual culture, they were often ambivalent about the nature of its significance. On this matter (as on so much else) Gauguin's own views were conflicting and contradictory. On one hand, he dismissed photography as an unexpressive medium, claiming that only academic masters like Ernest Meissonier, who cared about precise anatomical detail, could learn from it.[8] The mechanical nature of photography seemed to preclude any role for aesthetic play, subjective judgement, or individual imagination, all of which were values central to the symbolist credo. Gauguin's primitivism combined a romantic ideal of highly individual expression with the anti-modernist disdain of the symbolist generation for technology: 'Les machines sont venues, l'art s'en est allé; et je suis loin de penser que la photographie nous soit propice.'[9] For Gauguin, as for Baudelaire, seemingly objective photographic 'truths' could never surpass the beauties created by the imagination: 'La photographie des couleurs va nous dire la vérité. Quelle vérité? La vraie couleur d'un ciel, d'un arbre, de toute la nature matérialisée. Quelle est donc la vraie coleur d'un centaure, d'un minotaure, ou d'une chimère, de Vénus, et de Jupiter?'[10]

On the other hand, in spite of such contentions, Gauguin was clearly in awe of the speed and mimetic powers of photographic technology: 'Vous dirai-je ce qui serait l'oeuvre d'art la plus fidèle, la photographie, quand elle rendra les couleurs, ce qui sera bientôt possible. Et vous voudriez avoir un homme intelligent, transpirant pendant des mois pour donner la même illusion de réalité par une ingenieuse petit machine.'[11] The contemporary understanding of a photograph as an agent of subjectivity that always somehow bears the mark of its maker and its time was an insight that Gauguin never acknowledged.[12] Nonetheless, he seems to have known by intuition that a photograph is not transparently factual, that it has an independent agency to provoke and stimulate the beholder. He understood that a reproduction of a painting could teach him to see and appreciate that painting in a fresh way.[13] This modern machine had its uses, even for a 'sauvage civilisé,' as Gauguin sometimes called himself.[14]

In that era of fin-de-siècle colonialism, the medium of photography provided Gauguin with a crucial element of control and visual privilege. The photographic image assumed three important roles for him during his Polynesian sojourn: it was a convenient and affordable document to facilitate communication with the avant-garde community in Paris; it was a stimulating vehicle of art reproduction that allowed him to construct a *musée imaginaire* on the walls of his Tahitian studio; and it was an ethnographic source that authenticated the appearance and culture of the Other in the colonial sphere. Photography afforded Gauguin a mediating control over time and space, enabling him to engage in a decidedly modern, Western manipulation of the visible world. Photography also offered Gauguin a surrogate world of 'authentic' native experience in a colonial Tahiti that had disappointed him in its heterogeneity and modernity. Ethnographic and travel photography could stabilise and reify a perishing exotic world that was, to his European eye, in a tragic and inevitable process of dissolution and collapse in the wake of Western imperialism.[15] Photography was one tool of modernity that Gauguin chose not to leave behind.[16]

Gauguin's engagement with photography was a logical extension of his polymathic interests. At the centre of the avant-garde's re-evaluation of the role of traditional easel painting, he strove for innovation in every medium – devising new ceramic glazes, resurrecting the woodcut, painting directly on rough burlap rather than canvas, carving found branches in Tahiti into *ti'ii* ('receptacles for the Gods'), or mixing ethnographic photographs with water colours in his travel album *Noa Noa*. One of Gauguin's artistic strengths was his ability to forge unexpected connections by reconsidering the potential of materials and juxtaposing unusual combinations of motifs.

In the course of his Polynesian career, photography became an integral component of Gauguin's response to the exotic. He became an avid collector of photographs just as he had been a keen collector of impressionist painting when his income had permitted such a habit.[17] And while the historical record cannot confirm that Gauguin made photographs himself, both his ownership of a camera in at least three stages of his career and his friendships with at least three colonial photographers suggest that in the 1890s he was knowledgeable about the medium and probably experimented with it. Between 1895 and 1901, he may have made a few of the photographs that are now attributed to his friend Henri Lemasson.[18]

In all, at least fifty works of art that Gauguin created in Polynesia – paintings, sculptures, prints, illustrated manuscripts – are informed by his appropriation of poses or motifs taken from his large collection of photographic reproductions of art and from ethnographic photographs of indigenous people of Oceania.[19] Throughout his career Gauguin collected art reproductions; in Paris he covered the walls of his studio with reproductions of both Japanese prints and works by Manet and Puvis de Chavannes.[20] During his Breton period (1886–90), Gauguin did not rely on photographic sources for his compositions of peasants or landscapes. The most likely explanation for this difference may be both geographical and social. His frequent trips back to Paris from Brittany gave him constant access to original works of art (such as Manet's *Olympia,* which he copied directly at the Luxembourg museum). Also, while in Brittany, he was constantly surrounded by colleagues and younger acolytes. His intensely productive relationship with Émile Bernard is but one example of the creative stimuli Gauguin encountered at Pont Aven. Similarly, in Arles, he worked side by side with Van Gogh, and the two artists occupied each other in debate over stylistic and thematic matters. In Polynesia, however, Gauguin worked alone. In Papeete there were no European painters (other than amateurs) with whom he might work. As he stepped off the boat, he moved into an isolation unknown to him in his career in either Brittany or Paris. The only Western artists Gauguin appears to have been friendly with during his years in Tahiti were not painters at all but self-trained colonial photographers.[22] But as he prepared to depart for Tahiti in 1891, he declared to Redon his plan to take a 'whole little world of friends' in his collection of art reproductions and drawings: these images would be his comrades with whom he could chat every day.[21] At the end of his career, a photograph that shows his studio wall in Hiva Oa reveals that his little 'musée imaginaire' continued to play an important part in his studio life (fig. 3.1). For Gauguin, photographs became a surrogate art community.

But Gauguin's interest in photography can hardly be explained merely by the loss of his habitual cohort of painters in France. It is more productive to investigate his interest in the photograph as a key to exploring issues of memory, time, and space. These concerns emerge in key paintings completed well before Gauguin's departure for Tahiti in 1891. An early still-life composition of 1886, dating from his brief experimentation with neo-impressionist technique, makes explicit the eclectic nature of his exoticism. Gauguin connects the photograph to the worlds of the exotic and the historical in *Still-Life with a Horse's Head* (fig. 3.2): an exotic pastiche of decorative Japanese fans, a Japanese doll, and a cast replica of the head of a horse from the Parthenon displayed against patterned French wallpaper.[23] On a table at the base of the composition lies an open photograph album, its thick gilt-edged pages offering a sampling of photographs whose illegibility, in conjunction with the Japanese and Greek artefacts hovering above it, invite the viewer to muse over recollections and fantasies of travel and the exotic. Both the artefacts and the photographs are figured as resources of the imagination and as referents to idealised exotic locales.

Travel and relocation in the colonial world fuelled Gauguin's artistic energies. His early biography holds keys to his lifelong obsession with exotic locales. He spent six years of his early childhood in the lap of colonial luxury with family relations in Lima, Peru – an experience that conditioned him to the privileges of colonial life. In the final year of his life, Gauguin framed an account of his childhood with fond recollections of the colonial pleasure of being served by the Indian and Chinese domestics employed by his family.[24] In his early twenties, he travelled the world as a French merchant seaman. Later, as an artist, his first excursions out of Paris to Brittany led him in anti-pilgrimage away from the city to a realm of comparatively exotic Celtic culture within French borders. Pont Aven beckoned with fresh subjects, seemingly simpler patterns of life, and the potential of communion with like-minded artists. But once there, Brittany ceased to be exotic enough, and Gauguin hardly seemed able to stay put. Between 1886, when he first visited Brittany, and 1891, when he first went to Tahiti, he moved thirteen times, taking up residence in Paris, rural France, and abroad. In 1887, he travelled to Panama and Martinique, where he anticipated enjoying such colonial amenities as an inexpensive cost of living, friendly native women, and new artistic inspiration. In retrospect, he claimed 'I had a decisive experience in Martinique. It was only there that I felt like my real self.'[25] This notion of the discovery of one's 'real self' in the wake of the experience of an 'authentic' exotic locale is a hallmark trope of exoticism in the fin de siècle. Gauguin exemplified the disgruntled romantic individual who lamented his own alienation from the mass culture of modernity as characterized by the bourgeois urban experience. He longed to recuperate himself through an individualistic and idiosyncratic displacement in an exotic sphere. The desire was never completely fulfilled, however, and the project never completed (witness the escalating terms of Gauguin's geographic solutions). As Chris Bongie has observed, in the fin de siècle when the sheer existence of the Other was threatened by the presumed success of Europe's imperialist project, 'the exotic necessarily becomes, for those who persist in search of it, the sign of an aporia – a constitutional absence at the heart of what had been projected as a possible alternative to modernity.'[26] In other words, the exoticist goes searching for a self he or she will never find in a land that never seems to exist in the present except as a fading shadow of some earlier (and now irretrievably lost or degenerated) ideal state.

For Gauguin, the search took the form of an artist's ideal utopia, where a better life and a better art would result from the superior 'primitive' circumstances. His concept of a Studio of the Tropics derived from an earlier notion, the Studio of the South, first proposed by Van Gogh in 1886 to Émile Bernard and Gauguin. For Van Gogh, the light, natural beauty, and affordability of Provence seemed ideally suited to the establishment of an artistic commune. Van Gogh's Studio of the South was to be a productive and regenerative alternative to city life for the vanguard, where 'the poor cab horses of Paris ... could go out to pasture when they get too beat up.'[27] After their productive but volatile brief collaboration in Arles in 1888, Gauguin dismissed the idea of staying in Provence with Van Gogh, but he did not abandon the notion of a utopian studio, which he now envisioned as a Studio of the Tropics. Gauguin and Bernard proposed various remote locations for the dream studio, including three French colonies: Tonkin, Tahiti, and Madagascar. What Gauguin wanted was utopia, pure and simple. He wrote to Bernard of going where they could 'live in freedom and practice art. Without needing money, you will find an assured existence in a better world.'[28] Love would also be better and easier than in Europe: he fantasized about the women in Tonkin, whom he characterized as having good hearts and loose morals. His vision grew decidedly colonial: by the end of 1890, he was convinced that 'out there,' he could both 'renew his energies,' and his art.

While by this time Gauguin clearly demonstrated his penchant for seeking out the exotic, an event in Paris in 1889 turned him decidedly to the idea of immigration to the French colonies. That event was the spectacular Exposition universelle, a celebration of the centennial of the French Revolution. The Exposition elevated industry, commerce, and science as modern French triumphs and represented a massive effort in official propaganda. Political goals included the reconciliation of deeply divided factions of the Third Republic; a peaceful gesture to ease tensions with European powers; the stimulation of the domestic economy; and the assertion of France's imperial supremacy abroad.[29] On display for all of Europe was a France fully recovered from the Franco-Prussian war and led to renewed international prominence by the liberal republicanism of Jules Ferry and the opportunist Third Republic. The massive Eiffel Tower reigned supreme over the fairgrounds, its imposing height and graceful engineering serving as a monument to the powers of the rational, modern mind and to the dominance of bourgeois industrialism. Technology was the star; phonographs, improved gas lighting, new railways, telegraphs, and canal systems stole the show. Exhibits presented an accessible, peaceful, prosperous world of limitless possibility supported by the promises of modern science and industry and wrapped in a nationalistic confidence that touted France at the zenith of her commercial and creative vigour. In the Palais des arts libéraux, a large retrospective (fig. 3.3) canonized the history of photography, a rapidly developing technology that after just half a century now seemed 'already quite old thanks to the progress it has made.'[30] The era of the portable tourist camera had arrived: even the travelling amateur was promised the modern benefits of convenience, mastery, and efficiency in making visual records.[31]

Photography also figured prominently at the Palais des colonies, in displays that touted the success of France as Europe's leading imperial force in the colonial world (figs 3.4 and 3.5). The large exhibition of the colonies, linked with the glory of French military prowess by its location in front of the army's Hôtel des invalides, advertised France's newly revived colonial empire. As Debora Silverman has observed, the colonial exhibits were devised to bolster public interest and support for French colonial policies, which had been the focus of national debate in recent years.[32] Vast displays of 'authentic' native products (many of which were actually made in Paris to look like imported goods from the colonies) coupled with live exhibits of native persons at the various booths presented a commodified exoticism that could be viewed, handled, smelled, eaten, and taken home. Some visitors likened the fair's spectacle of exotic goods to the lure of the colourful displays at Parisian department stores.[33] This rampant consumerism extended to public demand for images of exotic places: visitors indulged in a visual covetousness that reduced global diversity to 'the world as postcard,' as a spectacle to be mastered through viewing and acquisition.[34] Scenic and ethnographic photographs of Tahiti on display at the Palais des colonies were so appealing that visitors repeatedly ripped them from the walls to take home, where they could fantasize in privacy. We might dismiss such shoplifting as meaningless petty vandalism, but these little thefts are telling analogues of greater acts of violation and appropriation enacted in a neocolonial age that still rang with the words, 'Prenez-la, prenez la,' Victor Hugo's exhortation to France to seize all available lands in Africa. Coveted and stolen photographs of the colonies were tangible souvenirs of trips not taken, mass-produced memories for travellers with no past. Purchased travel photographs made the exotic world both accessible and subservient to the desires of tourism and emigration; they provided the instant gratification for urban voyagers who spent a day – a vicarious short life – in the simulacrum of the exotic.

Gauguin's repeated trips to the colonial exhibition resulted in a few minor drawings made after the architectural exhibits – notably the full-scale reproduction of part of the Cambodian temple Angkor Wat.[35] Motifs lifted from the temple reliefs also informed a few of Gauguin's paintings and sculptures made prior to his departure for Tahiti. But of more lasting importance to his developing exoticism was his simultaneous exposure to the pre-packaged ideology of colonialism and to the collectible photographs of exotic works of art. The photographs Gauguin acquired at the colonial exhibition shared the same seductive quality of cultural authenticity that appealed to him in the displays. In writing to Bernard of his experience, he collapsed the distance between the Asian referents, the entertainment of the performance, and the photographic reproductions he had acquired: 'You missed something in not coming the other day. In the Java village there are Hindu dances. All the art of India can be seen there, and it is exactly like the photos I have ...'[36]

The colonial fair promoted shopping. Most visitors bought replicas of the icon of the future and of progress: miniature Eiffel Towers were the most popular souvenir of the 1889 fair. In buying photographs of ancient, exotic sculpture (fig. 3.6), Gauguin acquired the opposite: modern souvenirs of a vanishing world of ancient, hand-crafted, religious art. He transported these photographs, along with his reproductions of European paintings, to Tahiti in 1891 to set up his 'museum without walls' in his studio. These images inspired Gauguin for over a decade; he returned to them even in his last years in the Marquesas to mine them for poses. They offered all the convenience of the modern reproduction: a context-free detail drawn from a distant culture that could be viewed arbitrarily or juxtaposed with any other example of world art.[37] Gauguin's continuing attraction to the photographic reproduction lay in its infinite flexibility: it was a commodity over which he had ultimate control, because the photographic process decontextualized art objects and rendered a wide array of sizes, textures, and media in a relatively uniform, small, manipulable format. The reduction of hue to variations of black and white and of three-dimensional surfaces to a glossy flat picture homogenised a highly diverse group of objects into a single reservoir of visual ideas. The photographs also distanced both the authorship and the authority of the original object, and while Gauguin had never been an artist shy of 'plagiarizing' the work of another whose art he admired,[38] the use of photographs no doubt served to neutralize or even naturalize the act of borrowing pictorial ideas from the world encyclopaedia of art.

The full scope of Gauguin's 'musée imaginaire' will never be known, as only a small part of his photographic collection survives. But among the extant items are several photographs of relief sculptures from the ninth-century Javanese temple of Borobudur (fig. 3.6). A discussion of one of his many appropriations from these photographs will suffice here. Gauguin's canvas *Two Tahitian Women* (fig. 3.7) is often discussed as an example of his manipulation of the exotic female body to satisfy Western male voyeuristic expectations of viewing pleasure.[39] Certainly, the offerings of platter and flowers are consciously coupled with a bold proffering of female breasts, which Gauguin showcases in full sunlight, in contrast to the shadowed and recessive areas of the women's arms and heads. This titillation of sensual pleasures and invitations recalls the high romantic tradition of odalisques wallowing for the benefit of the male viewer in the hot-house sensorium of the harem. Yet the formal origins of these full-bodied hostesses in paradise is not within the French orientalist canon. It has escaped notice that these female figures, like so many in Gauguin's Polynesian oeuvre, derive from one of the photographs of the Borobudor reliefs (see fig. 3.6): the woman bearing the platter in Gauguin's canvas is a transcription of the second standing woman from the left in fig. 3.6 (see the detail in fig. 3.8).[40] The central theme of this Buddhist relief, the joyful greeting of a travelling merchant by a crowd of local women,[41] is subtly reiterated by Gauguin's painting, in which the direct gazes and welcoming postures of the two Tahitian women beckon the viewer as a newly arrived voyager to a foreign land of multiple delights.

Given Gauguin's isolation from art museums while living in Polynesia, it is not surprising he would create a surrogate gallery of world art to stimulate his imagination. Yet he turned to photography to help authenticate his experience of the local as well, collecting ethnographic photographs of Polynesian and other 'exotic' people. He used these photographs not only in the production of his art, but also in the negotiation of his own liminal position as what James Clifford has termed an ethnographic liberal, or an ironic participant in local culture who has cultivated an image of marginality that is at a certain remove from colonial authority.[42] Gauguin appropriated photographic clichés of imperialist voyeurism to negotiate his own social identity as bohemian and libertine within the restricted sphere of colonial society. A telling example of Gauguin's use of photography to manipulate his public image comes from his final year in the Marquesas, when he openly displayed pornographic photographs of North African women to irritate the morally self-righteous colonists in his community. He concluded that 'if you hang up a little indecency on your door, you will always get rid of the honest people, the most intolerable people God ever created.'[43] But while Gauguin was provoking the ire of local Catholics with his soft-core porn show, he was using a constructed, Western image of the exotic body to do it.[44] There is considerable irony here in the idea that Gauguin was deploying an orientalist's view of the exotic woman to critique Western notions of modesty and propriety, which were fostered by a European religion imposed on the island by colonists. The artist appropriated photographic clichés of imperialist voyeurism to negotiate his own social identity as bohemian and libertine within the restricted sphere of Marquesan colonial society.

Yet Gauguin also used photography to negotiate his attenuated relationship with the avant-garde in France. He appended photographs to his correspondence not just to convey specific information about his art, but more importantly, to reify his primitivist project. In this sense, his use of the photograph anticipates the ethnographer's use of photographs in the twentieth century to authenticate the author's experience as well as his text.[45] Gauguin used photographs to impress upon his distant colleagues the unfolding progress of his artistic mission. One such document is the only known photographic record of Gauguin's abodes in Polynesia (fig. 3.9), which he sent to Georges-Daniel de Monfreid in 1898.[46] The image, taken by Gauguin's friend Jules Agostini, who probably framed the view according to the artist's specifications, depicts the studio/home built by Gauguin in the Papeete suburb of Punaauia. The view so thoroughly imbeds the artist's hut in dense tropical vegetation that the verdant foliage collapses distinctions between structure and nature. Agostini used a crude pole structure at the edge of the garden to isolate and emphasise the central motif of Gauguin's landscape – a sculpted female nude, visible from the back. The photograph thus reiterates Gauguin's own recurring topos of the exotic Eve and promotes the mythology of Gauguin as artist-in-residence in a Tahitian Eden. Circulating such 'documents' allowed Gauguin to curate his reputation at a distance.

Gauguin also sent colonial photographs to reinforce his aesthetic agenda among his fellow artists. Invoking the symbolist terminology of synaesthesia, he wrote about the power of 'hearing' the music of a photograph of seated Tahitian women that he sent to a French friend in 1895. He praised the photograph for its barbarous or primitive rhythm and for the pleasing music the scene created for the beholder.[47] Gauguin concluded his letter with the lament, 'Ah, le rêve, comme il est facile de le trouver réel,' suggesting that the photograph offered reassurance and confirmation of an exotic world he sought but had not found. He also implied that it mattered little to him whether or not his poetic vision inspired by the compelling photograph was truthful or not: 'On dit que dans l'obscurité, on ne sait pas si on fume réellement son cigare.'

In spite of such disclaimers, however, Gauguin also admired photographs as sources of empirical knowledge, particularly in the wake of his frustration with the pervasive Westernization he witnessed in Oceania. In confronting the disappointing absence of the 'authentic' Tahiti he had expected to find, he often relied on the authoritative representation of a 'true' Polynesia as codified by ethnographic photography. Living in and near Papeete, Gauguin had easy access to the broad spectrum of representations of Tahitian culture produced by colonial photographers. Local businesses in Papeete produced four primary genres of photographs in the 1890s for sale to a growing local tourist market and for exportation to Europe and America as travel illustration. These included scenes of modern business and colonial settlement in Papeete; formal portraits of white colonists and affluent Tahitians who had assimilated European fashion (and apparently values); rural landscape and village scenes; and ethnographic studies of native 'types' posed in controlled studio settings that effaced most or all evidence of Tahiti's vast colonial history. Of these four categories of images, it was the ethnographic fictions, the frozen images of a pre-modern Tahiti, that most interested Gauguin; he used these images as the basis of numerous works of art.

Both ethnographic and travel photography of the fin de siècle tended to subjugate and categorize non-European peoples through several pictoral strategies. These strategies included the elimination of a competing cultural milieu and/or contemporary colonial detail that identified the subject as a member of a living, contemporary culture; the adoption of a stock repertoire of poses designed to display, measure, and objectify exotic bodies; and the reduction of facial expression to a vacuous, disinterested countenance that relieved Western beholders of the social responsibility of visually engaging an individual. Some or all of these qualities characterize the photographs Gauguin chose to collect in Tahiti.

Within weeks of his arrival in Tahiti, Gauguin purchased photographs of tattooed Marquesans in Papeete, probably at the Spitz Curio store (fig. 3.10), and from these found inspiration for the decorative patterns he applied to carved bowls and spoons during his first Tahitian trip.[48] The colonial photographer offered a controlled (and unthreatening) vision of the Marquesan body as yet another visual commodity the artist might collect and store in his repertoire of exotic phenomena. Such borrowings elucidate the mediating role of the colonial photograph for Gauguin's working process: it seems likely that Gauguin's exposure to the same Marquesan tattoos during his first days in Tahiti, had they been visible to him only on the moving bodies of people whom he could not control and with whom he could not communicate, would not have occasioned the same artistic appropriations. The Western image of the Marquesan in this ethnographic photograph – frozen in a contrived pose of contemplation in the perpetual ethnographic present and conveniently decontextualised from his social context – encouraged Gauguin's objectification of the exotic body. Like Cézanne's bowls of apples in the studio, photographs pinned to a wall did not talk back and did not distract an artist with the messy contingencies of human relationships with models.

Gauguin used an actual ethnographic photograph as part of a work of art in only one instance, but the example is significant because it is a work apparently made not for public consumption in a Parisian art gallery but only for the private perusal of the artist. This object is *Noa Noa*, the illustrated version of his fictionalised narrative of his first Tahitian trip. Between 1893 and 1896, Gauguin copied his text into a bound album, and illustrated scattered pages with a strikingly heterogeneous collage of images, including photographs, woodcuts, drawings, rubbings, watercolours, monotypes, and reproductions of his own art. A discussion of one of the four album pages that Gauguin decorated with photographs will suffice here (fig. 3.11). Gauguin's woodcut in the upper left depicts an encounter of two Tahitian deities, probably Hina and Tefatou.[49] The nature of their encounter has many possible interpretations, but it is obvious that Gauguin has reduced it to an iconic confrontation of male and female. Similarly, the watercolour in the bottom register of the page depicts mythic male and female personages drawn from Tahitian mythology – in this case, probably a scene from the narrative of Hiro, god of thieves, who rescues a virgin imprisoned in an enchanted forest guarded by giants. Gauguin's watercolour apparently illustrates Hiro's bare-handed destruction of the trees, an act that breaks the magic spell and liberates the woman.[50] Gauguin infuses this heroic scene with an undeniably erotic narrative: as the passive and diminutive captive watches, Hiro grabs an emphatically phallic branch of the tree in an ambiguous gesture that is as much a surrogate act of self-stimulation as it is the uprooting of the barrier between himself and the virgin. In such a context of sexualised male action and female passivity, the single photograph of the Polynesian woman glued on the upper right corner of the page plays an ambivalent role. She is at once the empirical evidence of the photographic referent – the exotic woman whom Gauguin encountered Out There – and the imagined subject of the amorous fantasies of the beholder. Her bare chest and grass skirt position her in the realm of traditional culture, yet her Christian necklace re-locates her in the present, in the mixed realities of colonialism. She inhabits the boundaries between the exoticist's realms of the experienced and the desired; she is Gauguin's feminised allegory of Tahiti.

The genesis of *Noa Noa* is usually linked with Gauguin's connections with the French literary circle of Symbolist writers and with his collaborator, the poet Charles Morice. But in conceiving *Noa Noa* as an illustrated travel journal, Gauguin was probably directly inspired by a more popular genre of souvenir albums of the sort compiled by French naval officers. On his return voyage from Tahiti to France via Noumea in 1893 on the cruiser Duchaffault, Gauguin (a former merchant seaman) kept close company with naval officers. One Officer Godey, whom Gauguin names as one of his travel companions, created a souvenir travel album that Gauguin no doubt examined.[51] A compilation of the officer's own sketches, purchased colonial photographs, and accounts of local lore and personal travel adventures, this album may well have served as a stimulus to Gauguin to begin his own *Noa Noa*.[52] The very title of Gauguin's narrative, the source of which has previously eluded scholars, may well derive from Godey's album, as the first page commemorates the ship's departure from Tahiti with a poem entitled 'Noa Noa' that identifies Tahiti as the happy land of love. Among the many photographs collected by Godey is a striking rehearsal of colonialist fantasy (fig. 3.12). For the benefit of the camera/beholder, a *pareu*-clad middle-aged sailor grasps the leg of his significantly younger *vahine* with a gesture that conveys as much confident possessiveness as affection. Following in the example of popular travel literature by such exoticist writers as Pierre Loti, this image codifies the pervasive male European fantasy of a passing dalliance with a native *vahine*. If we return to the photograph of the Polynesian woman in Gauguin's *Noa Noa* album in the context of such loaded imagery, we realise that the woman in the photograph is the only female on the page without a male partner. The photograph offers her up both as the tangible companion and as the reward for the artist's search for rejuvenation through contact with sexual and cultural novelty. Although his selection of the photograph was no doubt largely arbitrary, once chosen, this woman (nameless only in this context) assumes a key role of particularity – she is the exemplar of the Real, of compliant sexuality and of adventures in exotic wonderland. This interpretation is bolstered by Gauguin's use elsewhere in the album of similar photographs featuring young Polynesian women in indigenous costume. The only photograph of a Polynesian man to enter the pages has a historic specificity; it is the portrait of Pomare V, the last King of Tahiti, whose death at the time of Gauguin's arrival became one of the artist's metaphors for the state of degeneration and decline of Tahitian society as a whole.

Gauguin invests these ethnographic photographs with many meanings; they are nostalgic fragments torn from a vanishing paradise in decline and fixed to the bound pages of an album to give them improbable permanence. They reject the contingencies of real time and cultural transformation while still asserting the empirical truths of photographic evidence. Surrounded by Gauguin's watercolours and woodcuts, they easily enter the realm of personal association and memory; they are flashes of a dream given substance by the apparent veracity of ethnographic fact.

Gauguin used photographs as a direct medium only in the *Noa Noa* album, but several traces of the ethnographic authority of photography lie submerged in other works of art. He collected photographic images of Polynesian women throughout his career (and one might observe that he apparently collected actual women as well). One such photograph, made by an anonymous photographer, is of a Tongan girl living in Fiji (fig. 3.13); her elaborate dress, carved paddle, beaded necklace, and complex multi-layered hair style all set her apart, from Gauguin's perspective, as more exotic than the Tahitian women he lived among in Punaauia. In 1900, just prior to his departure for the Marquesas where he hoped to relocate among the 'purer' races of Polynesia, he used this photograph as the basis for at least two monotypes depicting a Polynesian woman accompanied by a male 'evil spirit' (fig. 3.14).[53] The spirit figure, based on one of Gauguin's sculptures, is mythic and fantastic. Yet here Gauguin grants a palpability and credence to his imagination through his juxtaposition of this incubus to a woman drawn from photography's ethnographic template. In his choice of this young Tongan girl as a model, Gauguin reinforced (perhaps unknowingly) the charged and slightly predatory sexual tensions implied in the image by the spirit's hovering presence at the girl's side: the hairstyle of the young Tongan girl is the traditional coif of a virgin who will relinquish her dangling braids to her suitor after consummation of their relationship.[54] While Gauguin's goal here was surely not ethnographic reportage, his monotype has the uncanny power of illusory realism; the beholder is propelled from the believable detail to the mythic implications of the image.

The ethnographic photograph also served Gauguin as the basis of some of his most mythic constructions of a primitive Tahiti. Perhaps the most famous (but surprisingly little examined) instance of his dependence on ethnographic photography dates to the first trip, when Gauguin was most concerned with recovering a traditional Tahiti he mourned as having arrived too late to witness. The painting *Pape Moe* (Sacred Waters) deserves analysis at length. Here, Gauguin lifted the central motif and composition from a photograph sold by Charles Spitz (figs 3.15 and 3.16).[55] The photograph provides a point of departure for Gauguin's hyperbolic tale, recounted in *Noa Noa*, of the magical transformation of a Tahitian princess into an eel. [56] Gauguin incorporates the idea of animistic transformation in two details of foliage in the canvas: the drinking figure looks up to meet the direct gaze of a fish that emerges from the contours of rock and foliage.[57] To the left of the fish, an embryo-like human figure, painted in the relative scale of a human infant, uncurls within the rock to also confront the drinker.[58] Gauguin brings to this image his knowledge of the Tahitian belief in the mutability of the spirit world, and visualizes a site of mystical transformation. The scene both invokes Tahitian cosmology and provides an analogue for the artistic processes of invention and imagination so revered by Gauguin.

But what of the relationship between the photograph and Gauguin's mythic scene at the waterfall? There are the superficial formal connections: Gauguin has clearly copied the thin stream of water, a few distinctive forms of vegetation, and the pose of the drinker. There are many additional layers of the relationship to consider as well. We could dismiss Gauguin's deference to the photograph as a method of verifying authentic Tahitian costume and scenery, although the photograph is actually of a Samoan. Or we might argue that Gauguin's attraction to the image derives from his pre-existing knowledge of European conventions of the feminine and the natural, and that his eye located this image in a continuum of essentializing views of women at waterfalls – a typology recurrent in French painting from Ingres to Courbet. A third possible interpretation might locate Gauguin's attraction to the image within its own intrinsic ambiguities. The face of the figure is hidden in the photograph; the hair is either short or is curled up around the neck; both the body and the costume of the figure could belong to either a Polynesian man or a Polynesian woman. Although the long hair in the painting clearly denotes Gauguin's drinking figure as a female, he retains the photographed figure's muscled body and thick waist in his rendering of the woman. Gauguin's adoption of a somewhat androgynous figure, partly inspired by the ambiguities of this photograph, might be interpreted as evidence of his appreciation of Tahiti as a realm where European gender stereotypes are relaxed and sexual identity is more mutable.[59] Moreover, the scene represents a waterfall in the rocky interior of the island, a mysterious area that the artist (in spite of his boastful tales of exploration in *Noa Noa*) did not know well, if at all, from first-hand experience. The photographer transports us to a forest scene that reiterates two essential characteristics of the European concept of the sublime in its shaded darkness and presumed inaccessibility; the Tahitian has had to scale a wall of rocks, and we as viewers are given no reassuring foothold in the foreground. The photograph thus enacts a veritable 'heart of nature' or 'heart of darkness' narrative for the viewer. Each of these models for considering Gauguin's interest in this particular photograph has some credibility, but additional considerations go beyond the appeal of this particular scene to lead us to some concluding observations about the more pervasive appeal of ethnographic photography for the fin-de-siècle primitivist.

The ethnographic photograph is a convenient and seemingly transparent filter of culture that functions in stopped time, not real time. Photography invariably dislocates time and space, as Susan Sontag has observed, freezing 'moments in a life or society [that] contradicts their form, which is process, a flow in time.'[60] This illusion of stopped time produces two subjective effects in viewing ethnographic photographs. On one hand, photography freezes its subject in time, suggesting that its referent belongs to a static realm of history rather than to the dynamic present. This is a particularly subversive quality in colonial photography, for as Johannes Fabian and others have argued, traditional ethnography, born in an imperialist age, practised a de-historicizing of its object that was reinforced by the photographic construction of an atemporal, unchanging Primitive pitted against the dynamic and progressive modernity of the observer's culture.[61] In the present example, the barefoot Samoan in the photograph is dressed in a plain fabric wrap (known as a *lava-lava*) that emulates the tapa *pareu* costume worn by Polynesians in the era of initial European contact; such unprinted fabric (whether real tapa or European-produced cotton) was not commonly worn as a daily costume by Tahitians in Gauguin's time. Thus the photograph invokes an idealised past. Yet there is another temporal fiction at play here, a fiction that we might term a cryogenic (or freeze-dried) transportation of the photographic referent to the viewer's own subjective present. The image's realism empowers the viewer to recall this frozen ethnographic sample to the present through the heat of subjective will. In the viewer's recovery of this moment, however, the subtle distinctions of how the image was made and for what audience – the contingent factors that gave it meaning at a particular time – may be swept away in an uncritical elevation of an image's claims to factual truth. As Barthes has characterized the seductive mechanism of photographic immediacy more generally, the 'there and then' of the moment when the picture was made becomes the 'here and now' of the beholder.[62] To summarize, in the case of colonial photography, the European viewer pushes the exotic subject back into a pre-contact zone of non-history, into a controlled and depoliticized position as the object of Western study and salvage. Yet the same viewer can then recall that distanced and voiceless Other back into a nostalgic reverie on the facticity of fading and lost cultures. The implications and convenience of the temporal dualism of photography for an artist are obvious: why should Gauguin, on a self-declared mission to recover primitive authenticity, deal with the messy contingencies of live models and the disappointing hybrid of colonialism when such an appealing simulacrum of the exotic was available to him in the imagery of colonial photography? Granted, neither he nor any other primitivist resorted exclusively to the authority of photographic renderings of the visible Polynesian world. But that Gauguin returned to this mediating image-world repeatedly throughout his Polynesian career suggests that in the realm of the photographic, he had found some satisfying comfort and reaffirmation of his vision of Tahiti as it should have been.

Yet photography's primitivist illusion is often not as seamless and monolithic as it may first seem. In the case of Spitz's waterfall image, the photograph compromises its own aura of timelessness. The source at which the Tahitian drinks is not a pure mountain stream, but the spout of a metal pipe, a modern product of hydraulic engineering. A less emphatic depiction of the pipe also appears in Gauguin's mythic painting. This detail reinserts real and historical time into both visual narratives, acknowledging a contemporary era that is inhabited by native and colonist alike. The telling detail of the water spout is located, not incidentally, at the centre of the photograph and at the centre of this temporal conflict. The falling stream of water, rendered in an inevitable blur by the limited technology of fin-de-siècle photography, is an appropriate analogue to Sontag's idea of the stream of time of photography: although the stream is arbitrarily and imperfectly fixed by the photographic image, it will, like the dynamic and unfolding culture of Tahiti under colonialism, establish its course beyond these imposed parameters of time and space.

NOTES

Portions of this essay appeared in my article 'Paradise Redux: Gaugin, Photography, and Fin-de-siècle Tahiti,' in *The Artist and the Camera: Degas to Picasso*, ed. Dorothy Kosinski (Dallas: Dallas Museum of Art with Yale University Press, 1999), 118–41, and are reprinted here with the permission of the Dallas Museum of Art. I gratefully acknowledge the support of my research on this topic by grants from the National Endowment for the Humanities and from the Center for the Advanced Study of the Visual Arts, National Gallery of Art, Washington D.C. This essay is dedicated in loving memory to Orlo E. Childs.

1 For a stimulating examination of the European primitivist impulse, see the anthology edited by Elazar Barkan and Ronald Bush, *Prehistories of the Future: The Primitivist Project and the Culture of Modernism* (Stanford: Stanford University Press, 1995), especially the introduction.

2 Gauguin's final days in the Marquesas have long received mythic embellishment, beginning with the essays written by Victor Ségalen immediately after the artist's death. Somerset Maugham recasts Gauguin's death in highly dramatic (even incendiary) terms in *The Moon and Sixpence* (1919). Even some recent scholarship, albeit well-grounded in biographical history and anthropology, indulges in romanticizing his death. Stephen Eisenman concludes his recent book *Gauguin's Skirt* (London: Thames and Hudson, 1997) with a novelistic account of Gauguin's progressively failing health.

3 For both a cogent summary of post-colonial theory and recent theoretical modifications of Edward Said's influential theory of the hegemony of imperialism set forth in *Orientalism* (New York: Vintage, 1979), see John M. MacKenzie, *Orientalism: History, Theory and the Arts* (Manchester: Manchester University Press, 1995), chapter 1. My discussion of colonialism and the politics of ethnographic investigation has been greatly informed by James Clifford, *The Predicament of Culture: Twentieth-Century Ethnography, Literature and Art* (Cambridge, Mass.: Harvard University Press, 1988).

4 A typical formulation of Gauguin's primitivism fuses the desire to return to childhood with a return to the origins of civilization: 'Je me suis reculé, bien loin, plus loin que les chevaux du Parthénon ... jusqu'au dada de mon enfance, le bon cheval de bois.' 'Diverses choses,' 1896–7, as quoted in Paul Gauguin, *Oviri, écrits d'un sauvage*, ed. Daniel Guérin (Paris: Gallimard, 1974), 158.

5 Bengt Danielsson, *Gauguin in the South Seas* (New York: Doubleday, 1966). A revised French edition (*Gauguin à Tahiti et aux Îles Marquises*; Papeete: Les Éditions Pacifique, 1975) offers important additional research. David Sweetman's ambitious recent biography, *Paul Gauguin: A Complete Life* (New York: Simon and Schuster, 1996), fills in many factual gaps in Gauguin's early life but is compromised by its

sensationalist treatment of Gauguin's sexual desires and motivations. See my review, 'The French Connection,' *The New York Times Book Review*, 31 March 1996, 22–3.

6 Abigail Solomon-Godeau, 'Going Native,' *Art in America* 77 (July 1989), 119–28, 161; and Griselda Pollock, *Avant-Garde Gambits 1888–1893: Gender and the Color of Art History* (New York: Thames and Hudson, 1992) consider Gauguin in the context of imperialist initiatives, and both authors emphasize Gauguin's physical and artistic exploitation of native women and the failure of his professed desire to assimilate into Tahitian culture. Stephen Eisenman strives to locate Gauguin more sympathetically in fin-de-siècle Tahitian culture, privileging the Tahitian content of the art and attempting to show how accurately Gauguin depicts the complexity of colonial identity.

7 Charles Baudelaire, 'The Salon of 1859: The Modern Public and Photography' (1859), reprinted in *Modern Art and Modernism: A Critical Anthology*, ed. Charles Harrison and Francis Frascina (London: The Open University, 1982), 19–21.

8 Gaugin's manuscript 'Diverses choses,' 1896–7, as quoted in Gauguin, *Oviri*, 158.

9 Gauguin, *Oviri*, 158.

10 Ibid., 174.

11 Quoted in S. Monneret, *L'impressionisme et son époque* (Paris: Robert Laffont, 1987), n.p. (photocopy in Musée d'Orsay documentation).

12 A useful discussion of the relativity of the verity of photography, particularly in cases of seemingly documentary photography of works of art, is found in Mary Bergstein, 'Lonely Aphrodites: On the Documentary Photography of Sculpture,' *Art Bulletin* 74 (September 1992), 475–98.

13 For example, he observes that a black and white reproduction of a painting by a colourist such as Delacroix can reveal that the charm of a painting lies not only in the colour but also in the tonality and the draughtsmanship. See 'Diverses choses,' 1896–7, as quoted in Gauguin, *Oviri*, 178.

14 Gauguin, *Oviri*, 11.

15 For a cogent formulation of fin-de-siècle exoticism in the context of imperialism, see Chris Bongie, *Exotic Memories: Literature, Colonialism and the Fin-de-siècle* (Stanford: Stanford University Press, 1991), chapter 1.

16 On photography, modernity, and progress, see 'Photography and the Modern in Nineteenth-Century Thought,' in *Photography and Its Critics: A Cultural History 1839–1900*, Mary Warner Marien (New York: Cambridge University Press, 1997).

17 On Gauguin's art collection, see Merete Bodelsen, 'Gauguin the collector,' *Burlington Magazine* 112 (September 1970), 590–615.

18 Bodelson proposed that Gauguin was an amateur photographer but offered no historical evidence to support the assertion (see Merete Bodelson, 'Gauguin and the Marquesan God,' *Gazette des Beaux Arts* 57 [mars 1960], 175). It is clear that Gauguin owned or borrowed cameras throughout the 1890s. He apparently left a camera behind in Paris in 1891, and once he found he needed the money in Tahiti he asked Georges Daniel de Monfried to sell it for him. See *Lettres de Paul Gauguin à Georges Daniel de Monfried*, 6th ed. (Paris: Édition Georges Crès, 1920), lettre IV (May 1892). Either the camera never sold, or Gauguin acquired a new one on his return to Paris,

since accounts of his studio at the rue Vercingetorix from September 1893 describe 'un énorme appareil photographique du format 18 × 26 monté sur pied' (see Jean de Rotonchamp, *Paul Gauguin* [Paris: Druet, 1903], 124). At his death, the estate sale of 1903 records several albums and boxes of photographs, plus 'un appareil photographique et accessoires' (G. Le Bronnec, 'Inventaire des biens de Gaugin, 27 mai 1903,' and 'Vente des oeuvres d'art, livres et objets ayant appartenu à Gaugin, 2 septembre 1903,' *Gazette des Beaux Arts* 47 [janvier–avril 1956], 201–4, 205–8). Bengt Danielsson thinks some of the lots probably contained both photographs that Gauguin collected and those he made himself. Danielsson interviewed the descendent of the buyer of the photographs (a Captain Martin of Papeete) but the material has vanished (oral communication, 1990).

Gauguin met Henri Lemasson and Jules Agostini, two amateur colonial photographers, on his return to Tahiti in 1895. They travelled together to Bora-Bora and took other excursions into the Tahitian countryside. See Henri Lemasson, 'La vie de Gauguin à Tahiti,' *Encyclopédie de la France et d'outremer* (February 1950), 19. Lemasson photographed Gauguin's hut in Punaauia as well as some of his sculpture; it seems likely that if Gauguin made photographs, he would have used his friend's expensive developing equipment. After moving to the Marquesas in 1901, he befriended yet another local photographer, Louis Grelet, who lived in Fatu Hiva. Grelet took numerous photographs of the artist at work in his studio/home, but these were lost in a shipwreck (Bengt Danielsson, oral communication, 1990).

19 It is outside the scope of the present essay to list these examples, but an analysis of these works of art will be included in my forthcoming book *In Search of Paradise: Painting and Photography in Fin-de-siecle Tahiti* (Berkeley: University of California Press).

20 Jean de Rotonchamp, *Paul Gauguin* (Paris: Druet, 1903), 68. For a discussion of the art reproductions Gauguin had seen though his godfather Gustave Arosa, a publisher, see Richard S. Field, *Paul Gauguin: The Paintings of the First Voyage to Tahiti* (New York: Garland 1977), especially 239 n50.

21 Gauguin to Redon, as quoted in Richard Brettell et al., *The Art of Paul Gauguin* (Washington D.C.: National Gallery of Art, 1988), 214.

22 These photographers included Charles Spitz, Henri Lemasson, Jules Agostini, and Louis Grelet. Gauguin never met John La Farge, the American painter whose visit to Tahiti ended only days before Gauguin's arrival in 1891. Given La Farge's open contempt for Gauguin's personal style, the two would hardly have become comrades had their paths crossed (John La Farge to Henry Adams, Newport Rhode Island, 8 November 1906, La Farge Family Papers, Sterling Library, Yale University, *LFFP* reel 2, frame 0444).

23 The Greek and Japanese elements in this painting and their possible relationship to Whistler's aestheticism are discussed by John House in the entry for this painting in *Royal Academy of Arts, Post-Impressionism: Cross-Currents in European Painting* (London: Royal Academy with Weidenfeld and Nicolson, 1979), cat. no. 80. House does not, however, discuss the significance of the photograph album in the still life.

24 'Avant et après,' 1903, as quoted in Gauguin, *Oviri*, 272. For accounts of Gauguin's travels, see Sweetman, *Paul Gauguin*.

25 Letter to Charles Morice, 1890, quoted in Brettell et. al., *Art of Paul Gauguin*, 60.

26 Bongie, *Exotic Memories*, 22.

27 Vincent Van Gogh, *The Complete Letters of Vincent Van Gogh*, 2nd ed. (Greenwich: New York Graphic Society, 1959), 2: letter 469.

28 Gauguin to Bernard, 1890, letter in *Paul Gauguin: Letters to his Wife and Friends*, ed. Maurice Malingue, trans. Henry Stenning (Cleveland: World Publishing Company, 1949), 139, no. 102.

29 For an excellent discussion of the fair and its political agenda, see Debora L. Silverman, 'The Paris Exhibition of 1889: Architecture and the Crisis of Individualism,' *Oppositions* 8 (Spring 1977), 71–91.

30 Louis Gonse, 'L'histoire retrospective du travail,' in *Revue de l'Exposition universelle de 1889*, ed. F.G. Dumas et L. de Fourcaud (Paris: Librairie d'art, 1889), 2:124.

31 See *L'Illustration*, 13 August 1889, 171.

32 Silverman, 'The Paris Exhibition of 1889: Architecture and the Crisis of Individualism,' 77.

33 T. de Wyzewa, 'Les Palais central des colonies,' in *Revue de l'Exposition Universelle de 1889*, ed. F.G. Dumas et L. de Fourcaud, 2:87.

34 For an interesting discussion of the commodification of exoticism and the idea of 'world as postcard,' see Ellen Strain, 'Exotic Bodies, Distant Landscapes: Touristic Viewing and Popularized Anthropology in the Nineteenth Century,' *Wide Angle* 18 (April 1996), 70–100.

35 See Douglas W. Druick and Peter Zegers, 'Le kampong et la pagode: Gauguin à l'Exposition universelle de 1889,' in *Gauguin: Actes du colloque Gauguin, Musée d'Orsay 11–13 janvier 1989* (Paris: École du Louvre, 1991), 101–42.

36 Letter of March 1889, in *Paul Gauguin: Letters to His Wife and Friends*, ed. Malingue, 118, letter 81.

37 An interesting comparison can be drawn here to Malraux's idea of a 'museum without walls,' a concept which encouraged the beholder of an art reproduction to deny the specific orientation of time and place – the cultural aura – that accompanies any original work of art if viewed in the context of its own culture. See Bergstein, 'Lonely Aphrodites,' 476.

38 The best discussion on this topic is Richard Field, 'Plagiaire ou créateur?' in *Paul Gauguin: génies et réalités* (Paris: Éditions du Chêne, 1986), 115–30.

39 The first influential feminist reading of this picture was Linda Nochlin's 'Eroticism and Female Imagery in Nineteenth-Century Art,' in *Woman as Sex Object* (New York: Newsweek, 1972), 11–12.

40 This identification is strengthened by a comparison of such details as the position of the right hand holding the.tray; notice that the fingers of the Tahitian woman wrap vertically around the lip of the tray as they do in the sculpture (see fig. 3.6). The breasts in the Borobudur relief are nestled even more provocatively over the edge of the tray, which is filled with flowers whose centers repeat the nipple shape on the breast. Moreover, there is a close resemblance of hand position between the woman standing at the far right whose hands are clasped in prayer and the woman at the right of Gauguin's painting whose raised, clasped hands hold pink flowers in greeting.

41 This identification of the subject of the relief follows John Miksic, *Borobudur: Golden Tales of the Buddhas* (Hong Kong: Periplus, 1990), 88.

42 See James Clifford, 'Power and Dialogue in Ethnography,' in *The Predicament of Culture*, 79.

43 He probably acquired these photographs in Port-Said, at the Suez Canal, on his return to Tahiti in 1895. See Gauguin, *Oviri*, 316.

44 While it is impossible to determine which particular photographs Gauguin bought in Port-Said in Egypt, examples of the genre of quasi-pornography that he acquired is reproduced in Malek Alloula, *The Colonial Harem*, trans. Myran Godzich and Wlad Godzich, Theory and History of Literature Series, vol. 21 (Minneapolis: University of Minnesota Press, 1986). Examples of pornographic photographs of Polynesian women no doubt existed in the 1890s, but the earliest examples I am aware of, by Lucien Gauthier, all post-date Gauguin's departure from Tahiti for the Marquesas in 1901.

45 See the excellent article by Chelsea Miller Goin, 'Malinowski's Ethnographic Photography: Image, Text and Authority,' in *History of Photography* 21 (Spring 1977), 67–73, at 67.

46 Letter 31, February 1898, *The Letters of Paul Gauguin to Georges Daniel de Monfreid*, trans. Ruth Peilkovo (New York: Dodd, Mead and Co., 1922), 95.

47 This unpublished Gauguin letter is quoted in an article by Théophile Briant in an obscure Breton journal, *Le Goeland*, 1 March 1938. Bengt Danielsson, who generously guided me to this article, believed the date of the letter to be 1895, not 1902, as stated in the article.

48 P. Jénot, 'Le premier séjour de Gauguin à Tahiti d'après le manuscrit Jénot,' *Gazette des Beaux Arts* 6 (janvier–avril 1956), 121–2. For examples of Gauguin's sculpture inspired by Marquesan tattoo design, see Christopher Gray, *Sculpture and Ceramics of Paul Gauguin* (Baltimore: The Johns Hopkins University Press, 1963), nos. 102, 104, 105, 144, 145. For further discussion of this connection, see Jehanne Teilhet-Fisk, *Paradise Reviewed: An Interpretation of Gauguin's Polynesian Symbolism* (Ann Arbor: UMI Research Press, 1983).

49 I follow here the identification of these two figures in a related drawing, as discussed by Teilhet-Fisk, *Paradise Reviewed*, 58–9, and ill. 20.

50 Gauguin's brief account of the tale probably derives from the longer version he read in J.A. Moerenhout, *Travels to the Islands of the Pacific Ocean* [1837] trans. Arthur Borden (Lanham: University Press of America, 1993), 226.

51 Gauguin named Godet (probably a misspelling for the proper name Godey) as one of his travel companions on the voyage in an appendix to the Getty manuscript of *Noa Noa* (begun in October 1893). See *Paul Gauguin: Noa Noa, Voyage to Tahiti*, ed. Jean Loize, trans. Jonathan Griffin (New York: Reynal and Company, 1961), 29. Gauguin noted that these officers welcomed him as a well-known artist and treated him with respect and friendship; given this recollection, it is probable that Godey showed Gauguin his souvenir album.

52 Although *Noa Noa: Gauguin's Tahiti* (ed. Nicholas Wadley, trans. Jonathan Griffin; Salem, New Hampshire: Salem House, 1985; 85) suggests that Gauguin began to

work on the text in earnest only after his return to France in 1893, there are indications that some of the initial text was drafted in Tahiti. I suggest those early passages probably date Gauguin's return trip to France.

53 See Richard Field, *Paul Gauguin: Monotypes* (Philadelphia: Philadelphia Museum of Art, 1977), nos. 66 and 67. Field identified a related photograph of this Tongan woman in his *Paul Gauguin: The Paintings of the First Voyage to Tahiti*, pl. 29, but the present photograph offers a more precise source for the physiognomic details, the hairstyle (particularly in the two tiny braids falling over the shoulder), the frontal standing pose, the beaded necklace, and flowered costume depicted in Gauguin's two monotypes.

54 Personal communication with Jehanne Teilhet-Fisk, May 1997.

55 The negative was made by an anonymous photographer in Samoa by 1887; an albumen print from it is preserved in the souvenir album compiled in that year by Reginald Gallop (in the collection of the State Library of New South Wales, Sydney). The image was also published in the French travel periodical *Autour du monde* in the early 1890s; there is a copy in the library of the Musée de l'homme, Paris. A slight variation of the composition is found in another photograph by Spitz in the collection of the Bishop Museum, Honolulu. This photograph was sold in the Spitz curio store in Papeete during Gauguin's stay in Tahiti.

56 Gauguin wrote his account of the picture in *Noa Noa* in part to justify the painting to his Parisian audience after its exhibition at Durand-Ruel in 1893: 'I had made no sound. When she had finished drinking, she took water in her hands and poured it over her breasts, then, as an uneasy antelope instinctively senses a stranger, she gazed hard at the thicket where I was hidden. Violently she dived ... I rushed to look down into the stream; – vanished. Only a huge eel writhed between the small stones of the bottom' (Getty manuscript of 1893, quoted in Wadley, *Noa Noa*, 32).

57 This head of a fish is a slight variation of the fish form painted on the inside cover of Gauguin's illustrated manuscript *Cahier pour Aline* (Fondation Jacques Doucet, Paris), begun in Tahiti in December 1892.

58 This figure may represent a variation of the man's head that emerges from the rock wall to the right of the drinker in a carved and painted oak relief version of *Pape Moe* (current location unknown); reproduced in Gray, *Sculpture and Ceramics of Paul Gauguin*, 129.

59 A discussion of Gauguin's writings and paintings in the context of the homosexuality of the Tahitian *mahu* (an idea first broached by Teilhet-Fisk) is developed by Eisenman in *Gauguin's Skirt*, chapter 2.

60 Susan Sontag, *On Photography* (Harmondsworth, UK: Penguin, 1978), 81 as quoted and discussed in Elizabeth Edwards, 'Introduction,' *Anthropology and Photography 1860–1920* (New Haven: Yale University Press, 1992), 7.

61 Johannes Fabian, *Time and the Other: How Anthropology Makes Its Object* (New York: Columbia University Press, 1983).

62 Roland Barthes, *Image Music Text*, trans. S. Heath (London: Fontana, 1977), 44.

CHAPTER FOUR

Emily Carr and the Traffic in Native Images

Gerta Moray

In these postcolonial times the ideological and political dimensions of artistic practice are more than ever under scrutiny. How do we read the work of an artist whose career and reputation were built on traffic in the Native image? This was literally the case with Emily Carr (1871–1945), a founding figure of modern art in Canada and a colleague of the legendary Group of Seven, who grounded an imagined modern-Canadian national identity in images of the landscape as a vast, alluring, and threatening wilderness. Carr herself contributed a further element to this foundational Canadian imagery: her paintings of the British Columbia landscape incorporated traces of what her white Canadian contemporaries saw as the ancient and exotic culture of the Northwest Coast Native peoples – what we see now as a colourful, local, and completely 'Canadian' heritage. In the years between 1907 and 1913 Carr made 200 paintings documenting the villages, the carvings, and the peoples of the Northwest Coast First Nations. In 1927, when she was in her mid-fifties, a large group of these paintings were shown in Ottawa at the National Gallery of Canada; the 'Exhibition of Canadian West Coast Art, Native and Modern' brought her into the national art scene. In 1941, her first published book, *Klee Wyck*, a collection of tales of her encounters with Native peoples, won the Governor General's Award and became a best-seller.[1] Carr's success as an artist was founded on the appeal of her Native images within a colonial context, the problematic history of which must be taken into account.

The Canadian settler community's enthusiastic adoption of Northwest Coast Native traditional artefacts as works of art (and, through the 1927 exhibition, as part of a *national* artistic heritage) becomes scandalous when we realise that Canadian government policy was at the same time intent on the forcible assimilation of Native peoples, on the eradication of their languages, beliefs, and traditions through compulsory residential schooling, and on the suppression of First Nations' political protest by making illegal any fundraising for the costs of pursuing land claims.[2] This was the culmination of a process that had begun during the seventeenth century on the east coast of what would become Canada and finally reached the west coast in the second half of the nineteenth century, a process through which aboriginal peoples were dispossessed of their lands and traditional livelihoods by an inexorable tide of settlers in an invasion that was, if relatively bloodless, nonetheless ruthless.

Developments in Canada were part of broader currents in a world increasingly interlinked by the domination of Western imperialism. The artefacts of non-European cultures became objects of European study and classification both in the métropole and in the colony. They were first collected as scientific specimens or ethnographic exotica for imperial museums. Later, through primitivism (an artistic current central to modernism), they were seen as the aesthetically superior creations of more 'authentically' artistic but 'uncivilised' non-European cultures that were doomed to extinction.[3] In the late nineteenth century, as urban industrial Europe reaped the wealth of global imperialism, the material products of other races became a consumer spectacle in the great world fairs and in department stores on both sides of the Atlantic.[4] In predominantly white settler colonies and in former colonies (such as the United States), as aboriginal peoples were subjugated and their land rights and traditional cultures eroded, they were classified as 'vanishing races.' This classification was accompanied by the construction of romanticized images of what was seen as their spirituality and rootedness in the land. Emily Carr's career unfolded within these international and colonial currents of response to non-European cultures, with their conflicting strands of romantic projection and exploitative plunder.

Drawing on recent critiques of the Eurocentric imperialist treatment and representation of non-European peoples, Marcia Crosby, an art historian of Haida-Tsimshian descent, has initiated a debate about Carr's images of Northwest Coast Native culture. She writes:

> There is a double edge to [Carr's] serious endeavour to record for posterity the remnants of a dying people: Carr paid tribute to the Indians she 'loved,' but who were they? Were they the real or authentic Indians who only existed in the past, or the Indians in the nostalgic, textual remembrances she created in her later years? They were not the native people who took her to the abandoned villages on 'a gas boat' rather than a canoe ... [H]er paintings of the last poles intimate that the authentic Indians who made them existed only in the past, and that all the changes that occurred afterwards provide evidence of racial contamination and cultural and moral deterioration ... The issue here is that the induction of First Nations peoples' history and heritage into institutions as a lost Canadian heritage should be considered within the context of the colonization of aboriginal land.[5]

Crosby's call for cultural processes to be seen in a political context is timely. Her verdict on Carr's paintings, however, rests on the picture of the artist that is current in narratives of Canadian art history and in popular culture, a picture that has constructed Carr as a mediator of Native traditions for Canada's white settlers. Carr has become a Canadian cultural icon and her work and persona have taken on an altogether autonomous and mythical life.[6] We must remember, however, that Carr produced her nearly 500 'Indian' paintings during a life and career that spanned a long period of change and development, and that her output went through distinct stages in both conception and reception. To illuminate the part played by her images of Northwest Coast culture in Canadian historical processes, and the specific position Carr herself took up within them, each stage of her career needs to be considered in its geographic, social, and political framework.[7] As Molly H. Mullin has written, 'Concern with *otherness* and its metonymic objects occurs in specific historical contexts, contexts that may be obscured by analyses of a more global nature and by such broad terms as *Primitivism* and *Orientalism*.'[8]

In this paper I shall argue for a methodologically complex approach to interpreting postcolonial situations. Carr offers a case study that calls for attention to issues of gender, of colonial identity and nation building, of regionalism, and of the crossing of cultural boundaries during periods of historical change. I shall engage these issues through an examination of Carr's image-making as it unfolded in three intersecting contexts: first, in her involvement with the international current of primitivism; second, in the position she staked out for her work amid the regional politics of settler–Native relations in British Columbia; and last, in the reception of her work and its evolution within the arena of the Canadian national art scene. My goal is not to contribute to Carr's legend as a heroic individual, but rather to recognize the complexities and contradictions of her involvement in various cultural currents, and the shifting meanings of her work in changing contexts. While Carr contributed to the traffic in Native images that accompanied the dynamics of colonial exploitation, I shall argue that her work was also a site of resistance to both predominant regional settler attitudes and the attitudes of nation-building elites in central Canada. Carr, as an agent, held a thoroughly ambivalent position in the traffic in Native images, and the situation is complicated by the fact that she herself has become an object in this traffic. I shall suggest that her treatment of the Native image has fresh relevance in light of the situation of First Nations communities and First Nations artists today.

Carr and International Primitivism

Emily Carr's paintings of Northwest Coast Native villages were transformed when she came in direct contact with the French current of artistic primitivism during her studies in Paris in 1910–11. Before this, her first Native images, made in the Nuu-chah-nulth villages around Ucluelet in 1899, had been finished mostly in pen and ink, the preferred medium of commercial illustration. Her studies in England during 1899–1903 enabled her to record the Northwest Coast landscape and local features of interest more ambitiously in large-scale naturalist watercolours. In 1907 she had the idea of creating a complete pictorial record of Native villages, a venture that shows the professional acumen and ambition of this young woman artist competing in the newly fledged Vancouver art scene. Sensing that her techniques were still not adequate to her task, she travelled to France in 1910 and studied in Paris with a number of teachers associated with post-impressionism and fauvism. The most important was the English painter Henry Phelan Gibb, a friend of Henri Matisse and Pablo Picasso, who, like them, was indebted both to Gauguin's eclectic formal borrowings from Japanese prints, archaic Greek and Egyptian art, and Javanese and Maori sources, and to Gauguin's assumption that the revitalization of European art could be effected through direct contact with art forms and lifestyles of what were seen as 'primitive' cultures.[9] For Emily Carr, initiation into Parisian primitivism meant that Northwest Coast totem poles, which had fascinated her since she began the project to document them in 1907, were securely ratified as works of artistic merit.

Carr returned from Paris a modernist with a conscious regard for the formal qualities of non-European art. As she wrote in a letter to the Vancouver newspaper, *The Province*, 'Art is art, nature is nature ... The Greeks and Egyptians did not copy nature in their works of art. The Japanese use nature, they do not copy it, and our native Indians do not copy nature, yet their carvings inspired by nature are wonderful.'[10] A comparison of two works by Carr shows the difference that the experience in France made to her mode of representing Native villages. *Potlatch at Alert Bay* (ca. 1909, fig. 4.1), is a watercolour painted in a late nineteenth-century naturalist style with an ethnographic interest in the appearance, clothing, and activities of people in the scene. In her autobiographical notes, Carr mentions that she took some of these watercolours with her to France and, after discussing them with her teacher, 're-painted them cooprating [*sic*] the bigger methods I had absorbed over here with the bigger material of the west.'[11] A small oil panel, *Totem Pole, Alert Bay* (fig. 4.2) is probably one of the works repainted in oils in France from her early watercolours. Carr has extracted the housefront and totem from a larger composition, placing them in a shallow plane parallel to the surface of the canvas, and enlarging them to fill the frame. The emphasis now is on the decorative forms of the pole and on the intense colour, which gives the image a fairy-tale quality. But Carr's interest in the poles as art did not lead her to elide the figures in the scene: the village is shown as peopled.

Something different was at stake for the colonial, Carr, than Gauguin's exploitation of an exotic Other as a means for the artist to escape his own stifling and bloodless European urban civilisation and to purvey fantasies of such escape.[12] Both Carr and contemporary artists in the United States were appropriating the cultural production of aboriginal populations residing within the borders of their modern nation states. These white settler nations had, by 1900, developed imagery and founding myths that gave a special role to the aboriginal peoples within their boundaries, making them emblematic both of the new land, and of a prehistory now superseded by the European introduction of progress and modernity.[13]

In the case of Carr, caught between European primitivist taste and the needs of her colonial homeland, we have a distinctive outcome. When Carr equated the aboriginals' use of abstracted and geometrically decorative form with a more primal creativity – an assumption at the root of the primitivist transvaluation of so-called tribal arts – she did not do so in order to appropriate the forms for exercises in autonomous formal experiment, like those of Gauguin and Picasso. She had other priorities, the most urgent of which was the need to experience, record, and learn to understand as well as possible the context and meanings of Native cultural traditions that were rapidly being modified by the introduction of Euro-Canadian industrial goods and political pressures. Having conceived the project of documenting 'totem poles in their own village settings,'[14] she committed herself to observing standards of accuracy that would satisfy current anthropological criteria. She developed a serious interest in Northwest Coast Native cultures (fed by reading ethnographic publications available in the Vancouver Public Library and Museum) and set out to represent the poles in each village with all their forms precisely rendered. Contrary to received art-historical wisdom, this did not present a conflict for Carr's painting after her French training.[15] The forms on the poles and the brightly coloured paint applied to them by Kwakwaka'wakw carvers were visually fascinating to her and they fitted the stylistic preferences she had learned from her teachers. In post-impressionist studio lore, which taught the exploitation of complementary and saturated colours and boldly generalized shapes, Carr found methods that enabled her at last to render both the intense colour and the vast scale of the coastal landscape. While making studies of the totem poles at Skidegate, Haida Gwaii (see figs 4.3, 4.4), Carr learned to draw the characteristic form language of Northwest Coast carving and to integrate that language with the landscape background through the use of arabesque lines. This led her to the idea that Native art was informed by close attention to the coastal environment. Carr thus took what suited her interests from the broader current of primitivism and applied it to distinctly local concerns. She created an artistic mode through which she could encounter and translate local realities, both geographic and ethnographic. For Carr, this process was at once subjective (in the choices of motif and emphasis that occur) and systematic (in her submission to the discipline of accurately recording Native designs). It was an outgoing process of exploration and learning that folded back upon itself as it offered Carr images through which she could express personal themes of local allegiance and sense of place.

Carr's Native Images in the British Columbia Context

The North American aboriginal peoples that were represented by artists in Canada and the United States were also the objects of local interaction and national politics, causing both conflicts of interest and humanitarian responses in the settler-invader communities. Artists making such images thus entered a politically charged domain. This was particularly so in the case of Emily Carr.[16] Unlike members of the New York intelligentsia who migrated for limited periods to the American Southwest in the 1910s, 1920s, and 1930s,[17] Carr was born, grew up, and worked in the same geographic space as the Native peoples whose cultural production she represented. During her documentary activity, she developed not only her artistic fascination with Native carvings, but also her strong views on Native–settler relations.

The time of Carr's childhood and adolescence was one of rapid change in the relations between Natives and invader-settlers in British Columbia. The completion of the Canadian Pacific Railway in 1886, when Carr was fifteen years old, provided a direct link with eastern Canada and heralded a period of dramatic growth. The 1881 Census of Canada put the Native population at more than half the total British Columbia population of 49,459, but over the following three decades the immigrant population grew to outnumber Native peoples by six to one.[18] The participation of the Native population was significant in many aspects of local economic development, especially in the early fishing, canning, and lumber industries. As Franz Boas wrote in 1889, 'Certain Indian tribes have already become indispensable on the labour market, and without them the Province would suffer a great economic damage.'[19] But as resource development companies grew larger and more capital-intensive, and as successive waves of white settlers arrived, the Native peoples were pushed out of developing sectors of the economy and off their traditional lands. Their presence came to be seen as an obstacle and an anachronism by the growing white community, which increasingly worked to confine them. A variety of institutions were developed to control and assimilate the Native population – Christian missions, Indian Agencies, residential schools – and Native grievances were often passed from one arm of government to another in a process of strategic evasion. Carr knew about the activities and attitudes of missionaries through her sisters' work for the churches and through her own travels. By 1912, when she was most actively engaged in her documentary work, conflict over land use in the province had escalated to become a burning issue. Native tribal groups were organizing and co-ordinating their land claims in petitions to the provincial and federal governments and to the Privy Council in London. The white community was uneasy about possible Native uprisings. In 1909 the Victoria *Colonist* reported:

> The isolated whites of the upper Skeena ... have, it is stated, less than one hundred men to protect their homes, their families and their settlement interests, little more than half of these being provided with rifles, and the supply of ammunition being limited. On the other hand, the affiliated Skeena tribes number some four thousand persons, of whom some five to six hundred are adult men, each of whom owns his own rifle or shotgun and is an adept in its use.[20]

Carr, who visited the Skeena area in 1912, tartly informed a Vancouver audience: 'I have spent long days and sometimes nights in lonely villages with no other protection than the worn teeth of my 13 year old dog. I never carry a revolver, being far more afraid of a gun than of an Indian.'[21]

Carr's documentary approach, as I have shown in detail elsewhere, involved a conscientious attempt to record the remaining poles in each village she visited, both in groups or singly, according to the necessities of the terrain.[22] In addition, convinced that the totem poles could not be understood outside their context within the community and the landscape, she painted views of the villages with their geographic settings. Two examples of the large canvases she painted in 1912–13 from her documentary field sketches are *Indian House Interior with Totems*, (fig. 4.5) and *Tanoo, Queen Charlotte Islands* (fig. 4.6). In both these paintings carved poles are the largest elements, dominating a scene that Carr has composed with the purpose of revealing how the poles express Native ideas or, as she would later put it, make 'strong talk' for the people.[23] The former (fig. 4.5) shows the interior of a Kwakwaka'wakw bighouse at Tsatsisnukomi, a warm enclosure of rich red-browns in which the house posts, huge carved eagles with grey-green wings, loom over the small human figures grouped around a green-shawled woman. The theme here is the protective power of the totem; Carr would paint a similar pair of eagles above her own bed in the attic of her house at a difficult time in her life when she had to earn her living by taking in boarders.[24] It is typical that Carr made this a scene of women and children – the aspect of Native life that was most accessible to her. In both her images and her writing we find many expressions of admiration for the role of women in Native society. In *Tanoo* (fig. 4.6), Carr depicts a section of a Haida village, deserted, as she was well aware, due to the decimation of the Native population by the later nineteenth-century smallpox epidemics. Drawing on three separate watercolour sketches, she composed a stormy scene in which three house poles stand up against a sky of turbulent clouds. Carr has drawn the animal forms on the poles with an emphatic line that records the staring eyes and the open mouths that swallow other creatures' heads or bare great incisors. Her animated brush work creates a movement in the landscape, one way in the long beach grasses and another way in the trees, suggesting a squall. Vertically braced against the elements, the poles demonstrate what Carr believed to be the moral dimension of the Native peoples' choice of their animal crests: 'Indians were proud of their totems, and were prone to surround them with attributes of bravery, strength, & talent, powers of endurance or other qualities ... In a general sense those animals which inspired fear, affection, or seemed to possess a high degree of intelligence or superhuman capabilities were regarded as their kindred.'[25]

Carr's attitudes towards Native peoples became highly nonconformist during the course of her documentary project, which coincided with the height of the McBride era of railway building and resource industry expansion in British Columbia.[26] Moving between Victoria or Vancouver and the remote villages at the frontier of settlement, she was continually confronted with the negative social and political tenor of settler–Native relations. Her documentary project became not only one of salvage (of the 'wonderful relics of a passing people')[27] but an assertion of the value of Native achievements, skills, and traditional culture. She was explicitly critical in her writings of the negative views propagated by individuals representing settler institutions: missionaries, Indian agents, politicians, and press. In 1913 she mounted a large exhibition of nearly two hundred documentary paintings in a public hall she rented in Vancouver, and she wrote a lengthy lecture that she delivered to the public at this show on two occasions in an attempt to explain the content of her images. In this lecture, in her pictorial representations of Native villages, and also in her later published travel tales in *Klee Wyck*, we find deliberate efforts to redress the effects of local ethnocentric discourses which dismissed Native traditions as dark and superstitious. In her lecture she insisted not only on the importance of understanding Native cultures and customs but also on the difficulties of attaining any such understanding. She acknowledged her debt to such guides as William and Clara Russ, the Haida couple who took her to deserted Haida villages (fig. 4.7). She attempted to explain to her audience the function and meaning of Native buildings and of the family crests and legends depicted on the totem poles. She commented: 'These are very very hard to learn. Many of the younger Indians do not know them: others again are unwilling to tell ... It is indeed always an honour & a privilege, to be taken into an Indian's confidence, for they are, and have good reason for being, suspicious of the whites.'[28] She expressed gratitude to Native people who had offered her friendship: 'It has been my privilege to know some Indians intimately (and it is necessary to know these people well before they will speak freely before you).'[29] In return she respected their desire to know why she was interested in their villages, and routinely tacked up exhibitions of her sketches for the people to see before she left, and offered to paint duplicates for any owners of poles and houses who wanted them or who were nervous that by painting them she was exercising some magic that might cause their poles to disappear. Her documentary project took on a civic and political dimension as she attempted to bring her newly acquired perceptions of Native cultures to the settler community through her work. No doubt naïvely, she hoped her paintings of 'our wonderful west and ... some of the relics of its first primitive greatness'[30] would become both a means of re-educating the settler community in its attitudes and a historical resource for the whole population of the province.

Carr's initiative was not welcomed by the settler society of British Columbia in 1913. Her work was neither supported nor purchased, as she requested that it be, by the provincial government for the museum that was being installed in the newly built Legislative Buildings in Victoria. Even had there been no recession in British Columbia in 1913, Carr's huge array of Native villages, most of them shown as inhabited, would not have appealed to white British Columbians. Many of the village names, familiar to citizens of Vancouver and Victoria from press reports of Native unrest over land development, were surely an unpleasant reminder of the presence and claims of the Native population in the province. Similarly, the critical sections in Carr's later writings that comment on institutional injustices to Native peoples and on the arrogant attitudes of missionaries have continued to be discomforting to Canadian institutions. A number of passages have been expurgated from all editions of *Klee Wyck* printed since 1951.[31]

Carr's work can instructively be placed in the context of the work of ethnographers active on the Northwest Coast. Anthropology as an institution tended generally to serve and reinforce the prejudices of colonizing societies, but there were also individuals who respected and helped the Native communities they studied.[32] Most notable of these was Franz Boas, who radically shifted anthropological theory from an evolutionist to a relativist paradigm.[33] Although she never met him, Carr's sketching trips coincided with the comings and goings of Boas, and her own comments and attitudes show many similarities with those Boas noted in his journals.[34] Both respected Native cultures as a coherent system that made sense in its own terms. Carr sought the acquaintance of Canadian ethnographers C.F. Newcombe and Marius Barbeau, and she received help from many of their aboriginal collaborators, among them George Hunt and William Beynon.[35] She also had much in common with ethnologists who lived on the coast and spent extended periods among the Native communities. One such individual was her acquaintance, the retired West Coast naval officer George Emmons, who had written wryly to Boas in 1897 of 'the custom in this country of ethnologists to study people from a long distance surrounded by the comforts and warmth of a Museum office.'[36]

Yet there are also significant differences between Carr's situation and theirs. When ethnographers came to Native communities, they had official introductions from Indian agents and sponsorship of important institutions. Thus, they were received and treated as men of influence and had access to the chiefs and leading families of the communities. They travelled with money in their pockets to pay informants and to purchase artefacts. Carr appeared in the villages without designated authority from her own community, and as a white woman travelling alone, she must have seemed a strange anomaly. She had to take her trips during her summer breaks from art teaching when, as she comments frequently in her writings, many villages were more or less deserted because the people were away working in the seasonal labour force for the canneries. She was hampered by her lack of funding; travel on the coast was expensive and visits to remote sites even more so, since they had to be made by private charter. It must be said that Carr managed extraordinarily well within these constraints. Occupying herself with her painting, she could account for her often lengthy presence in the villages and express her interest in Native culture in a relatively non-invasive way, allowing Native peoples to accept or ignore her presence.[37] It is clear from her accounts that she was often able to convey to them her real admiration for the artistry of their monumental poles, as well as her interest in and pleasure at being able to visit their villages.

Unlike artists working successfully at the time in the service of institutions such as museums or publishers, Carr did not represent Native peoples as timeless and essentialized. For example, in *Indian War Canoe* (1912, fig. 4.8), the canoe stands as a monument to Kwakwa̱ka̱'wakw history but is no longer in use.[38] Images of Native canoes by two other artists make an instructive comparison. American artist William Taylor painted a series of murals (fig. 4.9) for the American Museum of Natural History, after making sketching trips to many of the same villages during the same period as Carr. Taylor's paintings, which were recommended as a model for Carr's own work by Newcombe, were reconstructions of Native life that clearly implied that authentic Native culture inhabited a timeless past.[39] Taylor gave an astonishingly incompetent rendering of the forms on the Haida pole, despite both his travels and his access to photographs and museum specimens. Seattle photographer Edward S. Curtis, embarked at the same time as Carr on a project to document North American Native peoples.[40] In his images for volume ten of the resulting twenty-volume work, *The North American Indian*, he sought, in his treatment of the Kwakwaka'wakw people, to capture images of a dramatic primeval Native culture, carefully staged and aestheticized (fig. 4.10). He rented the same canoes Carr had sketched, and dressed up Kwakwaka'wakw actors in shaggy wigs and cedar-bark capes to reconstruct Native customs 'in the times of Captain Vancouver.'[41] Carr's images, while concerned with the accurate recording of the forms and features of Native designs on houses, canoes and totem poles, always also conveyed her personal encounter with a contemporary, contingent scene. Both her documentary paintings and her later stories about her travels show the villages as places where continuity and change were interwoven.

As an artist working in a colony that was in the process of rapid expansion and settlement, Carr created her images of Native peoples to address questions of local history and identity. The social and cultural implications with which Carr invested her images, her attempt to act as a 'missionary in reverse,'[42] and her refusal to observe the conventions for distancing her images into a remote past, made these images quite unacceptable in the province at the time. Carr often referred in her writings to the ridicule and incomprehension with which her images were met: Native traditions and carvings were regarded by the settler-invader community as evidence of barbarism, acceptable chiefly as curiosities, as relics of a dark and heathen past.[43] After the rejection of her huge and ambitious documentary undertaking by both the provincial government and the public, Carr continued to defend Native peoples and their traditions. In a newspaper article of 1918, for example, she was cited as describing 'her paintings of the B.C. Indians, their villages and their totem poles ... as the serious work of her life ... The painter hopes that some day her fine collection will become a national possession. Her ambition is that it will be a worthy tribute to the Indians that she loves so well.'[44] In the eyes of the majority of the conservative, British-dominated community of Victoria, Emily Carr, financially impoverished and socially embattled, brought down upon herself the same ridicule and contempt as that in which the Native population itself was held.

Carr's Images and Image in the National Arena

Emily Carr's fortunes changed in 1927 when her 1912 paintings became an important component in the project of building a Canadian national culture and consciousness, as these were conceived by leading intellectuals in central Canada, including the members of the Group of Seven and the staffs of Canada's National Gallery and National Museum. Carr served as an important recruit to their cause, eventually by creating a modern pictorial language for the coastal landscape and forests of British Columbia, but initially by facilitating their appropriation of the artefacts of Canada's Northwest Coast Native peoples into a narrative of the forging of a modern Canadian artistic culture. In the 1927 'Exhibition of Canadian West Coast Art, Native and Modern,' Carr's early paintings were hung alongside more recent paintings of British Columbia by A.Y. Jackson, Edwin Holgate, and other central Canadian artists. Here they reached a very different audience and took on different meanings. Carr's images of traditional Native villages, like paintings by members of the Group of Seven, appealed to a pattern of feeling among the educated Canadian elite that has been labelled 'anti-modern.' This pattern included both a yearning to recover bonds with nature threatened by urban industrial society and a cult of idealised images of 'the Folk' and of 'primitive' aboriginal peoples, who were imagined as living in creative harmony with a land that was uncorrupted by the modern industrial world.[45] This cultural current was reflected in Arts and Crafts revivals and harnessed by the tourism and heritage industries as recreation for city dwellers.[46]

The representation of Native artefacts as a Canadian national artistic heritage was accomplished by the 1927 exhibition, where for the first time in a major museum show, they were displayed side by side with modern paintings under the designation 'art.'[47] This was made possible, of course, by the primitivist aesthetic of European avant-garde art circles; more important still, it met the needs of Canadian nationalism. In the catalogue essays with which the curators, Eric Brown and Marius Barbeau, framed the exhibition they emphasized the 'world-wide fame' of Northwest Coast aboriginal art and its representation 'in the state museums of Europe and America,' but they also declared that the exhibition was 'entirely national in its origin and character.' As Barbeau put it, 'it is truly Canadian in its inspiration. It has sprung up wholly from the soil and the sea within our national boundaries.' Their stated goal was to 'enable this primitive and interesting art to take a definite place as one of the most valuable of Canada's artistic productions.' Northwest Coast Native artefacts, they proposed, should now become a source of inspiration to modern Canadian designers and painters.[48]

In their presentation of Native artefacts, the central Canadian curators divorced them from their ethnographic context and meanings. Carr, on the other hand, made an effort to contextualize the subjects of her paintings within Native culture both in her 1913 Vancouver exhibition and in her discussion of those paintings in the article published in the *McGill News* for her new central-Canadian audience in 1929, where she described the role of Native carvers and the meanings of their work.[49] A 1927 editorial reveals the central-Canadian urban response to Native artefacts in the 1927 Exhibition:

> In looking at the West Coast Indian art at the Toronto Art Gallery, one can easily share the enthusiasm of foreign authorities and critics over it. No knowledge of its ethnology is needed to enjoy the largeness of pattern and ingenuity of the carved and painted boxes, bowls, and rattles, the extraordinary combinations of conventionalized birds, animals, human figures, and the happy sweeping arm movements

> of the brush work in larger patterns. To one's fancy all lines have the roll and crescendo of waves and the swoop of great birds and fish. The play of art is not often better seen than in these grotesque carved and painted masks. These are children pretending, but what clever children. This work must undoubtedly go into the fabric of our Canadian art, but not too directly; our umbrellas and fountain pens are not blubber knives and harpoons.[50]

The *Canadian Forum* writer, patronisingly dismissive of Native peoples, flaunts the fantasy that the modern white settler community is the entitled heir of Native heritage. As Terry Goldie comments in his discussion of the 'incorporation' of the Native as a literary trope, 'Through the indigene the white character gains soul and the potential to become the land. A quite appropriate pun is that it is only by going native that the European arrivant can become native.'[51]

From this time on Carr herself would be described again and again by reviewers as such a 'gone Native' figure, a mediator for the settler community of the traditional wisdom of the aborigine. Take, for example, the romantic hyperbole of a youthful Robertson Davies, reviewing *Klee Wyck* in 1941:

> In her early days on the West Coast she penetrated almost unknown tracts of Indian country ... She knew the totems as an artist, not as an anthropologist, and it is an artist of insight who illuminates the pages of *Klee Wyck*, making it a great revelation of that secret Canada which is hidden for most of us pale sojourners in a strange land ... [T]he works of Emily Carr will be a permanent enrichment of our growing native tradition.[52]

Lawren Harris expanded this mythical figure of Carr into an image of her as a shaman-like mystic in deep communion with animals-Indians-Nature. In an article in the *Canadian Forum* in 1941 he writes:

> She has an uncommon bond with the animal world. She has had at different times a monkey, a chipmunk, white rats and all manner of birds as well as many dogs as companions ... She housed and handled them with a kind of careless, off-hand understanding which made one feel she knew every twist of their varied natures. Her bond with the Indians of the coast is of a similar nature.
>
> Her art in subject matter has no contact with white peoples. It is an art whose full sustenance is drawn from the soil and the sea ... [I]t embodies an almost primitive oneness with nature, identical one feels with the Indian sympathy with nature ... In the deep resonance of the paintings of Indian totems and villages set in the encompassing and sombre mystery of chromatic chords of green one is drawn into the very psyche of the Indian and made to feel the Indians' response to the prevailing mystery of great nature.[53]

Harris's characterization of Carr has passed into the writings of subsequent Canadian art historians.[54] Carr herself never made such grandiose claims, but her Native images did undergo a change as she took on the role in 1928 of creating paintings to represent the West Coast in the national arena.

While Carr espoused the ardent nationalist vision of the Group of Seven, she was diffidently self-conscious about what she could contribute to their agenda, about the responsibility of representing British Columbia, and about her status as a woman artist. As she wrote in her journal: 'These men are very interesting and big and inspiring ... I know they are building an art worthy of our great country, and I want to have my share, to put in a little spoke for the West, one woman holding up my end.'[55] Ending the long hiatus in her career, she enthusiastically returned to painting Native motifs as well as to the study of the Northwest Coast landscape. Native imagery, which she knew she was much better qualified to interpret than central-Canadian artists, became for Carr an indispensable marker of British Columbian identity.[56] Through her paintings of 1928–32 she amplified her earlier assertions of the validity of Native traditions; her images of lament for the destruction of the ancient sites are often of such intensity as to suggest her empathy with the trauma of loss.[57]

Many of her paintings now showed crest poles and single carved figures in monumental close-up, directly addressing the viewer. She clearly wished them to impart to an unfamiliar audience the particular Native values she believed important: pride in family lineage and ownership, courage and generosity, and the powerful roles of women. In one group of canvases, for example, Carr focuses on 'welcome figures.' These can be seen as emblems of the potlatch (the context to which these figures belonged), of the greatness and power of traditional Native chiefs, and of their role in activating social relations within and between Native villages.[58] A larger group of her paintings from 1928 on presents monumental female figures in the guise of Native carvings, images of both mothers with children and of Dzonokwa, the Kwakwaka'wakw wild woman of the woods.[59] Such images of powerful womanhood enabled her to address her preoccupation not only with her own threatening marginality as a provincial and as a woman artist but also with her problematic experience of her own femininity.[60] A painting that epitomises this is *Guyasdoms d'Sonoqua* (fig. 4.11), which shows a carving of the Kwakwaka'wakw mythological wild woman that Carr had first seen and sketched in the village of Gwyasdums in 1912. Significantly, Carr selected this motif as one of the first canvases to paint on her return from the visit to central Canada in 1928, where she first encountered the Group of Seven. The image of Dzonokwa offered the unconventional Carr a way to imagine a powerful alternative identity for herself. In her story 'D'Sonoqua,' she ascribes decisive moments in her own development to her encounters with the strongly ambiguous Dzonokwa, who became for her a mentor and guardian spirit.[61]

In Carr's late paintings and writings, she represented Native carvings as powerful and active sites of meaning and value for herself and her audience, but she did not divorce them from the Native present. In *Klee Wyck*, Carr connected her several paintings of 'Totem Mothers' on the poles at Kitwancool to her meeting with the powerful matriarch and chieftainess, Mrs Douse, who had offered her shelter.[62] It was in dialogue with Native peoples and with the artefacts that recorded their traditions that Carr was able to accept herself as a powerful, nonconformist woman, and to formulate a more inclusive vision of British Columbia society.[63] Her polemical statement to Eric Brown – 'I am a lesser artist than the red man'[64] – confirms the message of her late images: that Native culture has an enduring authority to address Canadians.

The implications of Carr's choice of images in her 'Indian' paintings of 1928–32, however, drew little comment at the time. Once again, I would argue, significant elements in her work exceeded what contemporaries wished to perceive. For Lawren Harris and for the American artist Mark Tobey (another of her mentors at this time), Carr's dedication to the Native image was excessive. Both men feared she was risking the 'authenticity' of her work by dependence on an already formed artistic language and urged her to move on to the painting of landscape. Her early salvage paintings were enough: now the programme of nation building required her to transfer the formal and spiritual insights gained from Native culture into modern landscape paintings that could express 'Canada.'

Imagining Difference Otherwise

While Carr contributed to the production of images of the aboriginal peoples of colonial Canada, her images were generally out of step with the prevailing demands of the settler community upon this 'traffic.' Her early work had presented a flagrant contradiction to the invader-settler community's edict that they were occupying a *terra nullius*. With the passage of time and changing political agendas, these images became useful to the central Canadian cultural elite, and a process was unleashed whereby Carr played a key role in establishing the 'imagined community' of the modern Canadian nation. Yet her 'imagined community' of Canada was significantly different.[65] It explicitly included Native peoples and respected both their past and their future. If the Vancouver Art Gallery now owns a great number of her documentary paintings, it is not because the Gallery purchased them but because Carr set the most important of them aside and gave them to the province.[66] She persistently insisted that her imagery was for the Native peoples as much as it was for the white community. In 1929 she wrote:

> [The Indians] always wanted to know what I was going to do with my pictures, and I tried to explain to them that I hoped that some day they would be put in a place where their children's children could see them and admire the work of their ancestors, which pleased them ... The old places and the old people are passing away rapidly. Last year I went north again, the first time for several years. Few poles were left, few old type houses, and very few old people. Yet the spirit of the Indian still haunts the old spots. What we are trying to remember they are trying to forget. The

young people are fast absorbing the white man's ways, and are half ashamed of these things now. But by and by when the white race has absorbed them, something deep down within them must surely respond to the great art of their past.[67]

Carr's contact with people in the northern villages had spanned a critical phase in their history. Her first visit to Haida Gwaii (the Queen Charlotte Islands) was made only thirty years after the first installation of a Methodist missionary at Skidegate. At the time of her second visit in 1928, Henry Edenshaw of Masset owned a motor car and his children danced the Charleston to records on their gramophone. Carr saw the inexorability of colonial pressures and of modernization, but she also anticipated that in the future aboriginal peoples would reassess their relationship to their traditions.

The depth of Carr's regard for Native peoples and the ways in which she expressed it in her work could hardly be taken seriously twenty years ago, before the rise of First Nations' political activism and cultural revival. The changing situation of the First Nations today has prompted the re-evaluation of Carr's relevance and the review of the specific, hitherto neglected, facts of her relations with Native peoples in British Columbia. This does not mean complacency about Carr's achievements, which were acutely limited by the conditions of her time, but it does mean challenging the image of her that was fabricated by central Canadian institutions and by later generations of British Columbians.[68] I have argued that, from early in her career, Carr was consciously involved in a social and cultural struggle in her attempt to change settler views of the Native population in British Columbia. If she lacked a direct connection with the arenas of provincial or federal politics, it must be remembered that from her mid-teens she was member of a family of church-centred impoverished gentlewomen, a family without men in a society where men controlled public and economic affairs.[69] In her formative years Carr observed British Columbia politics as an arena where well-connected settlers made fortunes through grabbing stakes in land and resource development.[70] It would have been surprising if Carr had looked to political institutions as a likely vehicle for progressive change, particularly for the cause of the Native population. But social and political convictions can be expressed in a variety of ways. Carr's documentary paintings, through their pictorial construction and public presentation, constituted a socially and politically contentious act at the time. Her later works asserted her belief in the enduring value of many Native traditions.

Carr's modernist faith in a universal formal language had enabled her to appreciate Native design forms. What Carr could not foresee was that, paradoxically, it would be the breakdown of modernism that would make it possible for Native artists both to reassert and to hybridize their traditional cultural expression, and at the same time to challenge the hierarchy that has placed the European tradition at the summit of an imagined progressive evolution. First Nations artists are now claiming voices with which to speak both within and beyond their communities. They draw upon a dual training, both through the deliberate reclamation of traditional values handed down by Native elders or found in anthropological records, and through study in Euro-Canadian institutions.[71] Their work today is varied but is distinctly tied to the continuing life of their traditions. It hangs in art galleries, including the National Gallery, where, as Charlotte Townsend-Gault has written, 'what emerges is the understanding that there is more than one kind of knowing: that there exists knowledge that can be shared, knowledge that may be intimated, and knowledge that should be withheld ... in respect for the final untranslatability of the essence of cultural difference.'[72]

The First Nations today have relinquished neither the right to their traditions nor the demand for autonomy and just settlement of outstanding land claims. The perpetuation of all of these is attested through continuing marks upon the territory that Carr painted in the 1910s and 1920s. In July 1987, a large Haida war canoe was pulled up on the beach in Skidegate, Haida Gwaii, its crew having just rowed the five hundred miles up the coast from Vancouver (see fig. 4.12). Luu Tas (or 'Wave Eater,' fig. 4.13) was built in 1986 to represent the Haida at the World's Fair in Vancouver, though there was no one still living with experience of the technical aspects of building a canoe on that scale. Its construction from a huge single red cedar trunk was conceived and supervised at Skidegate by Bill Reid (1920–98) who had already carved a new frontal pole for the Skidegate band council's longhouse.[73] This pole stood close to the village's last remaining nineteenth-century pole, the memorial pole of Itga (fig. 4.4). Emily Carr had painted that memorial pole, with its beaver crest, along with the eight other poles she saw at Skidegate in 1912. It collapsed in a storm in 1988 and, in accordance with Haida custom, was not re-erected. However, the blanket cloaks with family crests that Bill Reid and other participants wore at the welcoming ceremony for Luu Tas, Reid's carved bracelets and poles, and the work of other contemporary First Nations carvers on the Northwest coast (many of whom unlike Reid have grown up within their Native communities) are examples of the current blending of cultural continuities with deliberate reappropriation. Native artists such as the Kwakwaka'wakw David Neel are carving masks that address current experience in traditional language; Neel's *Injustice Mask* (fig. 4.14) is a portrait of Judge McEachern, whose dismissal of the Nisga'a land claim was recently successfully overturned. Today, Laurence Paul Yuxweluptun blends the languages of modern Surrealism and traditional Native form-line to make political statements about the environmental and social destruction that lurks below the surface of the contemporary Canadian landscape (fig. 4.15), a landscape whose distinctive qualities had been visually coded in Carr's own paintings of 1928–32 as already marked by the Native imagination.[74]

We can see today that Carr's late paintings of Native motifs carry a similar political address. The viewer is challenged by carved human figures, birds, and animals that declare Native values of strength, pride, endurance, and family inheritance. Throughout her career Carr's images were made with attention and respect for what she could learn of Native experience and values, a respect markedly different from the attitudes held by the majority of Euro-Canadians. As the Canadian state today faces the problems of ethnic co-existence,[75] Carr's work offers much more than a 'fantasised reconciliation.' It offers the challenge that Canadians accept the authority of Native traditions, as Carr herself did.

NOTES

I wish to thank Leslie Korrick and Oliver Botar for their comments on the first draft of this paper, and Charlotte Townshend-Gault, Robert Linsley, and Scott Watson for stimulating conversations on the issues with which it is concerned.

1 Emily Carr, *Klee Wyck* (Toronto: Oxford University Press, 1941). The period Carr covers in the book is from the 1880s to the early 1930s.
2 In British Columbia, few treaties for the surrender of land had been made with the aboriginal peoples, who were disenfranchised when the province entered the Canadian Confederation in 1871. A federal Special Joint Committee of the Senate and House of Commons in Ottawa delivered a final rejection of the British Columbia Native peoples' claims to aboriginal land title in 1927. See Wilson Duff, *The Indian History of British Columbia* (Victoria: British Columbia Provincial Museum, 1965), 69; and E. Brian Titley, *A Narrow Vision: Duncan Campbell Scott and the Administration of Indian Affairs in Canada* (Vancouver: University of British Columbia Press, 1986), 154–9. The political implications of the 1927 National Gallery exhibition have been fully discussed by Ann K. Morrison, 'Canadian Art and Cultural Appropriation: Emily Carr and the 1927 Exhibition of Canadian West Coast Art, Native and Modern,' (master's thesis, University of British Columbia, 1991). They will be further explored later in this paper.
3 For museum collecting see George W. Stocking, ed., *Objects and Others, Essays on Museums and Material Culture* (Madison: University of Wisconsin Press, 1985); George W. Stocking, *Victorian Anthropology* (New York: The Free Press, 1987); Douglas Cole, *Captured Heritage: The Scramble for Northwest Coast Artefacts* (Toronto: Douglas & McIntyre, 1985). For artistic primitivism, see Robert Goldwater, *Primitivism in Modern Art* (1938; reprint, New York: Vintage Books, 1967); William Jackson Rushing, *Native American Art and Culture and the New York Avant-Garde* (Ann Arbor: University Microfilms International, 1990); Molly H. Mullin, 'The Patronage of Difference: Making Indian Art "Art, Not Ethnology,"' in *The Traffic in Culture: Refiguring Art and Anthropology*, ed. G. Marcus and F. Myers (Berkeley: University of California Press, 1995); and James Clifford, *The Predicament of Culture: Twentieth-Century Ethnography, Literature, and Art* (Cambridge, Mass.: Harvard University Press, 1988).
4 Paul Greenhalgh, *Ephemeral Vistas: The Expositions Universelles, Great Exhibitions and World's Fairs, 1851–1939* (Manchester: Manchester University Press, 1988); Robert Rydell, *All the World's a Fair: Visions of Empire at American Expositions, 1876–1916* (Chicago: University of Chicago Press, 1984).
5 Marcia Crosby, 'Construction of the Imaginary Indian,' in *Vancouver Anthology: The*

Institutional Politics of Art, ed. Stan Douglas (Vancouver: Talonbooks, 1991), 276–7.

6 For a discussion of Carr's legend see Stephanie K. Walker, *This Woman in Particular: Contexts for the Biographical Image of Emily Carr* (Waterloo, Ont.: Wilfrid Laurier University Press, 1996).

7 A detailed study of Carr's work in its social and historical contexts (on which this paper draws) can be found in Gerta Moray, 'Northwest Coast Native Culture and the Early Indian Paintings of Emily Carr, 1899–1913' (PhD diss., University of Toronto, 1993).

8 Mullin, 'The Patronage of Difference,' 167.

9 See Kirk Varndoe, 'Gauguin,' in William Rubin, ed., *'Primitivism' in 20th Century Art: Affinity of the Tribal and the Modern* (New York: Museum of Modern Art, 1984).

10 *Province* (Vancouver) 3 April 1912.

11 British Columbia Archives and Records Service (hereafter BCARS), Carr Papers, 'Growing Pains,' MS (not paginated).

12 On the colonial power relations and sexual fantasies that underlay Gauguin's Tahitian images, see Abigail Solomon-Godeau, 'Going Native,' *Art in America* 77 (July 1989), 118–22.

13 The representation of Native peoples in Canada has been discussed by, among others, Terry Goldie, *Fear and Temptation: The Image of the Indigene in Canadian, Australian and New Zealand Literatures* (Kingston and Montreal: McGill-Queen's University Press, 1989); Robin Fisher, *Contact and Conflict: Indian-European Relations in British Columbia, 1774–1890* (Vancouver: University of British Columbia Press, 1977); François-Marc Gagnon, *Ces hommes dits sauvages* (Montreal: Libre expression, ca. 1985); Heather Dawkins, 'Paul Kane and the Eye of Power: Racism in Canadian Art History,' *Vanguard* (September 1986), 24–7; Marcia Crosby, 'Imaginary Indian'; Maureen Ryan, 'Picturing Canada's Native Landscape: Colonial Expansion, National Identity, and the Image of a "Dying Race,"' *RACAR* 27 (1990), 138–49; and Daniel Francis, *The Imaginary Indian: The Image of the Indian in Canadian Culture* (Vancouver: Arsenal, 1992).

14 Emily Carr, *Growing Pains: The Autobiography of Emily Carr*, 2nd ed. (Toronto: Clarke, Irwin, 1966), 211.

15 Modernist aesthetics have privileged the development of formal possibilities in pursuit of an original style as the criterion for the best art. Consequently, Carr's documentary paintings of 1912 were dismissed as artistically immature by the principal writers on her work. See Lawren Harris, *Emily Carr: Her Paintings and Sketches* (Toronto: Oxford University Press, 1945), 19; Doris Shadbolt, *The Art of Emily Carr* (Vancouver: Douglas & McIntyre, 1979), 30, 38–40.

16 Women artists and writers in nation-states that were established from European colonies often showed the greatest sympathy for the cultures and situations of aboriginal peoples, sometimes identifying or being identified with them to varied degrees. Examples are Emily Carr in Canada, Margaret Preston in Australia, and Frida Kahlo in Mexico. This identification fitted the moral role assigned to women in society at the time: middle class women often assumed the role of 'civilizing' and humanizing society in frontier regions while maternalist reform movements sought to alleviate the social problems of women and children and of the poor. See Seth Koven and Sonya Michel, eds., *Mothers of a New World: Maternalist Politics and the*

Origins of Welfare States (New York: Routledge, 1993), 1–31.

17 For these, see Rushing, *Native American Art*, and Mullin, 'Patronage of Difference.'

18 Population figures from Fisher, *Contact and Conflict*, 202, and Duff, *Indian History*, 44–5.

19 Ronald P. Rohner, *The Ethnography of Franz Boas* (Chicago: University of Chicago Press, 1969), 13. See also Rolf Knight, *Indians at Work: An Informal History of Native Indian Labour in British Columbia, 1858–1930* (Vancouver: New Star Books, 1978).

20 *Colonist* (Victoria) 21 November 1909.

21 'Lecture on Totems,' Carr Papers, BCARS, 16. This unpublished lecture was written in 1913 for an exhibition Carr held in Vancouver.

22 Moray, 'Northwest Coast,' 279–338.

23 Carr, *Growing Pains*, 213.

24 Ibid., 262.

25 Carr, 'Lecture on Totems,' 4–6 (underlinings by Carr.)

26 Richard McBride was Premier of British Columbia from 1903 to 1915.

27 Carr, 'Lecture on Totems,' 1.

28 Ibid., 14.

29 Ibid., 32.

30 Ibid., 52–3.

31 Major cuts to *Klee Wyck* include on, pp. 15–17, the last section of the story 'Ucluelet,' which defends native burial practices; on pp. 106–7, Carr's condemnation of the effects of residential schools; and on pp. 108–10, the story 'Martha's Joey,' about a native woman forced to give up her white foster-child. These excisions have not previously been noted, even by literary critics who analyse and interpret 'Carr's' text. See, for example, Hilda L. Thomas, 'Klee Wyck, The Eye of the Other,' *Canadian Literature* 136 (Spring 1993), 8; the 1941 edition of *Klee Wyck* is listed in the bibliography, but page numbers cited in the text correspond to the 1965 edition. In her otherwise excellent and complex discussion of *Klee Wyck*, Thomas overlooks Carr's explicit condemnation of the acts and attitudes of the settler community. A more complete reading of Carr's texts might have altered Thomas's mistaken view that, 'Had she lived to see it, Carr would probably have been neither surprised nor offended by Chief Justice Allan McEachern's *Reasons for Judgment in Delgam Uukw et al v. The Queen* (March 8, 1991) in which he characterizes the life in a native village as "nasty, brutish and short," ...' (p. 5).

32 An interesting survey of the ethnologists working in British Columbia at the time and their varying relationships with the Native groups they studied can be found in Ralph Maude, *A Guide to B.C. Indian Myth and Legend* (Vancouver: Talonbooks, 1982).

33 See George W. Stocking, *Race, Culture, and Evolution; Essays in the History of Anthropology* (New York: The Free Press, 1968), 213. Boas wrote several times to the Canadian federal government on behalf of the Kwakwa̱ka̱'wakw people to protest the anti-potlatch laws.

34 Their attitudes are compared in detail in Moray, 'Northwest Coast,' 196–200.

35 In 1912 Carr had sought out Newcombe, who lived in Victoria, after having heard about him from Native people (BCARS, Newcombe Family Papers, Emily Carr Letters). It was probably Tsimshian William Beynon who first informed Barbeau of

Carr's paintings. After meeting George Hunt in 1930, Carr corresponded with him. He apologized for his delay in answering her letter in December 1930 because he had been engaged in transcribing texts for Boas. See Moray, 'Northwest Coast,' 175–210.

36 Cited in Aldona Jonaitis, *From the Land of the Totem Poles: The Northwest Coast Indian Art Collection at the American Museum of Natural History* (New York: American Museum of Natural History, 1988), 158.

37 A good example of this is Carr's account of her 1912 visit to the village of Yan in the company of a Haida woman: 'We sheltered in a hut & made a fire, and the woman told me stories of her life, these are always worth hearing but you must not ask too many questions, or the story teller will become mute.' ('Lecture on Totems,' 39; Carr's spelling and punctuation have been retained).

38 This was one of three ancient canoes that stood at the end of Alert Bay village in 1910–12 and were heirlooms in potlatch exchange (communication from Peter MacNair, Royal British Columbia Museum).

39 Reproductions of four of Taylor's murals were published in an article, 'Foreword to the New Mural Paintings in the American Museum,' *American Museum Journal* 11 (1911), 129–36, which Carr was almost certainly shown by Newcombe.

40 Edward S. Curtis, *The North American Indian: Being a Series of Volumes Picturing and Describing the Indians of the United States and Alaska*, 20 vols. (1907–1930; reprint, New York: Johnson Reprint Corp., 1970), vols. 10–11.

41 This photograph shows the canoe as refurbished for Curtis's film 'In the Land of the Headhunters.' For Curtis's Kwakwaka'wakw photographs and film, see Bill Holm and George Irving Quimby, *Edward S. Curtis in the Land of the War Canoes* (Seattle: University of Washington Press, 1980). For a discussion of ways in which Curtis 'doctored' his photographs in order to create an illusion of a timeless, ethnographic present see Christopher Lyman, *The Vanishing Race and Other Illusions: Photographs by Edward S. Curtis* (Washington, D.C.: Smithsonian Press, 1982), and Bill Holm, '*The Vanishing Race and Other Illusions: Photographs by Edward S. Curtis*, by Christopher Lyman,' *American Indian Art Magazine* 8 (Summer 1983), 68–73.

42 The phrase is Monique Westra's. See 'Two Views of Emily Carr,' *artmagazine* (September–October 1980), 24.

43 Carr, *Growing Pains*, 227–8, 232–3.

44 *Western Woman's Weekly*, 9 November 1918

45 See T.J. Jackson Lears, *No Place of Grace: Antimodernism and the Transformation of American Culture, 1880–1920* (New York: Pantheon Books, 1983).

46 Anti-modernism in Canada is discussed in Ian McKay, *The Quest of the Folk, Antimodernism and Cultural Selection in Twentieth-Century Nova Scotia* (Kingston and Montreal: McGill-Queen's University Press, 1994); Donald A. Wright, 'W.D. Lighthall, and David Ross McCord: Antimodernism and English Canadian Imperialism, 1880–1918,' *Journal of Canadian Studies* 32 (Summer 1997), 12–48; and Lynda Jessup, 'Bushwackers in the Gallery: Antimodernism and the Group of Seven,' this volume.

47 Cole, *Captured Heritage*, 283–5. The 1927 'Exhibition of Canadian West Coast Art, Native and Modern,' preceded an important counterpart in the United States, the 'Exposition of Indian Tribal Art,' New York, 1931.

48 *Exhibition of Canadian West Coast Art, Native and Modern* (Ottawa: National Gallery of Canada, 1927), 2–4. It is significant, however, that after the 1927 exhibition, Native artefacts did not permanently enter the National Gallery, but remained in the ethnographic section of the National Museum.

49 Emily Carr, 'Modern and Indian Art of the West Coast,' *Supplement to the McGill News* (Montreal) June 1929: 18–22.

50 *Canadian Forum* 8 (February 1928), 525.

51 Goldie, *Fear and Temptation*, 16.

52 *Saturday Night* 8 November 1941, 18.

53 *Canadian Forum* 21 (December 1941), 277–8.

54 See, in particular, Shadbolt, *Art of Emily Carr*.

55 Emily Carr, *Hundreds and Thousands* (Toronto: Clarke, Irwin, 1966), 5.

56 She commented at the 1927 exhibition, '[T]hey all say I have more of the spirit of the Indian than the others' (Carr, *Hundreds and Thousands*, 9). During the years 1913–27 Carr had done very little painting, supporting herself by taking in boarders and breeding sheepdogs.

57 See canvases such as *Vanquished* (1929–30, oil on canvas, Vancouver Art Gallery), *Strangled by Growth* (1931, oil on canvas, Vancouver Art Gallery), and *Forsaken* (1937, oil on canvas, Vancouver Art Gallery). Much recent commentary on Carr has emphasized her obsession with ruins; see Scott Watson, 'Disfigured Nature: The Origins of the Modern Canadian Landscape,' in *Eye of Nature*, ed Diana Augaitis (Banff: Walter Phillips Gallery, 1991), 108–9. Her morbid preoccupation with death, linked to her experience as an orphan, is discussed by Catherine E. Mallory in 'Victorian and Canadian Worlds of Emily Carr: The Study of a Divided Imagination' (master's thesis, Dalhousie University, 1979). This said, it must be noted that the high mortality rate due to the infectious diseases brought by colonization and the rapid cultural change forced upon Native peoples entailed real losses on a traumatic scale, and Carr's acknowledgment of this should be seriously considered.

58 Paintings of welcome figures include *Potlatch Welcome* (1928–30, oil on canvas, Art Gallery of Ontario), *Sihouette no. 2* (1930, oil on canvas, Vancouver Art Gallery) and *Blunden Harbour* (1931, oil on canvas, National Gallery of Canada).

59 There are nine important paintings of female images, including *Dzunoqua* (1930, watercolour, Vancouver Art Gallery), *Indian Totem Pole (Dzonokwa)* (1930, watercolour, Mendel family collection), *Zunoqua of the Cat Village* (1930, oil on canvas, Vancouver Art Gallery), *Strangled By Growth* (1930, oil on canvas, Vancouver Art Gallery), *Totem Mother, Kitwancool* (1928, oil on canvas, Vancouver Art Gallery), *Kitwancool Totems* (1928, oil on canvas, Hart House, Toronto).

60 This aspect is more fully explored in Gerta Moray, 'T'Other Emily: Emily Carr, the Modern Woman Artist, and Dilemmas of Gender,' *RACAR* (forthcoming). It should be noted that early in her career, Carr decided to enter specifically those fields of artistic practice usually restricted to male artists, and she felt pride in the accolade 'painting like a man' that was frequently conferred on her by contemporary critics and artistic peers.

61 *Klee Wyck*, 47–58. Several other scholars have noted the significance of Carr's

images of *Dzonokwa* and of strong native women. See Roxanne Rimstead, '"Klee Wyck," Redefining Region through Marginal Realities,' *Canadian Literature* 130 (Autumn 1991), 41–4; and Thomas, 'Klee Wyck,' 12–15. I am grateful to Donna P. Pennee for drawing these articles to my attention

62 See 'Kitwancool,' *Klee Wyck*, 47–58.

63 For example, in 1932 Carr held exhibitions in her house, which she attempted to set up as a 'People's Gallery,' showing her own early images of Native villages along with work by successful Victoria artists and by artists, such as Chinese painter Lee Nam, who were debarred from the Island Arts and Crafts Society because of their style or their race.

64 National Gallery of Canada Library and Archives, NGC fonds, 7.1-C, 'Carr, Emily, correspondence with,' Emily Carr to Eric Brown, 3 June 1938.

65 Benedict Anderson has defined the modern nation as 'an imagined political community' in which citizens, who necessarily cannot all know one another, feel tied together by a shared image of their communion. See, *Imagined Communities: Reflections on the Origin and Spread of Nationalism* (London: Verso, 1983), 6.

66 Carr was long reluctant to sell the documentary works singly, and during the 1930s persisted in showing them alongside her new work even though they were stylistically outdated. These images will soon be accessible as a complete group (as Carr intended) through the illustrations in Gerta Moray, *Unsettling Encounters: The 'Indian' Pictures of Emily Carr* (forthcoming).

67 Emily Carr, 'Modern and Indian Art,' 22.

68 The debates about Carr's significance for British Columbia artists and critics have been summarized and reviewed by John O'Brian in *Gasoline, Oil, and Paper; The 1930s Oil-on-Paper Paintings of Emily Carr* (Saskatoon: Mendel Art Gallery, 1995), 7–17, 30–4.

69 Carr's younger brother, the only surviving male child in her family, made no contribution to the family's fortunes, dying in 1899 after spending many years in a sanatorium with tuberculosis. During the first half of Carr's life there was as yet no true party system in the British Columbia legislature, and women did not obtain the vote until Carr herself was nearly fifty.

70 See Martin Robin, *The Rush For Spoils: The Company Province 1871–1933* (Toronto: McClelland & Stewart, 1972).

71 Two major exhibitions of work by First Nations contemporary artists were held in Ottawa-Hull in 1992, the year of the five hundredth anniversary of Columbus's voyage. See Gerald McMaster and Lee-Ann Martin, eds., *Indigena: Contemporary Native Perspectives* (Hull, Quebec: Canadian Museum of Civilisation and Toronto: Douglas & McIntyre, 1992); and Diana Nemiroff, Robert Houle and Charlotte Townsend-Gault, eds., *Land Spirit Power: First Nations at the National Gallery of Canada* (Ottawa: National Gallery of Canada, 1992).

72 Charlotte Townshend-Gault, 'Kinds of Knowing,' in *Land, Spirit, Power: First Nations at the National Gallery of Canada*, ed. Diana Nemiroff, Robert Houle, and Charlotte Townshend-Gault (Ottawa: National Gallery of Canada), 86.

73 Son of a Haida mother and an American father of Scottish and German ancestry, Reid was raised in white settler society but later studied his Haida heritage and

learned the traditional skills of large scale wood carving at the British Columbia Provincial Museum from a Kwakwaka'wakw elder, Mungo Martin. See Doris Shadbolt, *Bill Reid* (Vancouver: Douglas & McIntyre, 1986).

74 Carr's drawings of 1928–9 show that she was experimenting with the application of Native form elements to stylized forest forms (see examples in Shadbolt, *Art of Emily Carr*, 107–10). Critical links between the work of Yuxweluptun and the British Columbia landscape painting tradition have been made by Robert Linsley, 'Yuxweluptun and the West Coast Landscape,' and by Scott Watson, 'The Modernist Past of Lawrence Paul Yuxweluptun's Landscape Allegories,' both in Scott Watson, ed., *Lawrence Paul Yuxweluptun* (Vancouver: Morris and Helen Belkin Art Gallery, 1995), 23–32 and 70–1 respectively. In view of Watson's discussion of the significance and limits of the Native Arts and Crafts movement, 'encouraged by whites for a multitude of purposes and uses of their own construction' (p. 62), it is interesting to note Carr's scepticism about that movement. She believed that Native people would have to find their own new, possibly hybrid forms, as George Clutesi was doing at the time.

75 I do not mean here a superficial 'cultural mosaic,' limited to culture divorced from politics, but rather an accord that acknowledges and redresses historical injustice. The question of First Nations sovereignty remains on the agenda for future reshaping of the Canadian constitution.

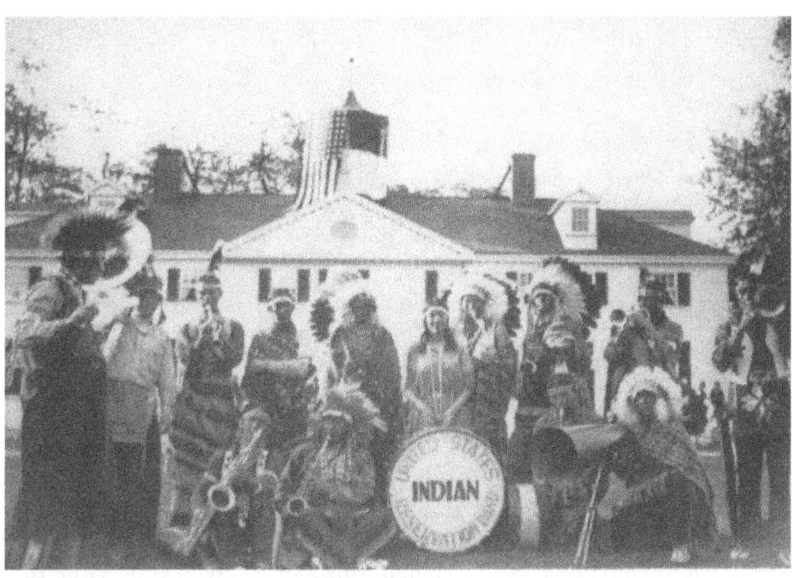

Fig. 2.1 Molly Nelson (Molly Spotted Elk) and other members of the United States Indian Reservation Band in front of the United States exhibit at the 1931 Colonial Exposition in Paris. The centrepiece of the exhibit was a replica of George Washington's Mt Vernon estate. Photo: United States National Archives, RG43.

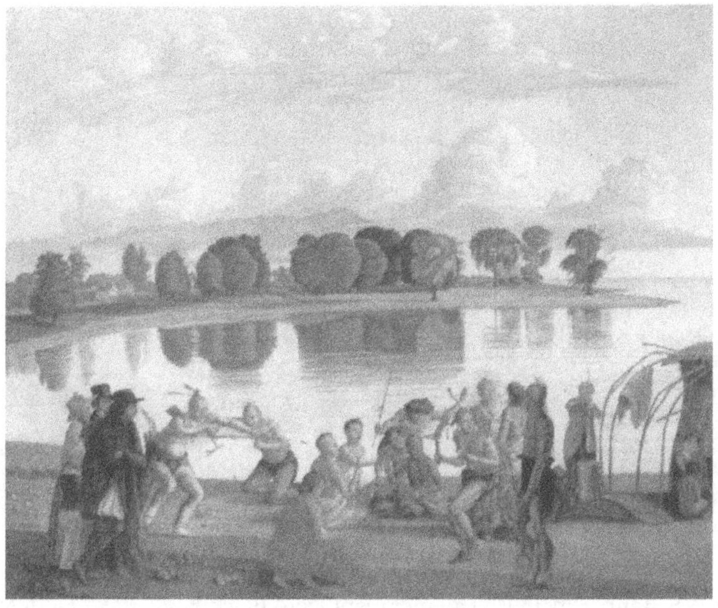

Fig. 2.2 William Bent Berczy, *Indian Dance at Amherstburg*, ca. 1825, oil on canvas (58.7 × 68.5 cm). Photo courtesy of the National Gallery of Canada, Ottawa, 30860.

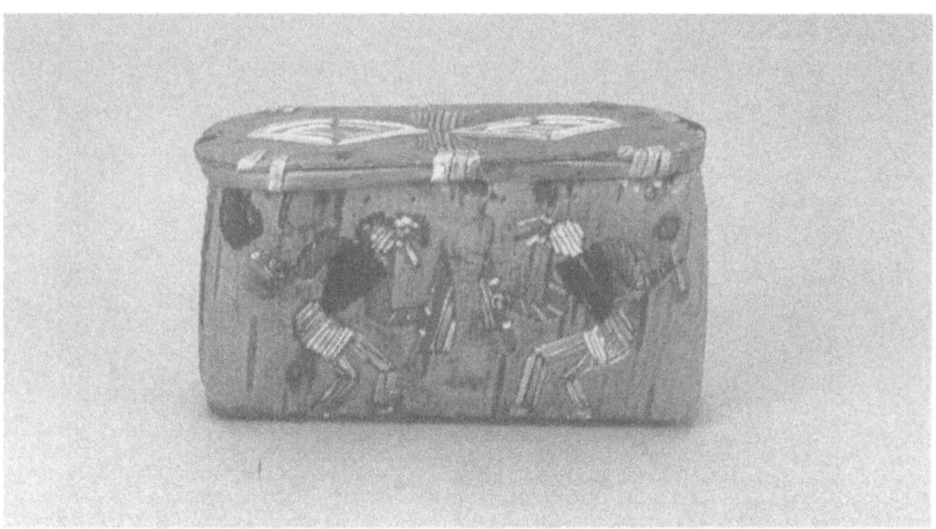

Fig. 2.3 Quilled birchbark *makak*, Canadian Museum of Civilization Hull, III-N-37a, b (photo S99-4755). The prominence of dance performance as a mode of self-representation and its popularity with early European visitors are suggested by its occurrence on souvenir objects, such as this ornamented container for maple sugar, made for the curio trade in the 1820s or 1830s.

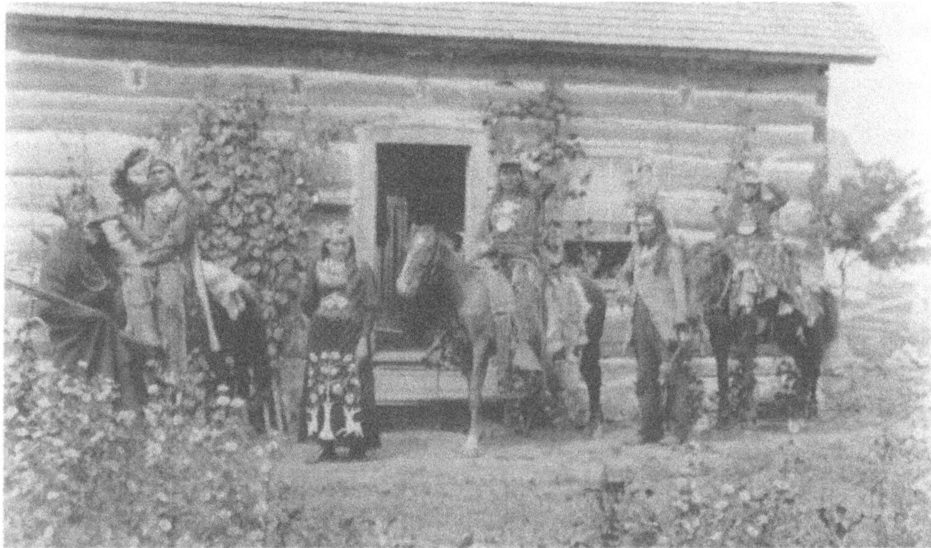

Fig. 2.4 The St Regis (Akwesasne) Indian Show Company photographed in Lawrence, Kansas, by W.S. Tanner in 1894. The members were Black Eagle, Jake Paul, Mary Ann Black Eagle, Chief Running Deer, Philip Big Tree, and Lily Deer. Photo courtesy of the Library of Congress, Washington, D.C., USZ62-42816.

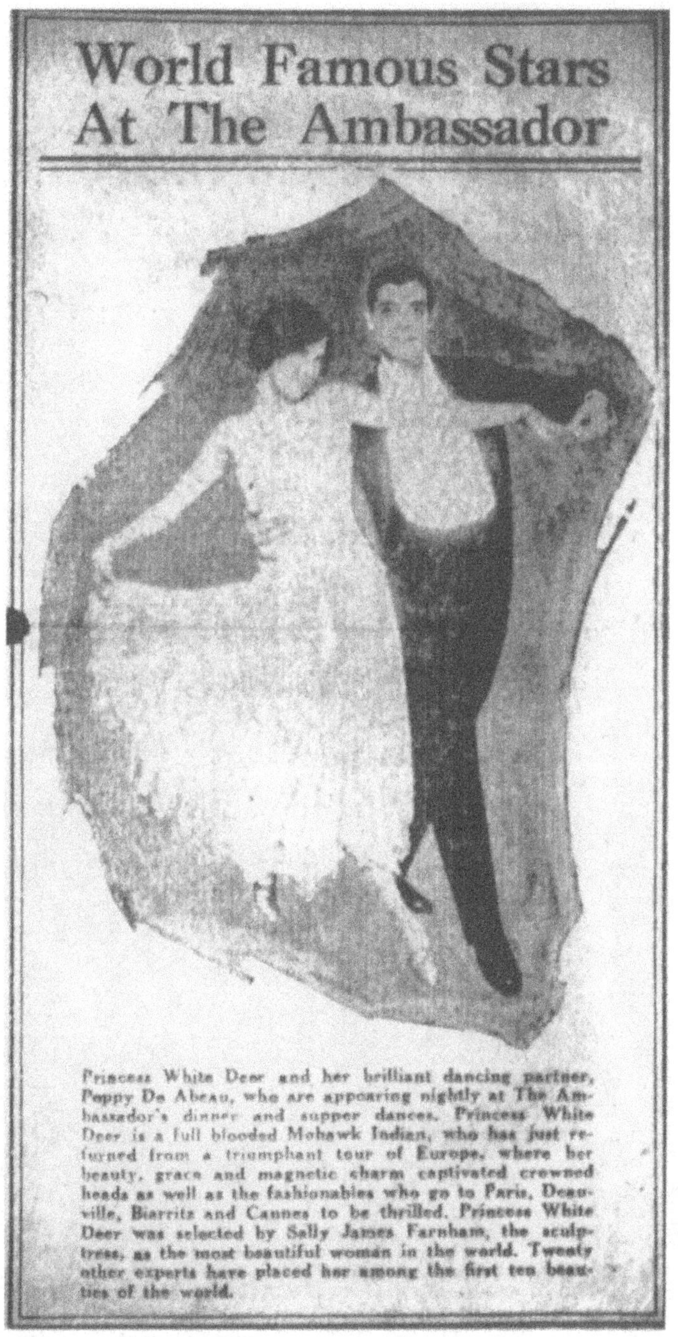

World Famous Stars At The Ambassador

Princess White Deer and her brilliant dancing partner, Peppy De Abeau, who are appearing nightly at The Ambassador's dinner and supper dances. Princess White Deer is a full blooded Mohawk Indian, who has just returned from a triumphant tour of Europe, where her beauty, grace and magnetic charm captivated crowned heads as well as the fashionables who go to Paris, Deauville, Biarritz and Cannes to be thrilled. Princess White Deer was selected by Sally James Farnham, the sculptress, as the most beautiful woman in the world. Twenty other experts have placed her among the first ten beauties of the world.

Fig. 2.5 Publicity sketch of Princess White Deer and her dance partner Peppy De Abrew preserved in Esther Deer's scrapbooks, 1920s. Photo: Ruth Phillips, courtesy of Sylvia Trudeau and Kanien'kehaka Raotitiohkwa Cultural Centre, Kahnawake.

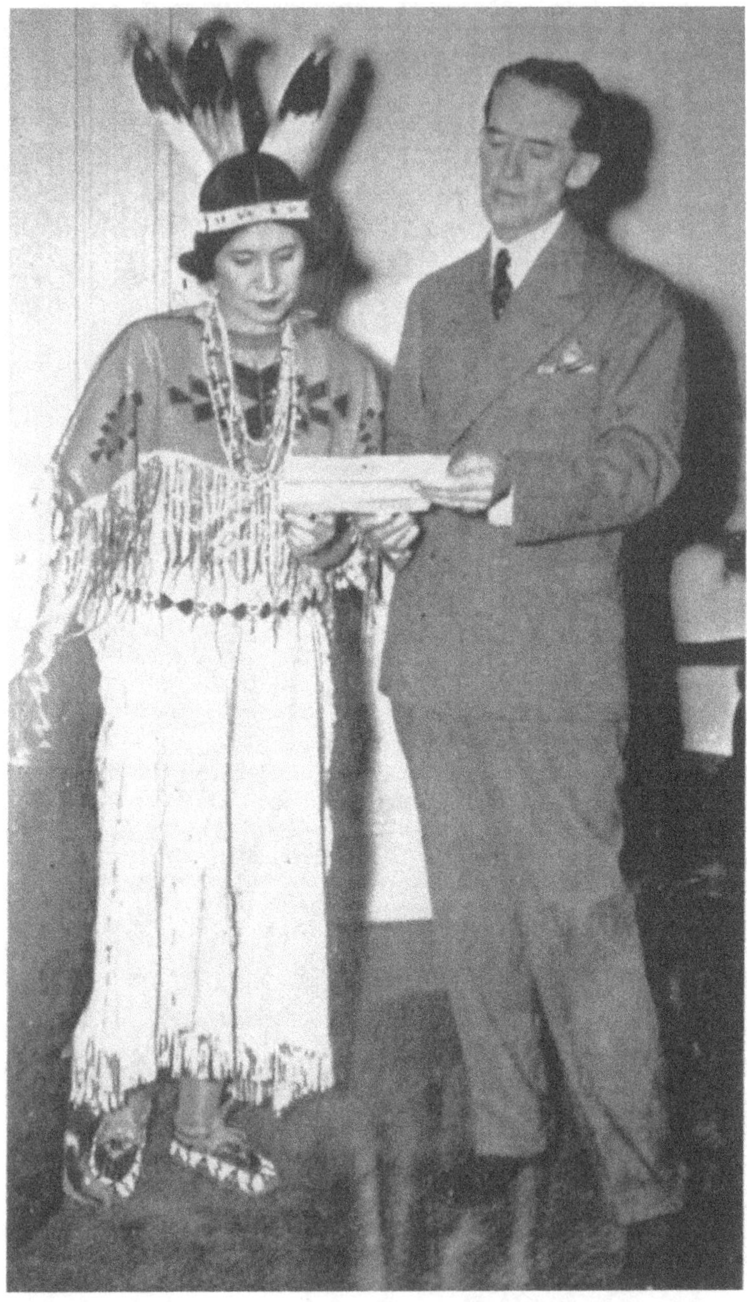

Fig. 2.6 Esther Deer at the White House in 1937, presenting a letter to President Roosevelt's secretary, Marvin Hunter McIntyre, inviting the President to attend a meeting of the Grand Council of Chiefs of the Six Nations of the Iroquois. Photo: Ruth Phillips, courtesy of Sylvia Trudeau and Kanien'kehaka Raotitiohkwa Cultural Centre, Kahnawake.

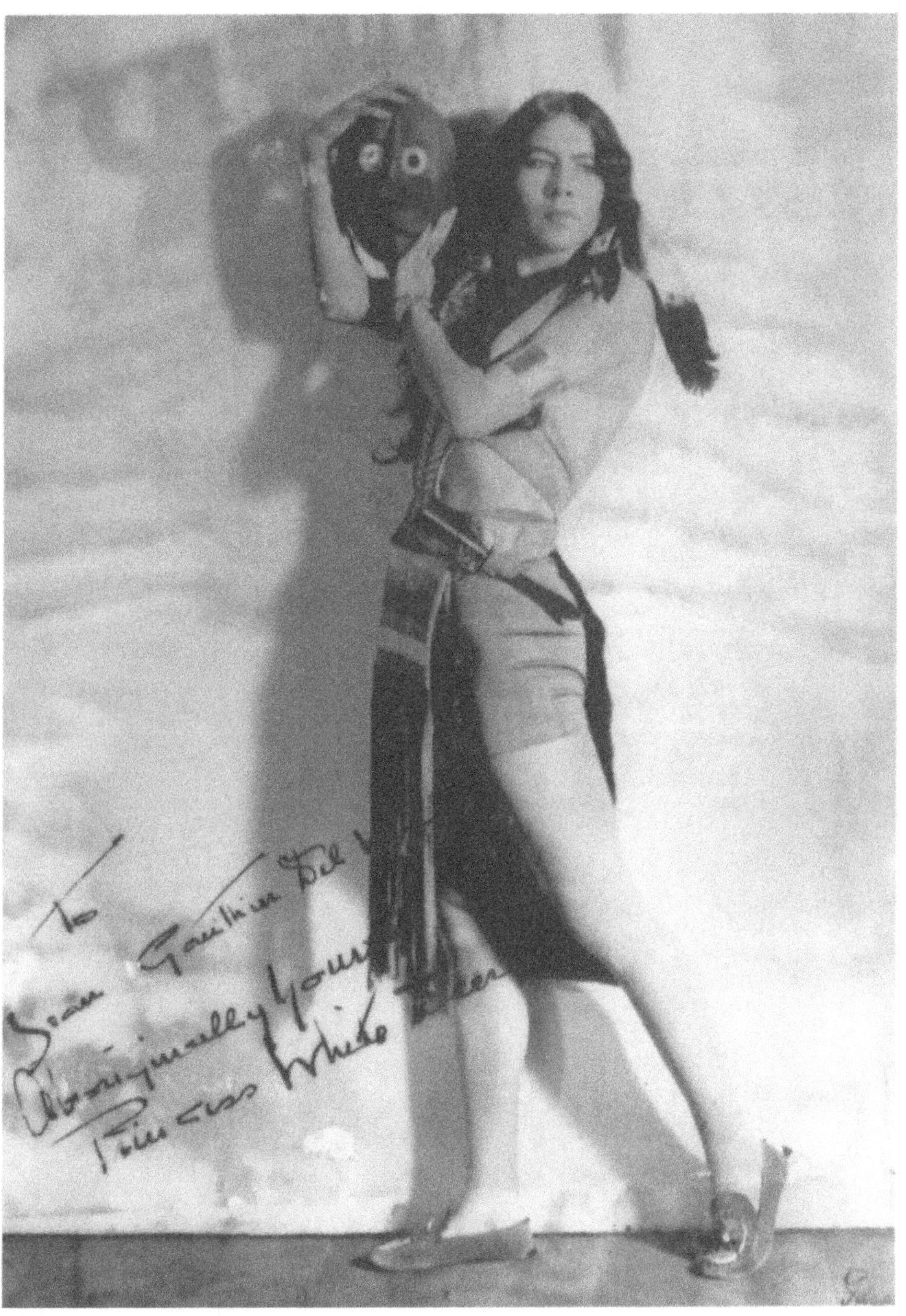

Fig. 2.7 Publicity photo of Princess White Deer holding an Iroquois False Face mask, 1921. Photo: Martin Loft, courtesy of Sylvia Trudeau.

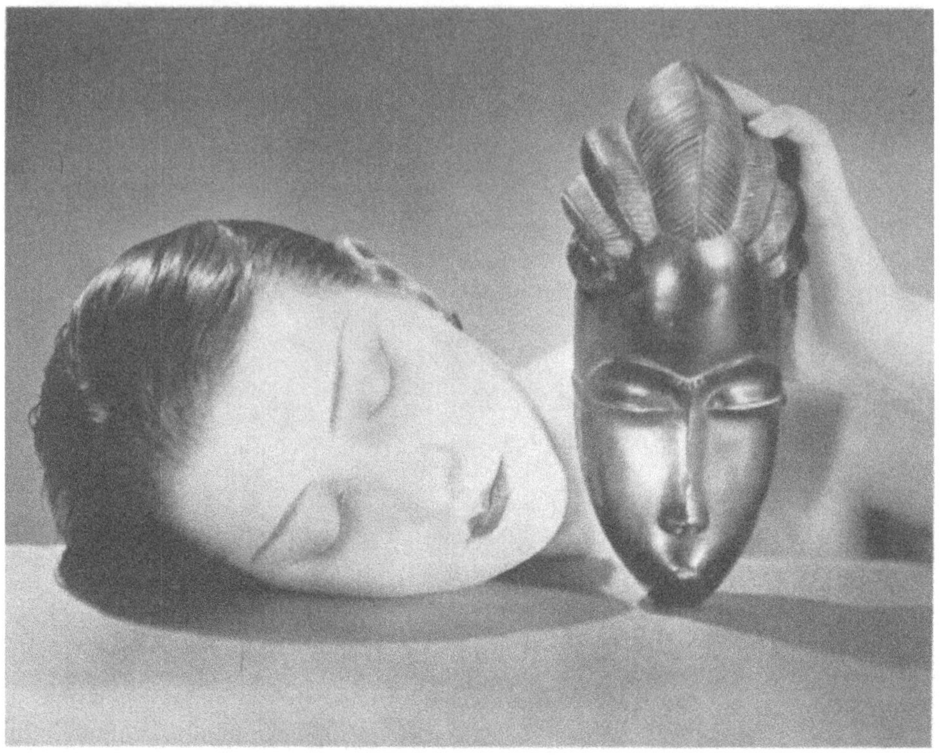

Fig. 2.8 Man Ray, *Noire et Blanche*, 1926. Photo copyright Man Ray Trust, Paris / SODRAC (Montreal) 2000.

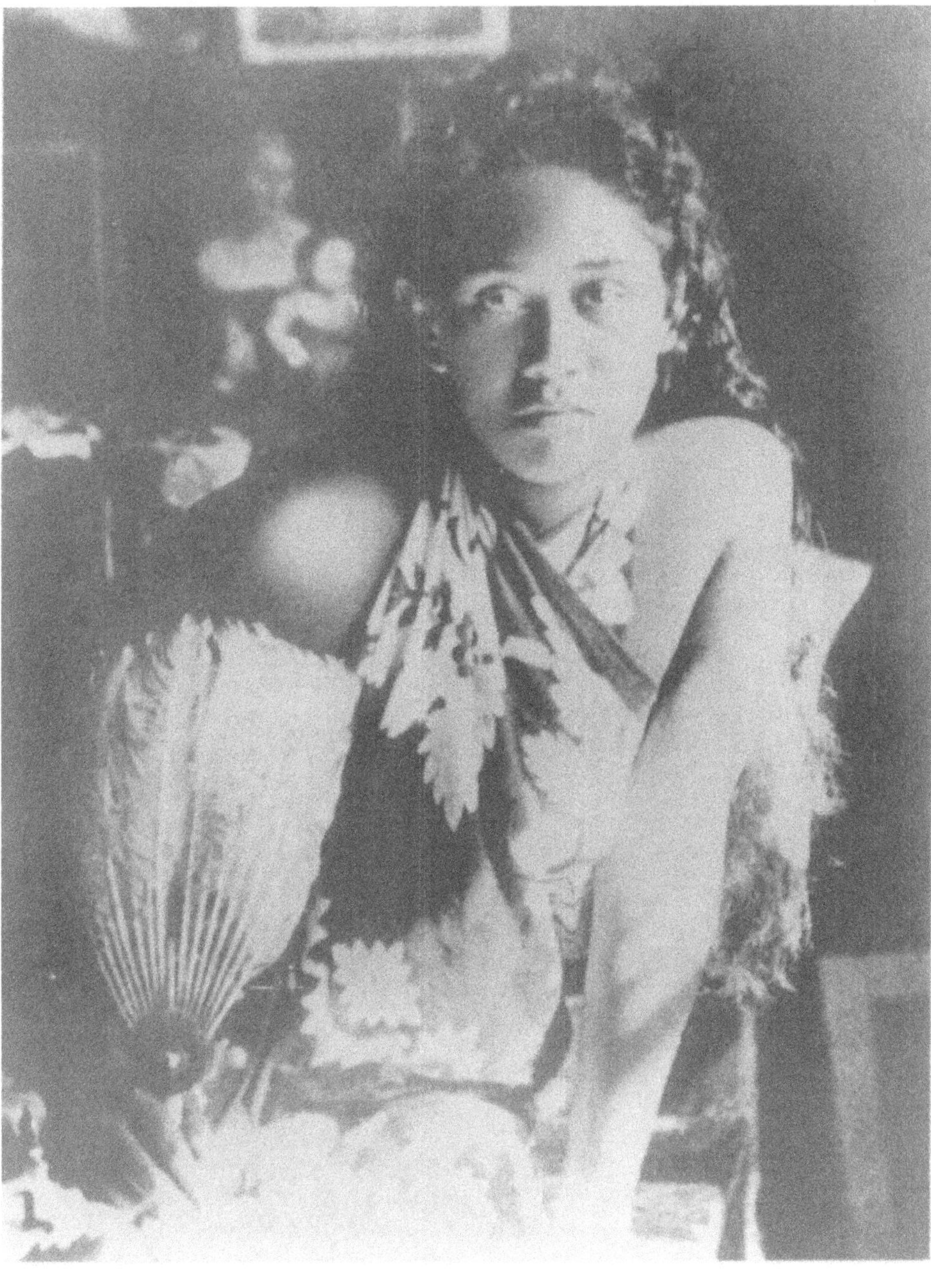

Fig. 3.1 Louis Grelet, *Tohotaua*, photographed in Gauguin's studio in Hiva Oa, Marquesas Islands, 1901. Visible on the back wall are reproductions of Hans Holbein, *Woman and Child*; Puvis de Chavannes, *Hope*; Edgar Degas, *Harlequin*; and a photograph of Buddha from the Borobudur sculptures (acquired by Gauguin at the Exposition universelle of 1889).

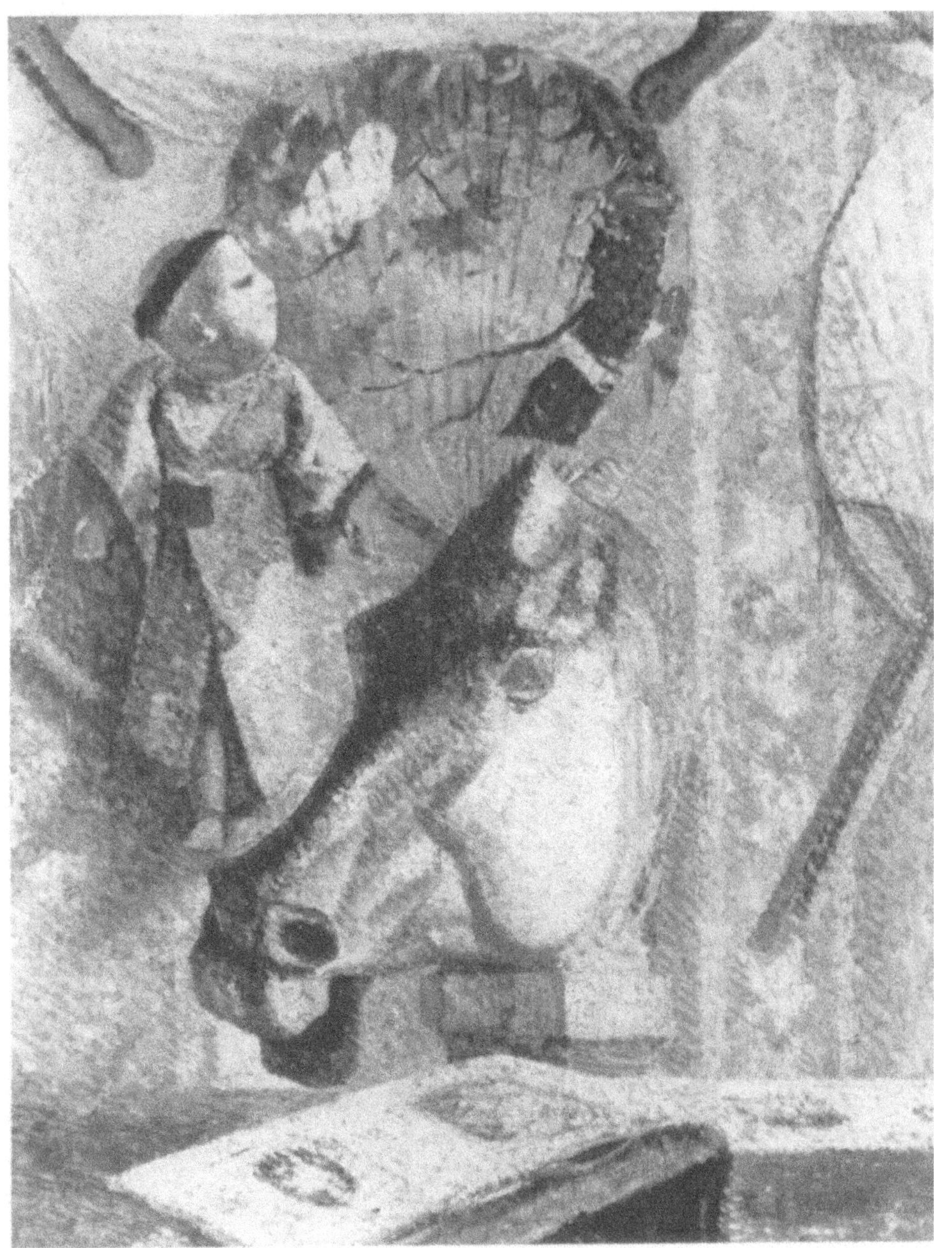

Fig. 3.2 Paul Gauguin, *Still Life with a Horse's Head*, ca. 1886. Oil on canvas, 49 × 38 cm. Bridgestone Museum of Art, Ishibashi Foundation, Tokyo.

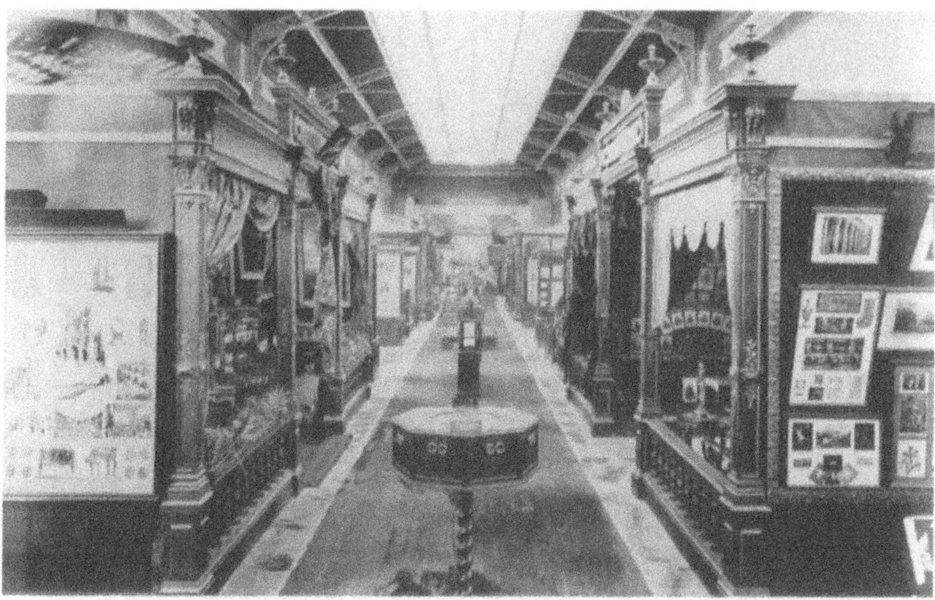

Fig. 3.3 J. Kuhn, *Exhibition of the history of photography, Exposition universelle de 1889.* Albumen print. Bibliothèque Historique de la Ville de Paris, Paris.

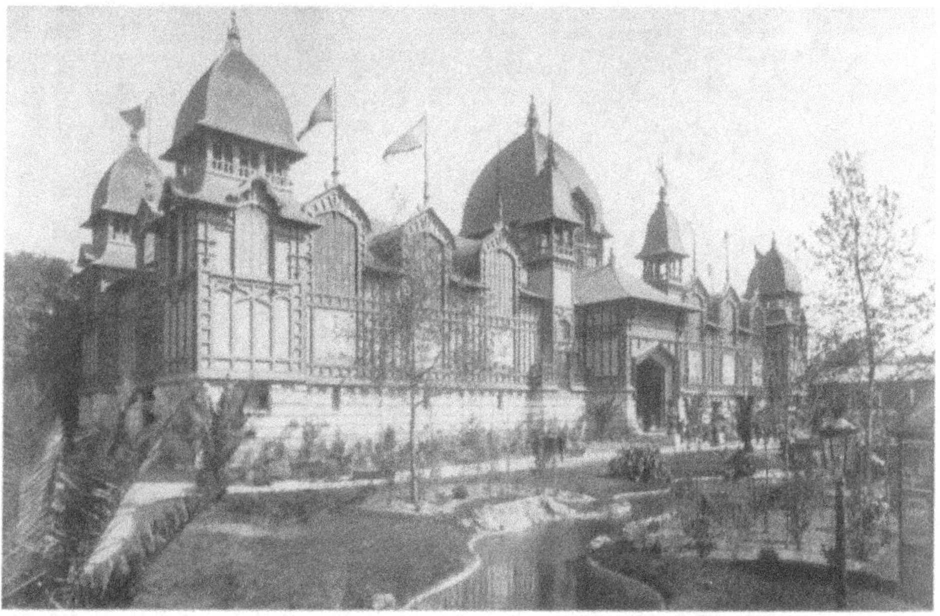

Fig. 3.4 E.H., éditeur, *Palais des colonies, Exposition universelle, Paris, 1889.* Albumen print mounted on board, 29 × 23.3 cm. Courtesy Photographic Archives, National Gallery of Art, Washington, D.C.

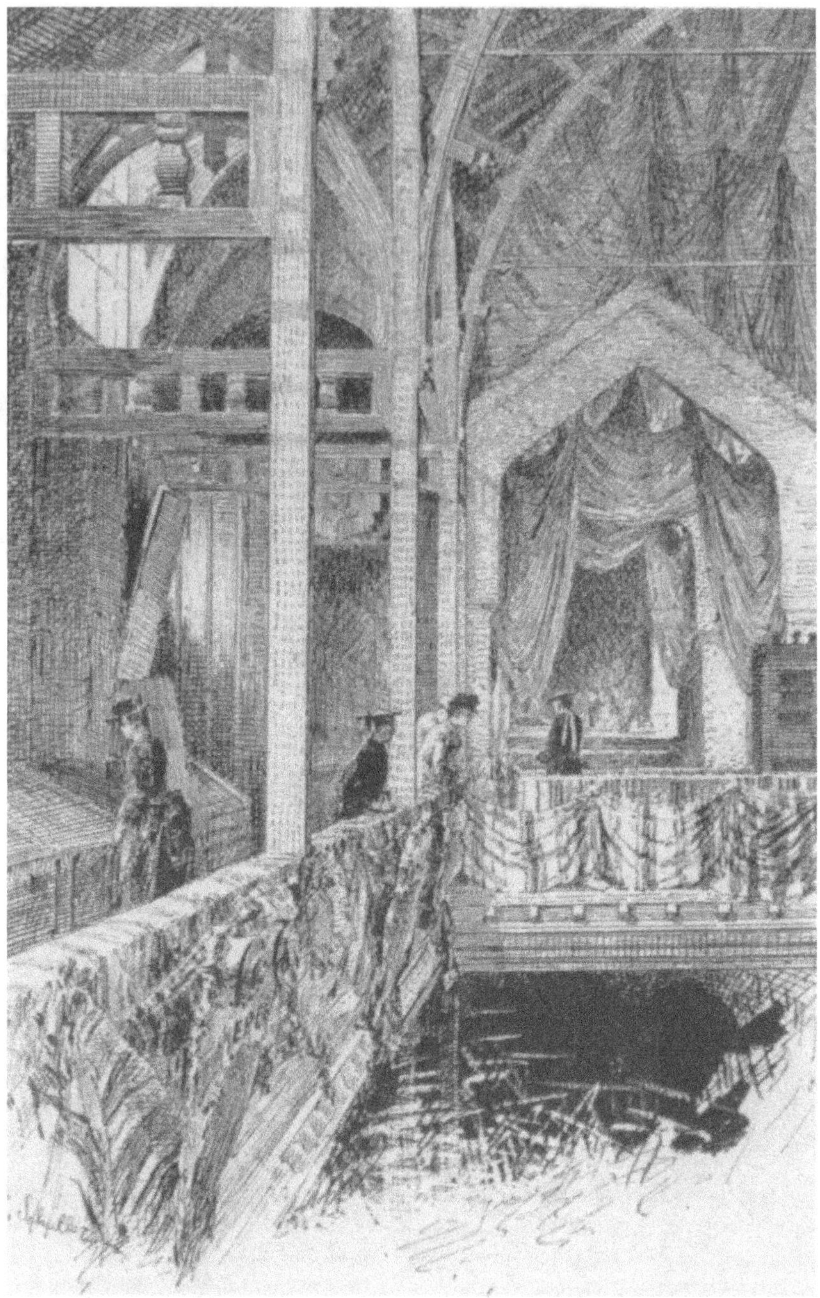

Fig. 3.5 Anonymous photographer, *Interieur du Palais central des colonies*. Engraving, 7 × 11 cm. Reproduced in F.G. Dumas and L. de Fourcaud, *Revue de l'Exposition universelle* (Paris: Ludovic Baschet, 1890), 90. Courtesy Photographic Archives, National Gallery of Art, Washington, D.C.

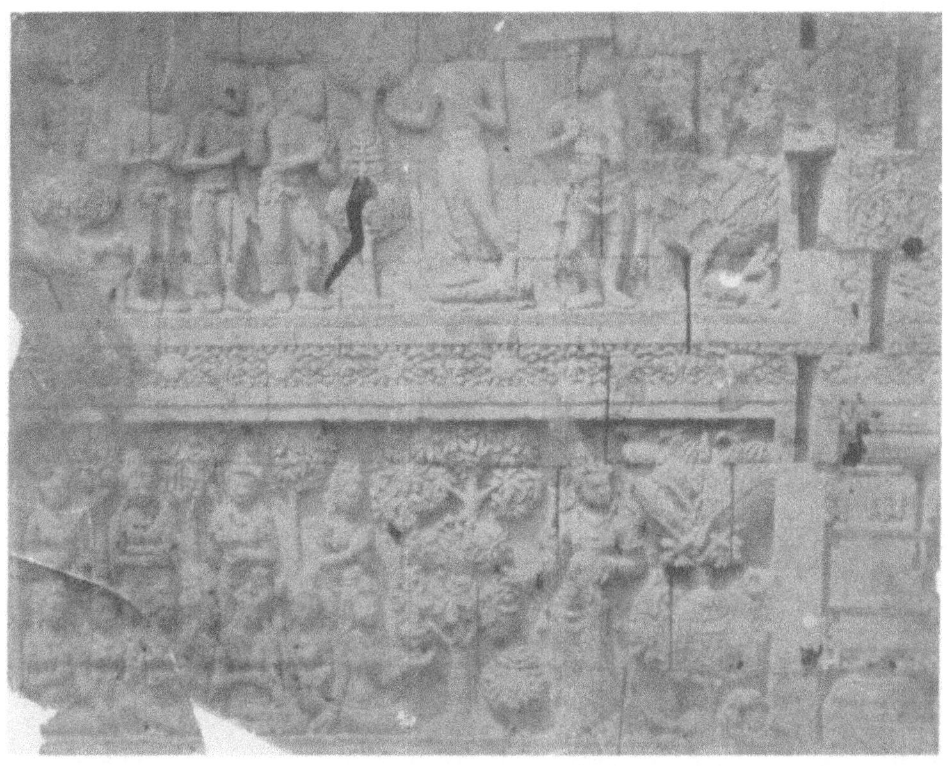

Fig. 3.6 Photograph of *The Arrival of Maitrakanyaka at Nadana* (a relief [panel I. b110] on Borobudur Temple, Java, 760–830 A.D.). French photograph, printed by 1889 and owned by Gauguin. Private collection, Papeete, Tahiti.

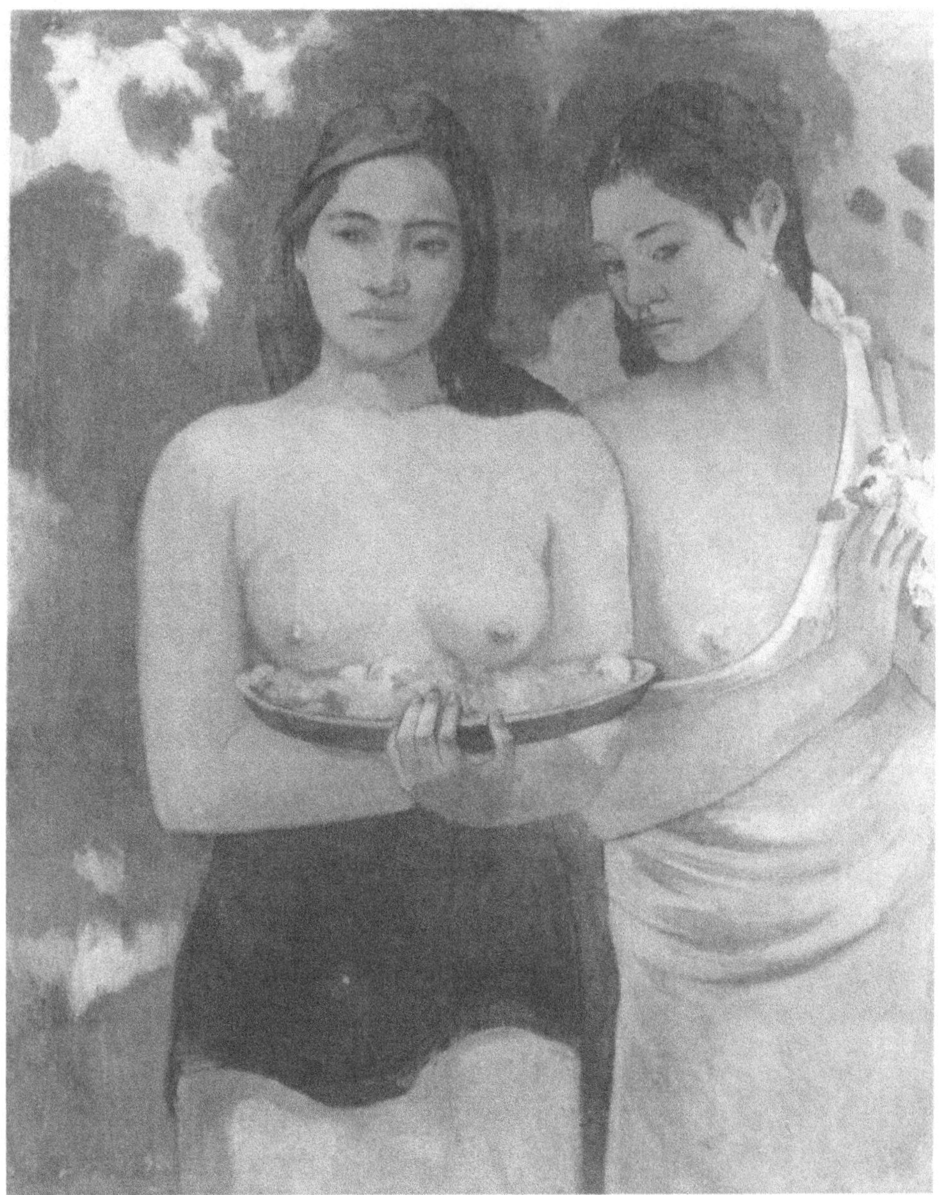

Fig. 3.7 Paul Gauguin, *Two Tahitian Women*, 1899. Oil on canvas, 94 × 72.2 cm. Metropolitan Museum of Art, New York, gift of William Church Osborn, 1949.

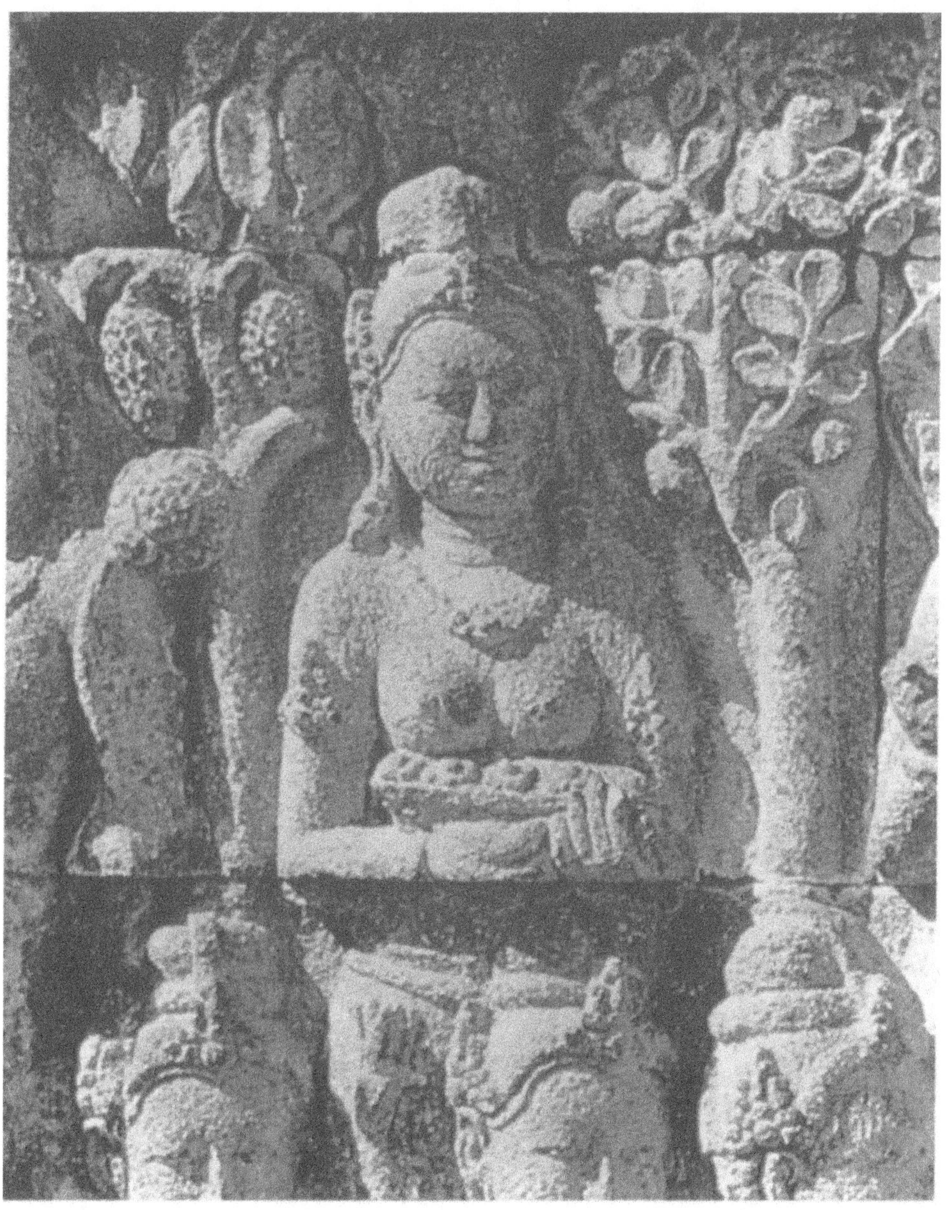

Fig. 3.8 Detail of figure 3.6, photograph of *The Arrival of Maitrakanyaka at Nadana* (detail of a relief [panel I. b110] on Borobudur Temple, Java, 760–830 A.D.).

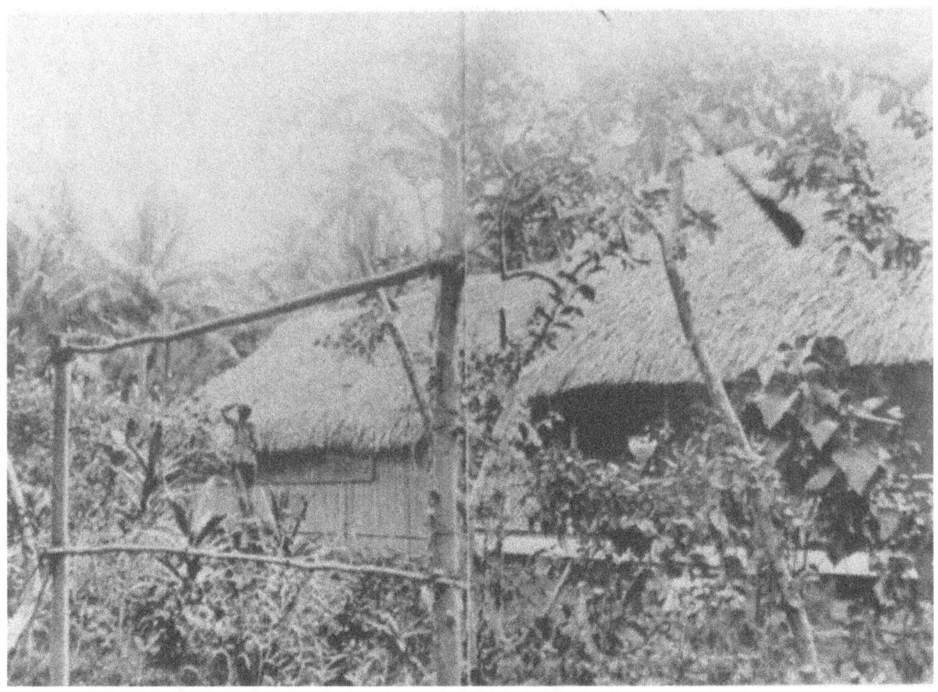

Fig. 3.9 Jules Agostini, *Gauguin's House and Studio in Punaaiua*, 1896. Albumen print sent by Gauguin to Daniel de Monfreid, November 1896; current location unknown. Reproduction published in Christopher Gray, *The Sculpture and Ceramics of Paul Gauguin*, ©1963 the Johns Hopkins University Press, 258.

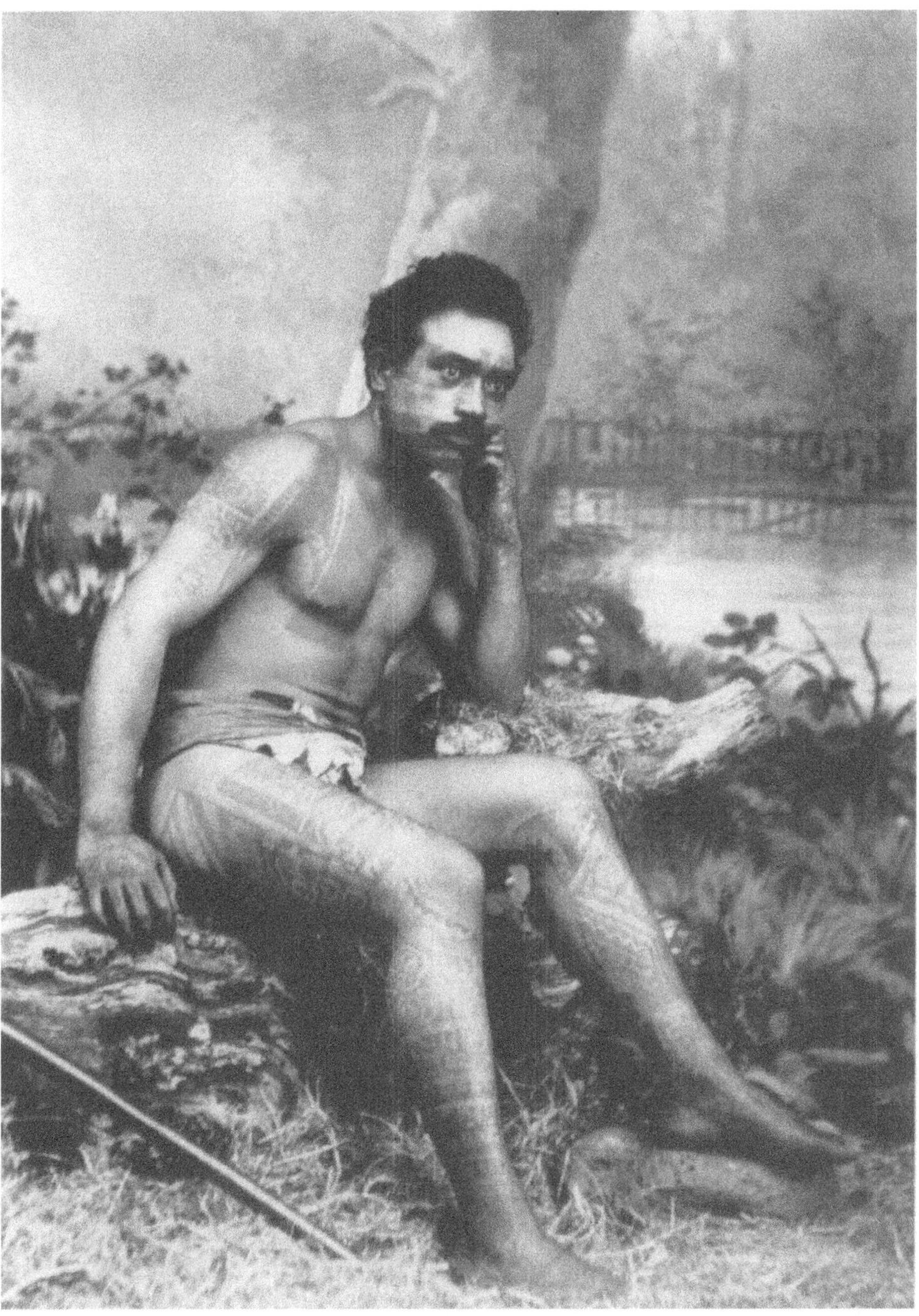

Fig. 3.10 Charles Spitz, 'A specimen of tattooing from the Marquesas Islands.' Albumen photograph made by 1887. Reginald Gallop manuscript, 1887, 49. Mitchell Library, State Library of New South Wales, Sydney.

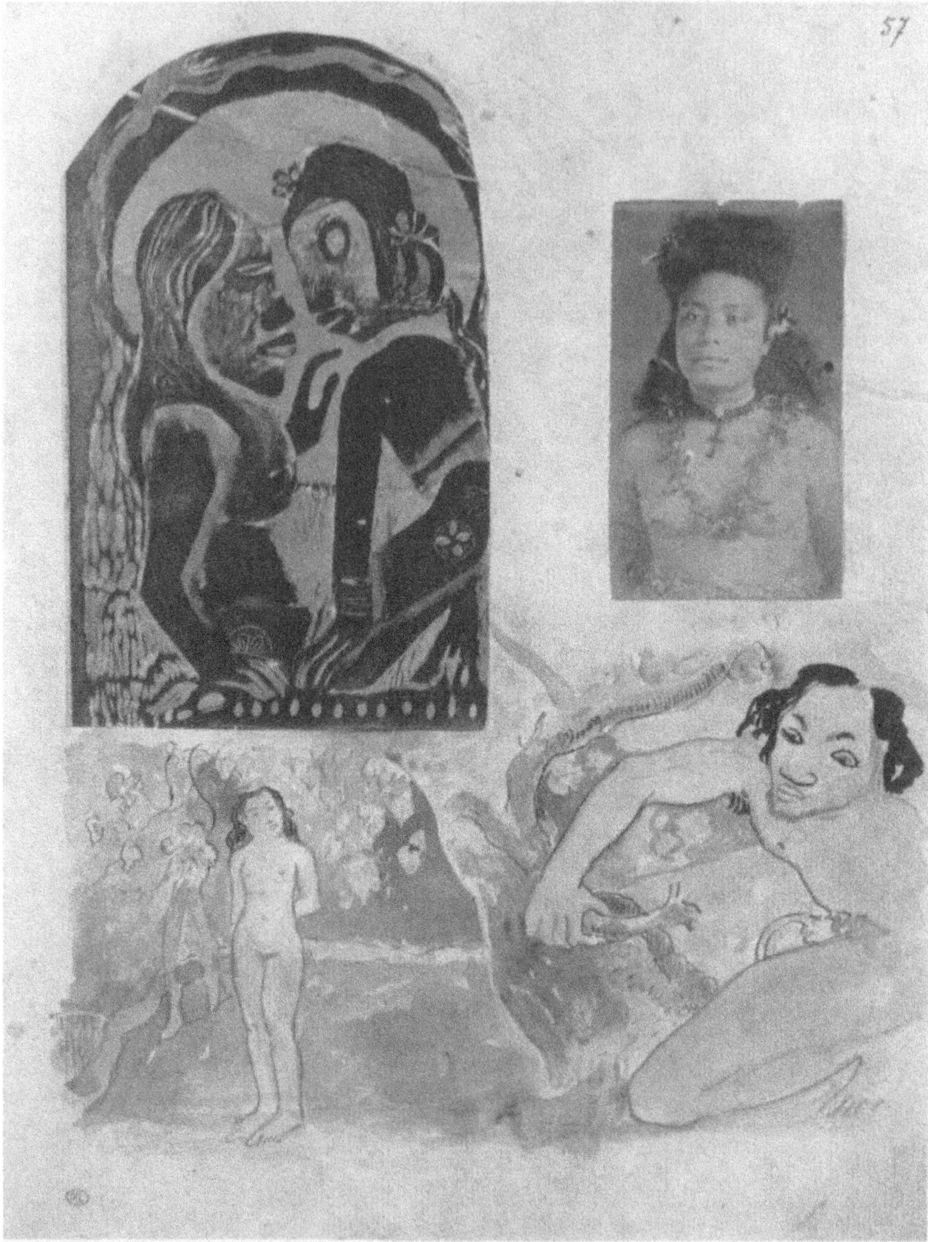

Fig. 3.11 Paul Gauguin, manuscript page from *Noa Noa*, 1893–7. Photograph, watercolour, and woodcut on paper, 34 × 26 cm. Département des arts graphiques, Musée du Louvre, Paris.

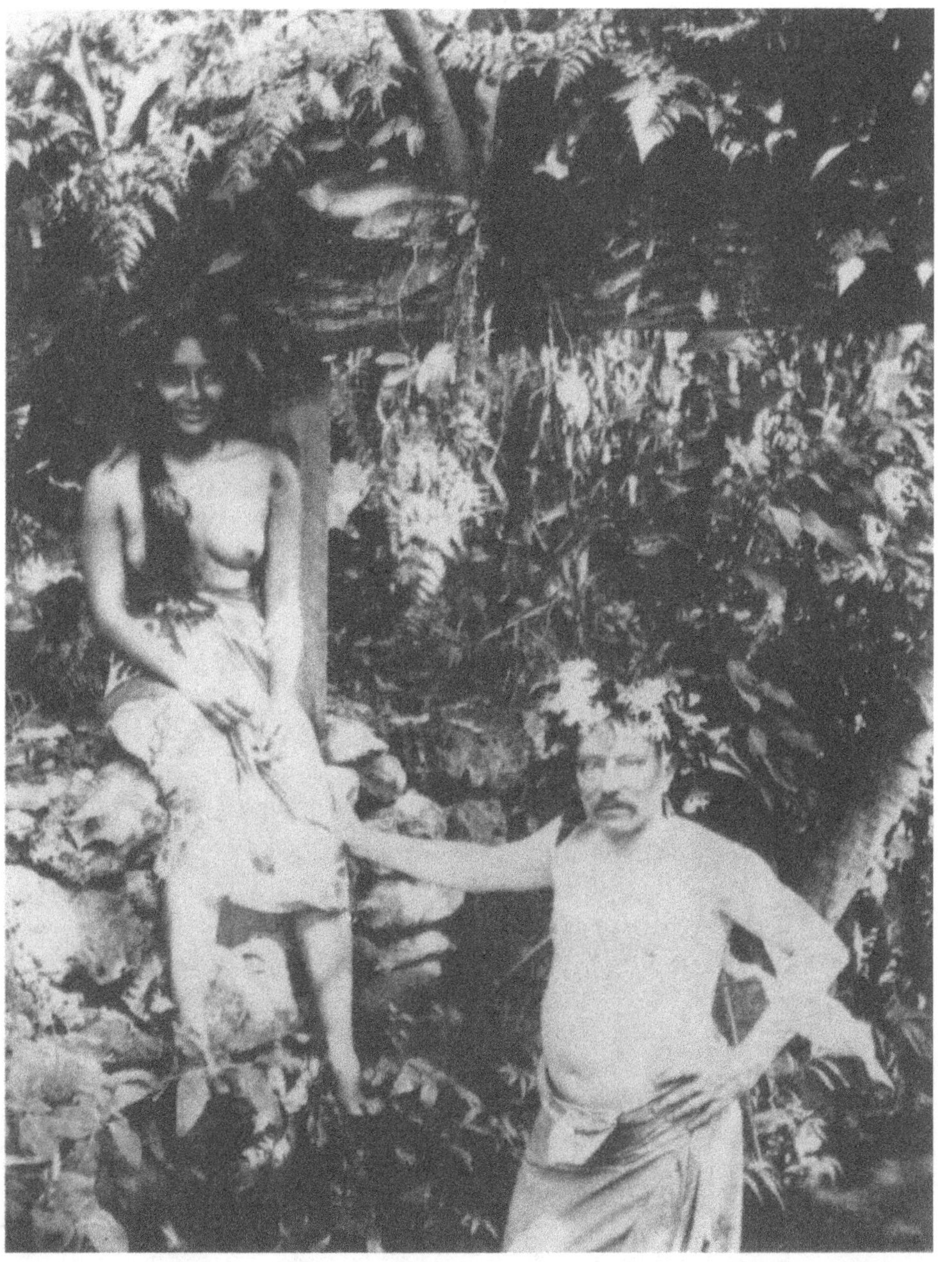

Fig. 3.12 Anonymous photographer, *Vahine I te pape*, in Album Godey, *Le Croisseur Duchaffault*, 1891–3, 25. Albumen print mounted in souvenir album. Cliché, Cabinet des estampes, Bibliothèque nationale de France, Paris.

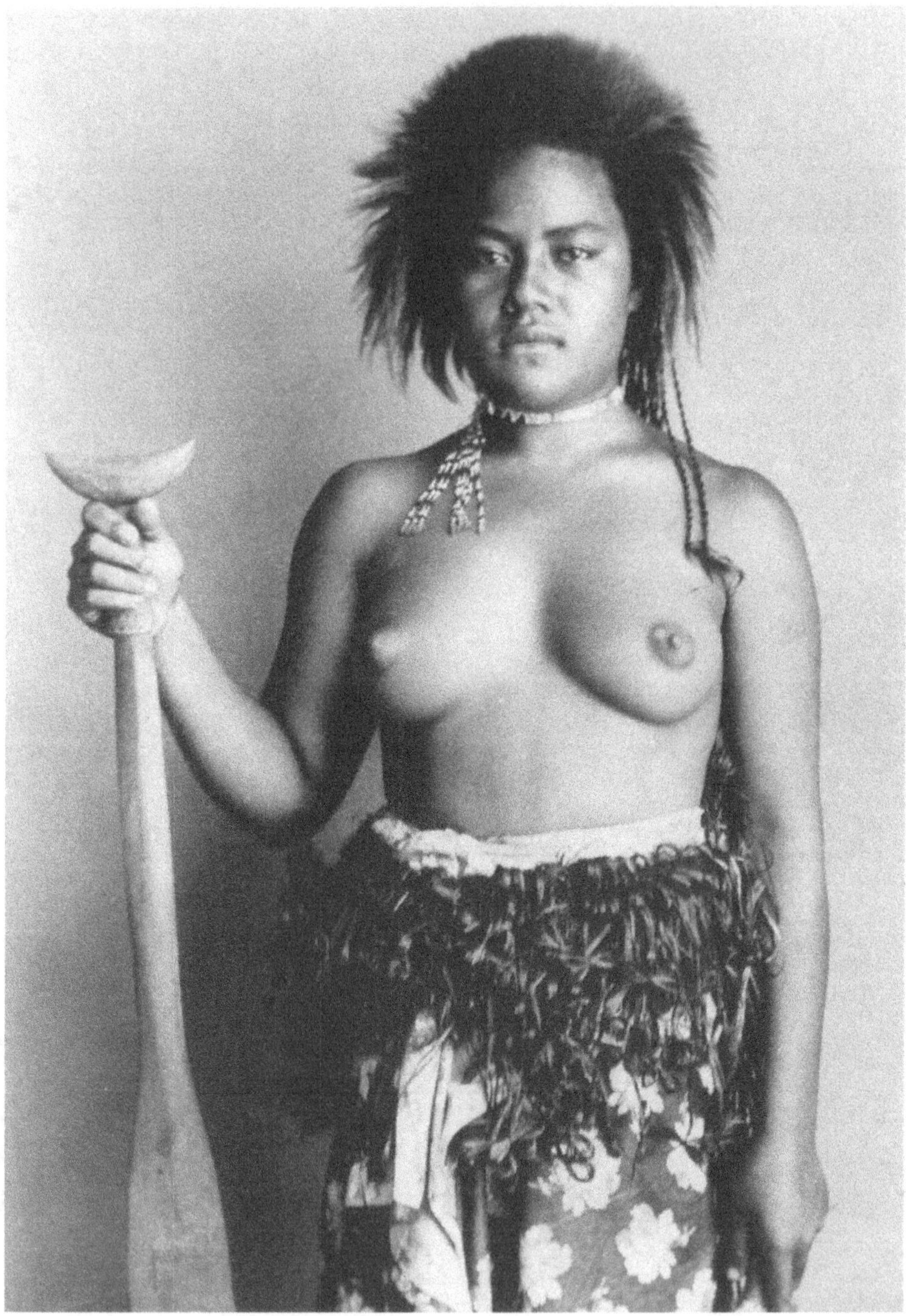

Fig. 3.13 Anonymous photographer, *Tongan girl living in Figi – Fehoko*, ca. 1900. Albumen print. Museum of Mankind, British Museum, London.

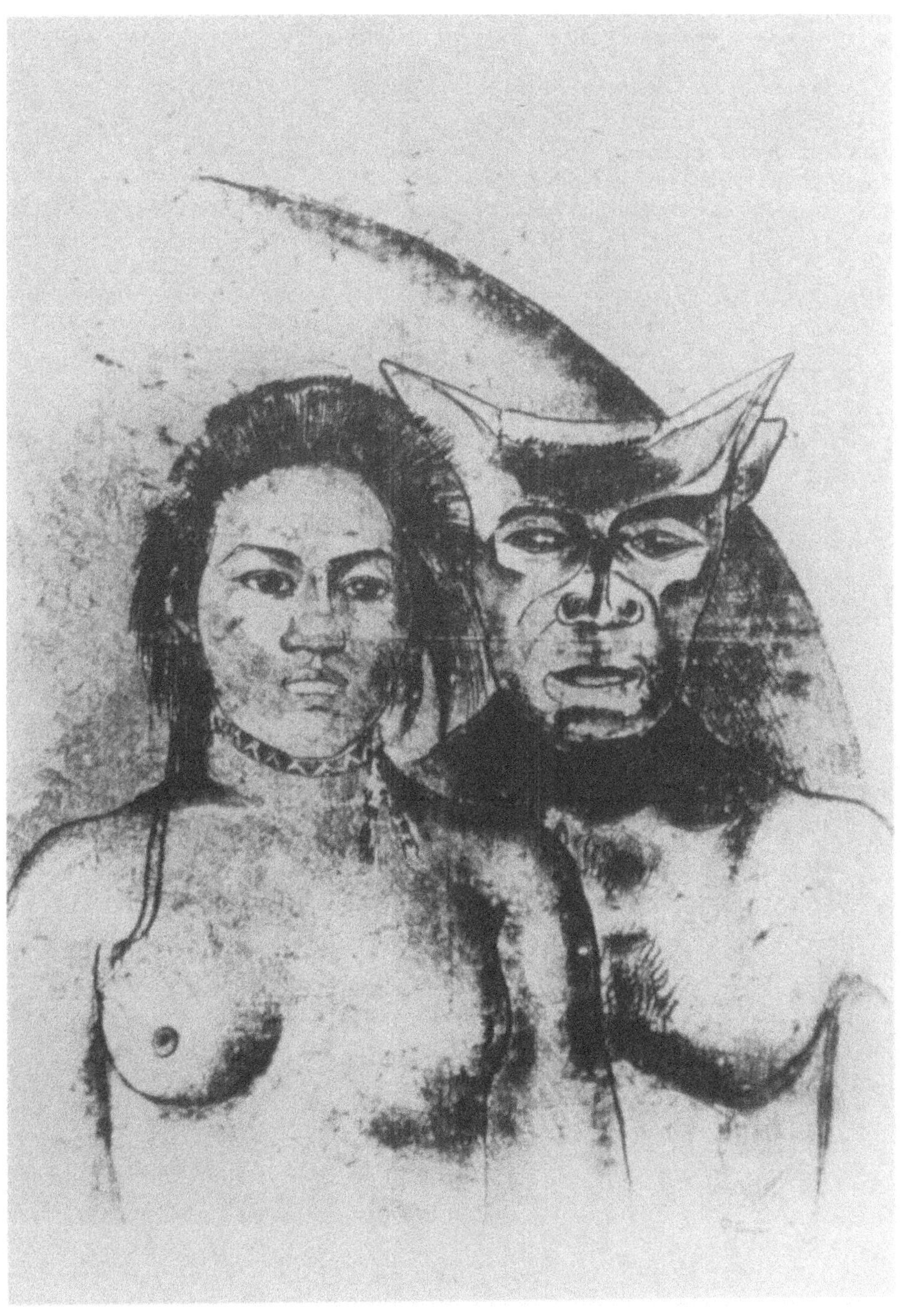

Fig. 3.14 Paul Gauguin, *Tahitian woman with Evil Spirit*, ca. 1900. Traced monotype, probably printed in brown and black, 65 × 46 cm. Private collection.

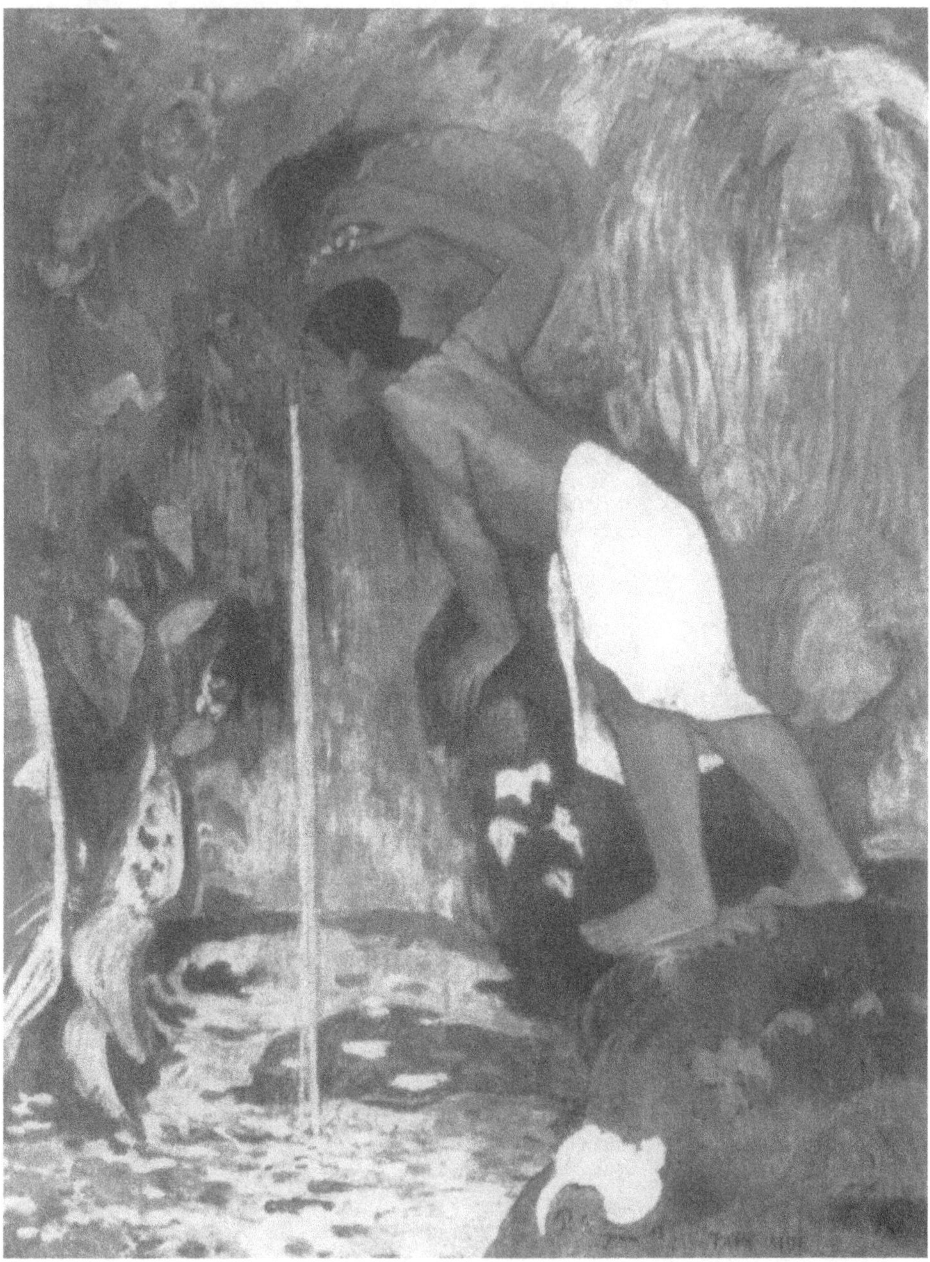

Fig. 3.15 Paul Gauguin, *Pape Moe* (Mysterious Waters), 1893. Oil on canvas, 99 × 75 cm. Private collection, Switzerland.

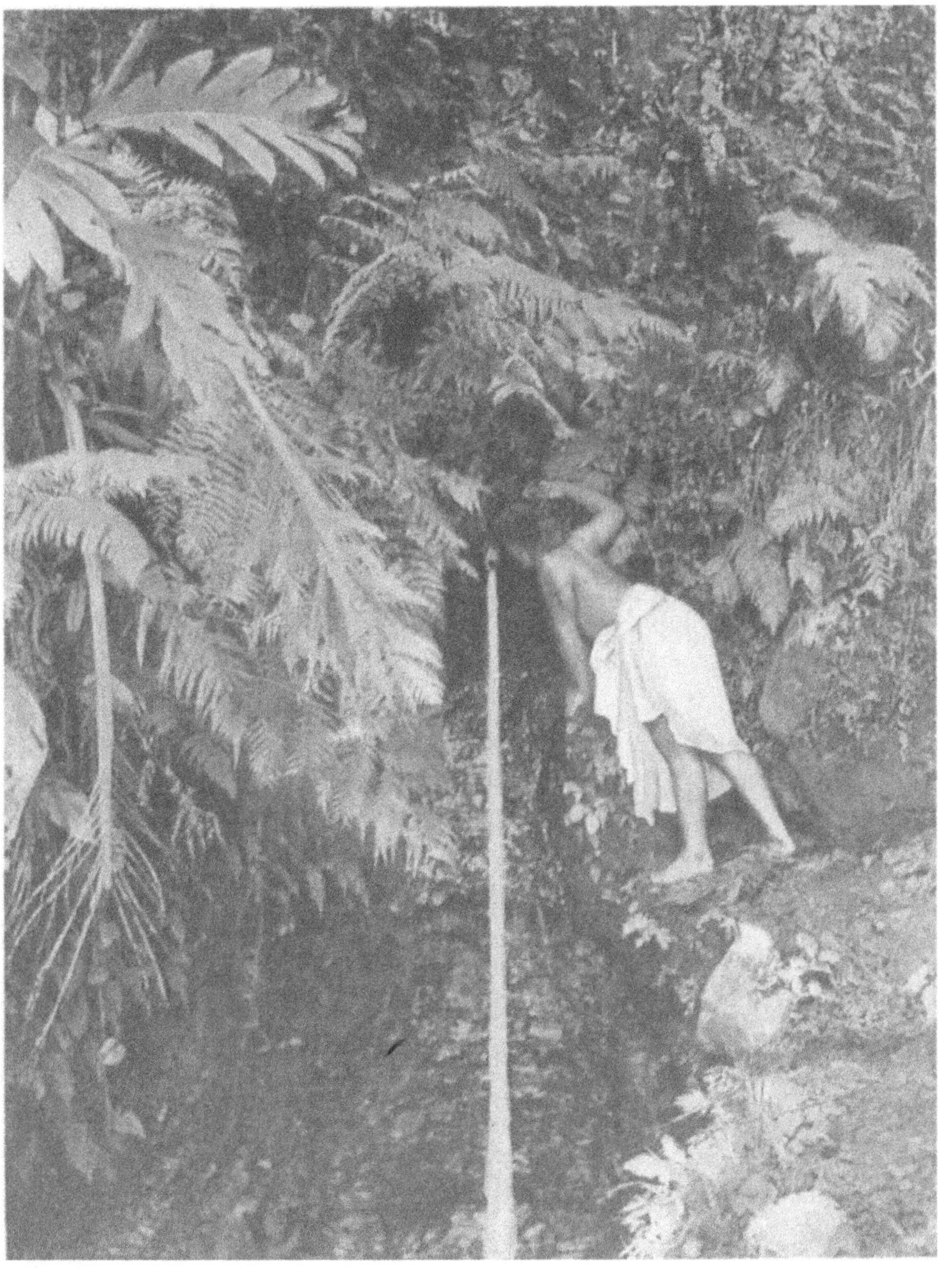

Fig. 3.16 Anonymous photographer, *Samoan at a Waterfall*, by 1887. Coloured gillotage reproduction of an albumen print, 23 × 18.4 cm. Collection of Christian Beslu, Tahiti.

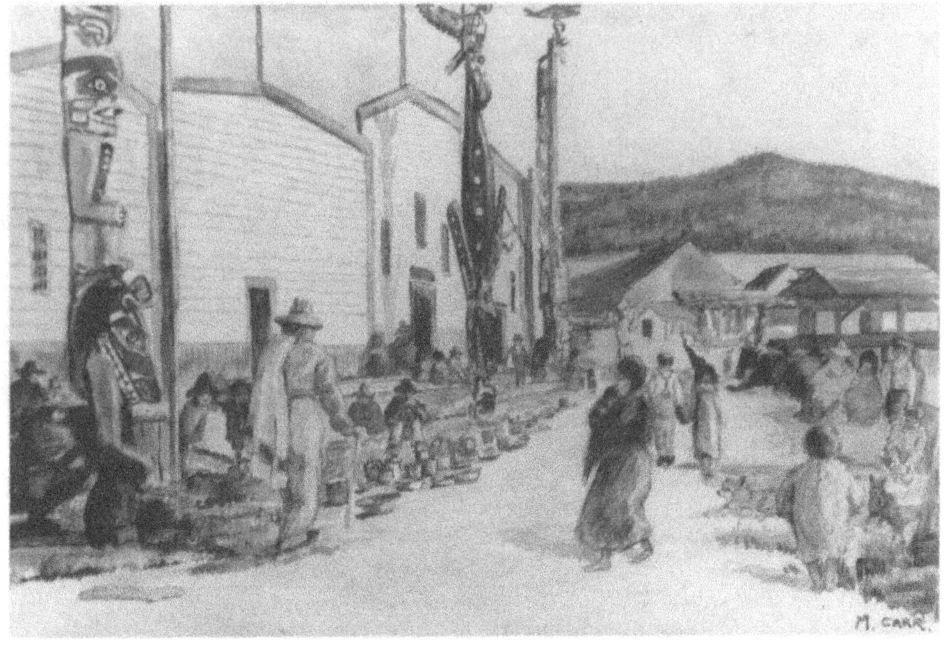

Fig. 4.1 Emily Carr, *Potlatch at Alert Bay*, ca. 1909. Watercolour on paper, 36.3 × 52.5 cm. Private collection. Courtesy Sotheby's, Toronto.

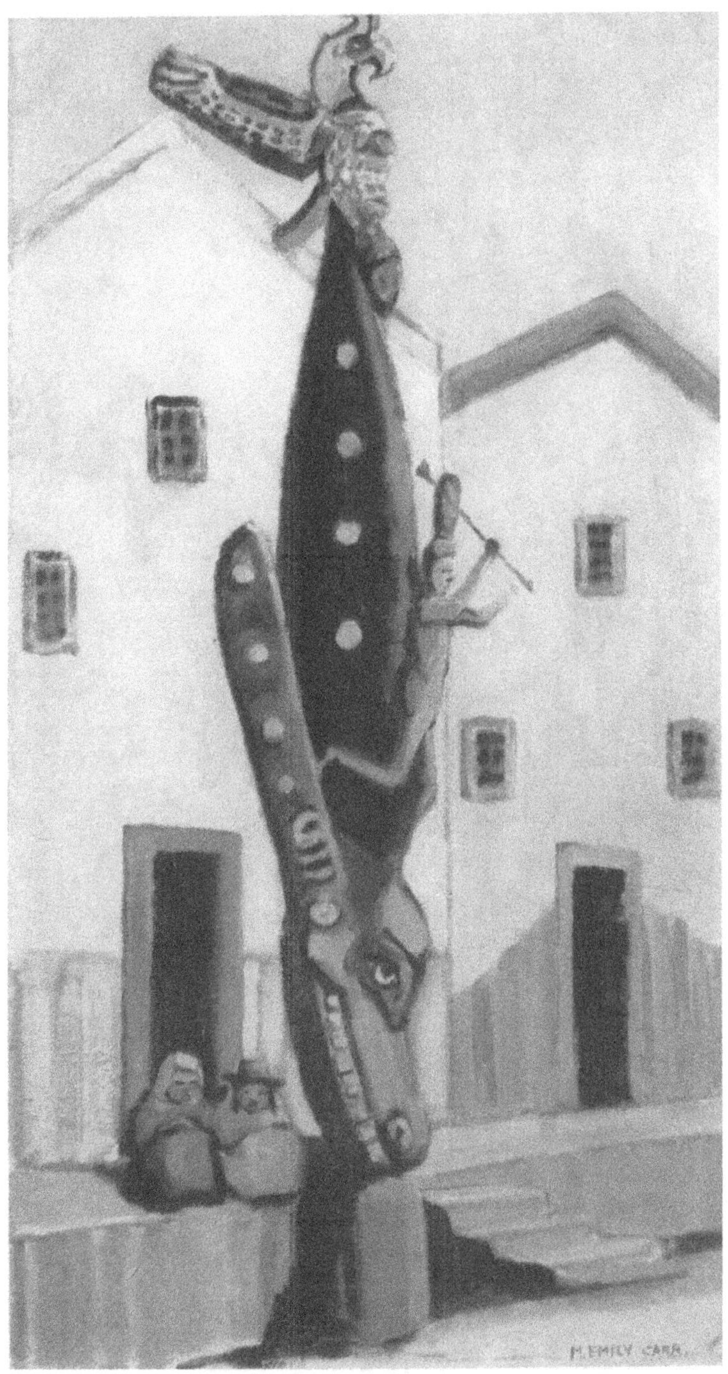

Fig. 4.2 Emily Carr, *Totem Pole, Alert Bay* ca. 1911. Oil on canvas, 68.6 × 35.9 cm. McMichael Canadian Art Collection, Kleinburg.

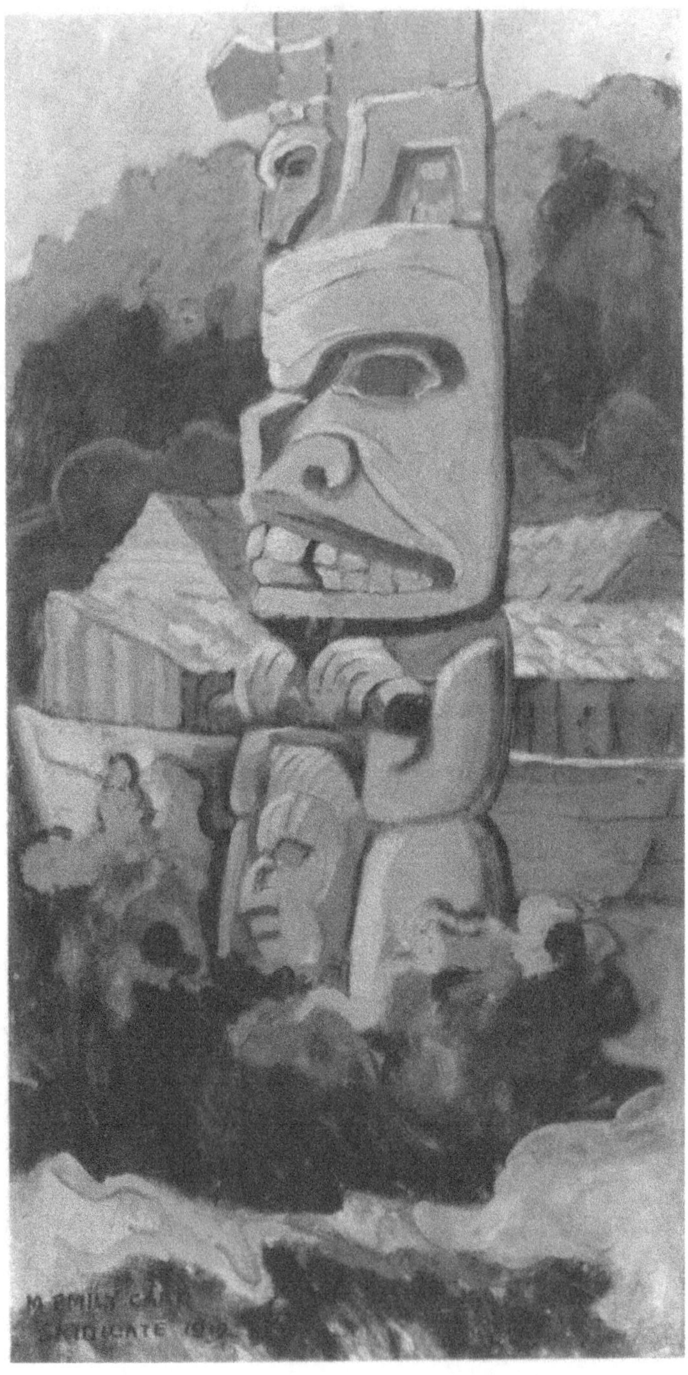

Fig. 4.3 Emily Carr, *Skidegate*, 1912. Oil on card, 64.5 × 32.5 cm. Vancouver Art Gallery, Emily Carr Trust, VAG 42.3.47.

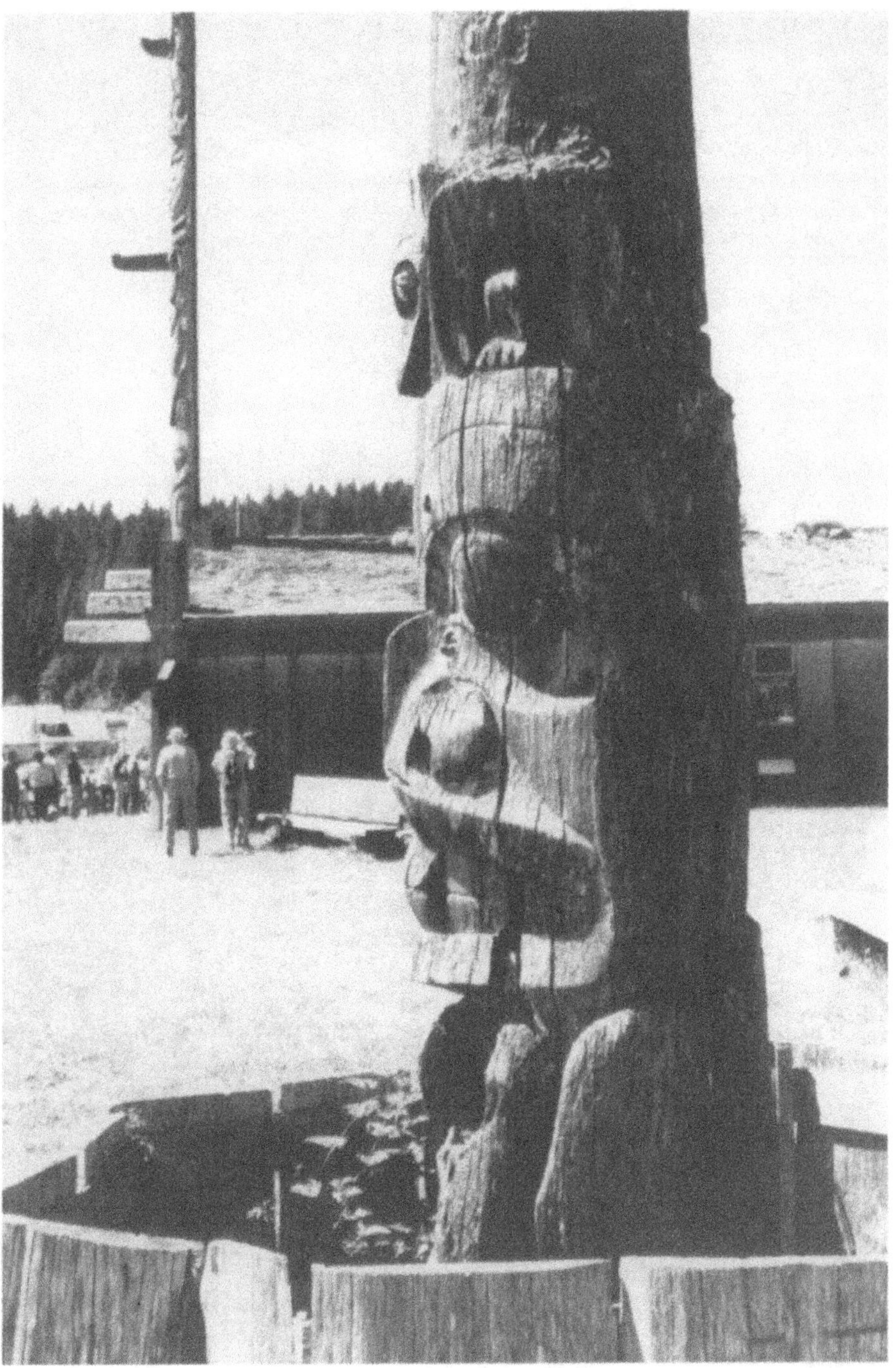

Fig. 4.4 Skidegate, 1987: foreground, pole of Itga; background, pole carved by Bill Reid for band council building. Photograph by Gerta Moray.

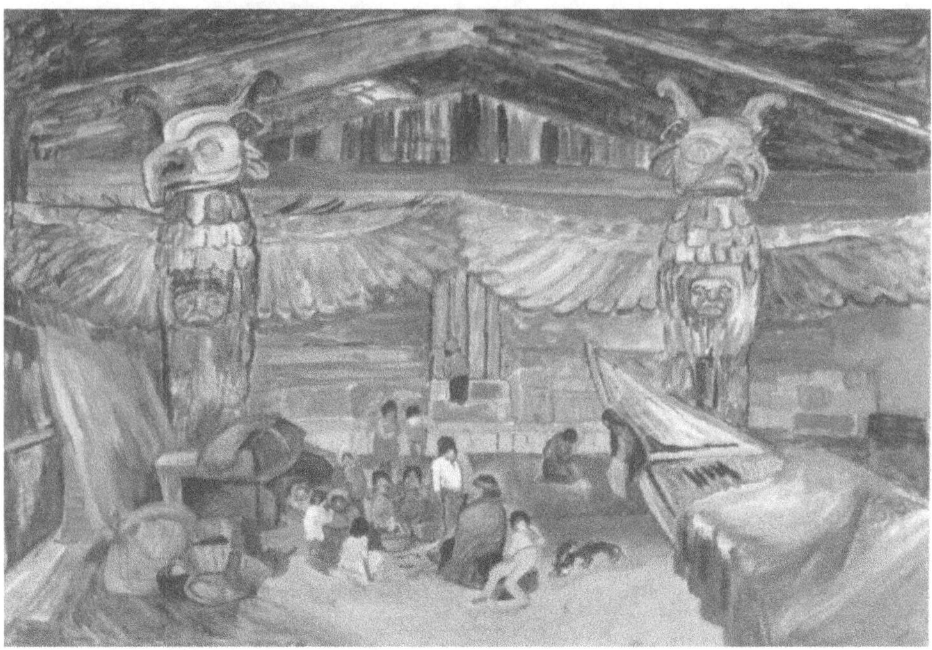

Fig. 4.5 Emily Carr, *Indian House Interior with Totems*, 1912–13. Oil on canvas, 89.5 × 130.5 cm. Vancouver Art Gallery, Emily Carr Trust, VAG 42.3.8.

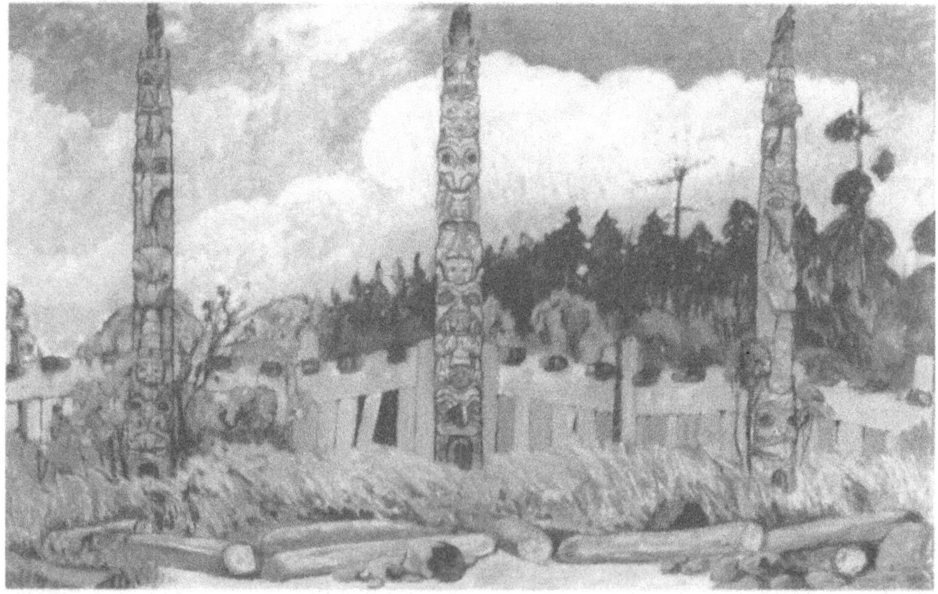

Fig. 4.6 Emily Carr, *Tanoo, Queen Charlotte Islands*, 1913. Oil on canvas, 110.5 × 170.5 cm. British Columbia Archives and Records Services, Victoria.

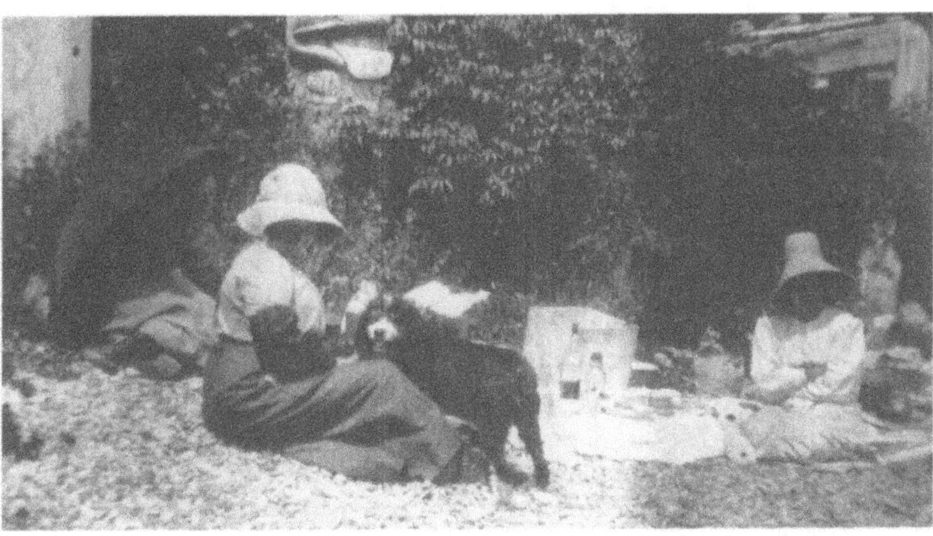

Fig. 4.7 Chaatl, 1912. Photograph by William Russ [?]. Left to right: Edna Leary, Emily Carr, Billie (Carr's dog), Clara Russ. British Columbia Archives and Records Services, Victoria (photo no. 94207).

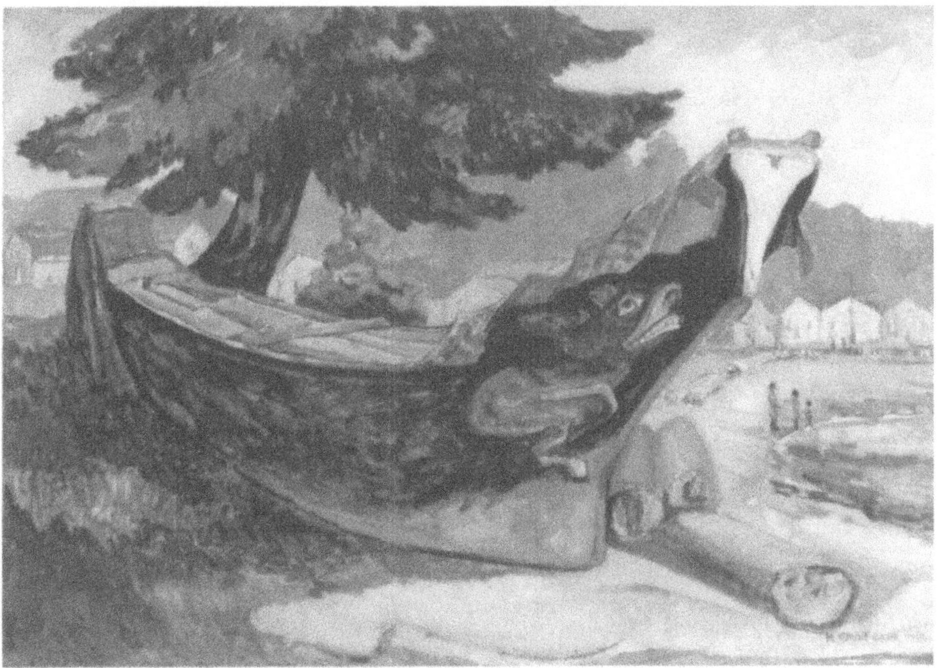

Fig. 4.8 Emily Carr, *Indian War Canoe*, 1912. Oil on board, 69 × 99.4 cm. Collection of the Montreal Museum of Fine Arts, Montreal. Gift of A. Sidney Dawes.

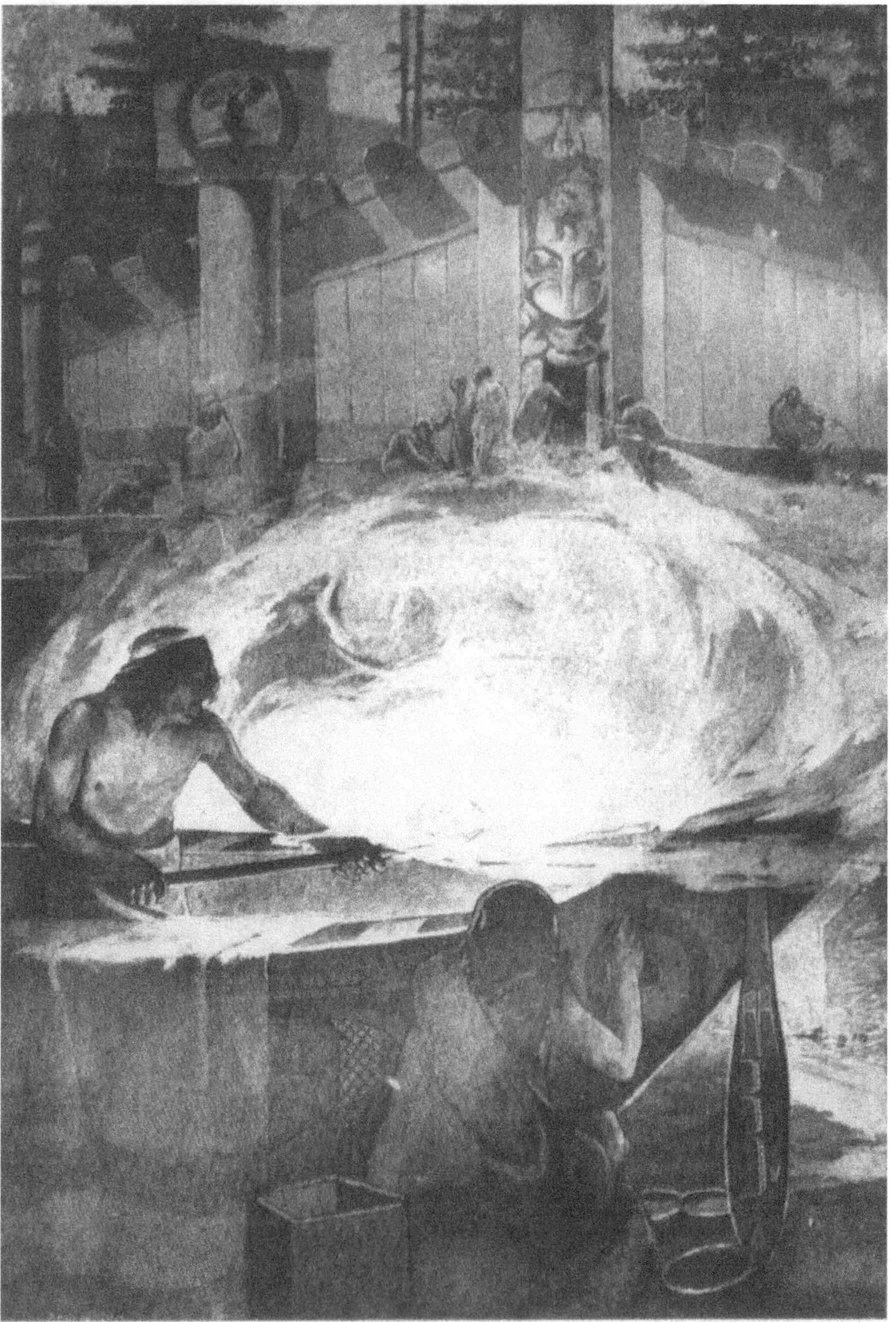

Fig. 4.9 William Taylor, *The Canoe Builders*, ca. 1911. Wall panel. American Museum of Natural History, New York (neg. no. 105411). Courtesy Department of Library Services, American Museum of Natural History, New York.

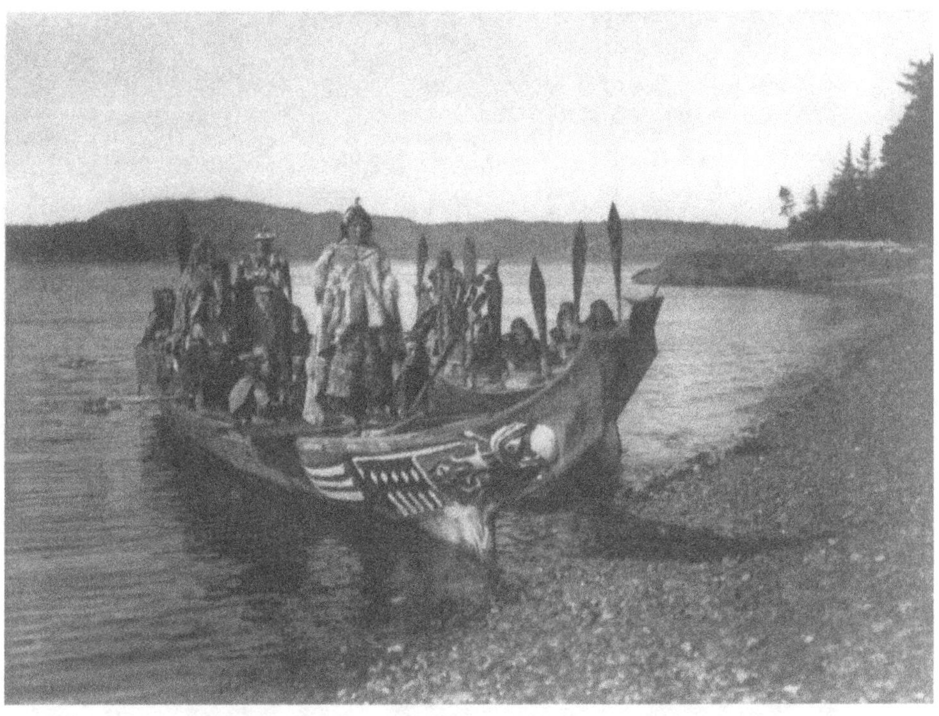

Fig. 4.10 Edward S. Curtis, *Wedding Party, Quyyuhl*. Plate from *The North American Indian: Being a Series of Volumes Picturing and Describing the Indians of the United States and Alaska*, Volume 10 (Norwood, Conn. 1915). Courtesy Department of Library Services, American Museum of Natural History, New York (neg. no. 335545).

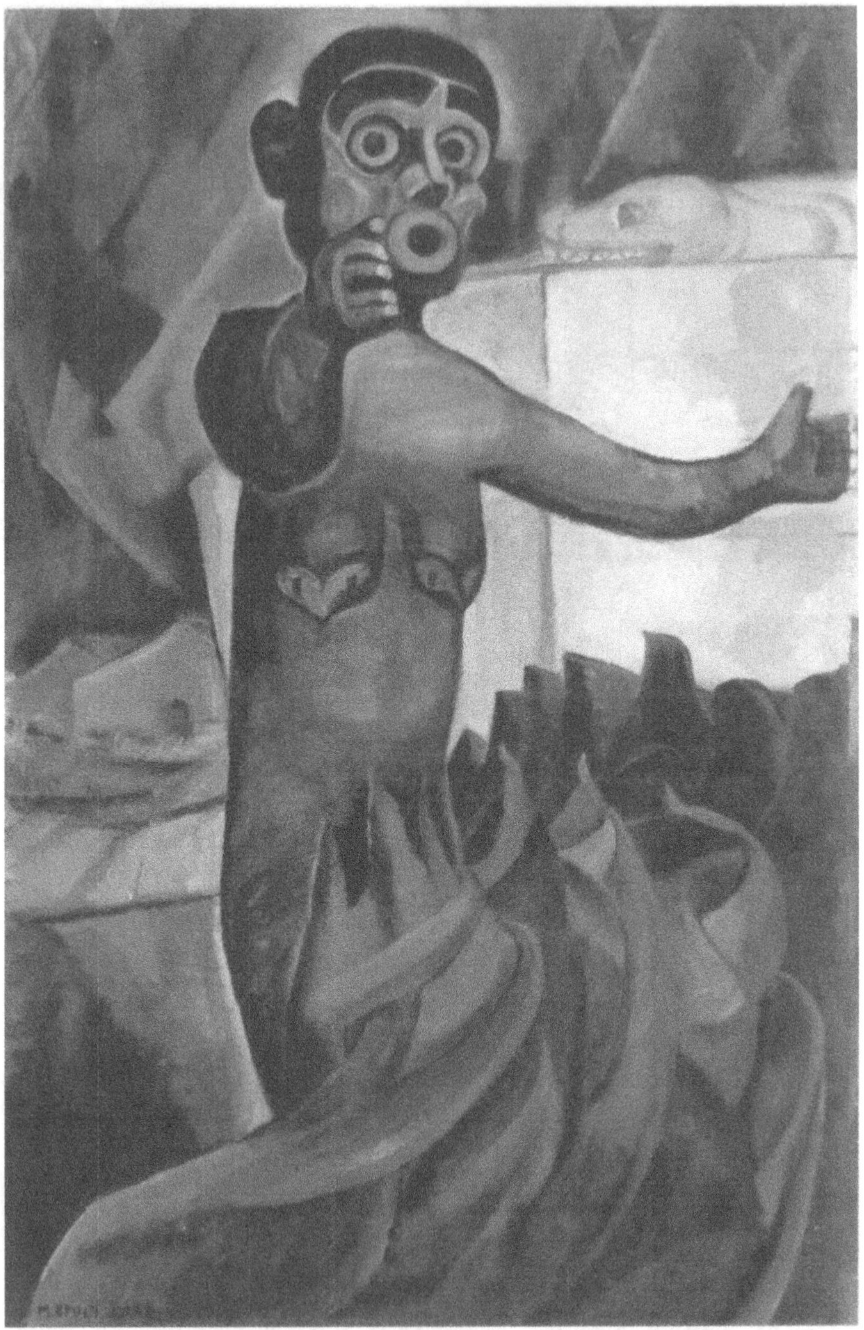

Fig. 4.11 Emily Carr, *Guyasdoms d'Sonoqua,* 1928–30. Oil on canvas, 100.3 × 65.4 cm. Art Gallery of Ontario, Toronto, gift of the Albert H. Robson Memorial Subscription Fund, 1942.

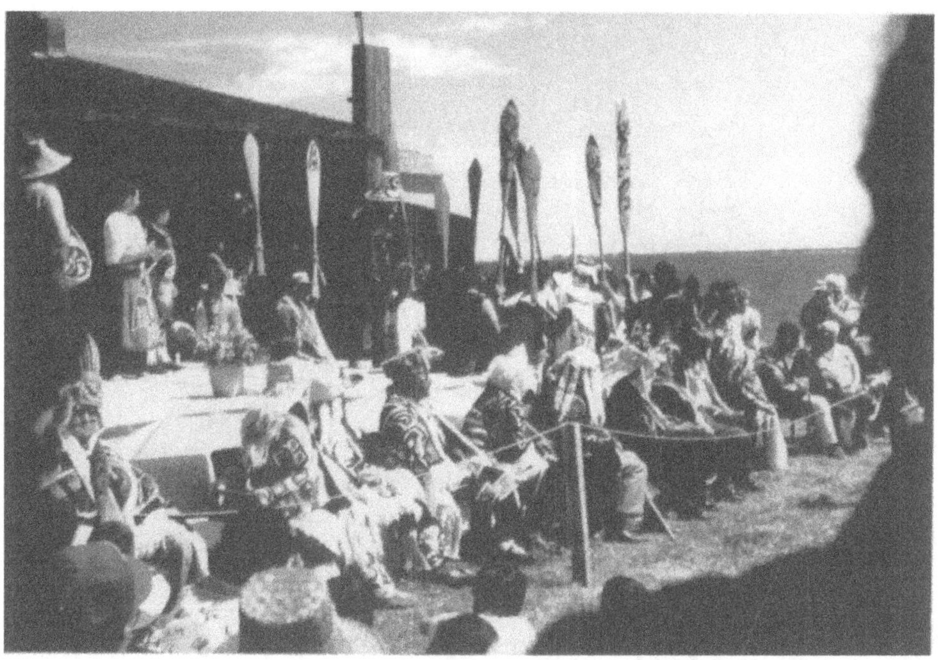

Fig. 4.12 Skidegate, 1987: welcoming ceremony for Luu Tas. Photograph by Gerta Moray.

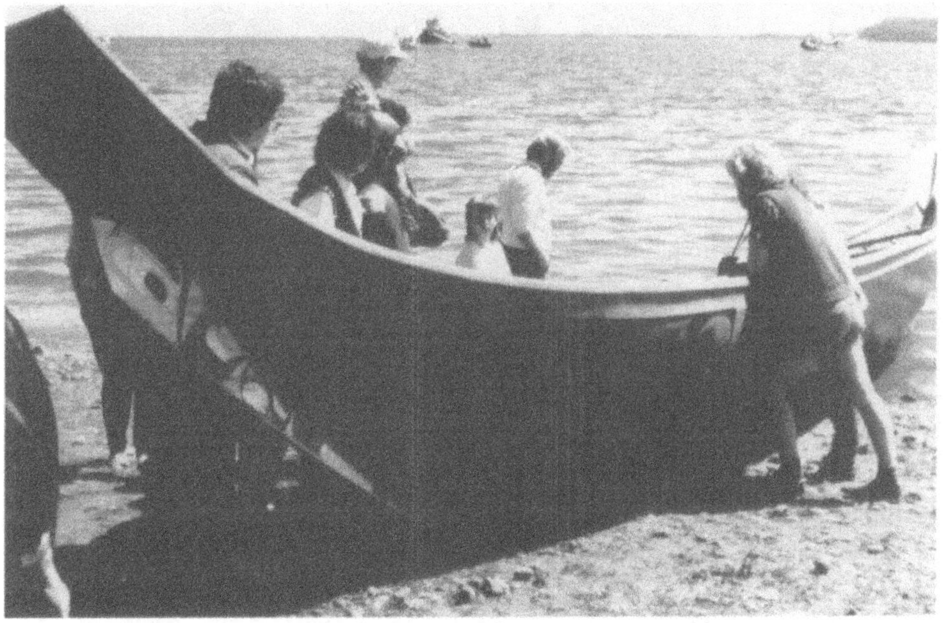

Fig. 4.13 Skidegate, 1987: Luu Tas canoe on the beach. Photograph by Gerta Moray.

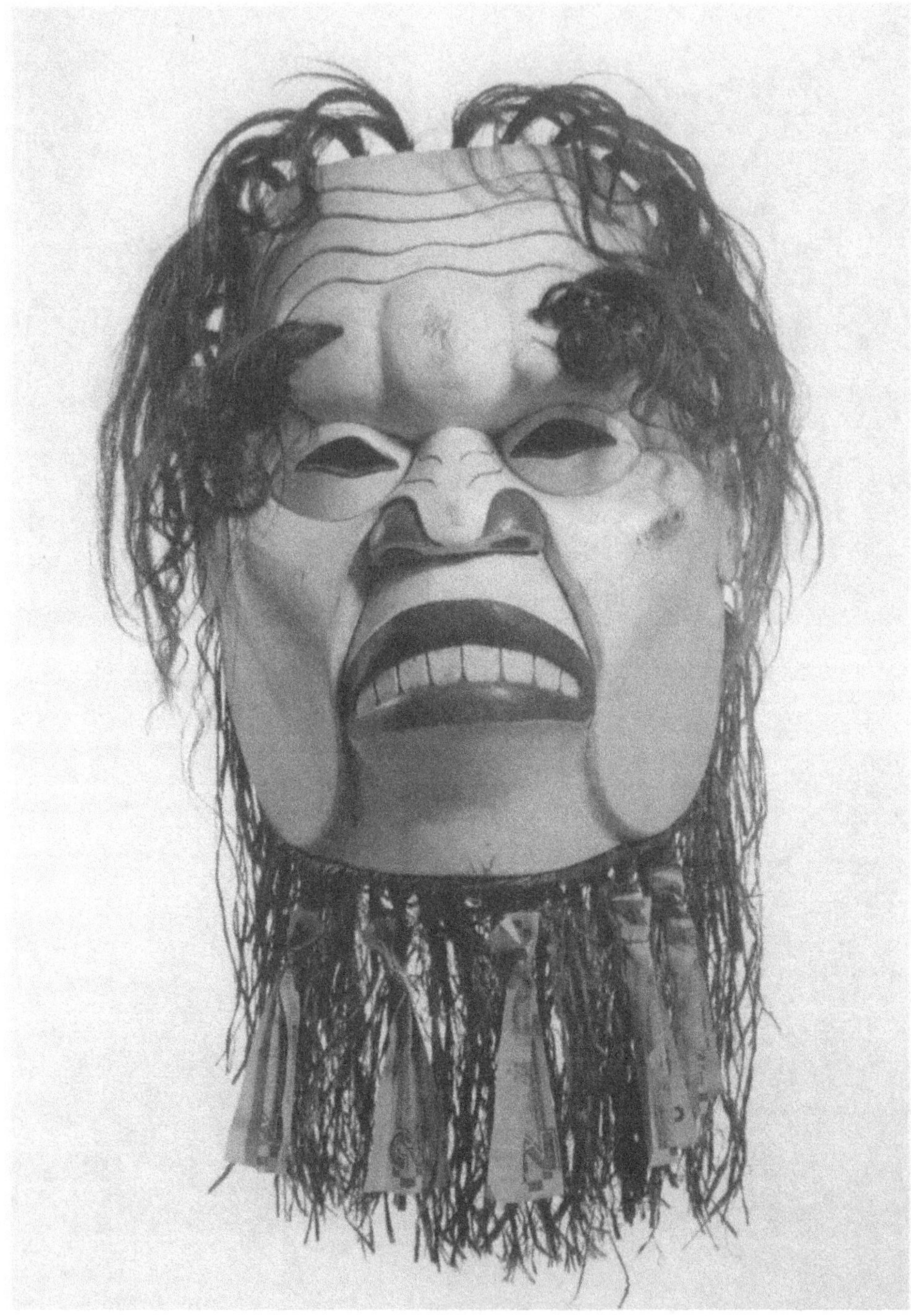

Fig. 4.14 David Neel, *Mask of the Injustice System*, 1991. Cedar, horsehair, paint, currency. Courtesy of the artist. Photograph by David Neel.

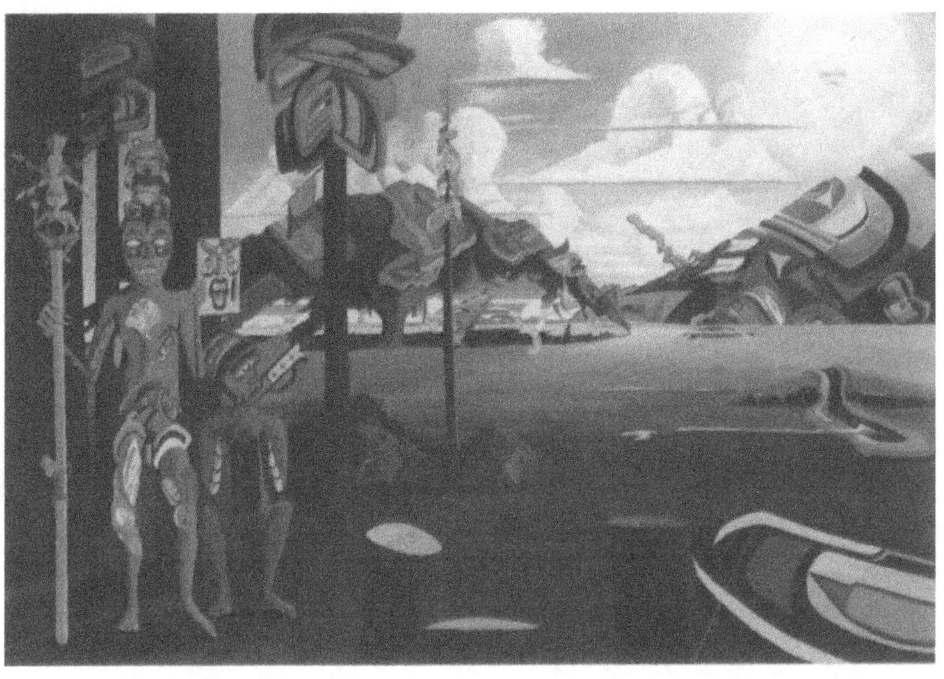

Fig. 4.15 Lawrence Paul Yuxweluptun, *Scorched Earth, Clear-Cut Logging on Native Sovereign Lands, Shaman Coming to Fix*, 1991. Acrylic on canvas, 196 × 276.5 cm. National Gallery of Canada, Ottawa.

Fig. 6.1 Anonymous (Québec artist), *Hooked Rug*, 1880–90, ca. 75 × 150 cm. Canadian Museum of Civilization, Hull. Courtesy Canadian Museum of Civilization, Hull, 81292.

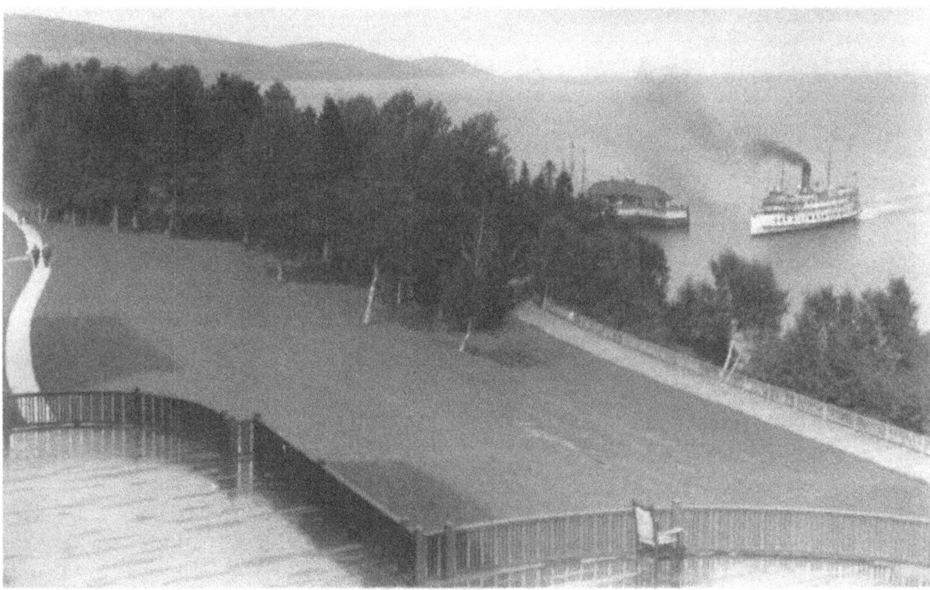

Fig. 6.2 William Notman & Son, *View From Manoir Richelieu, Murray Bay, P.Q.*, ca. 1912. Photograph. Notman Photographic Archives, McCord Museum of Canadian History, Montreal. Courtesy Notman Photographic Archives, McCord Museum of Canadian History, Montreal.

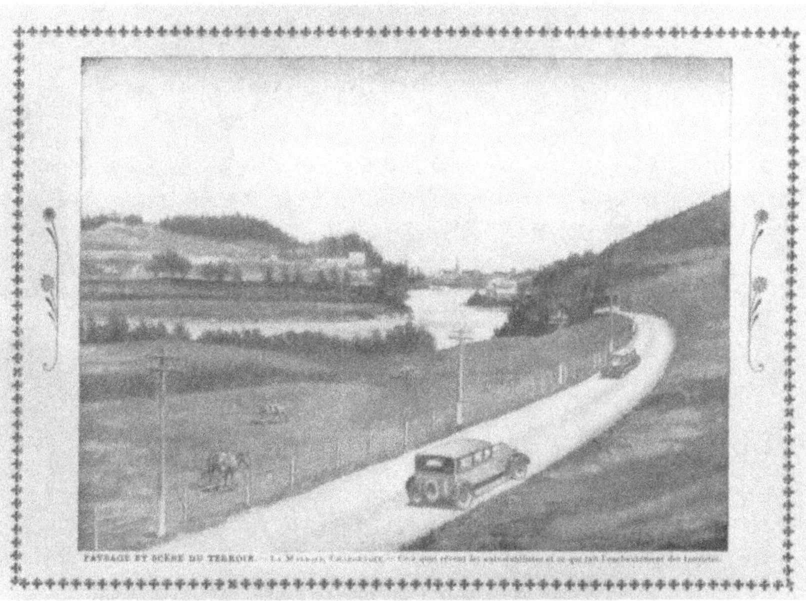

Fig. 6.3 'PAYSAGE ET SCÈNE DU TERROIR. – LA MALBAIE, CHARLEVOIX. – Ce à quoi rêvent les automobilistes et ce qui fait l'enchantement des touristes.' *Le Terroir* (Revue mensuelle illustrée) (Québec) VIII: 11–12 (mars–avril 1928), 199. Photograph by the Graphics Department, University of Toronto at Scarborough.

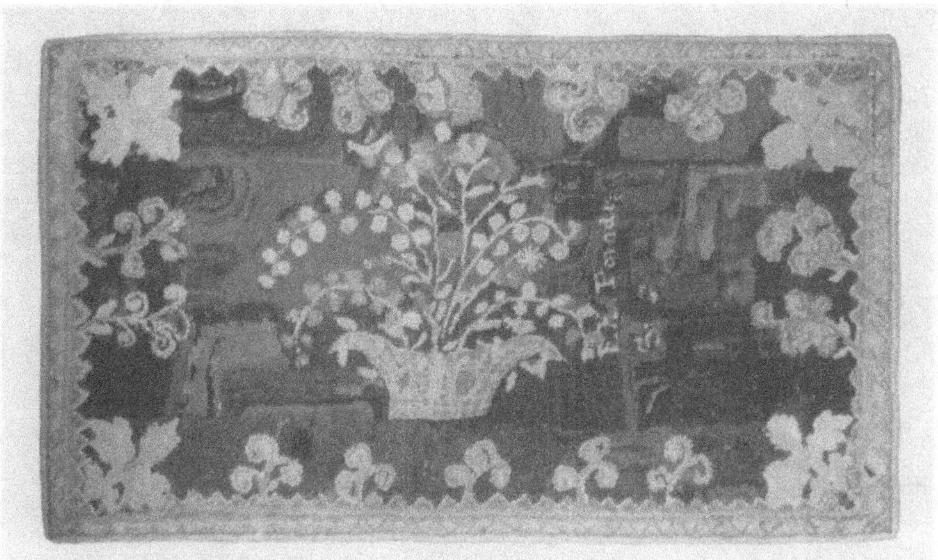

Fig. 6.4 F.-X. Paradis (Québec), *Hooked Rug*, 1855–65, ca. 152 × 229 cm. Canadian Museum of Civilization, Hull. Courtesy Canadian Museum of Civilization, Hull, 78079.

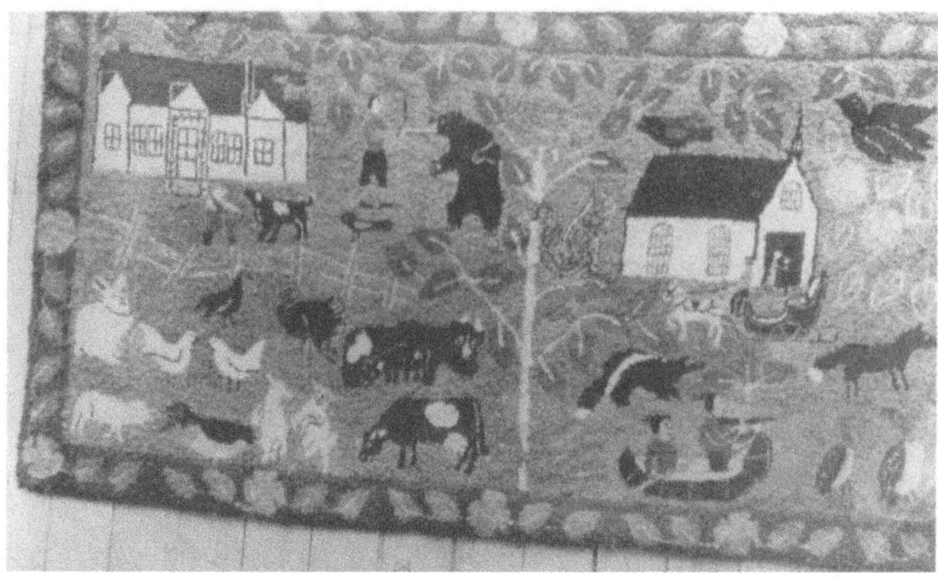

Fig. 6.5 Marie-Louise Hovington (Tadoussac, Québec), *Hooked Rug*, twentieth century (probably ca. 1930), ca. 183 cm. wide. Canadian Museum of Civilization, Hull (original photo probably by Marius Barbeau). Courtesy Canadian Museum of Civilization, Hull, 80047.

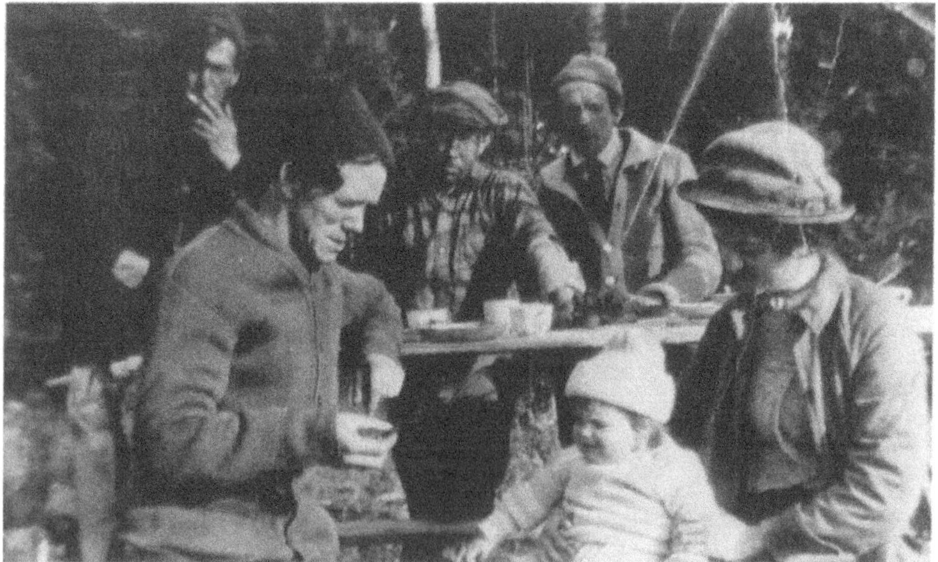

Fig. 8.1 Algonquin Park, October 1914, photographer unknown. Left to right: Tom Thomson, Frederick Varley, A.Y. Jackson, Arthur Lismer, Marjorie Lismer, and Esther Lismer. Photograph courtesy of the National Gallery of Canada, Ottawa.

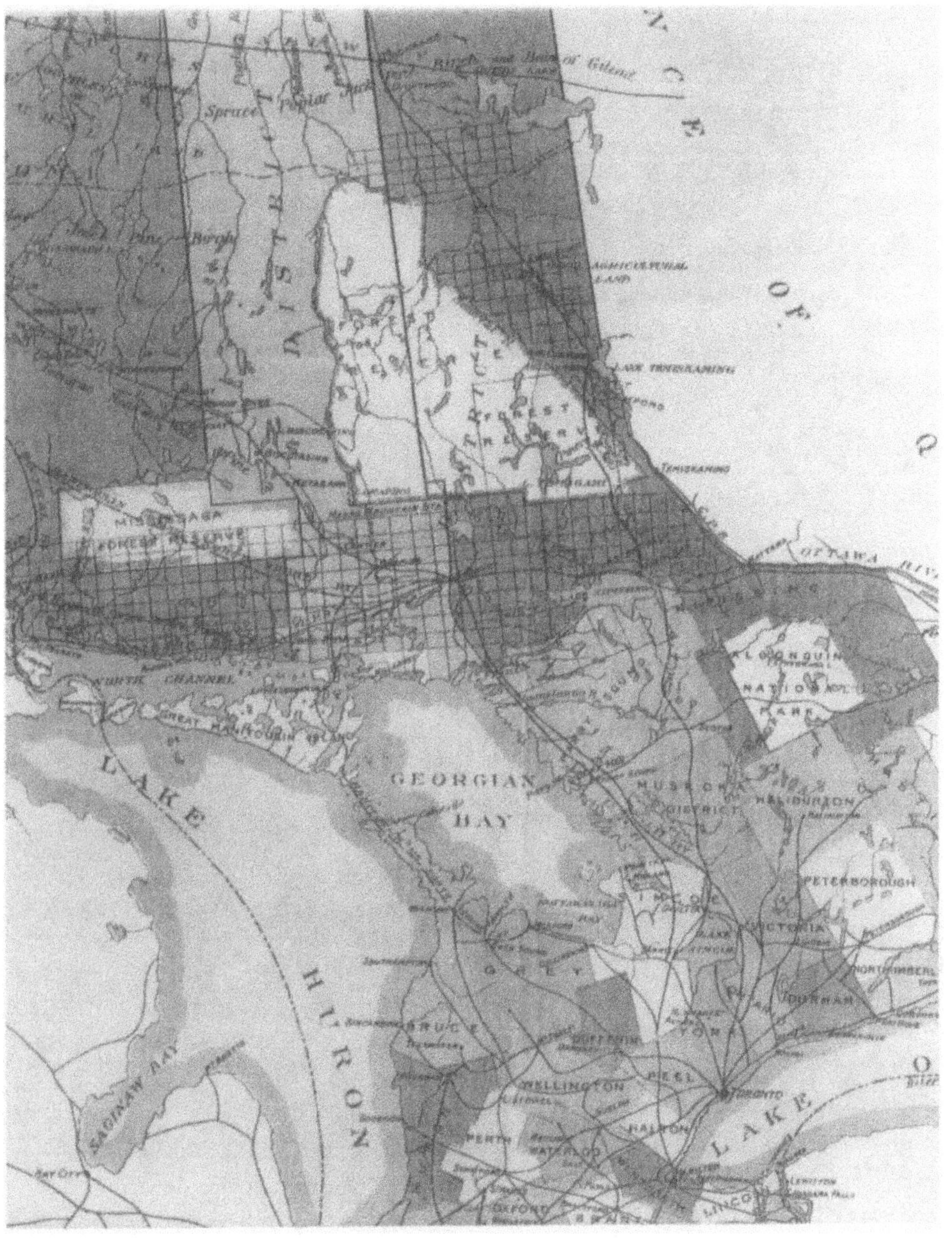

Fig. 8.2 Detail of map published in *The Province of Ontario* (Province of Ontario, Department of Agriculture, 1913) showing railroad lines from Toronto to Georgian Bay, the Muskoka District, and Algonquin Park.

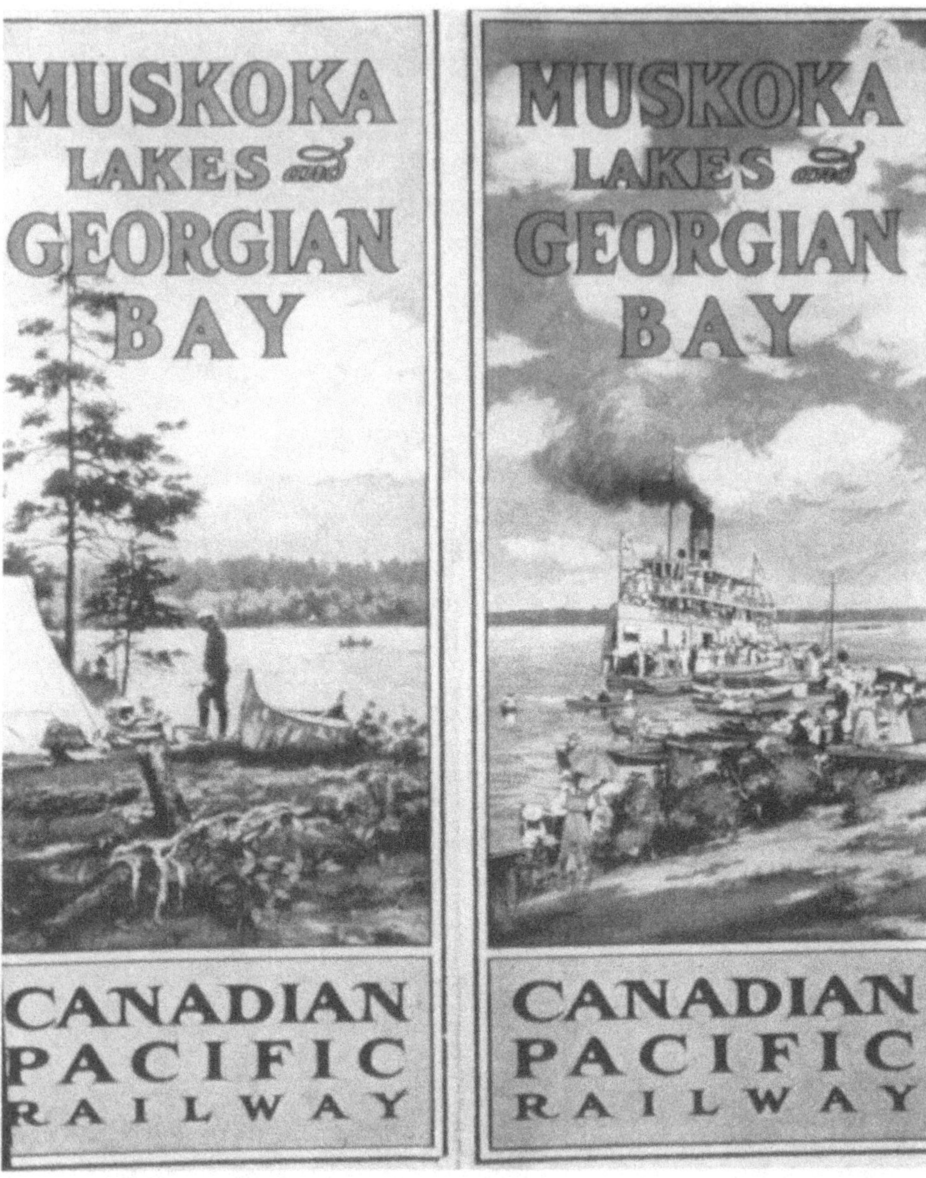

Fig. 8.3 Canadian Pacific Railway brochure, *Muskoka Lakes and Georgian Bay*, 1909.

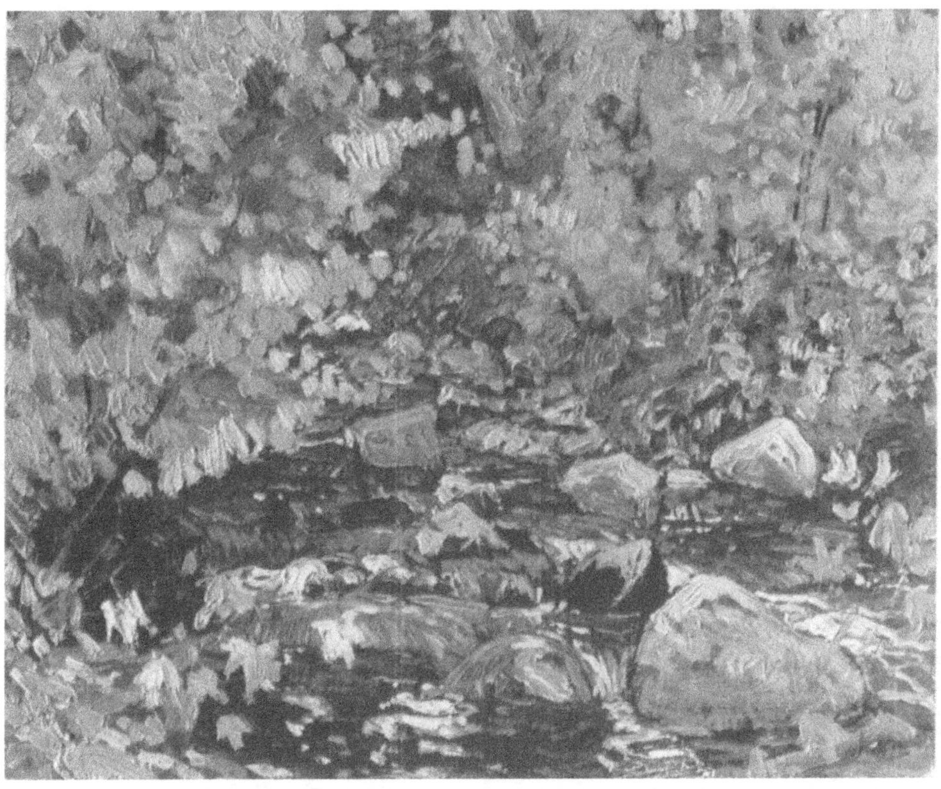

Fig. 8.4 J.E.H. MacDonald, *Autumn Leaves, Batchewana, Algoma*, ca. 1919. Oil on board, 21.6 × 26.7 cm. Art Gallery of Ontario, Toronto. Gift of the Student's Club, Ontario College of Art, Toronto, 1933.

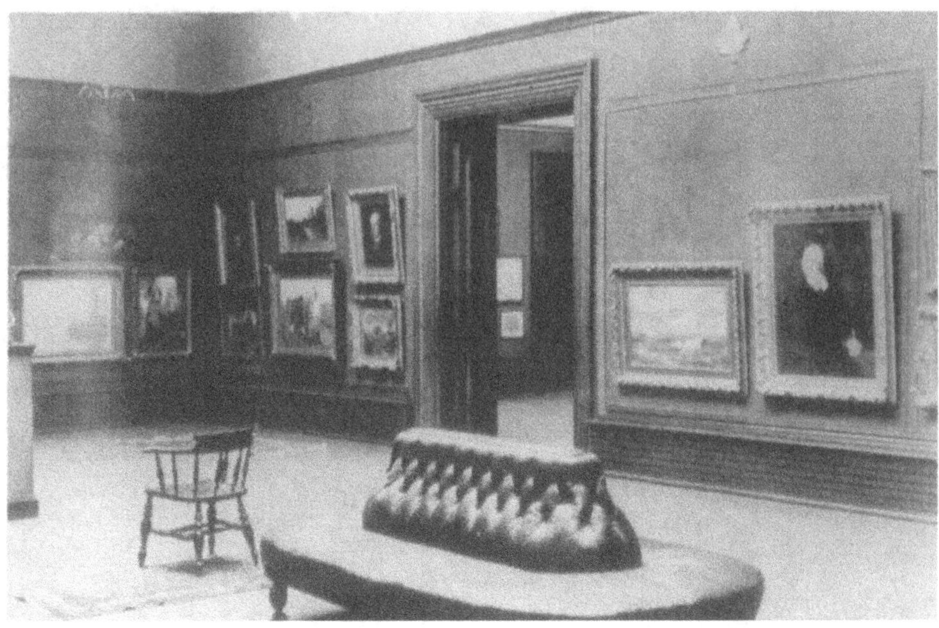

Fig. 8.5 Installation photograph, Canadian art exhibition, Walker Art Gallery, 1910. Courtesy of the National Archives of Canada, Ottawa C-098559.

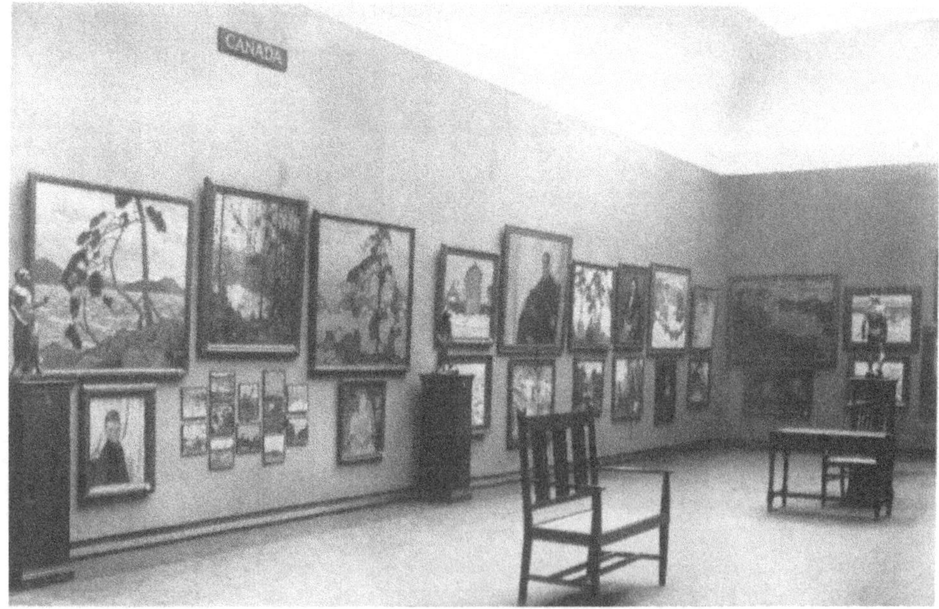

Fig. 8.6 Installation photograph, Canadian Section of Fine Arts, British Empire Exhibition, Wembley Park, London, 1924. Courtesy of the National Gallery of Canada, Ottawa.

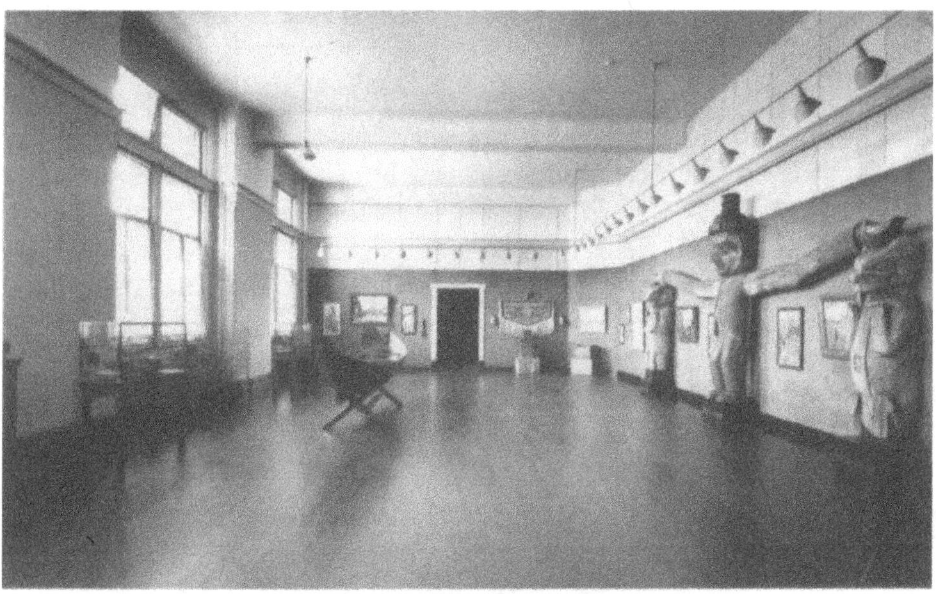

Fig. 8.7 Installation photograph, 'Exhibition of Canadian West Coast Art, Native and Modern,' National Gallery of Canada, 1927. Courtesy of the National Gallery of Canada, Ottawa.

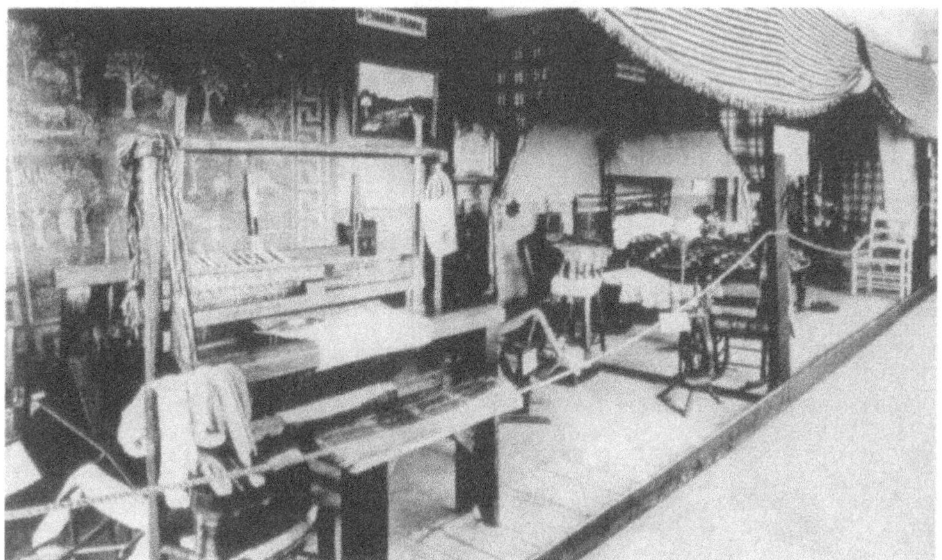

Fig. 8.8 'Workroom, Old French-Canadian Home, as shown at Exhibition, Quebec, 1924 (June).' Reproduced in *The French-Canadian Homespun Industry* (Canada: Department of Trade and Commerce, 1928), 18.

Ogata: Artisans and Art Noureau in Fin de siècle Belgium

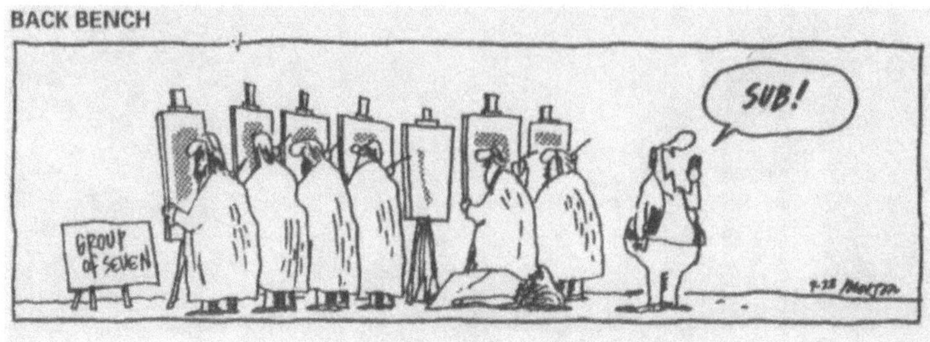

Fig. 8.9 Graham Harrop, 'Back Bench,' *Globe and Mail*, 23 September 1996, C8.

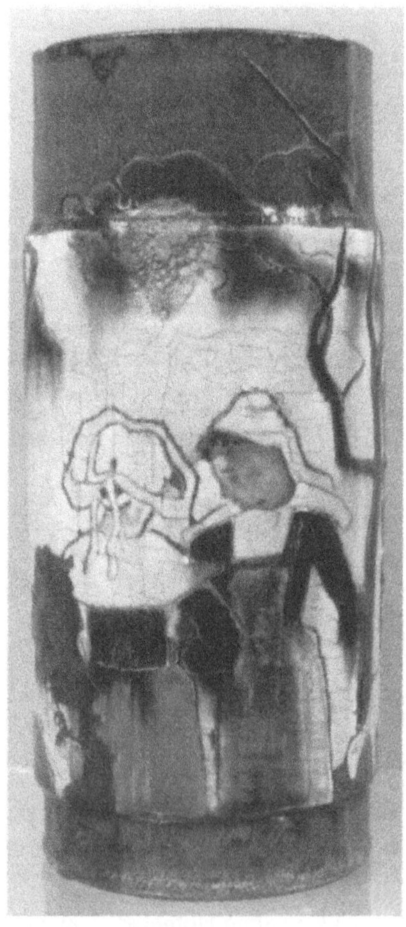

Fig. 10.1 Paul Gauguin, *Vase*, ca. 1886–7. Stoneware, 29 cm. Musées royaux d'art et d'histoire, Brussels. Copyright IRPA-KIK, Bruxelles.

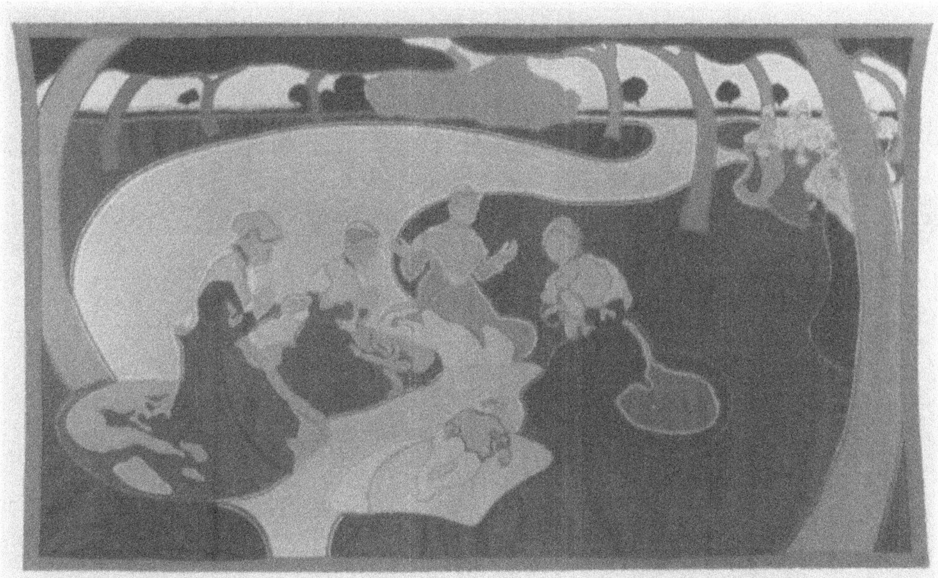

Fig. 10.2 Henry Van de Velde, *The Angels' Watch*, 1893. Hanging in wool and silk embroidered applique, 140 × 233 cm. Bellerive Museum, Zurich.

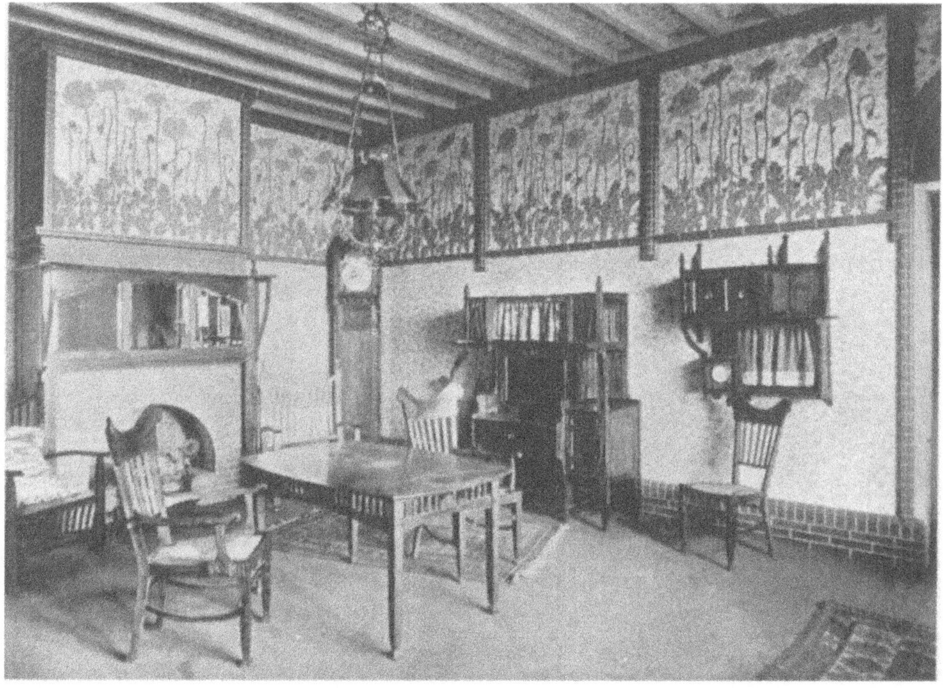

Fig. 10.3 Gustave Serrurier-Bovy, *Study*, 1894. *The Studio Magazine* 8 (1896).

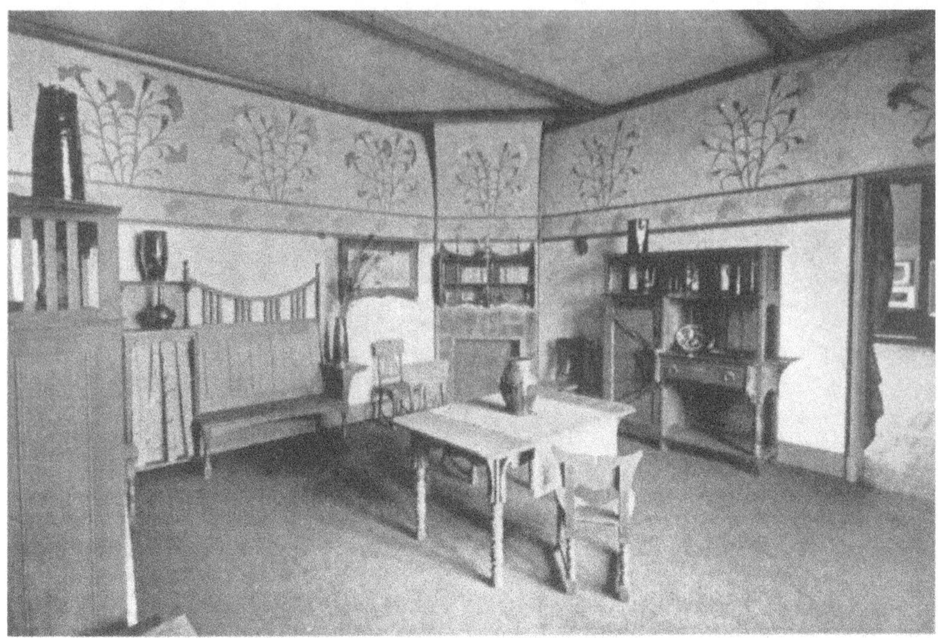

Fig. 10.4 Gustave Serrurier-Bovy, *Artisan's Room*, 1895. *The Studio Magazine* 8 (1896).

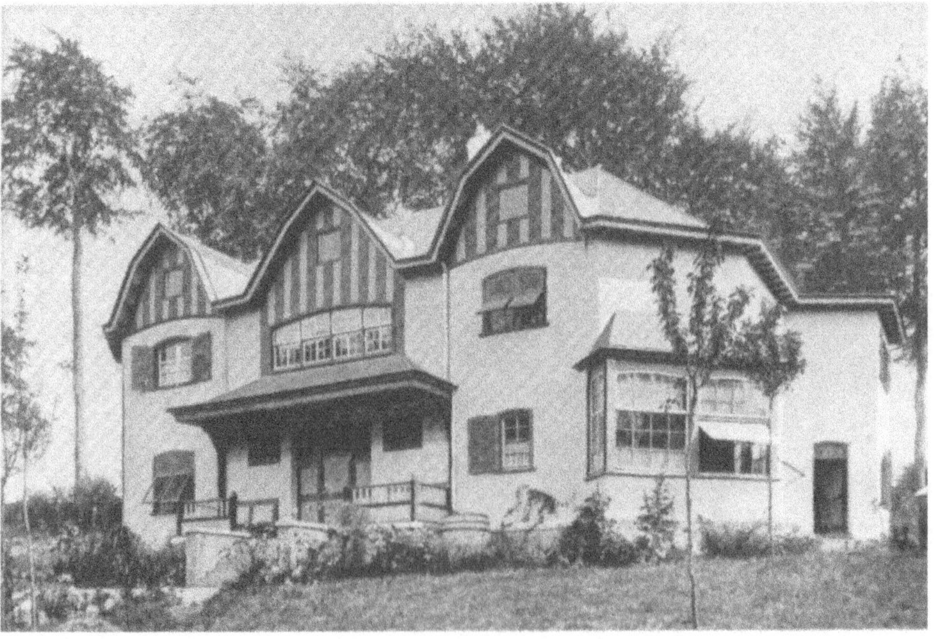

Fig. 10.5 Henry Van de Velde, Bloemenwerf, 1895–6. *Dekorative Kunst* 2 (1899).

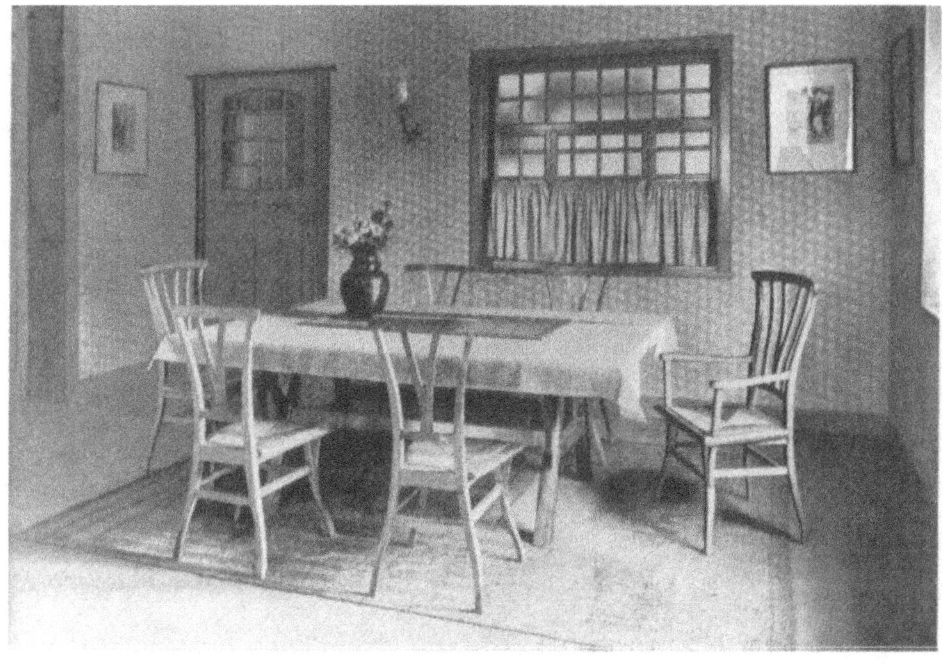

Fig. 10.6 Henry Van de Velde, Bloemenwerf interior, ca. 1896. *Dekorative Kunst* 2 (1899).

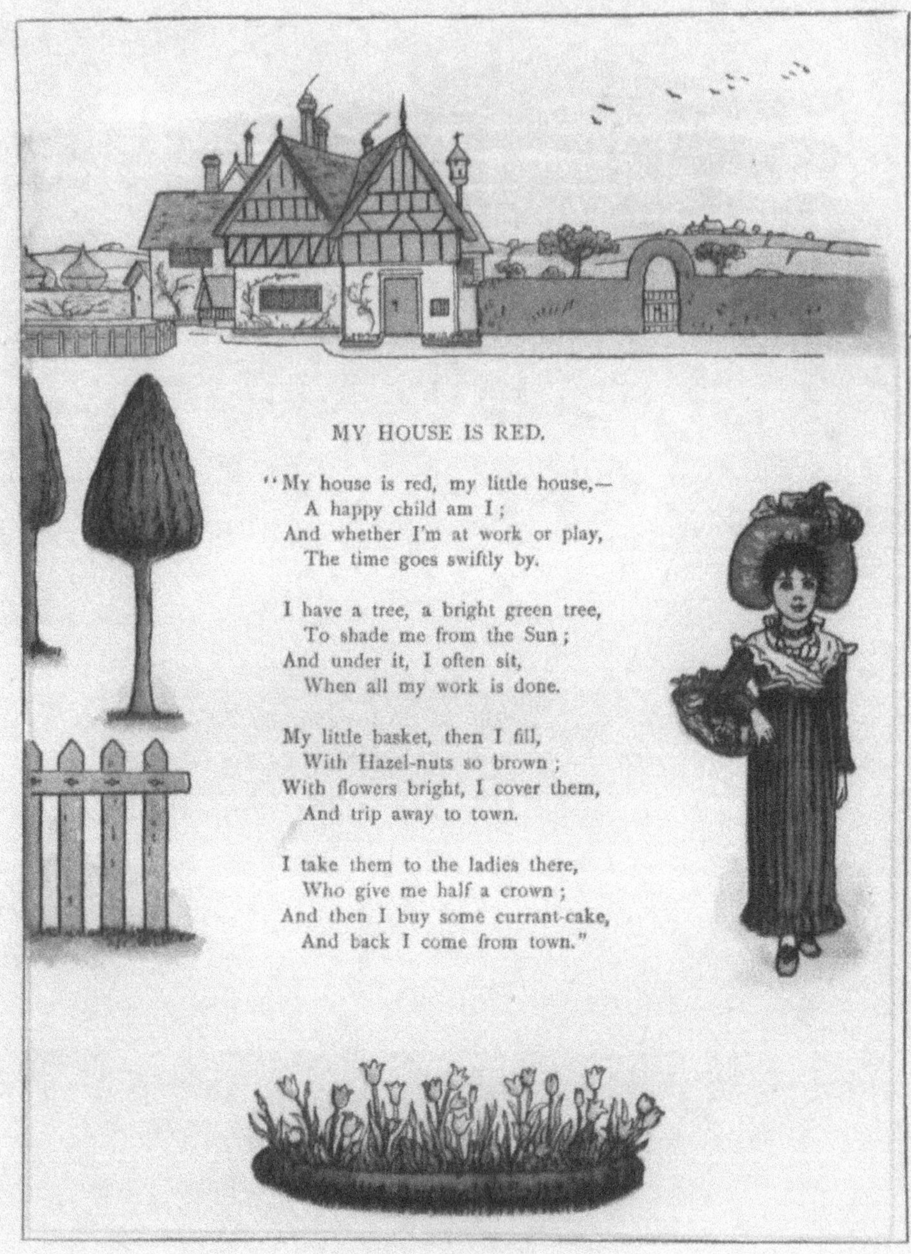

MY HOUSE IS RED.

"My house is red, my little house,—
  A happy child am I;
And whether I'm at work or play,
  The time goes swiftly by.

I have a tree, a bright green tree,
  To shade me from the Sun;
And under it, I often sit,
  When all my work is done.

My little basket, then I fill,
  With Hazel-nuts so brown;
With flowers bright, I cover them,
  And trip away to town.

I take them to the ladies there,
  Who give me half a crown;
And then I buy some currant-cake,
  And back I come from town."

Fig. 10.7 Kate Greenaway, 'My House Is Red,' in *Under the Window* (London: Edmund Evans, 1878). Department of Rare Books and Special Collections, Princeton University Library, Princeton.

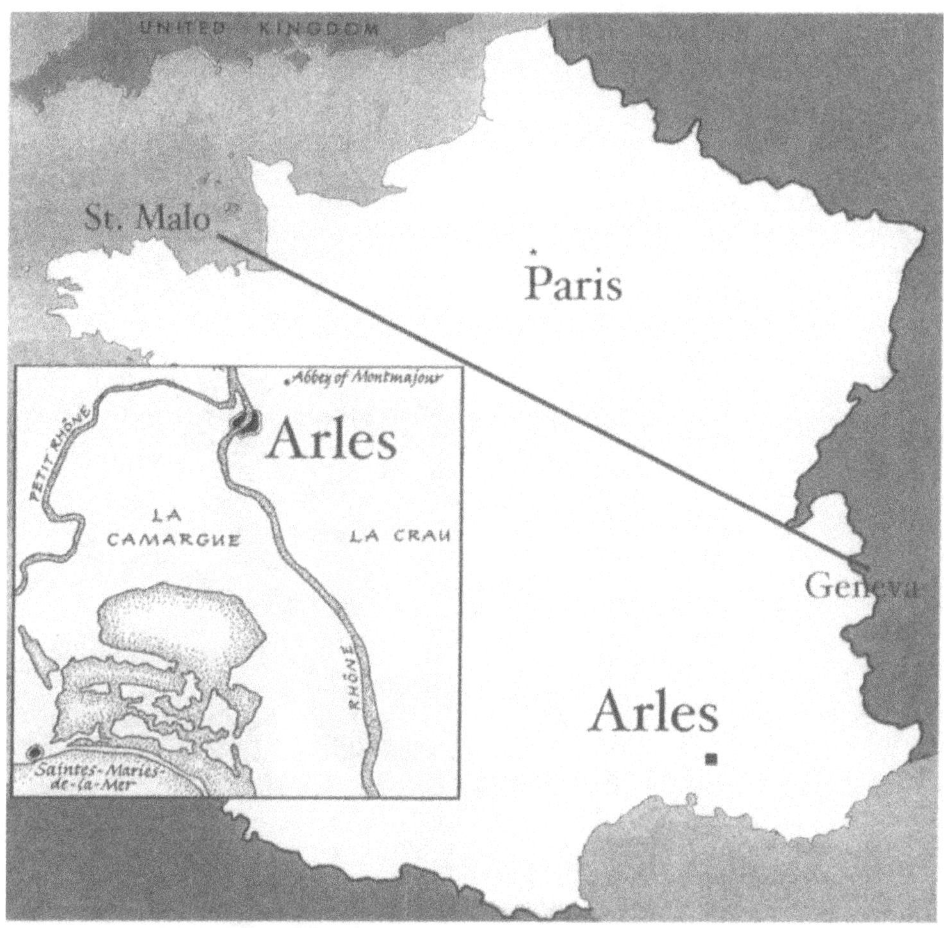

Fig. 11.1 Location of Arles in France with detail insert. S. and A. Gabov, based in part on R. Pickvance, *Van Gogh in Arles* (New York: Metropolitan Museum of Art/Abrams, 1984). Copyright Metropolitan Museum of Art, New York

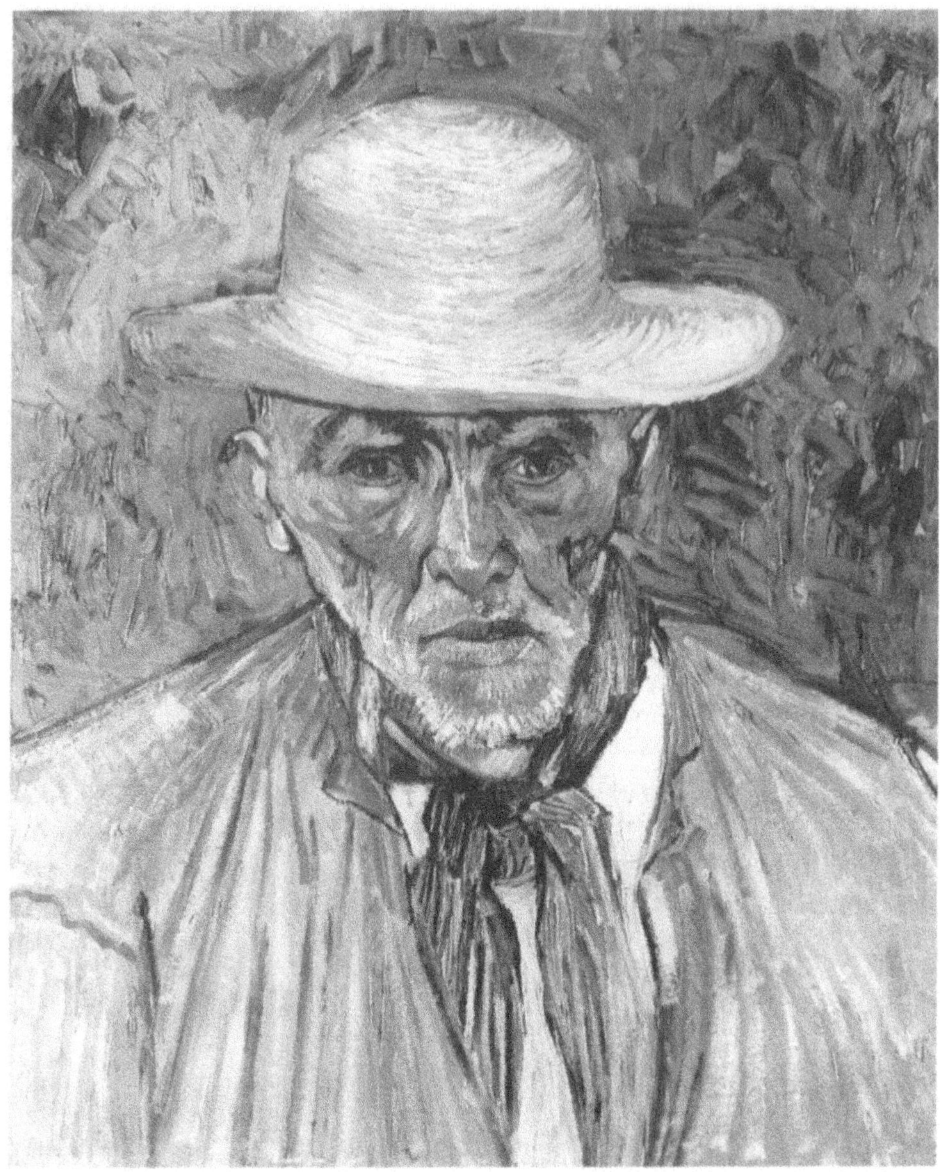

Fig. 11.2 Vincent van Gogh, *Portrait of Patience Escalier*, 1888. Oil on canvas, 64.4 × 54.6 cm. Norton Simon Art Foundation, Pasadena, California.

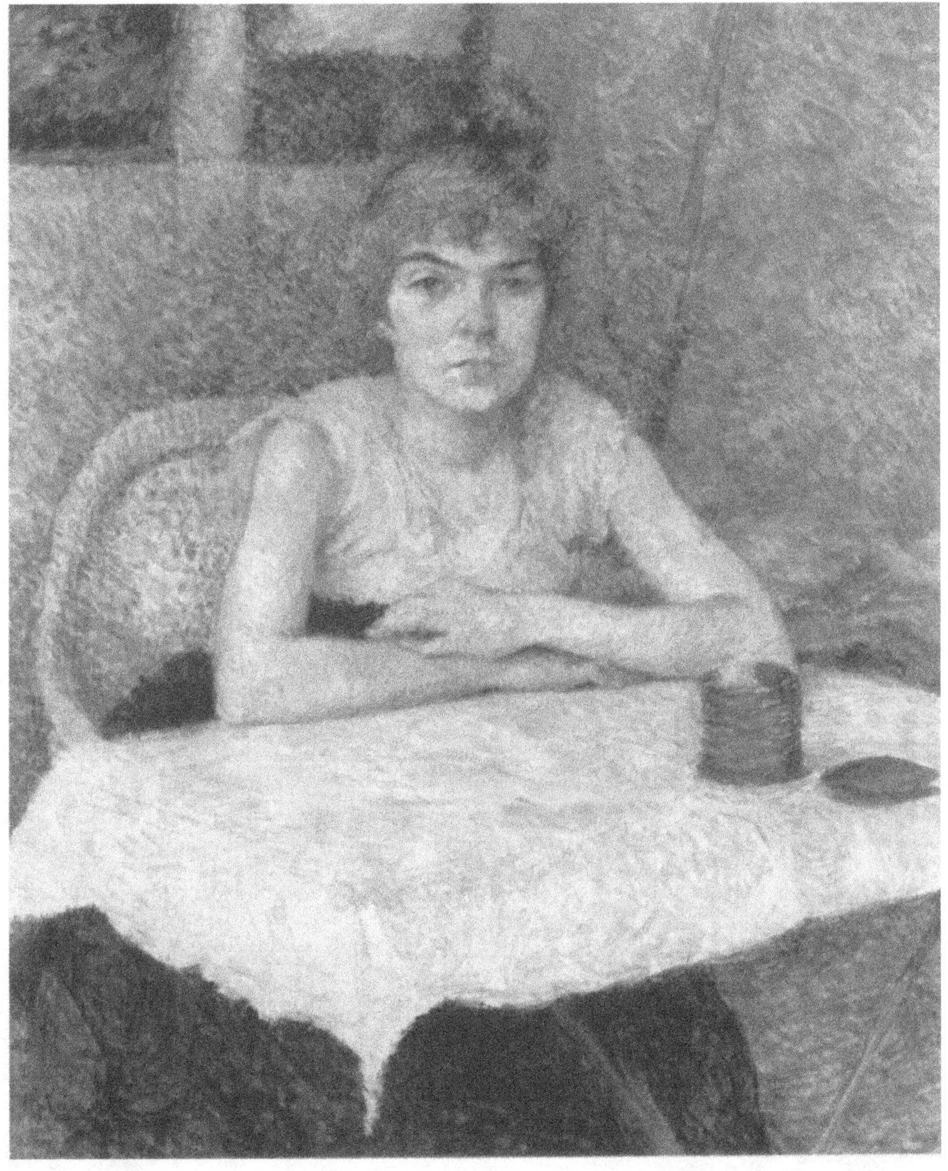

Fig. 11.3 Henri de Toulouse-Lautrec, *Poudre de riz*, 1887. Oil on canvas, 56 × 46 cm. Van Gogh Museum / Vincent van Gogh Foundation, Amsterdam.

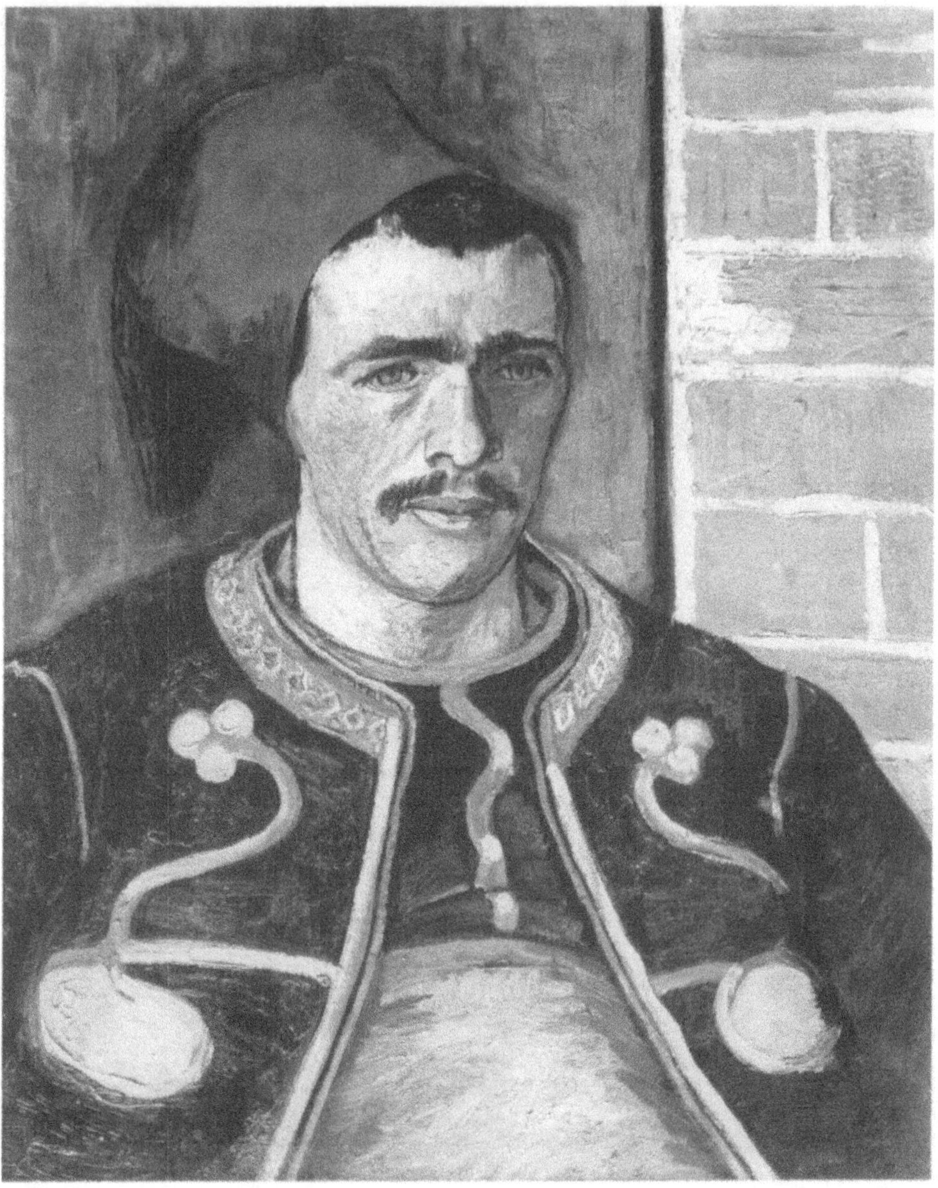

Fig. 11.4 Vincent van Gogh, *Zouave*, 1888. Oil on canvas, 65 × 54 cm. Van Gogh Museum / Vincent van Gogh Foundation, Amsterdam.

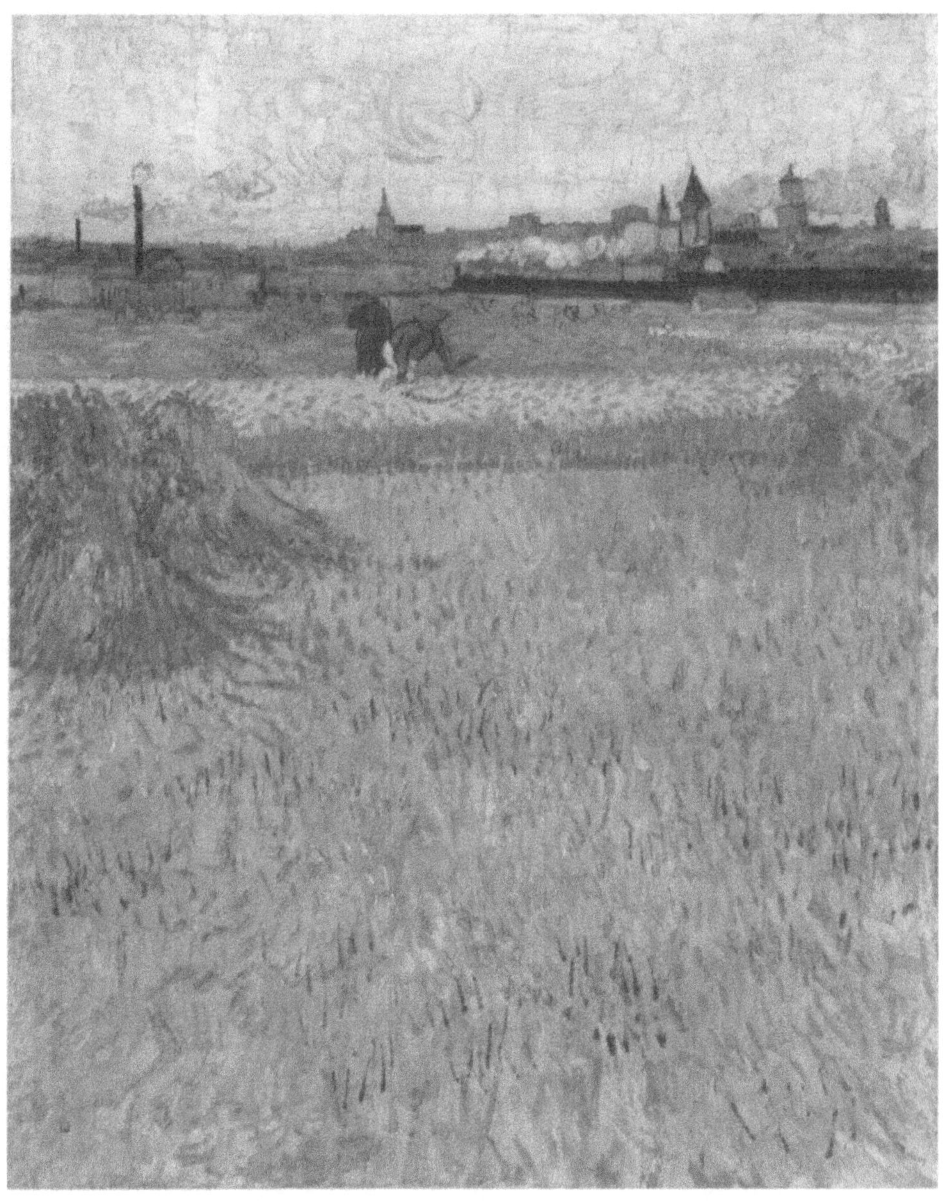

Fig. 11.5 Vincent van Gogh, *The Harvesters*, 1888. Oil on canvas, 73 × 54 cm. Rodin Museum, Paris. Photograph by Jean de Calan.

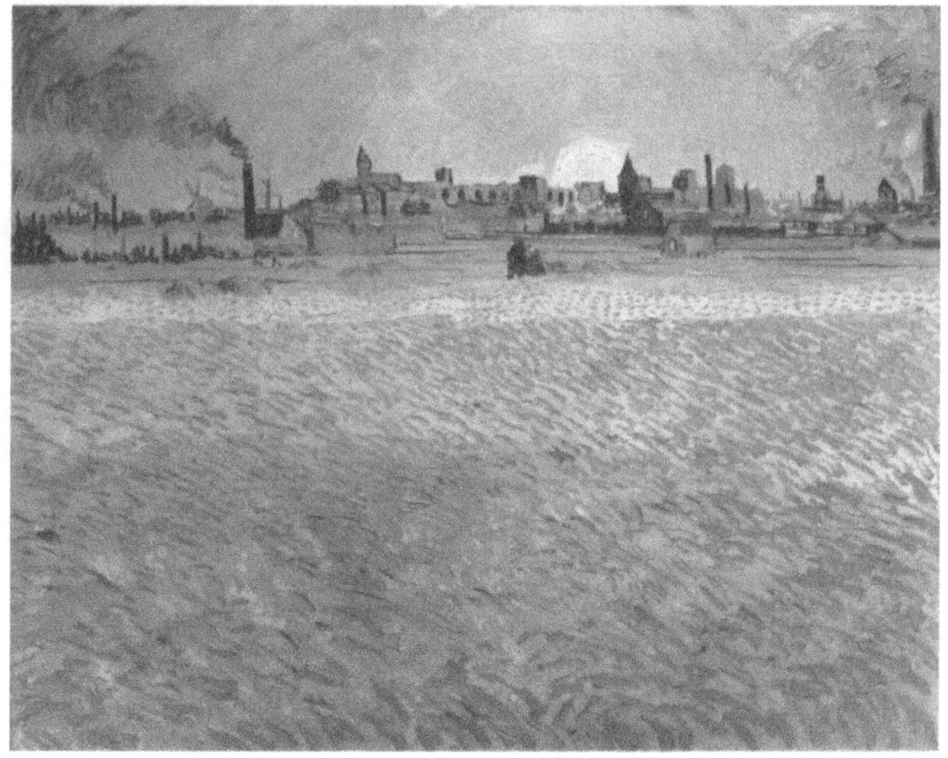

Fig. 11.6 Vincent van Gogh, *Summer Evening: Wheatfield with Setting Sun*, 1888. Oil on canvas, 74 × 92 cm. Winterthur, Kunstmuseum. Gift of Dr Emil Hahnloser.

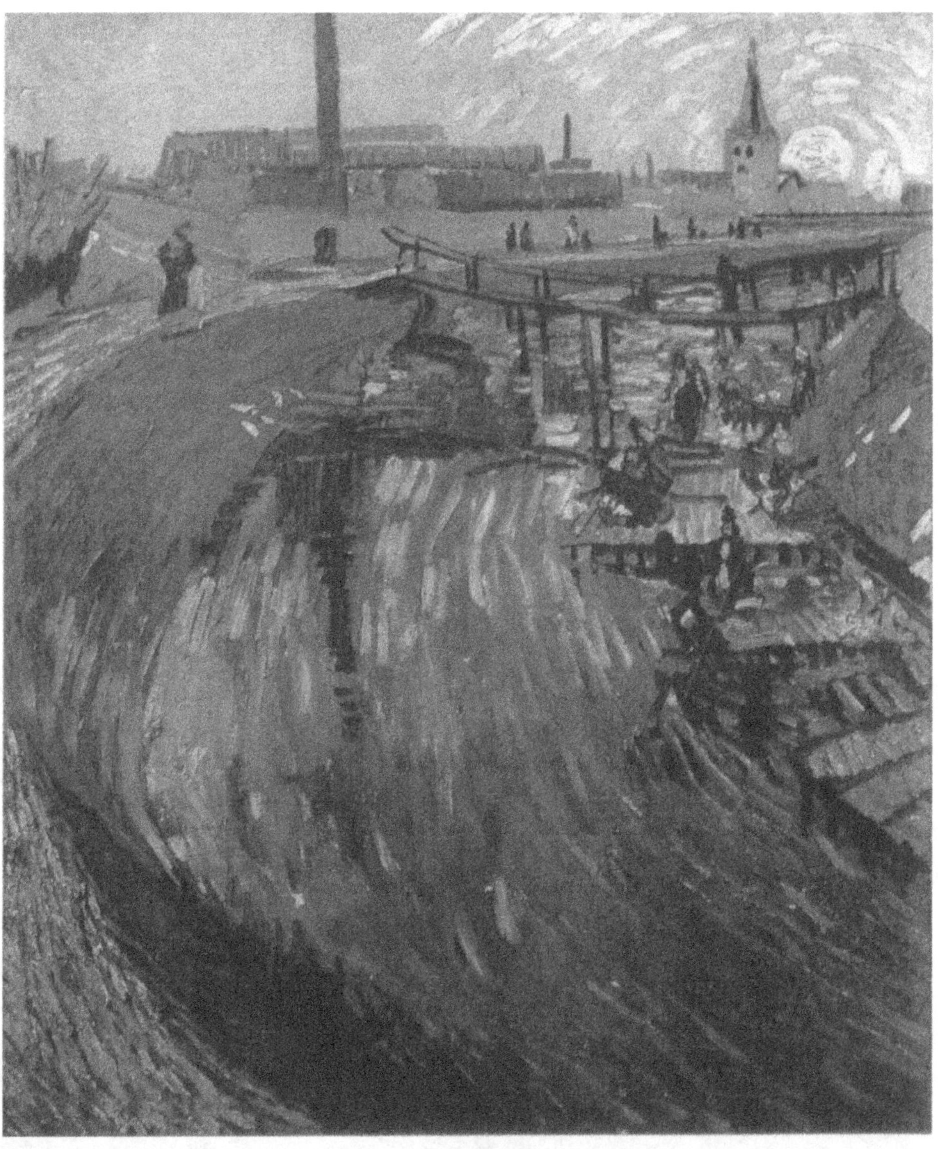

Fig. 11.7 Vincent van Gogh, *Roubine du roi*, 1888. Oil on canvas, 74 × 60 cm. Private collection. Reproduced from R. Pickvance, *Van Gogh in Arles*, Metropolitan Musum of Art, New York, 1984.

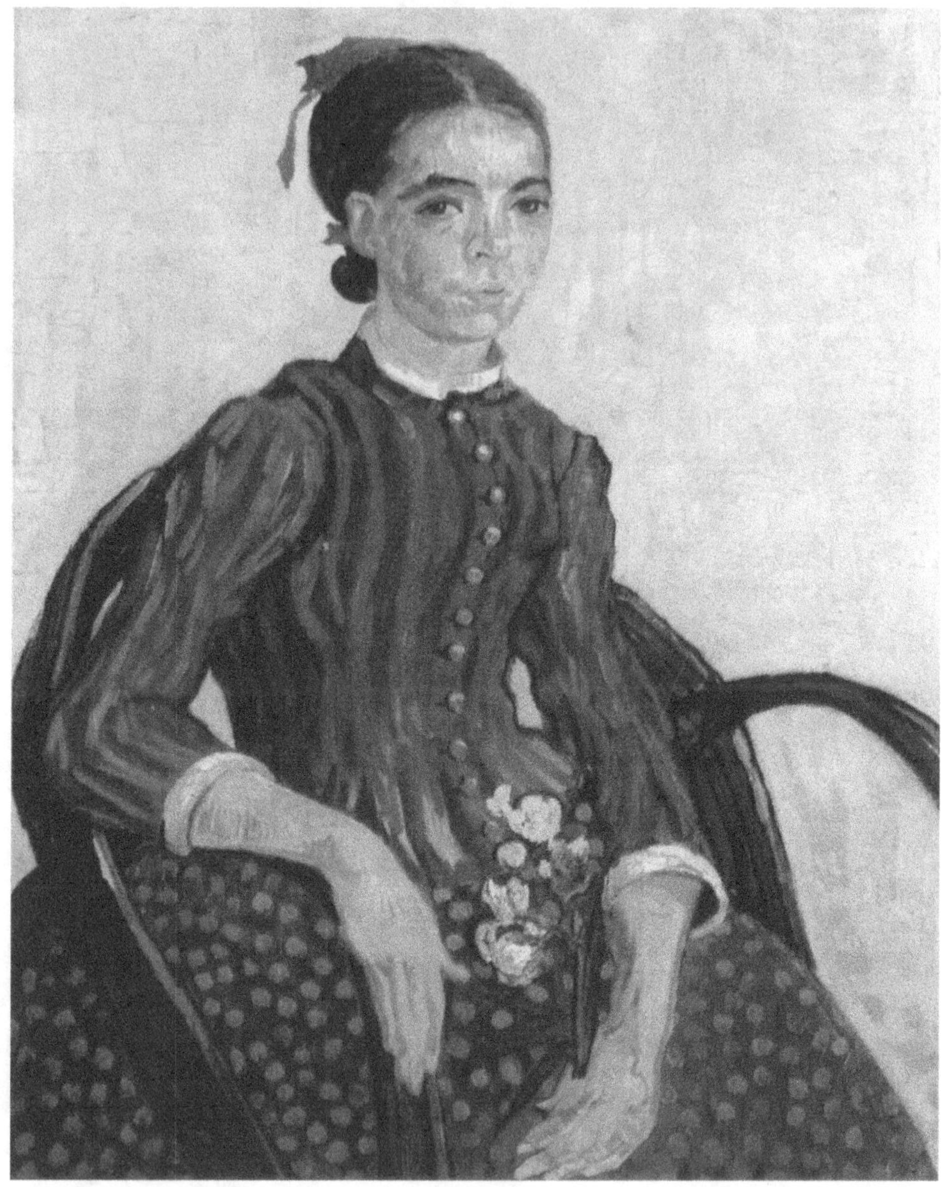

Fig. 11.8 Vincent van Gogh, *La mousmé*, 1888. Oil on canvas, 73.3 × 60.3 cm, Chester Dale Collection. © Board of Trustees, National Gallery of Art, Washington.

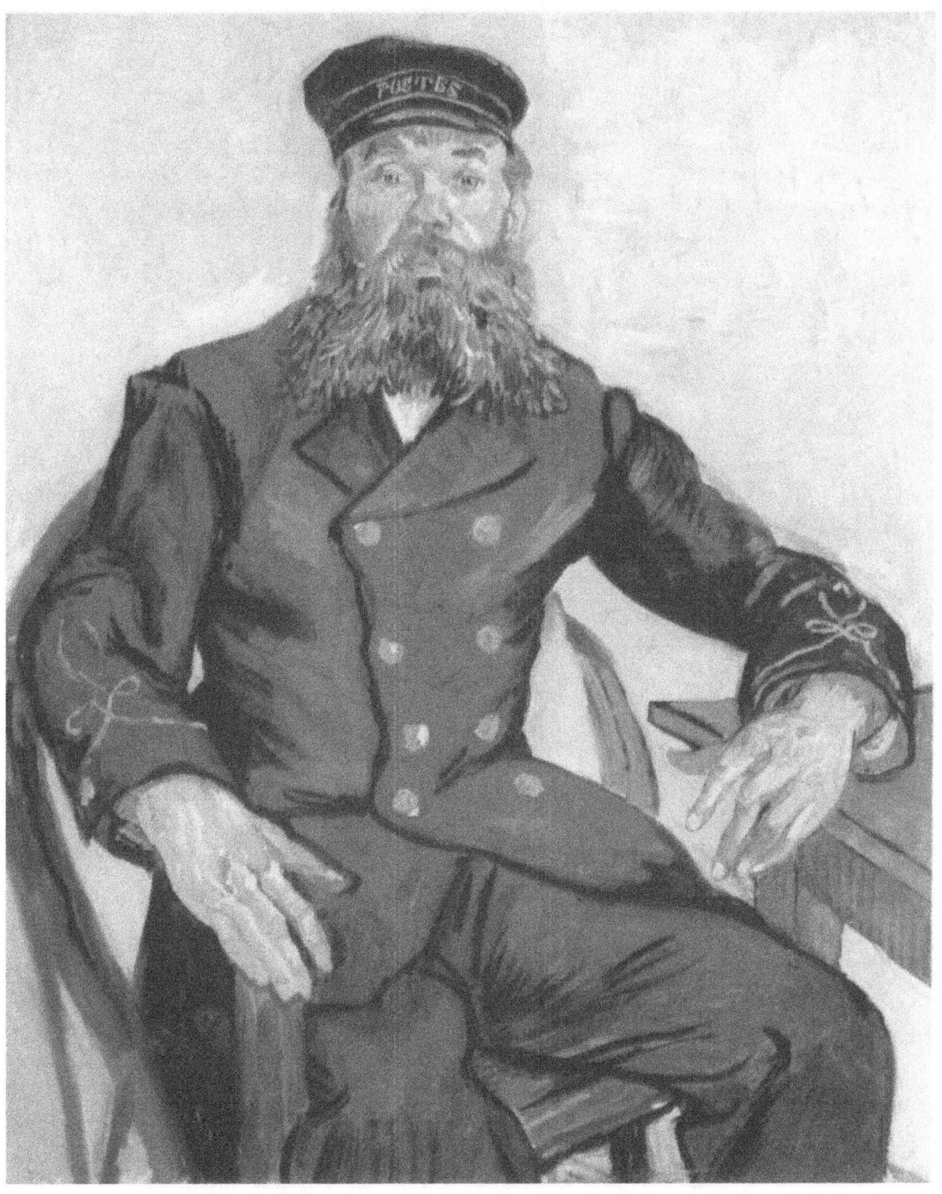

Fig. 11.9 Vincent van Gogh, *Portrait of Joseph Roulin*, 1888. Oil on canvas, 81.2 × 65.3 cm. Museum of Fine Arts, Boston. Gift of Robert Treat Paine II.

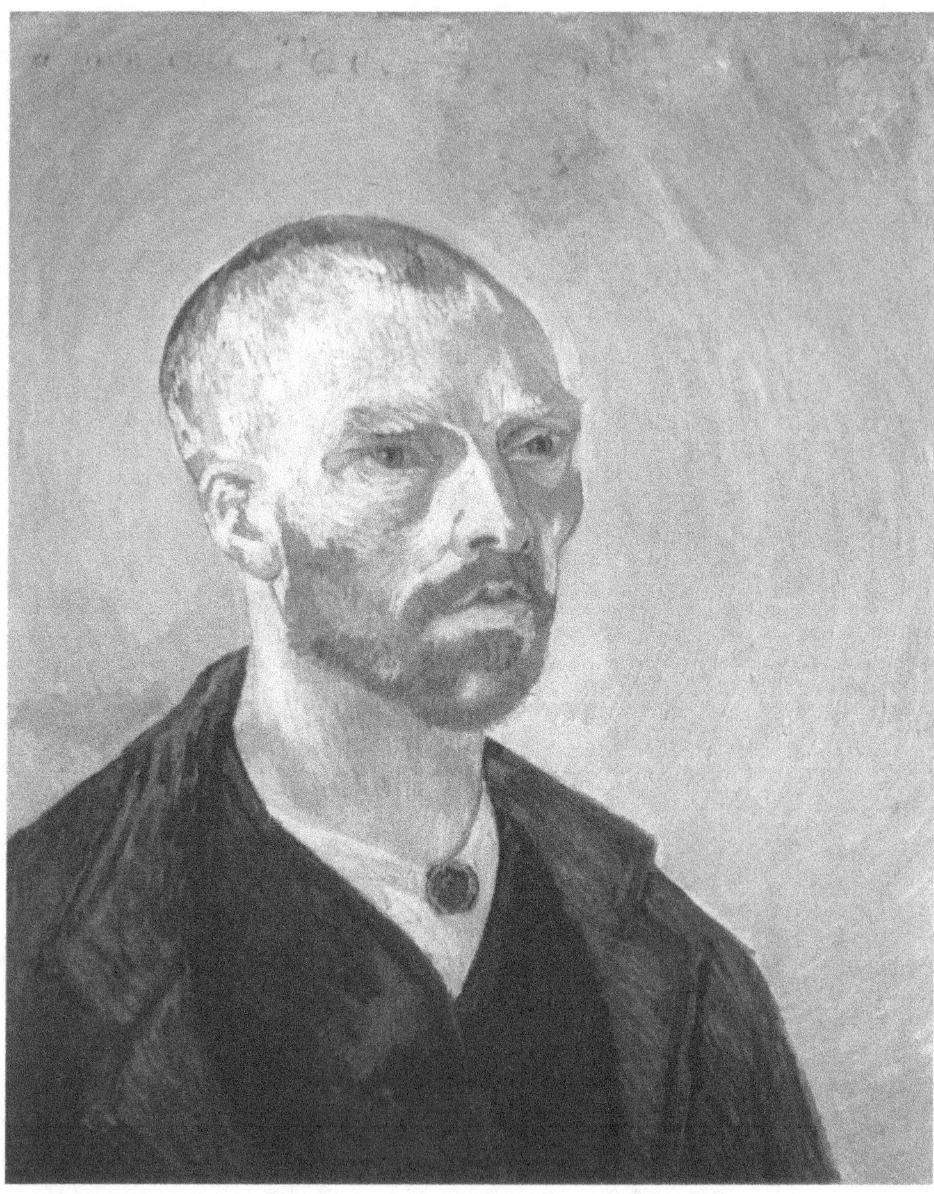

Fig. 11.10 Vincent van Gogh, *Self-Portrait Dedicated to Paul Gauguin*, 1888. Oil on canvas, 60 × 48 cm. Courtesy of the Fogg Art Museum, Harvard University Art Museums, Cambridge, Massachusetts. Bequest from the Collection of Maurice Wertheim, Class of 1906. Photograph by David Mathews.

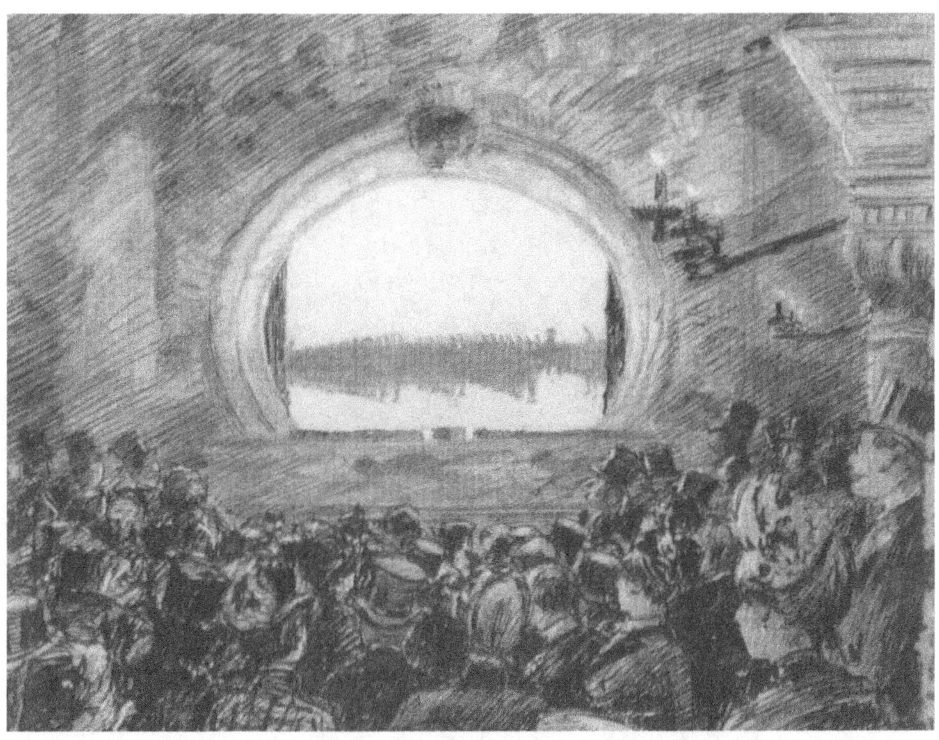

Fig. 12.1 Henri Rivière, *The Théâtre d'ombres at the Chat Noir*, ca. 1888. Pen, ink, and gouache, 20.5 × 15.7 cm. Jane Voorhees Zimmerli Art Museum, Rutgers, The State University of New Jersey, New Brunswick. Mindy and Ramon Tublitz Purchase Fund. Photograph by Victor Pustai.

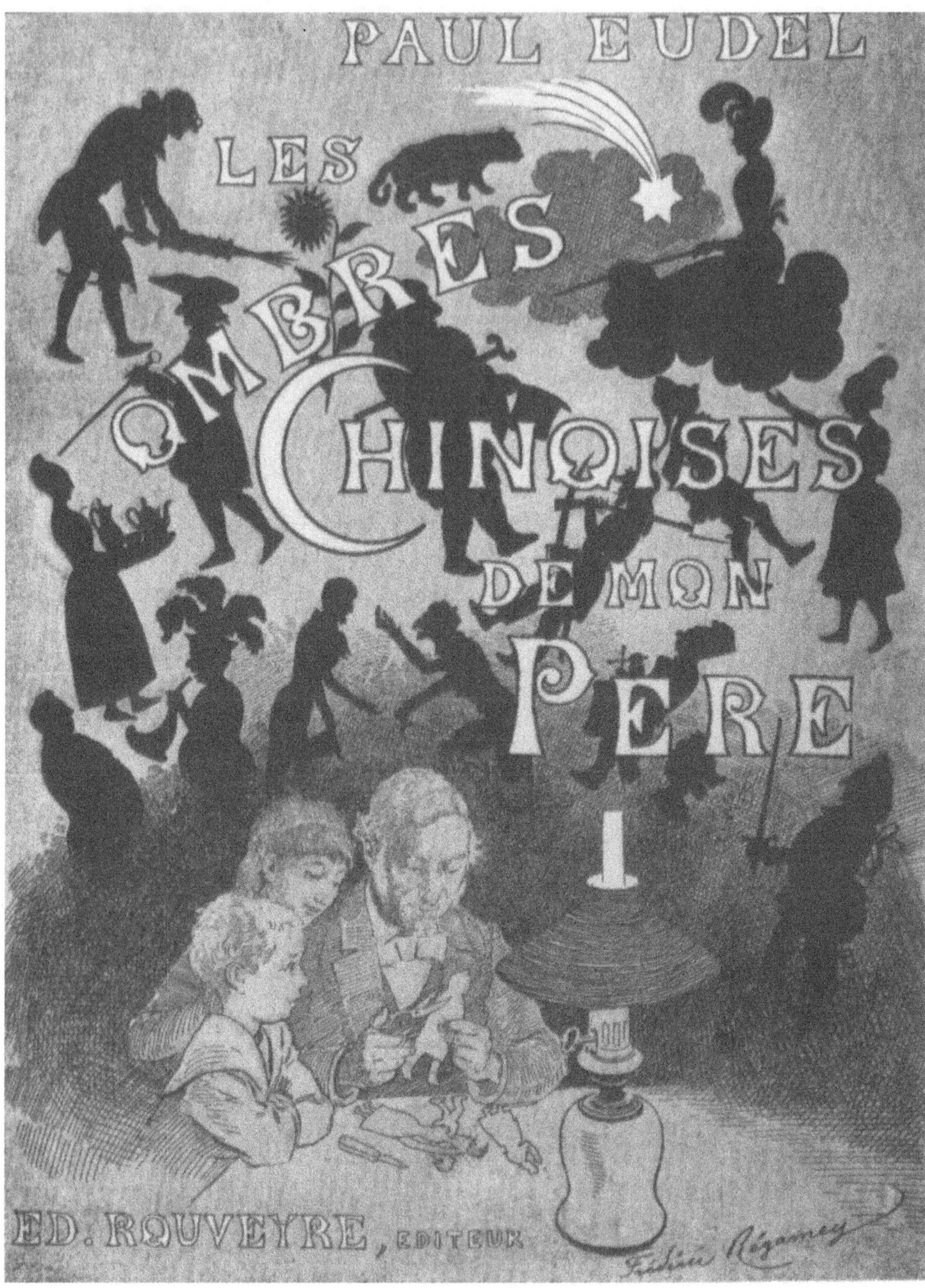

Fig. 12.2 Paul Eudel, *Les ombres chinoises de mon père* (Paris: Éditions Rouveyre, 1885). Book cover. Jane Voorhees Zimmerli Art Museum, Rutgers, The State University of New Jersey, New Brunswick. Gift of Herbert D. and Ruth Schimmel. Photograph by Jack Abraham.

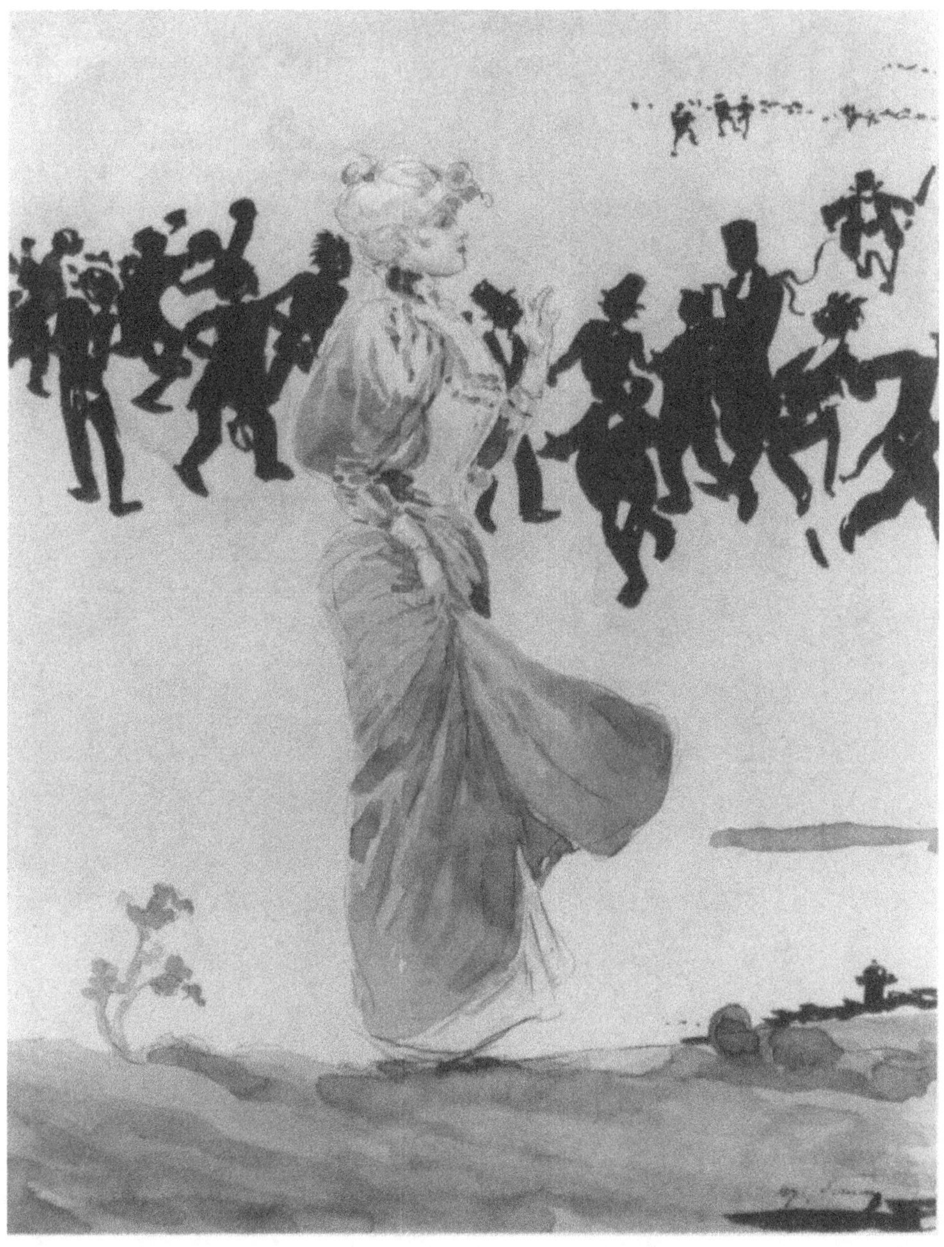

Fig. 12.3 Henry Somm, *Woman in Blue with a Shadow Theatre Effect,* ca. 1890. Watercolour and india ink, 20.5 × 15.7 cm. Jane Voorhees Zimmerli Art Museum, Rutgers, The State University of New Jersey, New Brunswick. Gift of Herbert D. and Ruth Schimmel Museum Library Fund. Photograph by Jack Abraham.

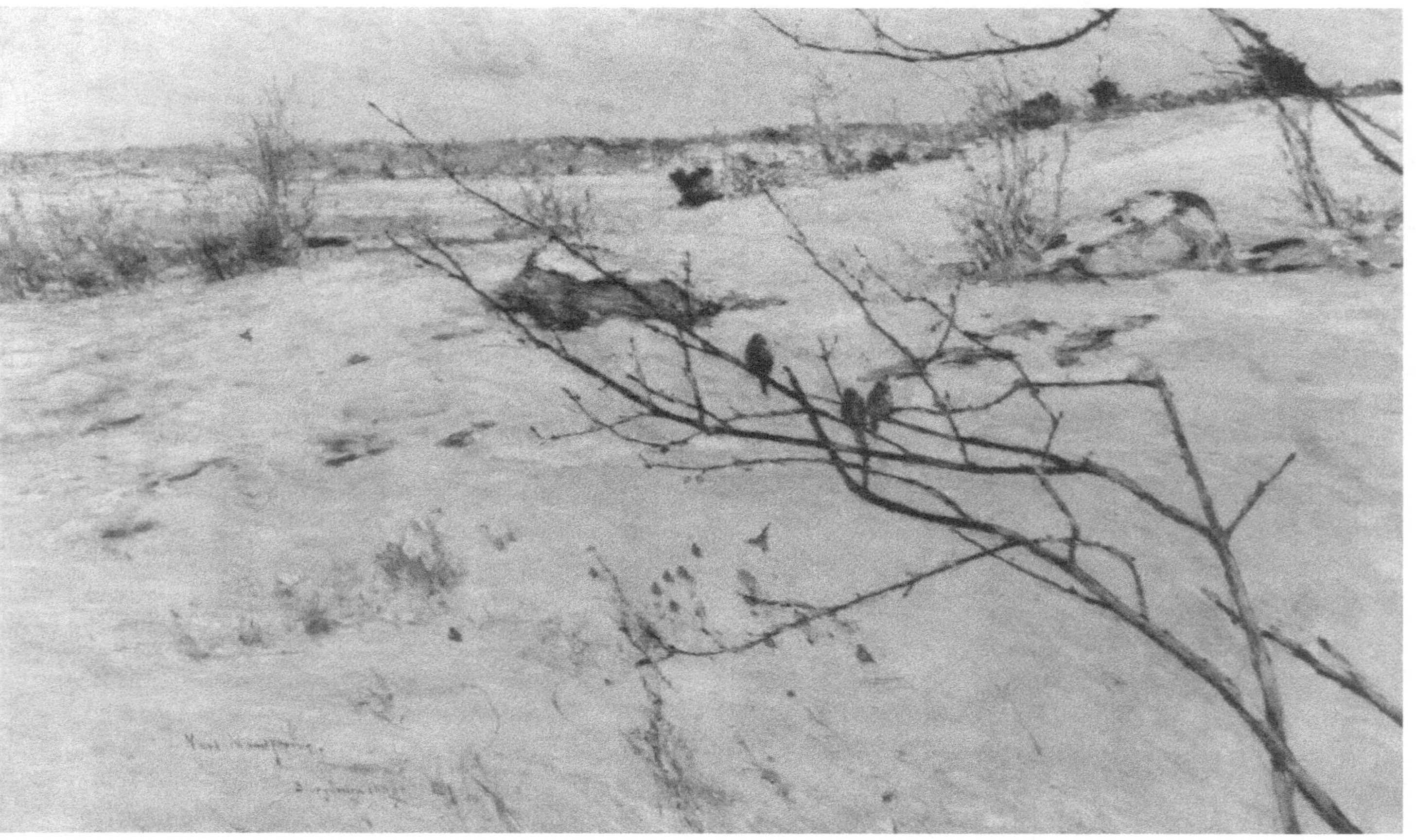

Fig. 13.1 Karl Nordström, *Winter Landscape – Djurgården*, 1889. Oil on canvas, 55 × 90.5 cm. Göteborg Art Museum, Göteborg. Photograph by Ebbe Carlsson.

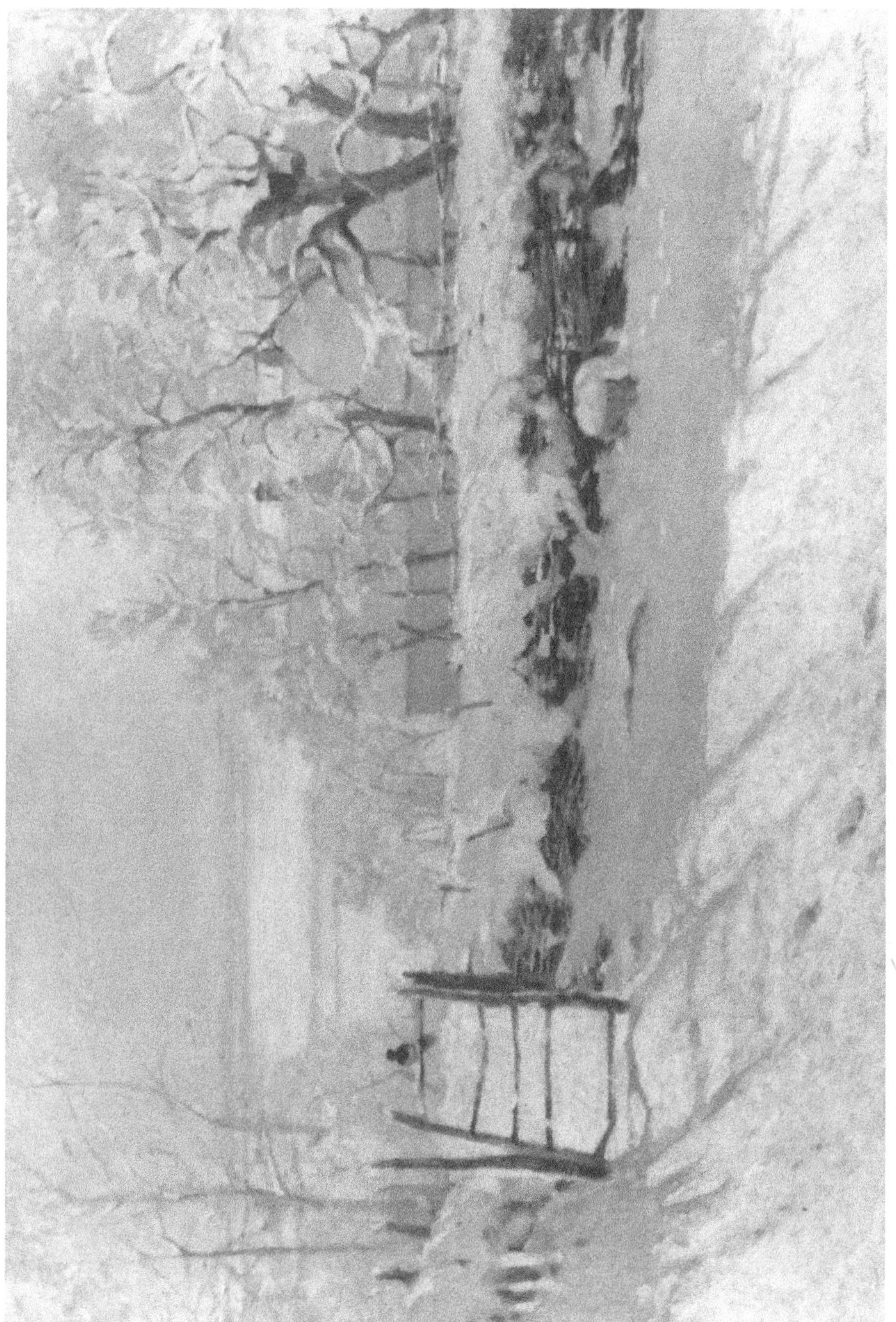

Fig. 13.2 Claude Monet, *The Skate*, 1869. Oil on canvas, 89 × 130 cm. Musée d'Orsay, Paris.

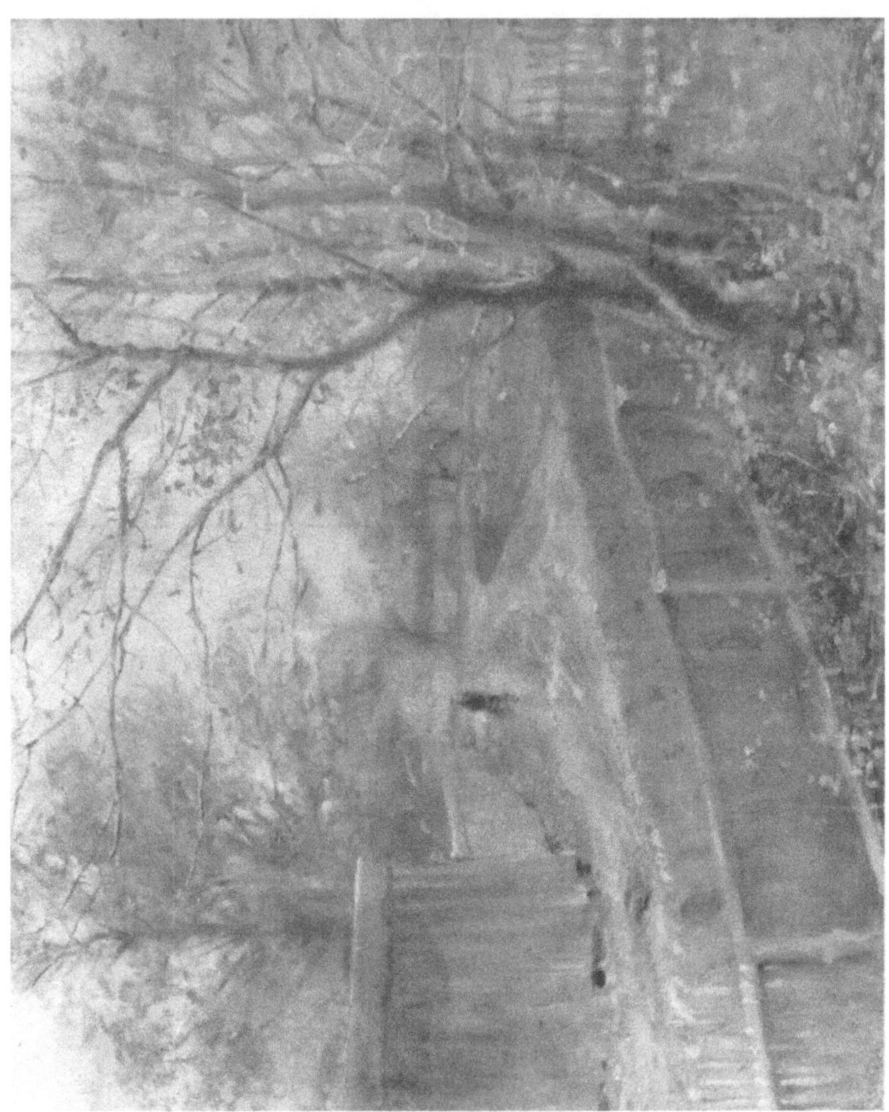

Fig. 13.3 Nils Kreuger, *Autumn, Varberg*, 1888. Oil on canvas, 32 × 41 cm. Nationalmuseum, Stockholm.

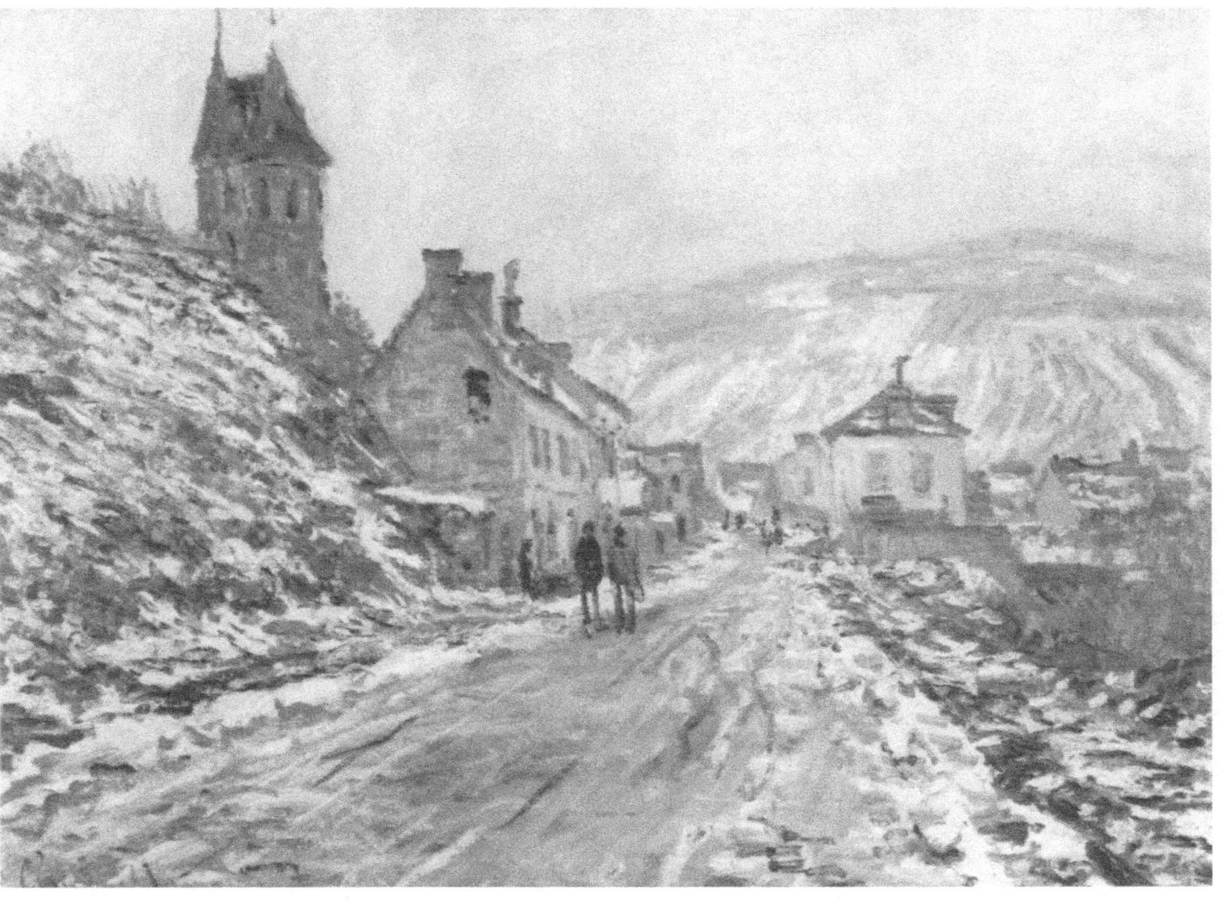

Fig. 13.4 Claude Monet, *Village Street in Vetheuil*, 1879. Oil on canvas, 52.5 × 71.5 cm. Göteborg Art Museum, Göteborg.

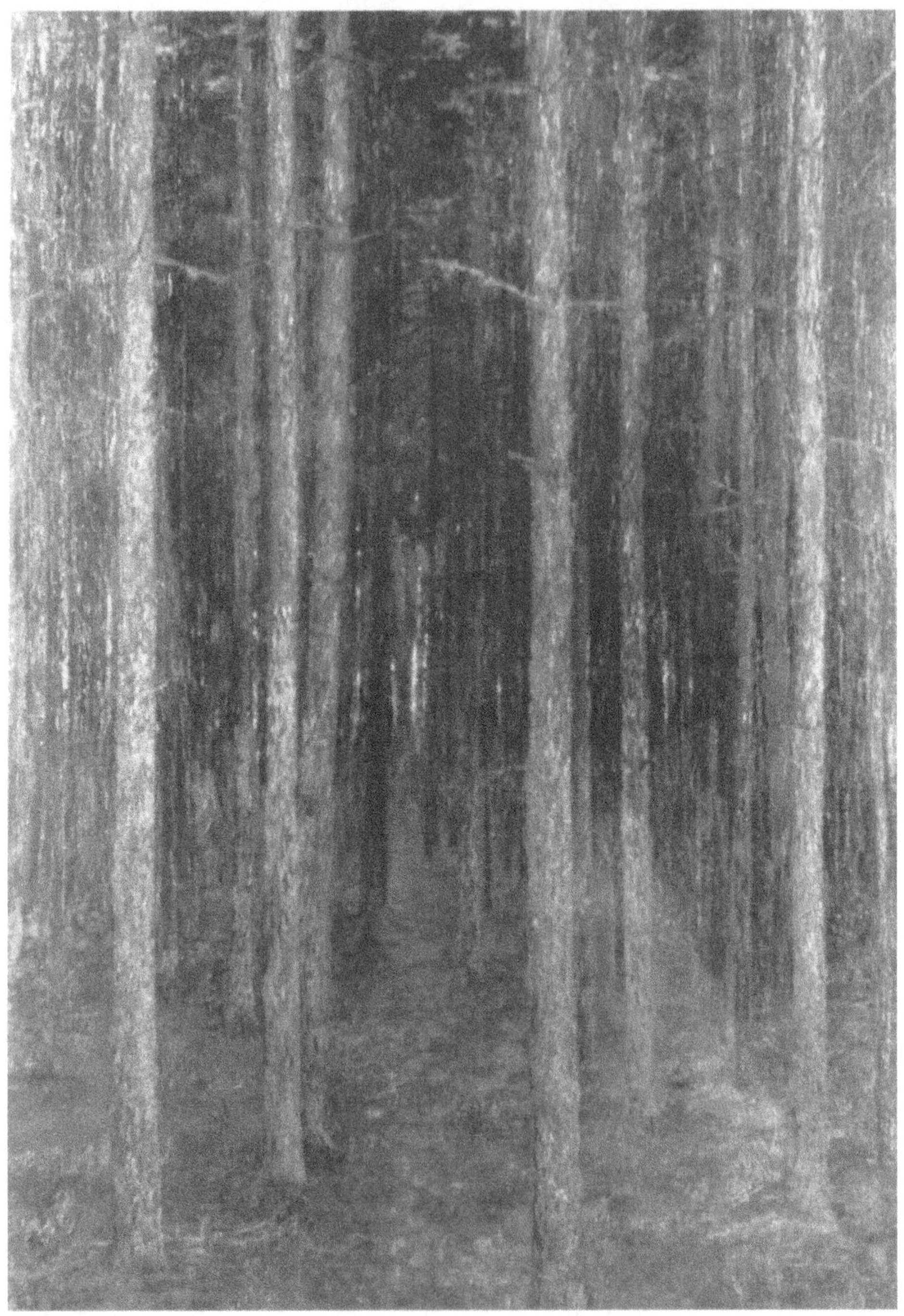

Fig. 13.5 Prince Eugen, *The Forest*, 1892. Oil on canvas, 150 × 100.5 cm. Göteborg Art Museum, Göteborg. Photograph by Ebbe Carlsson.

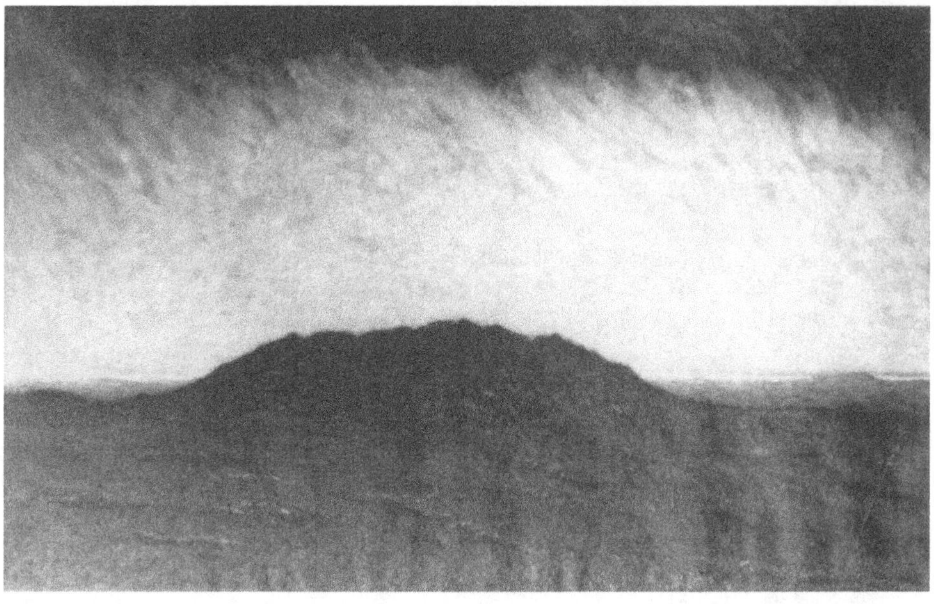

Fig. 13.6 Karl Nordström, *Grave Mound from Tjörn*, 1903. Oil on canvas, 106 × 170 cm. Norrköping Art Museum, Norrköping.

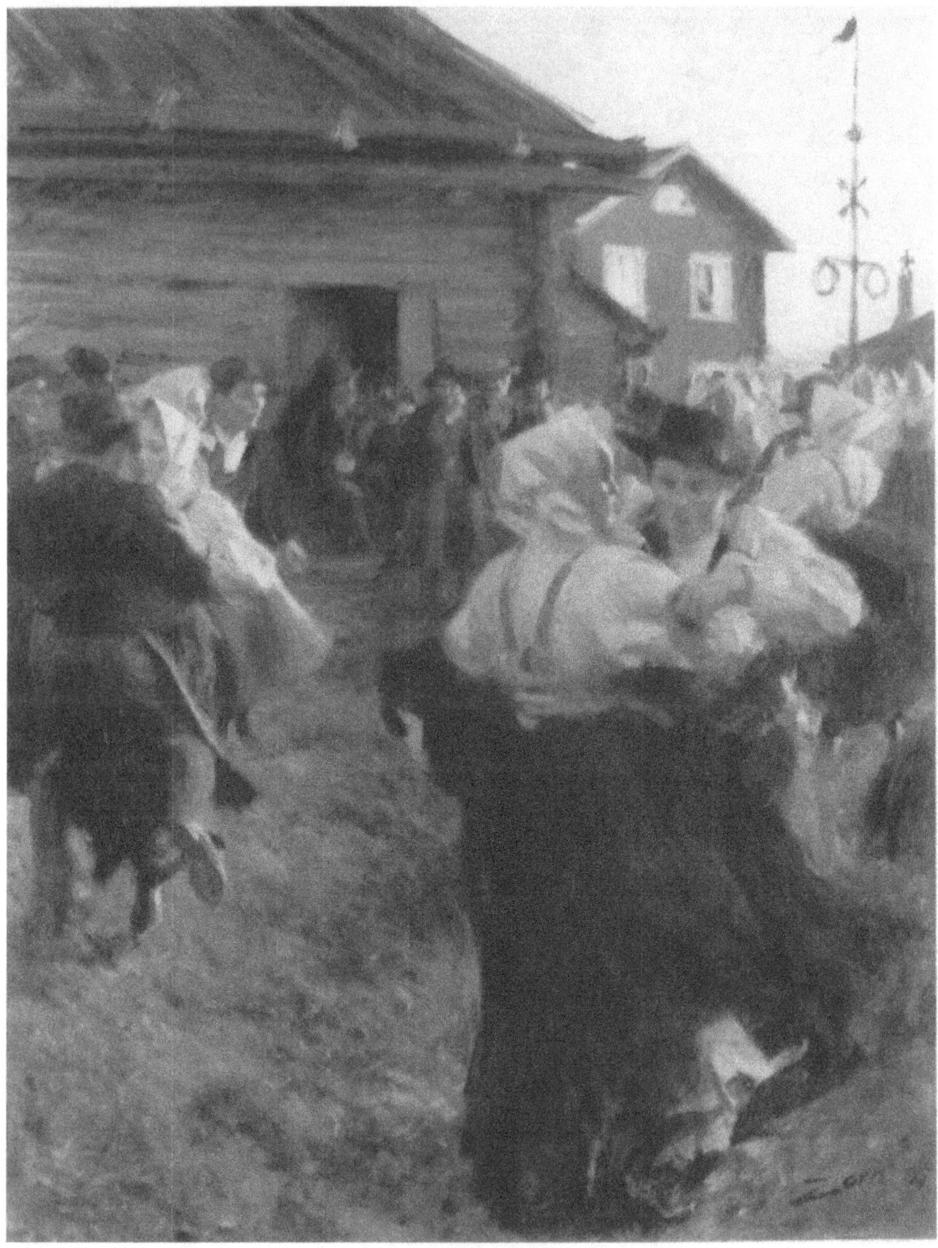

Fig. 13.7 Anders Zorn, *Midsummer Dance,* 1897. Oil on canvas, 140 × 98 cm. Nationalmuseum, Stockholm.

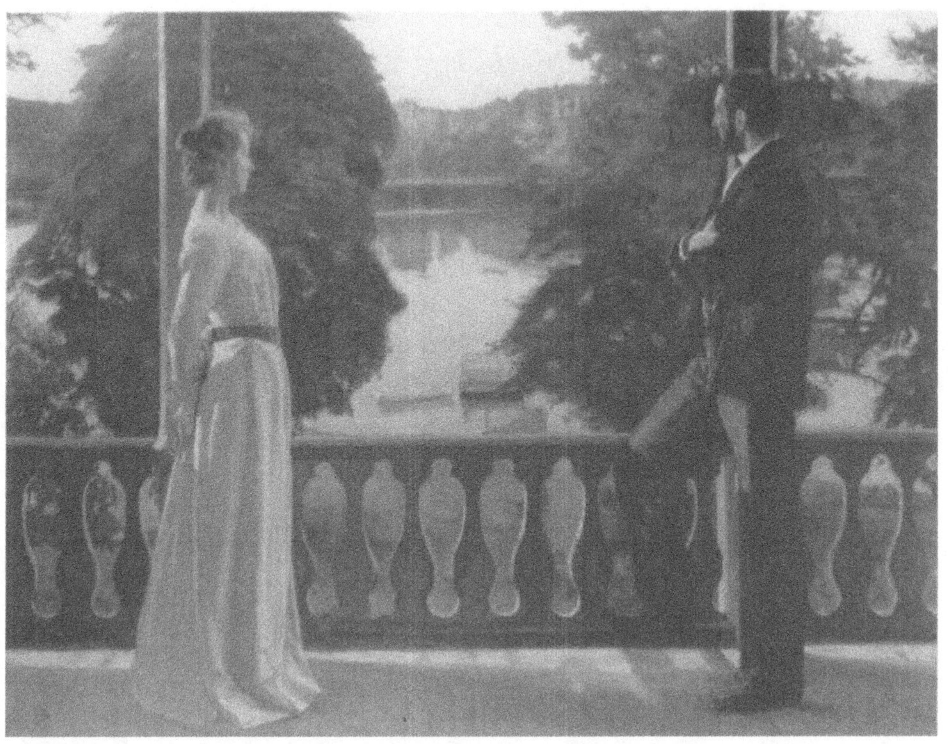

Fig. 13.8 Richard Bergh, *Nordic Summer Evening*, 1899–1900. Oil on canvas, 170 × 223.5 cm. Göteborg Art Museum, Göteborg. Photograph by Ebbe Carlsson.

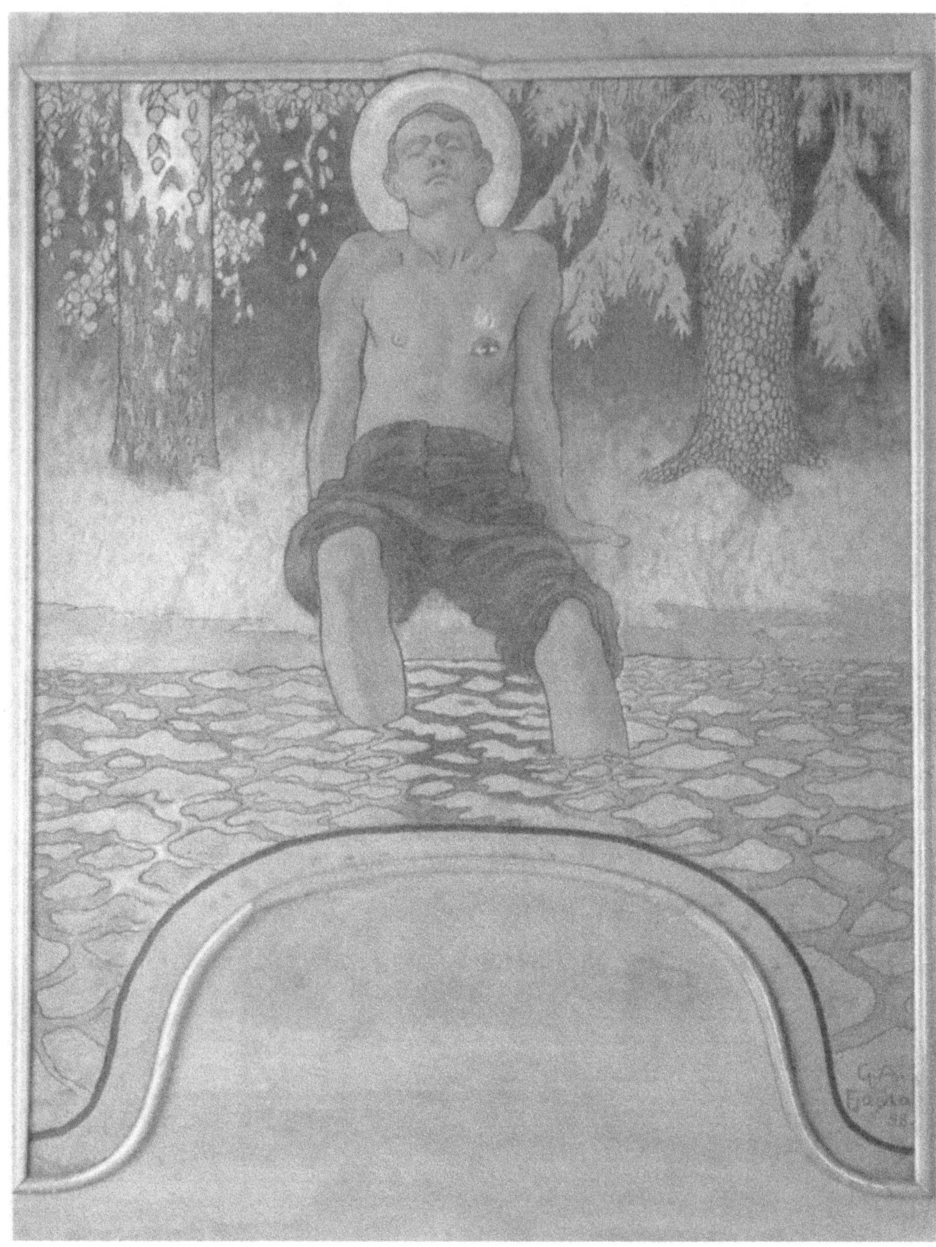

Fig. 13.9 Gustaf Fjaestad, *The Boy Who Sees With His Heart*, 1898. Ink, crayon, and body colour on paper, 94 × 76 cm. Moser and Klang Gallery, Stockholm.

PART TWO

CHAPTER FIVE

Introduction to Part Two: Staging Antimodernism in the Age of High Capitalist Nationalism

Benedict Anderson

It is perhaps easy to forget that in the first quarter of the twentieth century the entire population of Canada, geographically the second largest country in the world, was roughly the same as that of Greater London, the imperial capital. It is only a little harder to remember that until the Great War industrialism was something still largely foreign. Small wonder therefore that a Department of External Affairs was only created in 1909, a bare decade before the Group of Seven made their initial splash.

But in that decade, 'everything changed.' When the Empire went to war in August 1914, Canada automatically followed suit. Eventually, over 600,000 Canadians were either enrolled in Canada's own army and mini-navy or fought with the United Kingdom's air force. Two-thirds of these people served outside Canada, 60,000 were killed (more than all the Americans who died in Indochina) and 173,000 were wounded. In 1917 a conscription law was imposed for the first time, over the vehement opposition of many Québécois, following the extraordinary disfranchisement of all Canadians originating from 'enemy alien' countries who became naturalized citizens after 1902. The war also brought about a huge state-led change in the economy: between 1914 and 1918, industrial employment increased by more than a third, and between 1913 and 1920 the value of exports more than tripled. Meanwhile, a federal government facing large war-related debts, for the first time imposed both a personal income and a corporate profits tax. And by 1918, women could vote in federal elections.

Along with nationalization of violent death, nationalization of the economy, and nationalization of the voting-age citizenry, nationalization of culture too was inevitably under way, given the huge new demands made upon the subjects of the state. If the entire country counted only six museums in 1867 at the time of Confederation, this nullity would not do in the era of the tank, radio, cinema and the aeroplane. By the eve of the Second World War one hundred and fifty new museums had been created. Seen from this angle, the début of the Group of Seven in 1920 and its rapid ascension in Ontarian public esteem is not really surprising.

After its initial half-millenarian late-eighteenth-century stage, nationalism everywhere was expressed through a paradoxical binary that can be read, if one wishes, as what Ian McKay calls anti-modern modernism. On one side, the hunt was on for 'authenticity,' 'roots,' 'originality,' and 'history,' as nationalism's historically new consciousness created a radical break with the past. On the other side, nations were everywhere understood as 'gliding into a limitless future,' developing in perfect synchrony with the breakneck speed of Progress. Nineteenth-century Greek nationalists struggled both to revive the long-gone spirit of classical antiquity and at the same time to catch up with 'modern Europe,' and in this they were absolutely not unique.

In the nineteenth century, however, only a minority of existing states were nation states; most nationalist movements were directed against existing monarchical-imperial states, and drew their strength 'from below.' But there were deep trans-national tendencies at work throughout the century that would end this obsolete world-system and would create in 1920 – just months before the appearance of the Group of Seven – the unprecedented League of Nations as custodian of a new world order. Increasingly from that moment on, since all League members had to present themselves to each other as national, the state arrived to play a leading role in developing anti-modern modernism. The state was to be at once the rational planner and guardian of the nation's progress and at the same time the best guarantor of its originality – however this was conceived. What is most striking in retrospect is how unparadoxically these dual tasks were conceived. The term 'heritage industry' did not sound oxymoronic in people's ears.

The internal logic of a world of nations, understood at one level as a world of fundamentally similar, co-operating and rivalrous entities, also meant that nation states were required to display, for one another, their parallel differences. One almost always had to have, until very recently, rectangular flags; one had to have national anthems which were recognizable as such in their basic form (no triple-time waltzes). One had to provide, on a massive scale, national histories for young nationals in schools, and these histories had to be written in such a way as to show instantaneously their nature. One needed to foster national sports to make satisfactory showings at Olympic Games. And, of course, one had to have national handicrafts, literatures, arts, dances, etc. for display – in international competitions, Nobel Prize sweepstakes, exhibitions, trade fairs, and the rapidly ballooning struggle for advantage in the world-market of tourism. Seen this way, it is perfectly clear why the twentieth-century nation state has had so huge an interest in sponsoring, financing, steering, vending, stimulating, planning, and authenticating universally grounded particularity and originality.

Twentieth-century nation states came to face these paradoxically universal tasks with vastly different resources, histories, and difficulties. Among these states, the twentieth-century Dominions formed a very special minority. Spain had long since lost its Creolized colonies of settlement in South and Central America. In 1900, France's empire was overwhelmingly 'colonial' in the modern sense and was restricted to Asia and Africa; the only substantial overseas settlement of 'French' people was in parts of eastern Canada, and for well over a century this population had been firmly subordinated to London. The outcome of the Boer War finally put the main overseas area of Dutch settlement in the same position. Thanks to its historic naval supremacy and later industrial primacy, the United Kingdom was the only European imperial power that managed to create, and to maintain into near-contemporary times, racially based, politically dependent settler states: Australia, Canada, New Zealand, and, up to a point, South Africa.

If one asks the question of where, in these special states, national originality was to be looked for, one can see at once that in the first half of this century the choices were rather limited. As described with elegant asperity in Lynda Jessup's essay, the mythology of the Group of Seven, strenuously proclaiming the grandeur of the untamed wilderness of Canada, illustrates one possibility, which has its parallels in the nationalizing cultures of the other Dominions. The 'untouchedness' of the landscapes appeared to guarantee their aboriginal eternity, while their strangeness and scale marked them off decisively from anything British. (This perhaps mattered most to those of the Group of Seven who were first-generation immigrants from the United Kingdom.) In this light, one can see the Group's (modernist) antimodernism and anti-industrialism as a symbolic way of separating itself decisively from what, even as late as 1920, was one of the world metropolises of industrial modernity.

To be sure there was, so to speak, a catch. Truly 'untouched wildernesses' cannot, by definition, be national. Such wildernesses predate the human species, let alone nationalism, by eons. Their nationalization requires their human naming and their mapped location within a web of political territorialities (the Laurentians, not the Green Mountains of Vermont), and their representational subjection by nationalized artists, nationalized railway companies, and nationalized tourist agencies, who tend to think along the same lines. How is this function characteristically performed?

An enlightening comparison can be made with landscapes created by artists in different political situations and historic eras. In Hokusai's time (1760–1849), the peak of Mount Fuji was surely genuinely 'untouched' by human foot, but in his work it is never 'marked' that way; nor does it stand in for something else. Quite the reverse. It is typically embedded in an inhabited world which today we can say is 'Japanese,' but which there is no reason to think Hokusai understood as such. The great English painter John Turner (1775–1851), Hokusai's contemporary, was, in his early days, as happy to paint landscapes on the Continent as in Britain, and the inhabitants casually appear in most of these landscapes. When George Stephenson's railway appeared to scar the Midlands, the master welcomed it with his astonishing *Rain, Steam, and Speed: The Great Western Railway* (1844). And nothing suggests that the Mont St-Victoire painted so endlessly and lovingly by Paul Cézanne during the childhoods of the Group of Seven members was seen by the artist as either 'untouched,' or as a sign for something 'French.'

The peculiarity of the landscapes of the Group of Seven comes into high relief by such comparisons. Commercial postcards of *Rain, Steam and Speed* or *Mont St-Victoire* are always annoying because without the masters' paint strokes they are merely visual blurs. However, much of the work of the Seven survives postcarding quite well because of the national meaning that drenches its framing. The typical absence of people in their landscapes (only the lonely, hardy artist is 'out there') also has implications beyond the preservation of the 'untouched wilderness.' If there were people within the frame, who exactly would they be? Could they, in Anglophone Ontario, be guaranteed to be Canadian? Might they not be merely British? If this interpretation has some value it suggests that the solitude of the Group's landscapes also serves to occlude the ambiguous historical identity, in the 1920s and 1930s, of Dominion settlers, among whom the painters themselves had to be counted.

A second choice, shrewdly suggested by the essay of Ian McKay, involved a kind of metaphorical dissolution of the British United Kingdom into an English centre and a Celtic-Gaelic periphery. In historical fact, there was substantial emigration from Gaelic-speaking Scotland, (especially in the brutal aftermath of the failed Jacobite rebellion of 1745) as well as from oppressed, famine-stricken, Catholic Ireland. Also in historical fact, the Scottish Highlands and southern Ireland were largely bypassed in the United Kingdom's rush to industrial supremacy, and so, for generations of British romantics, these areas were regarded as storehouses of the authenticities that industrialism was so rapidly destroying. Could these authenticities have survived the Atlantic passage?

McKay's entertaining account of the handicrafts 'revival' in the New Scotland–Nova Scotia of the 1930s and 1940s and its Scotification in the 1950s shows the difficulties involved. The revival of cottage-weaving in the 1930s, on the basis of a long-fragile tradition in a province heavily subjected to capitalist development for over a century, was a project of the local state in the energetic person of a professional therapist, Mary Black. It was clearly designed to increase employment in a Depression-stricken region and to obtain a share of the tourist revenues being reaped by Québec and Ontario. The cottage industry was effectively 'nationalized' (in the local sense), modernized (in the introduction of the latest European techniques of design, production, and marketing), and finally quasi-nationalized, once Black had decided, along the lines of the Group of Seven, that the grand Atlantic-shore landscapes of Nova Scotia would be the weavers' cultural selling point. This was the background for the 1950s invention (by an Englishwoman and friend of Black) of the Nova Scotian tartan, which became a huge politico-cultural and commercial hit. It made no difference that there is little evidence for the wearing of tartans, even by the earliest farmer and shepherd immigrants from Scotland, or that in Scotland itself tartans are symbols of genealogical clans and not of political collectivities. The fact that this woven-handicraft tartan should have been so immediately popular even among those many Nova Scotians who had no plausible claims to Scottish ancestry, shows that an abstract, generic Scottishness was becoming available (like a parallel Irishness in Australia) as a valorized emblem of not-at-all-

Imperial-English Britishness. McKay goes on to make an important additional point when he notes that this kind of strengthening quasi-national identification had the national drawback of being explicitly local. (The Nova Scotian government of the 1950s emphasized this by placing tartan-clad bagpipe players on the border-crossing to New Brunswick.)

For the last sort of option the outstandingly 'successful' examples come from Mexico, and to a lesser extent other Latin American countries such as Peru, Paraguay, and Bolivia. This option is *indigenismo* of various sorts. Already in the eighteenth century there were clear signs that Creole elites in Mexico were seeking ancestries not in Madrid or Córdoba, but in Teotihuacan, and that this tendency was greatly accelerated during and immediately following the Revolution that broke out in 1910. One has only, in this context, to think of the great murals of the interwar years painted by Diego Rivera, José Clemente Orozco, and David Alfaro Siqueiros, featuring the struggles of the dark-skinned 'natives' against white-skinned oppressors from Spain and the United States. Although the Mexican ruling class has always been Spanish-speaking, Creole, and mestizo, the symbolic order of its official nationalism places every emphasis on pre-Hispanic traditions, rather than on Cortés and the other conquistadors. There are also practical and commercial conveniences involved, since it is precisely the grand ruins of the Aztec and Maya civilisations that are the country's major source of tourist prestige and revenues. That these 'antiquarian' nationalist policies go along (up to the present – see the crisis in Chiapas) with the oppression and marginalization of the real non-Spanish speaking descendants of Mayans and Aztecs does not seem a concern to the authorities, who have their modernizing eyes fixed elsewhere.

One can see a sort of quiet echo of the Mexican option in the work of Emily Carr, a contemporary of the Group of Seven, who was just as nationalist but scarcely enjoyed the sort of patronage that her male colleagues quickly captured. If one asks the question why, the most obvious answer is that the spectacular indigenous cultures on which she drew for inspiration were restricted to the far western shores of her country, utterly remote, in those days, from Ottawa, Toronto, and Montreal. But there is also the fact that the Protestant colonists from the United Kingdom did not have a tradition of mestization such as had long existed in the Iberian Catholic empires. Furthermore, as in the United States, indigenous populations were typically segregated off, if not eliminated, rather than being turned into – and integrated as – indentured labourers or peasant tenant farmers.

Closer to home, and also not without Mexican echoes, were the Québécois folk-handicrafts about which Lora Carney writes with sardonic brio. It is worth trying to imagine what kind of society would have developed in Québec had it not been subjugated by London's imperial power in the eighteenth century. Nothing seems less likely than that it would have become and remained so 'peasantized' until well into the twentieth century, or have waited till the 1960s to experience a Velvet Revolution. As in Mexico, the survival of folk art forms (in this case, hooked rugs of the late nineteenth century) was due to political control and economic subjugation by colonial elites and their local authoritarian collaborators.

In the end, of course, modernity could not be stayed. Lora Carney shows how Québec's strategic location marked parts of it for turn-of-the-century proto-industrialization and the subsequent creation of a *joual*-speaking urban working class. As elsewhere in Canada, the provincial state moved in quite early, in alliance with luxury hotel groups and the railways, to systematize, promote, standardize, and market folk art in various ecological niches between industrializing centres. So far, the situation in Quebec resembled that of New Scotland–Nova Scotia except that the cottage industries of Québec seem to have been more rooted in real rural society than anything to the east.

But there were, in Québec, peculiar problems that made both Nova Scotia and Mexico illusory exemplars. Carney inspects the late 1930s and early 1940s *de haut en bas* anxieties of modernist artist and critic John Lyman about the asphyxiation of Québécois 'peasant originality' through, as he saw it, commercialization and standardization. This was not language he would have used about Nova Scotia, or, most probably, about the indigenes of Emily Carr's Far West. The speakers of *joual* were, after all, 'Europeans' by descent; they formed a large part of the modern electorate and they had before them the possibility of national independence. (One notes, in passing, the eclipse of the Anglos in South Africa with the rise to power in the 1940s of the ex-Dutch-European, once-dominated Boers – peasants!) The end of 'traditionality' in Québec did not imply either provincial fun, as in New Scotland, or potential cultural implosion, as in the case of indigenous peoples, but rather a real challenge to Anglophone Canadian hegemony.

We can see this most clearly from Carney's account of Simone-Mary Bouchard, whose position shifted between 1937 and 1945 from roadside vendor of folk-kitsch hooked rugs for American and Anglo-Canadian tourists to regular prize winner at urban exhibitions even outside Canada. The ominous transformation is still more vividly evinced in Bouchard's late-in-life comment on her trajectory: 'Je vis par mes succès que ma nature artistique grandissait.' As an 'artist' she was poised to be for Québec what the Group of Seven had been two decades earlier for Ontario and Ottawa.

Once a year, on what serves as the national day of the People's Republic of China, the population is treated to an hours-long television spectacle featuring all the various peoples of the country performing in their own 'ethnic' fancy dress. The minorities are indeed as smoothly spectacular – and pre-modern – as the tourist brochures promise. The celebration runs into visible awkwardness only at the late-on moment when the dominant Han appear. How are they to dress and how are they to perform? It seems that 'traditional clothes' are out of the question: some are reserved for Chinese opera, others for the oddly dateless 'Old China' films that saturate cheap cinemas and television channels all over East and Southeast Asia. After all, the Han are modern, with a modernity that both specifies the pre-modernity of the minorities and underpins their own right to rule. A semiotic Great Wall of China must keep the two populations absolutely and unmistakably distinct. There is nothing for it – the Han are forced appear in drab Mao-era uniforms or, increasingly, in clothes which are indistinguishable, except in the quality of the tailoring, from those of contemporary bourgeoisies and bureaucrats almost everywhere in the world. One notes two obvious ironies: first, that the colourful minorities become visible thanks to the systematic efforts of the state and its mass-media to guarantee their permanent minority colourfulness; and second, that authentic Han modernity depends on the visual occlusion of any representation of the *haute-coûture* political finery of New York, Paris, Milan, Berlin, London, or perhaps even Tokyo. That the political elite of a society which, as many sinologists would affirm, has the oldest continuous history in the world, struggles for a modernity that is defined (who knows for how long) by Elsewhere, and that this elite also positions itself as the guardian of what is 'almost gone,' suggests that the modernist-antimodernist aporia of Anglo-Canada is by no means extraordinary. It also suggests that an independent Québec will not escape the same aporia – the fate of *joual* is already in the balance. Modernity has no stable ground and in the end is guaranteed only by political and economic power. Antimodernism is the dark-moon side of this fleeting modernity.

Nationalism, with its complex appeal to a vanished or imagined past and its ambitions for a limitless future, appears as the ordinary response to the aporia. (Postmodernism is merely a theoretical palliative.) Even in the singular Dominions. That Anglo–Australians seem ready for republicanism, and that at least some Anglo-New Zealanders are prepared to describe themselves, Maori-style, as *pakeha*, indicates the way the hurricane from Paradise is currently blowing. In the end, the Laurentian wilderness, 'Scotland,' the aboriginal West Coast, and Old Québec are mirages created both consciously and unconsciously by the *fata morgana* of the Future.

CHAPTER SIX

Modernists and Folk on the Lower St Lawrence: The Problem of Folk Art

Lora Senechal Carney

During the years 1936 to 1940 the Montréal painter John Lyman wrote an art column for *Montrealer*, a *New Yorker*–like magazine meant for Montréal's Golden Mile, the richest residential district in Canada. Lyman situated Canadian art along with United States and European art in an art world in which Cézanne, Renoir, and Matisse were the stars. He called often upon Clive Bell, Roger Fry, and other modernist writers as authorities supporting the claims he made for modern art. Like Fry, he insisted that what the artist feels about a subject is a picture's real subject, although some sort of recognizable representation remained important to him, as it did to Fry and to the French artists they both admired most. In fact, Lyman could be called the Roger Fry of Canadian critics, taking on a wide range of subjects over the years and submitting them to a powerful intelligence governed by the modernist principles that he frequently restated in his discourse.

Lyman had spent more than two decades in Europe and was personally acquainted with Matisse and other School of Paris artists. His *Montrealer* column brought into play his long experience of art and artists, his position at the centre of Montréal's developing modern art circles and desire to promote them, his privileged social standing with its resulting useful contacts and free time, his extraordinary ability to write, and his sharp wit. It was a high point in art criticism in Canada, and remains so.

Typically, the column commented on exhibitions in Montréal and elsewhere, and also on the occasional art book, but the 1 September 1937 piece was quite a different matter. It was about Québec hooked rugs, and Lyman titled it 'Poison in the Well.' It began: 'No one of taste has spent these summer months in our French Canadian regions without becoming conscious of the problem of folk art.' In fact Lyman's wealthy readers were quite likely to have spent the summer outside Montréal in 'our French Canadian regions,' as he himself did. 'Time was,' he mused, 'one could go into almost any farmer's home and acquire a few rugs, which, if not remarkable, had at least a naïve decorative charm.' Now the women were making 'monstrous rag pictures' representing village and rural scenes instead of the simple traditional patterns (for the latter, see fig. 6.1).

These *tapis murals* (wall rugs) were displayed on fences and clotheslines along the tourist routes and had 'turned the trip from Quebec to Montreal by road into a nightmare.' According to Lyman, however, the real villains were the handicraft organizations and the Québec government, who were making matters much worse by 'leading astray the unwitting country folk' with programs and exhibitions that rewarded entirely the wrong things. This sort of 'well-meaning but misguided "encouragement"' was only serving to 'poison the naïve sources of our folk arts.'

Lyman represented folk art as a thing completely spoiled by the involvement of a sophisticated outsider. 'If the would-be benefactors had tactfully acquired the flower of the natural crop, incidentally showing preference for good handiwork, materials and dyes' – if they had been as careful as Lyman was when he went into those farmhouses – 'the crop would automatically have increased and little harm would have been done.' Instead, they tried to cultivate a 'woodland flower that withers whenever a hand is laid on it,' and of course they failed.

James Naremore and Patrick Brantlinger, in *Modernity and Mass Culture,* note that the American modernist art critic Clement Greenberg, like so many other Western cultural theorists and critics in the first half of the century, lamented the destruction of folk art by modernization. Of course Naremore and Brantlinger find such laments suspect, for in their formulation 'folk art' is merely a rural or pre-industrial conceptual opposite to 'high art.' Folk art is always 'framed and represented by something other than itself,' endlessly reshaped in the minds of elites according to their particular needs and desires.[1] Similarly Richard Handler, who studied historical descriptions of Québec 'folk society,' concluded that these descriptions differ mostly according to the ideologies of their writers, which suggests that the whole notion of this folk society is mythical.[2]

Lyman's framing of folk art was driven by his modernist art–critical agenda, an agenda obviously interlaced with other elite agendas. As a critic he reserved his sharpest knives for conservative art academies (the Royal Canadian Academy still had a strong hold on Montréal). For him to write about folk art as art was to strengthen the idea that creativity did not depend on education, an idea that would render academies completely useless. But folk art had to be 'authentic,' innocent of debasing modern life and the capitalist marketplace.

In order to understand the interventions Lyman complained about so bitterly, I examined both newspaper and magazine accounts and books published in Québec and elsewhere from the 1920s onwards on hooked rugs and other Québec folk art. What follows is a response to Lyman's 1937 article in the light of certain of my findings about these interventions and about the circumstances in which they took place, with an emphasis on what happened in Charlevoix County.

On 18 March 1919, Victor Morin, president of the Société historique de Montréal, commented that the old traditions and manual arts, once so vital to many Québec villages that were forced by their isolation to be self-sufficient, had suddenly been swept away by industrialization and commerce. Anglicization or Americanization had set in without anyone seeming to have noticed. Some villages and rural areas were not yet submerged by the invading wave of mass culture and technology, but even in these places old objects had passed to the status of relics, destined for dealers, collectors, and vandals.[3] The occasion for these remarks was a public 'Soirée des traditions populaires canadiennes,' an evening of Québec songs and stories at the Bibliothèque Saint-Sulpice in Montréal, organised by National Museum of Canada ethnologist Marius Barbeau and a collaborator, E.Z. Massicotte. They were promoting among educated francophones what Barbeau described as a patrimony, preserved unconsciously by the rural population for the regeneration of the race, a patrimony that these urban francophones had long rejected as 'savage' in favour of literary models from France.[4]

By 1900 industrialization was well established in the Montréal area, but in the early twentieth century, as long-distance power transmission became feasible, large projects financed mostly by American, British, and Anglo-Canadian interests were undertaken in rural areas. Dams and hydroelectric stations were built on the big rivers flowing down from the Laurentians to the St Lawrence; huge pulp and paper mills and aluminium and chemical processing plants soon followed (a trend which would gain even more momentum in the 1920s). The value of Québec's manufactured goods went from about $150 million in 1900 to more than $1,050 million in 1920,[5] and the population balance began to tip toward urban areas.

In spite of this industrial growth, Victor Morin's vision of a traditional culture suddenly swept away by modernity is a construction like those of many modernists, influenced perhaps by Barbeau's project to salvage its artefacts. Some contrasting accounts claimed that traditional French Canadian culture survived in pristine condition in the old parishes of the lower St Lawrence from Québec City to Rivière du Loup on the south shore, and to the Saguenay River on the north shore. These accounts, of course, also had some stake in the vision they presented. In 1924 Toronto's *Canadian Magazine* published a travel piece on 'the Quaint Old French Settlements Along the North Shore of the Lower St. Lawrence,' its writing grounded both in Anglo-Canadian nationalism and in stereotypes of rural Québec:

> The little white village ... The rolling meadows ... A dusty road ... On one of the balconies sat a pretty young girl in a dress of blue homespun, at her feet a basket of soft rose-colored wool, which she was spinning into yarn. On another sat a woman hooking a mat ... It might have been a little village of Normandy away back in the seventeenth century ... But no, for in Canada we found it ... Whether we stand on the ramparts of Quebec, in the amphitheatre of mountains at Baie St. Paul or on the grim cliffs of Isle aux Coudres, and gaze down the proud river towards the Gulf and along the majestic north shore, we feel a new exaltation in our Canadian birth, a fresh interest in the history of our country ...[6]

'Be happy this spring,' said a 1927 Canadian Pacific Railways advertisement for the Chateau Frontenac hotel in Quebec City, 'among people who still dwell in a romantic age.'[7]

Such images of the lower St Lawrence overlooked a railroad that had been running since 1859 from Rivière du Loup to Sarnia, Ontario, providing service to towns on the south shore. Railroad connections also gave access to manufacturing centres in New England, to which hundreds of thousands of Québec francophones emigrated permanently or temporarily for economic reasons after the mid-nineteenth century.[8]

Traffic had moved up and down the St Lawrence for centuries, but regular steamboat service along the north shore from Quebec City to the Saguenay River and the nearby area around the village of La Malbaie in Charlevoix County began in 1853 when a quay was built at Pointe-au-Pic, the promontory at the mouth of the Malbaie River. This quay was expanded in 1865 to accommodate the 'floating hotel' cruise ships which brought summer residents and tourists to Murray Bay, as the area was known to anglophones. From 1875 railroad connections from New York and Boston to Rivière-Ouelle on the south shore of the St Lawrence linked with a ferry to Pointe-au-Pic. The area around La Malbaie (which happened to be the 'little white village' in the *Canadian Magazine* article) was thus a summer destination for the rich of Montréal, Québec, and the Northeastern United States well before the twentieth century. Philippe Dubé writes in *200 ans de villégiature dans Charlevoix* that for well over a century great families of the Northeast summered here – Blakes, Cabots, Tafts, Fitzpatricks, Taschereau, and Gouin.[9] President Taft spent more than forty summers at Murray Bay.

Many of these people, Americans in particular, built their own villas overlooking the St Lawrence, and great gardens were created around these villas; Frederick Law Olmstead, of New York's Central Park fame, designed one. Dubé notes that American guests were dismayed by industry's destruction of the green spaces around their own urban areas. For them 'Charlevoix doit être préservé du modernisme afin de conserver le plus longtemps possible sa virginité.'[10]

There were hotels too, for both francophone and anglophone clientele; the grandest was the 250-room cedar-sided Manoir Richelieu, built in 1899 by the steamship line serving Pointe-au-Pic (fig. 6.2). The Manoir had its own orchestra, which played for bathers on the terrace in the afternoons and also presented four evening concerts a week throughout the season. The hotel burned in September 1928, but a new, all-concrete Manoir Richelieu, 100 rooms larger and built in a Norman chateau design, was ready for the 1929 season.

Marius Barbeau commented in 1935 that Charlevoix had become famous for its traditional homespun textiles only after the steamship line built the Manoir Richelieu and another magnificent hotel at nearby Tadoussac, advertised the area in Canada and abroad, and brought in tourists who sought out local crafts.[11] Some of these crafts were exhibited and sold at the Manoir Richelieu, and in 1929 Canada Steamship Line co-operated with the Québec Department of Agriculture to produce the Murray Bay Festival, a large exhibition of Québec 'handicrafts' at the new concrete Manoir.[12] Certainly, as Dubé notes, Charlevoix was 'a privileged point of contact' between the rural francophone culture and a primarily Anglo-Saxon urban culture via the authentically modern activity of tourism.[13]

Twenty kilometres up the north shore from La Malbaie was Baie-Saint-Paul, a community less frequented by tourists but favoured by artists. Clarence Gagnon visited in 1902 on the advice of his Montréal teacher William Brymner, who made summer visits there in the 1890s.[14] Gagnon lived in Baie-Saint-Paul on and off until 1924 and made its district the central subject of his painting career. He also became very interested himself in the local rugs and homespuns, assisting the area's producers by finding them markets in Québec and Ontario and dyeing wool himself for pieces he commissioned from local weavers. He made designs for hooked rugs that were similar to his paintings, one of which, a Charlevoix village with turkeys in the foreground, still exists.[15]

Group of Seven painter A.Y. Jackson visited Baie-Saint-Paul in 1923 and reported that there was 'a good deal of the primitive here yet, thatched barns and many timber houses and a few old stone ones. It is a very beautiful place, almost too much so for painting.'[16] However the railroad had come through a few years earlier, bringing 'civilising influences which will not improve it inwardly or outwardly. Already there are four or five houses in stock catalogue architecture and they are likely to set the style and the Ford car will supersede the old cariole.'[17]

During the years before the Second World War many other Canadian and American artists spent summers or long visits at Baie-Saint-Paul or at Saint-Urbain just up the road, as Victoria Baker reports in *Images de Charlevoix*.[18] The Canadians included Albert Henry Robinson, Randolph Hewton, Robert Pilot, Jori Smith, Jean Palardy, Jean-Paul Lemieux, André Biéler, Stanley Cosgrove, Charles Goldhammer, Peter Haworth, Bobs Cogill Haworth, Caven Atkins, Marc-Aurèle Fortin, Kathleen Daly, and George Pepper. Among the American painters were Frederick W. Hutchison and Edward Boyd, who attracted fellow members of New York City's Salamagundi Sketch Club as well as William Glackens of Ashcan School fame.

Lynda Jessup has noted that in the mid-1920s the Canadian Pacific and Canadian National railway companies began to market the 'folk culture' of Québec and to advertise the historic Québec sites found on their railroad and ship routes. The CNR provided passes to A.Y. Jackson, Arthur Lismer and others involved in a visit to the lower St Lawrence organised by Barbeau in the summer of 1925. These companies understood well the publicity value of art and the advantages of working with governments in projects such as Barbeau's.[19]

Jessup relates that Arthur Lismer approached the curator of the Art Gallery of Toronto soon after that 1925 summer trip about an exhibition on Québec. Jackson wrote to Barbeau that the Gallery was eager: 'get alot of stuff from the Women's art, pictures by Gagnon, Robinson, Cullen, Coté, Henri Julien etc. and have you give a couple of lectures on folk songs or folk lore and bring a singer with you. It should be very popular.'[20] The Art Gallery of Toronto presented this exhibition the following spring in a space adjoining the annual Group of Seven show. The common catalogue for the two shows listed contemporary paintings of Québec scenes together with traditional wood sculpture, fabrics, and an unnumbered group of hooked rugs and homespuns lent by the Woman's Art Association of Toronto. The text of the catalogue referred to Québec as the cradle of Canadian art but lamented that Quebéc's beautiful old house architecture was losing ground, and that its rug-making and weaving were 'only kept alive through the efforts of art societies and a few connoisseurs.'[21] Again the argument was made that a traditional culture was disappearing or at best surviving on artificial support systems, and that a salvage project was in order. This time, as Jessup concludes, the project appropriated French-Canadian work into the established, largely Anglo-Canadian nationalist movement in a way parallel to the nationalist appropriation of 'primitive' native work for the 1927 National Gallery 'Exhibition, Canadian West Coast Art, Native and Modern.'[22]

Also in 1927, the Canadian Pacific Railway hosted a 'Canadian Folksong and Handicrafts Festival' at the Chateau Frontenac under the auspices of the National Museum of Canada, Barbeau's home institution. The festival featured Québec crafts such as textiles and carving as well as Québec paintings by Jackson, Lismer, and others, and song and dance performances arranged by Barbeau and John Murray Gibbon, a CPR publicity agent and folk song enthusiast. The thirty-two-page program[23] combined pleasant light information on crafts and songs with photographs of rural Québec people, largely from Barbeau's collection. For this event Gibbon advertised widely and attracted an audience from New York, Boston, and Toronto; there was even a special Festival Train from Boston.[24] In 1928 the CPR mounted another, larger Québec festival for which singers and costumes were brought in from New York's Metropolitan Opera Company; and a third festival followed in 1930.

It is no surprise that in the discourses surrounding such events, the concepts of Primitive and Folk are linked, and that children are often thrown into the bargain. Lismer, musing after his Québec trip about the farm women and their rugs and homespuns, wrote, 'Primitive, or let us say, simple people feel beauty naturally. Children are like this. It is not acquired. It is not merely taste. It is intuitive.'[25] Victor Morin, opening a 1931 Canadian Handicrafts Guild show at the Art Association of Montreal, was quoted as saying that handicrafts in Canada had a notable record, from the 'wampum and beadwork of the original children of the soil to the lovely things collected in the Guild exhibition.'[26] John Lyman's 'Poison in the Well' assigned the folk artist 'that sense of rhythm and balance instinctive in those who remain close to nature, instinctive also in the cultivated artist and in children who have not been corrupted by their environment or education.'[27]

Meanwhile, access to many parts of Québec increased. Road construction was going on at a terrific pace. Between 1923 and 1931, the Québec government built or improved some 12,000 miles of highways and paved roads and 20,000 miles of good earth roads (scarcely a tenth of that existed before 1923) using profits from the government-run liquor business during American prohibition. As the government had hoped, the roads further encouraged Prohibition-era visitors. By the early 1930s, tourism, by road (fig. 6.3) and by boat, had become Québec's biggest business and it continued to grow.[28]

This was when Lyman's 'problem of folk art' appeared. The Québec government, also perceiving a problem, ordered an investigation into handicrafts in the province in 1929, in the context of an ambitious pre-election agricultural improvement program, and concluded that old craft techniques were disappearing, old looms were inadequate, and a 'lack of artistic taste was noticeable' in spite of the obvious ability of the rural women. The Québec Department of Agriculture's Rural Economy Service opened the École provinciale des arts domestiques in Quebec City;[29] vegetable dyeing, design preparation, and fabrication techniques were taught to hundreds of women each year, who in turn taught thousands more at existing regional household science schools. Oscar Bériau, the Director-General of Handicrafts for the province (a newly created position), stressed that the products of this program 'must be truly Canadian in execution, material and expression.' The Department of Agriculture also held exhibitions all over Québec, aided in distribution, and sent instructors out to the Cercles des fermières – local branches of the rural women's association that the Department had founded during the First World War in the government's first major effort to promote crafts and rural life, and that now increased greatly in number.[30] The government officially hoped that this activity would help slow the exodus from farms to cities and to the United States, bring money to Québec farm families (whose land values and farm product incomes had fallen by as much as half in the Depression), and provide a useful and pleasant pastime during the long winters.

Of course it is precisely this government initiative that John Lyman denounced. Governmental taste was apparently based on 'characteristic interest' rather than 'authenticity.' They discouraged the use of commercial patterns for hooked rugs, but house and village scenes were fine: nothing could be more characteristic.

The Canadian Handicrafts Guild, also denounced by Lyman, carried on the work it had been doing since the very beginning of the century: collecting, teaching, exhibiting (at the Art Association of Montreal as well as nationally and internationally), and lecturing about and selling handicrafts. Like the Québec government, they seemed to consider landscape rugs worthy of highest honours. In fact, the Guild had recently taken it upon itself to renew among Charlevoix hooked rug makers the naturalistic themes that were to the taste of the American tourist in order to improve Depression-era sales.[31] This commodification of the locally 'authentic' rug was part of a larger pattern in north-eastern North America. Private dealers and collectors had been mining the best sites in the United States since the end of the First World War. One American writer noted in 1927, 'The hooked rug mania is sweeping the country with as much spirit as the interest in early American glass. You have only to try to collect rugs to find out how everybody is out looking for them.'[32] Ian McKay quotes poet Margaret Lathrop Law, who in 1928 described rug collectors coming to Canada as 'antique dealers, interior decorators, and summer cottagers from the States, all possessed of the hooked-mat mania.'[33]

I myself find house and village scenes no less 'authentic' than the earliest patterns, which in any case were local reworkings of such things as the patterns in imported rugs and tapestries (figs. 6.4 and 6.5). The commercial stamping of designs onto burlap rug foundations dates back to the nineteenth century. The first examples appeared in Maine around 1870, and within two decades many such prepared foundations and design catalogues were available throughout the northeastern part of the continent. In fact, hooked rugs were not made in any quantity until about the mid-nineteenth century, following the introduction of commercial burlap from British factories in India, and the pre-industrial history of hooked rugs only began a few decades before that at the most.[34] However, in his 1937 article Lyman treats hooked rugs as a timeless and natural part of an ageless culture.

Both the Liberal government of Québec and the Canadian Handicrafts Guild probably acted out of a real desire to help rural people. I am convinced, however, that a major underlying reason for the government's enthusiasm for 'characteristic interest' was that tourists were attracted to 'truly Canadian' products and tourism meant economic growth. In any case, Québec's Minister of Agriculture declared in 1934 that:

> there is improvement, that taste is developing, and that a Canadian art is rapidly forming. Our rural homes are being embellished with draperies, bed-covers and Canadian carpets which harmonise with the styles of our old houses, and we can count thousands of farmers' families now exclusively dressed in cloth woven at home from wool and flax raised on the farm. The surplus supplies of such production is finding a ready market amongst tourists and our urban populations.[35]

The idea of a natural surplus of hooked rugs and homespuns was also invoked by Lyman when he talked about increasing production by taking 'the flower of the natural crop'; but obviously the rugs that Lyman liked to acquire when he drove up to a farmhouse were available because he and tourists like him were expected.

John Lyman should not have presumed, in 1937, to find French Canadians living in a mythical pre-industrial past. It is especially odd that he mentioned the trip from Québec to Montréal because Trois-Rivières, a town along the north shore between the two cities, had, in addition to other manufacturing, the largest paper mill in the world. Lyman should have realized that rural people, like everyone else, respond to transitions towards modernity with new attitudes toward clothing, house furnishings, and the use of their time. He should have understood that as a tourist he himself was gradually changing life and work in rural Québec. But Lyman was dreaming the modernist dream of an ageless world purer than his own, to which he could still feel superior.

In *Gone Primitive: Savage Intellects and Modern Lives*, Marianna Torgovnick attacked British critic Roger Fry for wrongly assigning to African cultures the 'want of a conscious critical sense and the intellectual powers of comparison and classification.'[36] Fry allowed them intuition and creativity but denied them 'culture.' Culture needed a system of aesthetics: it needed him. Lyman's concept of the folk artist is just like Roger Fry's concept of the primitive – she is an uncultivated visionary whose work, Lyman claimed, sprang from native impulses and instinct, and was 'supported by so little power of conscious thought that any attempt to interfere with its natural processes must dislocate the conditions of creative production.'[37] A being close to nature, Lyman's folk artist could be understood on an aesthetic level only by someone as sophisticated as himself.

'Poison in the Well' failed to mention Simone-Mary Bouchard, who lived near Baie-Saint-Paul and who, along with her sisters and mother, made hooked rugs for sale to tourists at a shop in Pointe-au-Pic. Rug-making was one of several strategies the family had for surviving the Depression.[38] Simone-Mary Bouchard drew rural scenes for these rugs, and eventually, while keeping up the rugs, started painting as well.

Bouchard repaired some old textiles for Barbeau in 1936 and she also made some rugs for Jean Palardy, a painter and a friend of Lyman. Palardy had explored Charlevoix for three summers in the early 1930s as Barbeau's assistant and he also designed hooked rugs, some of which were made by Charlevoix women for the department store owner Henry Morgan (Lyman's Montréal cousin).[39] Palardy and Barbeau saw Mary Bouchard's paintings at her family home in 1936. Barbeau put her in touch with American artists Maud and Patrick Morgan (more relatives of Lyman) who summered at La Malbaie and who gave exhibitions of Charlevoix painters there from 1934 to 1939.

When the Morgans showed some of the Charlevoix 'modern primitives,' including Bouchard, at a New York City gallery in December 1937, Lyman complained in his *Montrealer* column. 'The chief value of these manifestations is to underline the fact that the creative impulse is a very different thing from learning how to paint or model according to school formulas ... But the absence of conventional proficiency is not equivalent to the unified force of primitive tradition. In reality the modern primitives are not primitive at all; they could be more correctly called elementary. They are on the margin of a self-conscious society.' Lyman found these artists neither pure and natural enough to be folk nor sophisticated enough to be modern. One, Yvonne Bolduc (who happened to be a friend of Bouchard), even 'began by making hooked rugs in imitation of pictures by Mr. Coburn and Mr. Clarence Gagnon, which is about as far as possible from simple-minded candour.'[40] Evidently Lyman did not know about the rug connection in Bouchard's case, nor did he refer to another exhibitor, Georges-Edouard Tremblay, a neighbour of Bouchard who began by drawing designs for his fiancée's hooked rugs, went on to paint designs, and, with the encouragement of Oscar Bériau, eventually became not only a painter but head of a hooked 'wall rug' business as well.[41] Clearly Lyman wanted to keep his categories and his cultures separate and distinct; but that was his problem, not the problem of these painters. Making pictorial hooked rugs, which after all are easel-sized rectangles, could easily slide over into painting if you were not worried about one being folk art and the other art.

Mary Bouchard's paintings appeared at the Art Association of Montreal in 1940, and the following spring she showed in Québec and Montréal with ten of Canada's most modern artists, including Paul-Émile Borduas, Alfred Pellan, and Lyman himself. That fall she became a member of the Contemporary Art Society in Montréal, and a mere two years later she was described by a Montréal writer and critic as one of the Contemporary Art Society's eminent senior artists.[42] The artist Françoise Sullivan, in the Université de Montréal's *Quartier latin* magazine, named her 'our most powerful woman painter' and writer Gilles Hénault applauded her 'truly miraculous' pictures.[43]

Two pictures by Mary Bouchard were included in the exhibition 'Aspects of Contemporary Painting in Canada' that opened at the Addison Gallery at Phillips Academy in Andover, Massachusetts, in September 1942 and later travelled to a number of cities in the United States. Seven other Charlevoix artists, including Yvonne Bolduc, Georges-Edouard Tremblay, and Bouchard's sister Marie-Cécile, were also represented among the sixty-seven paintings. John Lyman's review of the exhibition, 'Canadian Art Show in US is Best Yet Sent Abroad,' was published a Montréal newspaper. Lyman was now less negative, wanting to support the show overall: the Charlevoix side of the show may have been 'a little overdone, but if so we can easily accept it as a wholesome corrective, for the light-fingered imagery of these untaught artists, though uneven, has far more of the true creative spark than plenty of more knowing work that is often seen in our exhibitions.'[44] Nevertheless his tone was still condescending, and he still maintained boundaries between the knowing 'moderns' and the instinctive 'primitives' as did most of his peers.

There is no evidence that this concerned Mary Bouchard at all. She continued to exhibit and win prizes in urban exhibitions until her death in 1945. In an autobiographical note, she wrote, in her idiosyncratic style:

> je fis d'autres peintures pour les expositions de Montreal et de Québec et la plus par de mes tableaux fur vendu à New York par M. Morgan. En dix-neuf-cent-trente-six Japportait pour les tapis crocheter le premier prix à Montréal, l'ané suivante à Québec et dans la suite pour la peinture. A l'exposition provinciale de Québec dix-neuf-cent-trente neuf, le troisième prix pour la peinture l'ané suivante le deuxieme et en quarante un le premier pour la peinture. Je vis par mes succès que ma nature artistiques grandissait ...[45]

NOTES

1 James Naremore and Patrick Brantlinger, 'Introduction: Six Artistic Cultures,' in *Modernity and Mass Culture*, ed. James Naremore and Patrick Brantlinger (Bloomington and Indianapolis: Indiana University Press, 1991), 11–12.

2 Richard Handler, 'In Search of the Folk Society: Nationalism and Folklore Studies in Québec,' *Culture* 3 (1983), 107.
3 Victor Morin, 'Nos Traditions populaires,' *Veillées du bon vieux temps à la bibliothèque Saint-Sulpice à Montréal, les 18 mars et 24 avril 1919 sous les auspices de la Société historique de Montréal et de la Société de folklore d'Amérique (section de Québec)* (Montréal: G. Ducharme, 1920), 94–5.
4 Marius Barbeau, preface, *Veillées du bon vieux temps*, 1; and Laurence Nowry, *Man of Mana: Marius Barbeau* (Toronto: NC Press, 1995), 186–9.
5 Wilfrid Bovey, *The French Canadians To-Day: A People on the March* (Toronto: J.M. Dent & Sons [Canada], 1938), 118; and Paul-André Linteau, Réne Durocher, and Jean-Claude Robert, *Québec: A History 1867–1929*, trans. Robert Chodos (Toronto: James Lorimer & Company, 1983), 324.
6 Constance Cromarty, 'Seigniories – Weaving-Looms and Homespuns: An Article on the Quaint Old French Settlements along the North Shore of the Lower St. Lawrence,' *Canadian Magazine* 63 (August 1924), 198.
7 *Canadian Folk Song and Handicrafts Festival, under the Auspices of the National Museum of Canada, Chateau Frontenac, Quebec, May 20–22, 1927* (pamphlet), inside cover.
8 Yolande Lavoie, *L'émigration des Québécois aux États-Unis de 1840 à 1930* (Québec: Conseil de la langue française, Gouvernement du Québec, 1981); and Yves Roby, 'Un Québec émigré aux Etats-Unis: bilan historiographique,' in *Textes de l'exode: recueil des textes sur l'émigraton des québécois aux États-Unis* (XIXe et XXe siècles) (Montréal: Guerin littérature, 1987), 113ff.
9 Philippe Dubé, avec la collaboration de Jacques Blouin, photographe, *200 ans de villégiature dans Charlevoix* (Québec: Les Presses de l'Université Laval, 1986), 6.
10 Ibid., 132.
11 Marius Barbeau, 'L'artisanat chez nous: une industrie à developper,' *L'Événement* (Québec) 23 janvier 1935.
12 William Carless, 'The Murray Bay Festival,' *Canadian Homes and Gardens* 6 (November 1929), 82–4.
13 Dubé, *200 ans de villégiature*, 1.
14 Victoria A. Baker, with the collaboration of Richard Dubé and François Tremblay, *Images de Charlevoix 1784–1950/Scenes of Charlevoix 1784–1950* (Montréal: Musée des beaux-arts de Montréal, 1982), 25, 27.
15 René Boissay, *Clarence Gagnon*, trans. Raymond Chamberlain (Ottawa: Marcel Broquet, 1988), 181 and 106, plate 50; and Hugues de Jouvancourt, *Clarence Gagnon* (Montréal: Éditions La Frégate, 1970), 50–62.
16 A.Y. Jackson to F.B. Housser, quoted in F.B. Housser, *A Canadian Art Movement: The Story of the Group of Seven* (Toronto: Macmillan, 1926), 201.
17 Ibid., 201.
18 Baker, *Images de Charlevoix*, 37–57
19 Lynda Jessup, 'Canadian Artists, Railways, the State and "The Business of Becoming a Nation,"' (PhD diss., University of Toronto, 1992), 48–9.
20 Canadian Museum of Civilization, Marius Barbeau Collection, Barbeau Correspondence, f. 'A.Y. Jackson,' Jackson to Barbeau (late 1925); quoted in Jessup, 'Canadian Artists,' 53.

21 *Exhibitions of the Group of 7 & Art in French Canada* (Toronto: Art Gallery of Toronto, 1926), 8.
22 Jessup, 'Canadian Artists,' 7–8, 58–98.
23 *Canadian Folk Song and Handicrafts Festival*
24 Nowry, *Man of Mana*, 284.
25 Arthur Lismer, 'Art a Common Necessity,' *Canadian Bookman* 7 (October 1925), 159–60; also published in *Edmonton Journal*, 14 November 1925.
26 Victor Morin, quoted in anon., 'Suggests Museum for Handicrafts,' *Montreal Gazette*, 19 October 1931.
27 John Lyman, 'Poison in the Well,' in 'Art,' *Montrealer* 11 (1 September 1937), 17.
28 Wilfrid Bovey, *Canadien: A Study of the French Canadians* (London, Toronto & Vancouver: J.M. Dent and Sons, 1933), 137, 152; and Michel Bérard, *Les Routes du Québec* (Quebec: Ministère de la Voirie, 1964).
29 Oscar A. Bériau, 'The Handicraft Renaissance in Quebec,' *Canadian Geographical Journal* 7 (September 1933), 147.
30 Bériau, 'The Handicraft Renaissance in Quebec,' 148–9; Bériau, 'Domestic Crafts in Quebec,' *Quebec* 9 (April 1934), 38.
31 Richard Dubé and François Tremblay, *Peindre un pays: Charlevoix et ses peintres populaires* (Ottawa: Éds. Broquet, 1989), 8.
32 Ella Shannon Bowles, *Handmade Rugs* (1927), quoted in William C. Ketchum, *Hooked Rugs: A Historical and Collector's Guide: How to Make Your Own* (New York: Harcourt Brace Jovanovitch, 1976), 63.
33 Margaret Lathrop Law, 'The Hooked Rugs of Nova Scotia,' *House Beautiful* (July 1928), 58; quoted in Ian McKay, *The Quest of the Folk: Antimodernism and Cultural Selection in Twentieth-Century Nova Scotia* (Kingston and Montrèal: McGill-Queen's University Press, 1994), 162.
34 This is the consensus both of sources in Lyman's time and of more recent writers on the subject. See Elizabeth Waugh and Edith Foley, *Collecting Hooked Rugs* (New York & London: The Century Co., 1927); Marius Barbeau, 'The Hooked Rug – Its Origin,' *Transactions of the Royal Society of Canada*, 3rd Series, 36 (1942), 25–32; Ramsay Traquair, 'Hooked Rugs in Canada,' *Canadian Geographical Journal* 36 (May 1943), 240–54; Ketchum, *Hooked Rugs*; and Max Allen, 'Canadian Hooked Rugs,' *Artisan News* 3 (Spring 1980), 10–12.
35 Hon. Adélard Godbout, 'Agriculture of Québec Moves Towards New Era of Well-being,' *Quebec* 9 (September 1934), 119.
36 Marianna Torgovnick, *Gone Primitive: Savage Intellects, Modern Lives* (Chicago: University of Chicago Press, 1990), 93–4; Roger Fry, *Vision and Design* (London: Chatto & Windus, 1920), 68.
37 Lyman, 'Poison in the Well,' 17.
38 Dubé and Tremblay, *Peindre un pays*, 64.
39 Jean-Marie Gauvreau, *Artisans du Québec* (Trois-Rivières: Les Éditions du bien public, 1940), 87.
40 John Lyman, 'Hunting the Primitive in Canada,' *Montrealer* (1 January 1938), 19.
41 Dube and Tremblay, *Piendre un pays*, 129–34.
42 Pierre Daniel [Robert Elie], 'De Borduas à M. Bouchard: Exposition de la Société d'Art contemporain à la Galerie des Arts,' *La Presse (Montreal)*, 14 novembre 1942.

43 Françoise Sullivan, 'La peinture féminine,' in 'La peinture canadienne,' *Le quartier latin* 26 (17 décembre 1943), ii; Gilles Hénault, 'La question du primitivisme' in 'La peinture canadienne,' *Le quartier latin* 26 (17 décembre 1943), vii.

44 John Lyman, 'Canadian Art Show in U.S. Is Best Yet Sent Abroad,' *The Standard* (Montreal), 24 October 1942.

45 Mary Bouchard, manuscript ca. 1940–5, private collection, 44 pp. Simone-Mary Bouchard's idiosyncratic spellings and grammar are at least partly the result of her lack of education. She left school at age 14 to help her mother manage their family (typescript biography of Simone-Mary Bouchard by her sister Edith Bouchard, artist's file, National Gallery of Canada Library).

CHAPTER SEVEN

Handicrafts and the Logic of 'Commercial Antimodernism': The Nova Scotia Case

Ian McKay

The postcolonial dilemma confronting inter-war Canadian nationalists was this: how to develop a powerful set of stories and symbols through which a British 'Dominion' – by definition, a territory held by force of British arms, a polity whose separate political existence was legitimized in terms of dynastic power and British imperialism – could become a Canadian nation. Their mission was to evolve an official nationalism through which (in Benedict Anderson's words) 'the short, tight skin of the nation' could be stretched over the old, gigantic, transcontinental body of empire.[1] To meet this challenge, such cultural producers as the Group of Seven, new-liberal and Laurentian historians, and political novelists (running the gamut from Hugh MacLennan to Dorothy Dumbrille) began to 'narrate the nation' in ways which stressed the inevitability and goodness of Canada. A general strategy was to ground this new 'Canada' on the bedrock truth of the landscape; equally pervasive was a rhetoric of blood, soil, nordicity, Folk, and so on. There was little here that any student of twentieth-century nationalism would find surprising, except, perhaps, the fact that with the exception of a few areas and people, the new definitions did not really take hold. Canadian novels did not, by and large, set the framework within which a majority of Canadians 'imagined' a new community; Canadian paintings, although frequently found on the walls of banks (as a 'natural' part of standardized corporate iconostases) did not establish a consensus about the ultimate 'natural' signifier of Canadianness. This failure to 'naturalize' Canada makes the lavish Ontario celebrations of the Group of Seven in 1995 an ironic and melancholy exercise in nostalgia – a visual homage, one might almost say, to the official nationalism of the Former Canada.

Why did this moment of nationalism leave such a minor legacy? Leaving aside the difficult geopolitical challenge of imagining a new national community in northern North America, one can note three pivotal weaknesses of the nationalists: their elitist preoccupations, along with their insistent focus on safeguarding high culture and their place within it, which distanced them from most Canadians with their unregenerately 'popular' tastes; their hesitant and partial imagined break with Britain, which distinctly limited the extent to which they could articulate a convincing new concept of Canada; and finally, their failure to construct a truly hegemonic discourse of nation, founded on both cultural consent and state coercion, in which the disparate *ethnies*, territories, provinces, regions (not merely a self-selected central Canadian elite) could all recognize themselves. Building with internationally accredited materials – the Call of the Blood, the Voice of the Folk, Nature, Race, Land, and so forth – the organic intellectuals of the putative Canadian 'nation' failed to articulate these ideas to the projected 'people-nation' on whose behalf they claimed to speak.

Because of the strikingly limited success of this new Canadian nationalism, even in the short term, cultural historians interested in twentieth-century antimodernism would be ill-advised to concentrate exclusively on the well-known nationalist cultural producers of central Canada. In the absence of a hegemonic national myth-symbol complex, in Canada one found a profusion of national, regional and provincial identities. Some of these were competitive with the new Canadian national definition (as in an emergent Québec nationalism with its Laurentian myth-symbol complex and its potent myth of *La race fondatrice*); others (such as emergent regionalisms in the West and in the Maritimes, which might be better seen as competitive versions of the new nationalism) were more ambiguously placed. All, it seems, drew on the same international current of antimodernism, which coincided exactly with the advent of the question of postcolonial identity in Canada. Commodification, the turn to a bedrock essentialist rhetoric, the pivotal role of the state in reshaping the symbolic order, even certain important cultural producers (such as Marius Barbeau and John Murray Gibbon): these are themes that can be traced on Canada-wide, regional and provincial levels. It would seem, however, at least to generalize from the Nova Scotia case, that symbolic landscapes (for example, Peggy's Cove), new definitions of ethnicity, and new concepts of the Folk and its culture were all constructed more successfully within the regions than in the country as a whole.

Handicrafts – an important a part of national and ethnic identities in Europe and North America – provide an interesting case in point. The history of the Canadian Handicrafts Guild was that of attempting to articulate to the Canadian project the many cultural traditions brought by recent immigrants. But the more penetrating and powerful interventions by cultural producers took place on more local levels. By the early twentieth century, most traditional handicrafts in Nova Scotia had been rendered obsolete by industrial capitalism: contrary to the pastoral myth of rural self-sufficiency, in many parts of Nova Scotia virtually nothing remained of the earlier 'older' ways. Prior to the 1940s, there had been isolated and sporadic attempts at a craft revival, which in the context of the collapse of many of the province's industries had emerged as one possible strategy for economic survival. The rise of the tourist industry in the interwar period (which in the Great Depression was greatly accelerated by a highly active state) created a new emphasis on crafts – especially carpets – as souvenirs. (So pronounced was the so-called hooked rug mania of the 1920s that one purist was already complaining about 'commercial dealers, of the lower sort,' many of them from the United States, descending upon the fishing villages in droves.) There was nonetheless an acute awareness that the province had lagged behind other North American jurisdictions; Québec and New Hampshire were commonly cited as places where handicraft revivals had been successfully engineered. When Québec handicrafts purists warned that traditional forms were being compromised by the pressures of feeding the insatiable appetite of American tourists, Nova Scotian craft revivalists may have seen this 'warning' as a promising indication of the economic growth handicrafts might prompt in their own province. At a time when the male breadwinner economy was in crisis, a Gaelic revival (which led to the creation of a Gaelic College at St Ann's) was underway in Cape Breton, and many rural women were actively scouting for ways of surviving, handicrafts seemed a logical and inexpensive avenue for a liberal (and for the most part Liberal) government to pursue. Tourists in search of an 'authentic souvenir,' and often enticed to Nova Scotia by the prospect of experiencing the older and better ways of the province, were ironically in the vanguard of commodifying activities which had been previously oriented to domestic use.

Despite some promising beginnings, there was a sense – which found acute expression at a large 1942 craft conference spearheaded by Catholic social activists – that the province was missing out on major revenues by failing to promote crafts. It was in response to this demand for action, and doubtless prompted by the prospect of doing something that appeared to be a response to the grave economic and social problems that were stimulating the rise of the socialist CCF party, that the Liberal government decided to act. In 1942, it issued a call to Mary Black, who was like so many Nova Scotians an economic exile from the economically troubled province, to return to organize an effective state-sponsored craft movement.

Mary Black (1895–1988) was an occupational therapist who became a world authority on weaving. She was a tough-minded and pragmatic professional, and had spent much of her career in the United States; in 1942 she returned to Nova Scotia to confront a sexist bureaucracy and indifferent, sometimes hostile, politicians. Her work in mental hospitals and other institutions had given her a profound respect for the wonders occupational therapy could achieve: it could rescue individuals from alcoholism, neuroses, and the effects of trauma. She did not hesitate to suggest that entire societies could also benefit in much the same way. Just as occupational therapy helped individuals recover from personal disorders, the development of crafts might help Nova Scotia recover from economic disaster.

Thus in one sense Mary Black shared with many other Canadian cultural producers of the 1930s and 1940s an antimodern sense of restoring the pride of craft and of regenerating the community; she unmistakably belongs in the same generation as Helen Creighton, Marius Barbeau, and Ramsay Traquair – all of whom also wrote on the handicrafts revival – not to mention equally interested members of the Group of Seven. In another respect, however, she suggests just how complex inter-war antimodernism could be, for she also drew directly on progressive arguments based on efficiency, productivity, and planning.

There was remarkably little nostalgia in Black's program for crafts in Nova Scotia. Her revealing diary notes contain slashing critiques of almost everything that 'craft workers' had achieved thus far in Nova Scotia. Black saw a province in which handicrafts had been marginalized by the factory and the department store – unsurprisingly, for by the 1940s Nova Scotia had experienced more than a century of sustained capitalist development. From mitten-making to weaving, Black found little that she liked: even the rugs, which had been sold to American tourists during the 1920s 'hooked rug mania,' received only a lukewarm endorsement. Most of these products, judged according to standards she believed to be universally valid, were poorly designed and hard on the eye. In many cases, one had to start over from scratch, to create handicrafts that attained an international standard.

The Nova Scotia craft movement was of a piece with so many other acts of retrieval and redescription in inter-war Canada: a *gemeinschaftlich* vocabulary of family, community, and intimacy was (through state policy and the conscious imposition of an ideology of absolute standards) made accessible to the *Gesellschaft* of modern capitalism. As an occupational therapist, Black had seen the hospital as the engine of redemption, and now the market came to play that same role: only through deeper and more profitable integration with the market (primarily through the sale of craft souvenirs to tourists) could the province's self-esteem be raised. Black did indeed champion 'older and better ways,' but she did so as a liberal progressive professional, guided by ideals of efficiency, competitiveness, moral therapy, and commerce. In her radical program – which was never realized through the small 'Handcrafts Division' she headed – the design and production of Nova Scotia crafts would be centrally co-ordinated; one could not really entrust to the rank-and-file Nova Scotia craft worker the intricacies of craft design. The mild version of this vision, which was brought into effect, was to make her Halifax office into something of a clearing house for craft designs; the stronger version was to require craft workers in outlying areas to work to the specifications of Halifax planners. Black also sought to modernize marketing, integrating handicrafts more completely into the existing machinery of tourism, and to subject craft workers to her own down-home version of panopticism, which she developed, not on the basis of Jeremy Bentham's prison system, but on the examples of the Duncan Hines inspectors. No doubt one can get into extraordinary convolutions when thinking about 'modernity,' modernism, and antimodernism, but in this case a rather convoluted expression – modernizing antimodernism – seems necessary and valuable in order to capture a reality in which a novel degree of market-driven state dictation and direction was seen as a decisive weapon in a struggle to invent new handicrafts, to reform the rest, and to make this new sector efficient and productive – all in the interests of providing tourists with material articles that spoke reassuringly of the older, better, more spacious days in which handicrafts flourished within pre-industrial communities.

Black's modern antimodernism influenced her specific prescriptions for the craft sector. Romantics had seen (and still see) one of the great attractions of craft production as being the integration of the public and the private realms: workplace and home, work and recreation. In contrast to the alienated wage worker abandoning his or her home and family for hours on end, the artisan (as wistfully imagined by the urban romantic) is a person for whom the pace of work is determined by the nature of the task at hand, and who works within the warm and friendly confusion of the household or workshop where firm lines between home and work are not drawn. Whatever the plausibility of this vision of 'pre-industrial labour,' which unrealistically forgets the role of the market economy in enforcing deadlines and exerting pressures, it left Black completely cold. Craftspeople selling from the home or guilds selling from their centres of production, should, she argued (in a programmatic statement of the 1940s) sell their products in the antiseptic settings that twentieth-century consumers demanded:

1. A special room or building with an entrance directly from the street should be set up and retained for the sale of handicrafts;
2. There should be no visible signs of living in the room or building nor sight of household activities being carried on through open doors;
3. There should not be any mingling of animals of [or] children with customers. Premise and goods must be clean and goods attractively displayed, preferably in cases.
4. Sale of goods should be restricted to own products of which a fair size stock must be carried at such times as the outlet is advertised as being open.[2]

Such modern marketing methods effectively cleansed the craft product of the taint of humble labour. The craft commodity's beauty could be appreciated abstractly, without the distraction of its real conditions of production in a (household or workshop) labour process. It could become a purer, better commodity, if it were decontextualized, freed from the burden of its history. Crafts could be relieved of their (unacknowledged) collective history, and be reborn as instances of romantic individualism: as isolated, spontaneous acts of individual creativity. 'Myth,' wrote Roland Barthes, 'deprives the object of which it speaks of all history. All that is left for one to do is to enjoy this beautiful object without wondering where it came from.'[3] And around these purified and beautiful commodities would grow up a scientific technology of marketing, a 'system ... whereby definite orders will be placed and a steady market assured,' a 1951 memorandum from the Division urged.[4]

Yet, if the handicrafts were to be deeply influenced by European (often Scandinavian) traditions of design and sometimes actually made by European craft workers (whose techniques were especially cherished by the Division), and if they were to be no less shaped by the preferences of the American tourists, what would be Nova Scotian about any of them? How could one indigenize what was, in essence, a set of newly invented craft forms? If they looked liked crafts found anywhere in the world, how could they function as 'signifiers' of Nova Scotianness for the souvenir-buying travelling public? The resolution of this dilemma could be found in *nature* itself. Black argued that, for generations, Nova Scotians had not correctly seen the landscape around them. They had been blind to the 'natural forms' of their own province, and – here was an opening for professional handicrafts workers – they required a sort of aesthetic therapy before they could be truly enlightened. Once Nova Scotians had been taught to see the natural forms around them and instructed on the ways in which these natural forms could best be represented in handicrafts, they would produce articles which were simultaneously *European* in design and *Nova Scotian* in inspiration. Like the Group of Seven, Black was concerned to develop a form in which one could see nature's true essence captured, as in a magic mirror.

We may conclude with two case studies of handicrafts and cultural transformation in twentieth-century Nova Scotia. The first comes from Chéticamp, on the western shore of Cape Breton Island. Before 1927, the women of Chéticamp had made bright rag carpets, often depicting local vessels and other aspects of their community life, which they sold to tourists but also used themselves. It was only with the visit of Lilian Burke that the women of Chéticamp 'learned how to see.' Burke was an occupational therapist from the United States – another one! – who was a guest of her friends, the Alexander Graham Bell family at their substantial summer home in Cape Breton. Burke's biggest innovation involved changing the designs and colour schemes. The bright primary colours disappeared as the women were taught to mix their colours to produce pastel tints. Their rugs were transformed from brightly coloured and locally designed products carrying images of fishing life to pale, understated symbols of Victorian formality and refinement. As the *National Geographic* enthused, 'Under the guidance of Miss Lilian Burke, a New York designer ... [g]arish, hard colors have been replaced with soft-toned pastels; stark, angular designs exchanged for graceful antique motifs of flowers, animals, and birds, or classic patterns.'[5] Everything about Chéticamp rug-making was transformed. The labour process was completely revolutionized, as Burke gradually increased the size of the carpets, brought more and more craft workers together under one roof, and firmly separated conception and execution: conception of the carpets' design took place in her New York office, while the detailed execution was left to the supervised workers in Chéticamp. It was, in essence, a reinvention of rural manufacture, and involved a stark discrepancy between the craft workers' risks and labour and the craft entrepreneurs profits and prestige. In the course of a strike in 1936–7 against low wages and high financial risks, Lilian Burke would argue that the ungrateful Chéticamp craft workers had in a sense engaged in a politics of cultural appropriation – an arresting moment in the province's history of antimodernism. But for all this turmoil, the new 'antique' form succeeded where it most had to succeed: among the tourists and in well-to-do homes up and down the Atlantic seaboard.

Important as the Chéticamp case is in suggesting the underlying logic of the interwar craft revival – that of inventing new 'antique' craft traditions in order to more firmly integrate local communities into the market – the more suggestive case, because it involved a form designed to represent the cultural essence of the entire province, was that of the Nova Scotia tartan.

The notion that Nova Scotia was in some essential sense 'Scottish' attained great influence in the second quarter of the twentieth-century. Angus L. Macdonald, the most influential premier of the period, was committed both to tourism and to a particularly romantic reading of Scottish history. Under his leadership, provincial funds were given to the Gaelic College (headed by a man who could not in fact speak Gaelic), key provincial tourism sites were 'tartaned' with Scottish names, and a brawny Scots piper was stationed at the Nova Scotia border. 'Tartanism' – the reading of Nova Scotia as a sort of Scott-land across the waves – triumphed; this concept of the Scottish essence (or 'Highland Heart') of Nova Scotia was accepted even by Nova Scotians who did not claim Scottish descent.[6] The actual 'tartan' at the centre of tartanism, however, was the direct outcome not of this labour of ethnic redescription but of the handicrafts revival. The Nova Scotia tartan was invented by an Englishwoman in 1953. It originated in Black's Handcrafts Division and represented its moment of triumph.

Although the Nova Scotia Sheep Breeders' Association was not renowned as a force for cultural innovation in the province, it was this Association's desire to mount an exhibition devoted to the uses of local wool that made the Nova Scotia tartan possible. The Handcrafts Division was invited to organize a special display as part of the exhibition. Black decided on a panel depicting archetypal Nova Scotians amid the changing seasons. Work began on 9 June 1953. Few problems were posed by the Acadian girl 'in traditional dress,' or the United Empire Loyalist surrounded by 'his wife and child, a hen and pet cat.' Then came the autumn panel of the mural, and with it a serious difficulty: a kilted Scottish shepherd – such as had probably never been seen in Cape Breton – was minding his sheep, duly assisted by his sheepdog, with the lone shieling in the background. (The shieling was a deft way of tying Scots romanticism in with handicrafts: a simulated 'lone shieling,' a humble shepherd's lodge commemorated in a famous poem expressing nostalgic longing for the Hebrides, had recently been reconstructed in Cape Breton.) Obviously a Scottish shepherd lolling about in front of a lone shieling in Cape Breton had to wear a tartaned kilt (although it was in fact highly doubtful if Cape Breton shepherds had ever actually done so). Which clan tartan should he wear? Confronted with this same dilemma in Cape Breton Highlands National Park, Premier Angus L. Macdonald had inclined, for reasons which were compelling for him, towards the Macdonald tartan. For the Halifax craft revivalists, however, the question seemed more difficult to resolve. It was a knotty problem, and neither 'tradition' or present practice offered many solutions. There was simply not much of a tradition of tartan weaving in Nova Scotia. As Florence Mackley notes in *Handweaving in Cape Breton*, although one 'would probably expect to find many of the old tartan setts in Cape Breton homes,' this was simply not so. Most of the early settlers were not accustomed to tartan weaving.[7]

Part of the handcraft revival involved the establishment by the Gaelic College at St Ann's of a handicraft centre that concentrated on weaving; the centre was officially opened by Premier A.S. MacMillan in July 1944. Black herself had taught at the College in the summers of 1943, 1944, and 1945, and had been distinctly unimpressed by the quality of the weaving. The College's tartan output received mixed reviews. Angus L. Macdonald, who had received a Clan Ranald couch throw compliments of the Craft Centre, gave the local product a glowing review.[8] Those more expert in the field were somewhat less generous. An expert Scotswoman visiting the province informed Black that the colours were 'rather garish.'[9] Yet garish or not, the tourists loved them. As early as 1947, demand far exceeded supply,[10] and by the mid-1950s, thanks to extensive state financial assistance and Black's sponsorship of the project, the weavers at St Ann's were turning out tartan by the ton.

But the growth of tartan production at St Ann's did not clarify the problem of which clan tartan the fancifully conceived Scottish shepherd should wear. It fell to Bessie Murray, an English embroiderer from Crewe, to tackle the issue. As was so characteristic of the entire craft revival, she found the answer not in any actual history of Nova Scotia or Cape Breton, but in nature itself. The Nova Scotia tartan, as she conceived it, was to be the direct imprint of the Terence Bay landscape, with its deep-blue lake set in a circle of bleached white granite. It would be Scottish in form, but natural in essence, its authenticity founded on the rockbound coast. As one account explains:

> Ah! Now things began to fall into place for her [Murray]. The blue of that water was the blue of the sea and the sky, with the autumal [*sic*] softness about it to suggest the name 'October blue' and the beautiful clear blue of the cross on the Nova Scotia flag. And there were also the dark and light greens, for the evergreen and deciduous trees characteristic of the province by the sea. The white of the rocks was in the flag too, as background, and in the surf that pounds the Nova Scotia coastline on all its sides except for a narrow band of land that binds it to the rest of Canada. It remained only to add the gold to represent Nova Scotia's Royal character and the red to symbolize the lion rampant on the Nova Scotia crest on the flag.[11]

This historical account by Marjorie Major of Mrs Murray's ecstatic vision is itself an interesting attempt to develop a romantic narrative of romantic individualism within the context of a state cultural enterprise. Whether it happened in just this visionary way is doubtful. Black later observed that Murray had had some sort of 'Nova Scotia tartan' design in her mind sometime before the project came up, and Major herself notes the extensive book study of tartans the English embroiderer required in order to produce the tartan in time for the display.[12] Neither the English-born Murray nor the American-born Black were in any sense experts on Scottish tartans.[13]

What is more important, the 'Eureka!' version of the history of the Nova Scotia tartan understates how deeply structured this happy accident was. Had it occurred in another context (say, in a private workshop in Chéticamp or in a purely commercial setting such as Eaton's), the tartan would never have been 'naturalized' as a symbol of all Nova Scotia. But this invention occurred within (and by means of) a division of the state, which had been preoccupied for over a decade with creating an 'authentic' Nova Scotian handicraft tradition that would be simultaneously 'natural' and 'commercial.' The tartan was the precise exemplification of the ideals of handicraft development that Black had been working towards since the 1940s. It was professionally designed, European in its origins and structure, supposedly a direct reflection of nature, and devoid of even the slightest connection with Nova Scotian history. Bessie Murray, in a heartfelt thanks to Black for her support, wrote in 1961: 'I want you to know that I shall always feel that you were the real one who started the tartan.'[14] This modest acknowledgment of her friend's assistance contained a real insight: without Black and the state presence in the Handcrafts Division, this invented tradition would likely never have emerged in the first place.

Nor would it have ever been naturalized except in a tourism state mobilising Scottish forms for the purposes of promotion. Although the shepherd's costume occupied only a minuscule portion of a very large mural, the tartan stole the 1953 show. By the time of the 'Craftsmen-at-Work' exhibition in Antigonish in July 1954, the Division had made enough tartan to dress models in the material: soon there were requests for curling skirts and slippers. Black and Murray repaired to the office of Premier Macdonald. The Premier – also known as The Grand Noble Chief of the Clans of Nova Scotia – was, unsurprisingly, very sympathetic to the idea of a Nova Scotia tartan. The Tartan Question – should this tartan receive state recognition? – went to the provincial cabinet. After due deliberation, the idea was favourably referred to the Lord Lyon, King of Arms, the Scottish official in charge of such matters. The Lord Lyon found the idea rather unusual. Tartans were supposed to stand for clans, not political units, and a tartan for a province was a novelty. It was all rather perplexing, but in the end he approved the tartan, with the quaint proviso that a 'governmentally-sponsored tartan should not come into conflict with the clan system and sentiment.' The anxious Lord was reassured that none of the supposed Nova Scotia 'clans' would be compelled to wear the tartan at pistol-point, and the tartan was duly registered. A symbol supposedly confined to pre-industrial clans had now been appropriated by a modern state.[15] Over the next forty years, provinces, cities, and even Queen's University would be clamouring for the honour of their own recently invented tartans, all indirectly thanks to the small Handcrafts Division headed by Mary Black.

In the summer of 1954, less than a year after the little tartan patch had appeared on the tiny figure of the Cape Breton shepherd in the Sheep Breeders' Mural, it was draped over the six-foot-four body of the brawny Scots piper who piped tourists across the New Brunswick/Nova Scotia border. For Mary Black, the sight was a revelation: 'When you first saw the piper at a distance his kilt and plaidie blended into a lovely soft blue-grey but as your car came up the slope the blue brightened and all the greens took on their own individual values and then the colours in the smaller units came into focus and there was the much-discussed new Nova Scotia Tartan.'[16] Although there was an element of serendipity in the emergence of this particular tartan at this particular time, there was nothing accidental about the existence of a state oriented to tourism, willing and able to redefine the meaning of the tartan. It had the means and the will to make the Nova Scotia tartan more official than any number of floral designs in Chéticamp, going so far as to incorporate the tartan into the Armorial Bearings of the province in 1964. (It can now be used only with the Province's permission.) And it had the means and the will to broadcast news of the tartan far and wide. The Handicrafts Bureau fed articles to the CBC, to the *Family Herald* and *Weekly Star*, and to *Newsweek*; it adopted the tartan for the July 1954 issue of *Handcrafts*. Soon the tartan was everywhere – on books, on Bulletins of the Board of Trade, on the provincial *Journal of Education*, on the jackets of the Tourist Bureau Staff, and on a new set of contour maps put out by the Mapping Division of the Department of Mines. When the Liberal member for Pictou West entered the Legislature in 1955, on St Patrick's Day, to launch an appeal for an 'authentic Scottish or Hebridean village' in Pictou County, he took care to wear the Nova Scotia Tartan. The tartan's commercial success was assured: the Division was soon fielding requests for use of the tartan from a English playing card company and a Manhattan manufacturer of bath robes. Its political success was no less dramatic. When the Liberals met to select a successor to Angus L. Macdonald, they requested a piece of tartan for the centre table at their banquet. Political acceptance could go no further.[17]

The business response was no less enthusiastic. The Eaton's department store helped transport yarn to Terence Bay for the first consignment of men's tartan ties and marketed tartan clothes aggressively.[18] A company, the Nova Scotia Tartan Limited, was formed on 6 August 1954, with Bessie Murray as president and holder of a controlling interest of the stock. By 1955, the new company was in business, employing about 45 people in manufacturing, supervising, selling, and bookkeeping. Later the operation moved to Yarmouth, where it was eventually absorbed by Bonda Textiles Ltd. In 1964, a new 'dress tartan' was introduced by the company and officially registered in Canada, Great Britain, the United States, West Germany, and elsewhere.[19] The tartan had cash value. In 1973, Bessie Murray rejected an offer that Bonda Textiles pay the annual registration fee for Nova Scotia Tartan Limited in return for the option to purchase the name. 'I have ascertained from several sources that the tax loss is worth a minimum of $5,000 and that the name itself is worth a considerable amount. It has been suggested that a reasonable amount would be the equivalent of the tax loss making a total of $10,000.'[20] This was a tidy sum for a piece of cultural property and a name, both of which had been developed with public money and under state guidance. The state had smoothed the path to profits and hastened the pace of commodification.

Here was Chéticamp commercialization writ large, a tribute to Mary Black and the cultural power of the twentieth-century tourism state. In both cases, traditions that marginalized older forms in the interests of commercialisation had been invented in the name of 'recovering' a lost handicraft essence. As had been the case in Chéticamp, the new form encountered resistance. The Nova Scotia Association of Scottish Societies withdrew its recognition of the tartan, and the senior Scottish society in the province, the Antigonish Highland Society, expressed its adamant disapproval at a meeting on St Andrew's night in 1954:

> A warm discussion arose over the merits of the new Nova Scotia tartan. Most members disapproved of the tartan as an innovation too likely to spread and be abused. They felt that if a Nova Scotia tartan could be arranged, then why not a New Glasgow tartan or an Antigonish tartan or a Halifax tartan. Some also frowned on the marketing of the tartan as being too monopolistic. The tartan can only be obtained from one source, while older and authorized clan tartans could be manufactured by any number of firms ... One member gained much support when he protested the clothing of the piper at the N.S. border in the new tartan. The incoming president, Rod C. Chisholm, stated his opposition to the tartan on the grounds that anyone in the province could wear it, whether of Scots descent or not.[21]

This by no means exhausted the objections – economic, political, aesthetic – of the Antigonish Highland Society. The members of the Society had grasped a key point: the tartan no longer signified anything about the Scottish traditions to which the Society was attached. They glimpsed what full commodification would do to something that they, as cultural conservatives, cared about. But their words were easily forgotten and marginalized in a wave of favourable, state-orchestrated publicity. One of the great paradoxes of intervention-induced cultural change, David Whisnant argues suggestively, 'is its very durability and the degree to which imported forms and styles are accepted and defended by local people whose actual cultural traditions they altered or displaced.'[22] The tartan is now an uncontroversial (if not quite the ultimate) signifier of Nova Scotia, and it has indeed been copied far and wide throughout Canada within competing regional vocabularies of tourism. Freed from its (tenuous) moorings in the clan and redescribed as a mirror of the province's (newly) archetypal rockbound coast, the tartan had been fully commodified and was now far beyond the reach of those for whom tartans had once meant something specific. It had become a key element in an imagined Nova Scotia that the tourism state was calling into being.

A characteristic of Canadian antimodernism – this recoil from modernity and the pursuit of true essences, untainted pasts, heroes of the race – was the extent to which the search for cultural 'bedrock' so often took the form of the representation of the actual landscapes that brought one back, if not to bedrock, then at least to 'nature' stripped of humanity, reduced to its vital essentials, unforgiving and unrelenting in its superhuman agency and power. Perhaps we already know some of the places to look for this sensibility and the critical statements that must now be made about this so-called 'Art for a Nation.' But the Nova Scotia case suggests that we should also look in less obvious places. Antimodernism deeply influenced Canadian cultural life, but it did so in ways that confirmed rather than effaced the many other-than-national identities across the Canadian subcontinent.

NOTES

The core of this paper is drawn from chapter 3 of my *The Quest of the Folk: Antimodernism and Cultural Selection in Twentieth-Century Nova Scotia* (Montreal and Kingston: McGill-Queen's University Press, 1994), to which the reader in search of fuller references is referred.

1 Benedict Anderson, *Imagined Communities: Reflections on the Origin and Spread of Nationalism* (London and New York: Verso, 1983), 86.
2 Public Archives of Nova Scotia [hereafter PANS], Mary Black Papers, MG1, vol. 2878, f. 28, Mary Black, undated memorandum to S.J. Montgomery.
3 Roland Barthes, *Mythologies*, trans. Annette Lavers (Frogmore, St Albans: Paladin, 1973), 151.
4 PANS, Black Papers, vol. 2878, f. 29, memorandum of D. MacDonald, 21 March 1951.
5 Andrew Brown, 'Salty Nova Scotia: In Friendly New Scotland Gaelic Songs Still Answer the Skirling Bagpipes,' *National Geographic* 77 (May 1940), 614.
6 See Ian McKay, *In the Province of History* (forthcoming).
7 Florence Mackley, *Handweaving in Cape Breton* (Sydney: privately published, 1967), 43.
8 PANS, Angus L. Macdonald Papers, MG2, vol. 921, f. 31–9h/62, Mrs. A.W.R. (Angie) MacKenzie to A.L. Macdonald
9 PANS, Macdonald Papers, MG2, vol. 921, f. 31–9L/56, Mary Black to Angus L. Macdonald, 20 November 1946.
10 Nova Scotia, *Journals of the House of Assembly* (Industry and Publicity) 1947, 112.
11 Marjorie Major, 'History of the Nova Scotia Tartan,' *Nova Scotia Historical Quarterly* 2 (June 1976), 197.
12 PANS, Black Papers, MG1, vol. 2880, f. 62, Mary Black, 'To Whom It May Concern,' n.d., 'Re Origin of the Nova Scotia Tartan.' Black's concern was to defend the sole authorship of Bessie Murray.
13 PANS, Black Papers, vol. 2142, f. 3, Mary Black to Eleanor C. Hayes, Lily Mills Co., 22 January 1957.
14 PANS, Black Papers, vol. 2880, f. 63, Bessie Murray to Mary Black, 14 September 1961.
15 Major, 'History of the Nova Scotia Tartan,' 198–9.
16 PANS, Black Papers, MG1, vol. 2878, f. 30, Mary Black, 'The Nova Scotia Tartan and a Cloth of Gold Dress.'
17 Major, 'History of the Nova Scotia Tartan,' 206–7; PANS, Black Papers, Black Diary Notes, 19 August 1953, 1 May, 4, 23, 26 August, 3 September, 1954; Nova Scotia, *Journal of the House of Assembly* (Trade and Industry) 1956, 56–7.

18 'Nova Scotian Products Featured at Eaton's Right Now!' *Halifax Mail Star*, 7 July 1967.

19 PANS, Black Papers, vol. 2880, Minutes of the Annual Meeting of Nova Scotia Tartan Limited, 18 August 1964. For the purposes of identification and advertising, it was not possible to state explicitly that the dress tartan was the 'dress version' of the official Nova Scotia Tartan, because the rights in connection with the official tartan had been vested by Statute in the Government of Nova Scotia. This was neatly and misleadingly circumvented by a card attached to the garments in the dress tartan, which read, 'Dress Tartan, Nova Scotia Tartan Limited.' See PANS, Black Papers, vol. 2880, no. 63, f. 'Nova Scotia Tartan Ltd. (Halifax): 1955–1973.'

20 PANS, Black Papers, MG1, vol. 2880, f. 63, Bessy Murray to Mr J. DeGooyer, Bonda Textiles, 29 September 1973 (copy).

21 *Antigonish Casket*, 2 December 1954.

22 David Whisnant, *All That Is Native & Fine: The Politics of Culture in an American Region* (Chapel Hill and London: University of North Carolina Press, 1983), 100.

CHAPTER EIGHT

Bushwhackers in the Gallery: Antimodernism and the Group of Seven

Lynda Jessup

As far as Canadian Art concerns me, it can go to - - -. There never will be a school of Canadian art. The natural centre for Eastern Canadian artists will be New York, and it will be better for themselves and their art when they realize it.

A.Y. Jackson, 1 October 1910[1]

Decorum likely dictated Jackson's use of three dashes instead of 'hell,' but I suspect his words are nonetheless shocking to Canadians steeped in the mythology of the Group of Seven and its fight for 'a distinctively Canadian art.' Coming from one of the foremost members of the Group and, for a large part of the twentieth century, Canada's poster boy for cultural nationalism, these words rank with his now famous 1910 comment that the Georgian Bay landscape, which the Group would later celebrate, was 'not quite paintable.'[2] Both suggest a counternarrative to the accepted story of the Group of Seven, the story most recently advanced by the National Gallery of Canada in its 1995 exhibition 'The Group of Seven: Art for a Nation.' The accepted account posits the idea that the Group of Seven was, and is, populist; that they were advocates of cultural democracy, and that theirs was an art expressive of an essential Canadianism. In the 1995 show a reformulated version of the story served as underpinning to the idea that the Group of Seven was a beleaguered avant-garde, fighting the academy and, in doing so, struggling to bring art to the Canadian people. Thus the artists' subsequent victory, we are told, was, and continues to be, that of all Canadians.[3]

As feel-good history of the inclusive sort, this story also asserts the importance of the National Gallery of Canada, which has consistently identified itself with the Group's populist position. In the 1995 show this was perhaps nowhere more apparent than in the description of the 1924 controversy surrounding the Gallery's selection of works for the Canadian Section of the British Empire Exhibition at Wembley, England. There, arguing in a manner consistent with his thesis that 'the real battle was between the ancients and the moderns,' exhibition curator Charles Hill represented the recorded conflict arising from the Royal Canadian Academy's association of the National Gallery both with the

Group members' interests and with efforts to diminish the Academy's previously unchallenged authority to choose representative Canadian works for international exhibitions. 'At issue,' he explained of what amounted to a public struggle for power, 'was whether artists (the Academy) or lay people (the board and director of the National Gallery) should establish standards for Canadian art.'[4]

His choice of words, it seems to me, is important, for it could just as easily, and at this juncture perhaps more appropriately, be argued that what this transfer of authority to the National Gallery exemplified was not the democratization of aesthetic opinion, but rather the professionalization of the cultural field and the shift evidenced elsewhere during this period to bureaucratically oriented, hierarchical cultural institutions modelled on the modern business corporation.[5] Such an approach would set the Group of Seven's activities, which were more often than not intimately connected with such institutions, in the context of a broader, international experience in the early twentieth-century Western world. That experience is clearly associated with the process of rationalization characteristic of the transformation of nineteenth-century entrepreneurial capitalism to the modern corporate capitalism of the twentieth century. In a word, we call that experience 'modernity' – what Ian McKay has succinctly described as 'the lived experience of [an] unremitting process of rapid change and its social consequences.'[6]

Reluctance to see the Group of Seven in relation to such broader trends in the history of culture in the West – to see them instead only in the context of a Canadian scene isolated from larger international currents – perpetuates the self-fulfilling claim witnessed in the literature to date that the artists were, and thus remain today, 'distinctively Canadian.'[7] Apart from the fact that it smacks of parochialism, the problem with this limited perspective is that as a result the role of the Group of Seven in the history of Canadian art has been misunderstood. Simply put, the Group was not, as we have been told, demotic in its stance. Nor was their work expressive of an essential Canadianism. On the contrary, the Group, affected by the managerial restructuring of Western society in a manner similar to that of their counterparts on both sides of the Atlantic during these years, actually helped to reformulate the cultural authority of the nation's Anglo-Canadian elite.

Of course, one reason it is difficult to see the Group of Seven in the light of early twentieth-century modernity is that the artists positioned themselves so stridently in opposition to it. Consider the Group's polemic, which was largely fashioned in a flurry of publications by future members A.Y. Jackson, Arthur Lismer, and J.E.H. MacDonald prior to its collective, and often cryptic, presentation in the Group's exhibition catalogues of the 1920s.[8] Based on a conflation of avant-gardism and arts-and-crafts aestheticism, it was nothing less than an all-embracing critique of modern production, both artistic and industrial. 'We [Canadians] are the poor victims of standardization,' Lismer argued in 1919, 'the acceptors of the impositions of so-called experts, and at the mercy of whatever kinds of goods the manufacturers and distributors wish to impose ...'

goods 'that reflect neither taste nor utility.'[9] The only difference between industrial products and fine art in Canada was the cost, a point Jackson whimsically brought to the fore at about the same time in his story of the Buckeye Picture Company, a pot-boiler factory on Toronto's Yonge Street where the then-current taste for quasi-nineteenth-century-European art was met by paintings replicated in quantity and priced accordingly at about twenty dollars each. As the pragmatic manager of the shop was made to explain:

> Most painters work with one eye continually on the prospective buyer. Their product is commercial but not commercial enough ... By systematizing their output and not wasting time mooning around for an individual subject they can while selling their product at an honest price treble their income. An uninspired product is merely a manufactured product. The Buckeye Coy sell [*sic*] them as such.[10]

In fact, the Group members' definition of themselves as authentic, original artists, and thus as authentically uncommercial artists, rested on this critique of imagined art production in Canada, which set them in opposition to market-driven art. In keeping with many arts-and-crafts ideologues in the northeastern United States earlier in the century, they also tied their aestheticism to social conditions, seeing the ugliness fostered by commercialism as leading to the deterioration of society. To combat the decline in taste that caused the public to abandon older models of beauty and utility – or, as Jackson would have it, the rural Canadian to favour ugly housing inappropriate to his needs while '[looking] back condescendingly to the simple home-like old log cabin his grandfather built'[11] – they called for the reintroduction of aesthetic concerns to society. Like the object of arts-and-crafts reform elsewhere, art was 'common meeting ground for all the classes,'[12] its usefulness in suppressing social unrest and building community compounded in 1920s Canada by the Group's association of the latter with the growth of nationality. Elevating standards of taste, the artists argued, would ultimately foster nationality by creating a market for articles of beauty and utility (including goods such as theirs), which like the product of the Ruskinian craftsman promised renewal in the midst of degenerative modernity.[13]

In other words, the Group were antimodernists; their suspicion of so-called progress was one of a number of responses that tied them to a more general fear in Western society from the end of the nineteenth century that the unprecedented social changes wrought by industrial capitalism – among them the shift to routinized work and bureaucratic rationality – were removing the possibility of 'authentic' experience.[14] Their other responses are definitional of antimodernism as well, which can be described, according to Jackson Lears, as 'the recoil from an "overcivilized" modern existence to more intense forms of physical or spiritual experience.'[15] Key among these responses was the fiction of the authentic Canadian painter as a premodern man seeking, in the imagined premodern environment of the Canadian wilderness, the physical and emotional intensity identified with authentic experience.

The figure of the Canadian artist, derived from the artists' sketching trips (which actually began in 1914 with their first joint excursion north of Toronto to Algonquin Provincial Park, fig. 8.1), was invariably described as that of a prospector, bushwhacker, woodsman, or child. Writing in Toronto-based *Saturday Night* in 1916, journalist Peter Donovan described 'the coming Canadian artist' as 'a husky beggar' who 'puts on a pair of Strathcona boots, rolls up his blanket and beans enough to last three months, takes a rifle and paddle, and hikes for the northern woods.' Toronto journalist Fred Housser, writing his 'biography' of the Group ten years later, described 'a new type of artist; one who divests himself of the velvet coat and flowing tie of his caste, puts on the outfit of the bushwhacker and prospector; closes with his environment; paddles, portages and makes camp; sleeps in the out-of-doors under the stars; climbs mountains with his sketch box on his back.' To Arthur Lismer, speaking of the 'natural and spontaneous impudence of the Canadian type' in his 1926 address to the Canadian Club in Toronto, the Canadian artist was one who loved 'to stick his tongue out at tradition and go gaily on his own livelier road through his own native bush instead of following the shady, flower strewn ways of older countries.'[16] In every case, the 'real' Canadian artist stood outside the constraints of civilization, whether socially (in the guise of the prospector, bushwhacker, or woodsman) or developmentally (in the figure of Lismer's impudent child). The landscape surrounding him was also conceptualized in developmental terms, both in youthful opposition to so-called older, cultivated lands and (as Lismer would have it in almost the same breath) as a landscape with a past itself – a 'boundless background of lake and stream, forest and prairie, mountain and coast, each with precious memories of pioneer, explorer and prospector.'[17]

This 'real' Canadian artist can also be associated with what Patricia Jasen has recently identified as the wild man of Toronto's recreational hinterland, the product of the urban middle-class wilderness holiday that grew in popularity from the end of the nineteenth century in Ontario along with the growth of cities in the province and 'fears about effects of overwork and "overcivilization" on personal and racial health.'[18] To begin with, the painters identified with the archetypal Canadian artist began the sketching program that would eventually take them across Canada and to the Arctic with a number of short trips by rail to camp in this tourist area, which comprised Georgian Bay, Muskoka, and Algonquin Park (fig. 8.2). In doing so, they participated in a journey much touted by contemporary advocates and advertisers of the area. Jasen has mapped it in a survey of contemporary tourist literature and travel accounts as 'a journey inwards to discover the primitive self, and back to a time when "the race" as a whole was more vigorous, more self-reliant, more alive to its place in nature.'[19] Given what Carl Berger has identified as a growing association in Canadian nationalist thought at the end of the nineteenth century between the idea of Canada as a northern wilderness and the health of the so-called Canadian race, it should not be surprising that, once there, urbanites searching for the wild man within found him in the 'natural,' 'authentic,' 'real' experience offered in the intimate wilderness encounter that was promoted in tourist literature of the period as 'typically Canadian.'[20]

Of the possibilities that existed for such an encounter, moreover, the artists were identified with the most rigorous – the camping and canoeing trip associated at the time with the male domain – in contrast to the cottage or resort vacation normally identified with the family (fig. 8.3).[21] What distinguished them from the urban middle-class tourist was the product of this encounter: small 8 × 10 inch oil sketches (see, for example, fig. 8.4). Jackson described them as 'hard won impressions of places where the going was tough,'[22] casting them in terms familiar to vitalist antimodernists who equated strenuous physical activity with authentic emotional response.[23] Of course, his comments were also in keeping with the avant-garde theory inherited by the artists along with the tepid post-impressionism that characterized their landscape paintings by 1920. According to this thinking, originality was the defining quality of the work of art. It made itself felt in distinctive pictorial effects, which were seen as the product of the creative impulses of the original, or authentic, artist. In this case, it was also understood that the formal qualities that seemingly registered these creative impulses simultaneously embodied the artists' emotional response to the landscape. What has not been so clearly understood, however, is that in doing so, these formal qualities also invested the landscape in the sketches with characteristics associated at the time with wilderness.

To put it another way, what has not been stressed in discussion of the artists' landscape paintings to date is the fact that landscape does not inherently possess character; it is invested with character. We cannot simply assert, as Hill has recently, that 'the rough wildness of the landscape, its raw, dramatic austerity, coupled with breathtaking colour and light spoke far more directly of Canada for these artists than anything to be found in the cities or settled areas.'[24] As Roderich Nash points out, although 'wilderness has a deceptive concreteness at first glance ... [t]here is no specific material object that is wilderness.'[25] It is a concept, or, I would argue in keeping with Nash's discussion, it is part of a larger concept of which civilization and overcivilization are mutually constitutive parts. As a term, he observes, wilderness 'designates a quality ... that produces a certain mood or feeling in a given individual and, as a consequence, may be assigned by that person to a specific place.'[26] Thus, wilderness in the artists' paintings, through its inextricable relationship to the formal, pictorial effects of post-impressionism, not only embodied the artists' response to the landscape, but was also the object of emotion itself, and thus was capable of stimulating a response from the viewer that, although triggered by pictorial effects, was seen to be an emotional reaction to the landscape depicted.

The nature of this relationship between pictorial elements and image is apparent in the repeated use, by the artists and their supporters, of the same type of adjectives to characterize the formal qualities of the artists' work – primarily the brushwork, colour, and design – as those used to describe wilderness. 'Bold simplification,' 'emphatic design,' 'strong,' 'vibrant,' 'vivid' colour became common in descriptions of the artists' work, providing a framework for such particularized versions of this vocabulary as that offered, for example, by Toronto *Mail and Empire* critic Fred Jacob, who wrote of 'the glaring, vital, rigid studies of Canadian solitudes that Mr. Harris paints.'[27] The effect, while investing the formal qualities of the works with character, was simultaneously to invest the image with similar character – the boldness, ruggedness, vitality, and vibrancy that defined the real wilderness landscape and, for that matter, the 'authentically Canadian' artist. 'The north country is by no means a timid painter's paradise,' as Lismer put it,[28] signalling once again the circular relationship the painters had established between artist, landscape, and art. At a time when urban middle-class Ontarians identified wilderness with an essential Canadianism, the artists located the national feeling it stimulated firmly in the formal qualities of their work, making their art as seemingly 'Canadian' as the wilderness it pictured.[29] As early as 1911, in his review of an Arts and Letters Club exhibition in Toronto of oil sketches by future Group member J.E.H. MacDonald, fellow artist C.W. Jefferys asserted simply, 'so deep and compelling has been the native inspiration that it has, to a very great extent, found through him, a method of expression in paint as native and original as itself.' MacDonald's art was 'native,' Jefferys insisted, 'as native as the rocks or the snow, or pine trees, or the lumber drives that are so largely his themes ...'[30]

Dennis Reid has pointed out that the definitional framework Jefferys presented for a national style of painting was probably a response to a review of an exhibition of Canadian art held the year before at the Walker Art Gallery in Liverpool (fig. 8.5).[31] The writer, a reviewer for the Liverpool *Morning Post*, had felt that although 'observation of physical fact' in the Canadian works was strong, 'the more immutable essence of each scene is crushed out by foreign-begotten technique.'[32] It seems likely that Jeffreys was responding to this statement in his own review of MacDonald's sketches. If this is so, Jeffreys's use of reviews of the 1910 Liverpool show in relation to the work of Group artists predates the formation of the Group in 1920. These reviews were also used by both Jackson and Housser – the latter in his influential 1926 book *A Canadian Art Movement: The Story of the Group of Seven*.[33] Following suit in his 1995 catalogue, Hill seemingly sets the stage for a tale of the Group as an anti-academic avant-garde when he points out that Housser actually 'begins the story' of the Group of Seven with the 1910 Liverpool exhibition that (we are told) consisted of works selected by the Royal Canadian Academy.[34] However, Hill prefaces the *Morning Post* review Housser used with a quotation from a review in the *Art Chronicle* that, like many of the almost forty reviews of the Liverpool show, situates the art firmly within a colony-to-nation narrative. 'Canadian painting has not yet grown beyond the assimilative stage of youth,' it reads; 'its painters still look to Europe for initiative, its students go to London and Paris for the training and the inspiring associations that the artist-life of the Old World alone can provide. The sapling, however, is a vigorous one,' the text continues, 'and all that is now being grafted on it will in due season bear rich fruit.'[35]

It is appropriate commentary, particularly given what Hill does not tell us:

that the works in the 1910 exhibition were originally selected under the auspices of the Royal Canadian Academy only because they were intended as part of a Canadian display in an international exhibition – in this case, significantly, an imperial exhibition called the 'Festival of Empire,' which would have been held had not the death of King Edward caused its postponement for a year.[36] Setting aside the ensuing 1911 exhibition (which celebrated imperial solidarity along with the coronation of King George V), the next and, as it turned out, last of the large imperial exhibitions was the 1924–5 'British Empire Exhibition' at Wembley. This show marked 'the almost unanimous' praise of the British press for the work of the Group of Seven, and with it, what the National Gallery of Canada saw as approval of both its unstinting support of the artists for the decade or so prior to the show and, connected with this support, the Gallery's battle to control the selection process for international exhibitions of Canadian art (fig. 8.6).[37] In other words, what these shows make abundantly clear is the fact that progress in art in Canada at the time was tied in a concrete way to its evaluation in an imperial context. In this sense, it is not surprising that the Group responded to a definitional framework for Canadian art suggested in reviews of the 1910 show. Jackson saw the relationship between the two as pivotal; his reference to reviews of the 1910 exhibition, which he made in a 1925 talk to the Empire Club in Toronto, included a corresponding reference to a favourable review of the Wembley show as evidence of the Group's triumphant emergence as a 'national' school of art.[38]

Simply put, the colony-to-nation narrative championed by the Group and its supporters reveals their essentially British Canadianism, which in its appearance of inclusiveness – its claim to speak for the country as a whole – is characteristic of what can be more precisely defined as Ontario regionalism.[39] This is significant, because this regional ideology was institutionalized in the second and third decades of the century through the Group's close association with authoritative cultural institutions ranging from the Art Gallery of Toronto to the National Gallery and National Museum of Canada. Like other cultural bodies with 'national' mandates, these institutions were instrumental in legitimating the cultural authority of this regional identity on a national scale.[40] Of course, part of the institutionalization of Ontario's British Canadianism involved the definition and subordination of what in the process became other, mutually constitutive identities – a project undertaken to some degree by Group members in conjunction with these institutions in the mid-1920s. This was done in a gallery context for the first time in the exhibition 'Art in French Canada,' a display of paintings, woodcarvings, and rural Québec homespuns that was held alongside the 1926 Group of Seven exhibition at the Art Gallery of Toronto. This was followed in 1927 by the 'Exhibition of Canadian West Coast Art, Native and Modern,' which toured from the National Gallery in Ottawa to Toronto and Montréal; this show combined the work of North American aboriginal cultures of the Pacific Northwest with paintings and sculptures by Euro-Canadian artists, prominent among them, members of the Group of Seven (fig. 8.7).[41]

Although celebrated in the recent Group of Seven exhibition as evidence of an expanding definition of national culture in the 1920s, one that provided 'a new lineage' for the Group of Seven,[42] these two exhibitions can also be seen as a way of reformulating and naturalizing this regional ideology as a cultural hierarchy with clear ethnic, gender, and class divisions, and with the Group of Seven firmly at the top. We have only to acknowledge the way in which such exhibitions worked to exclude certain groups from consideration as equal participants in 'modern' life by representing them as peoples 'of the past' – peoples existing outside the historical present in that indeterminate time we call 'the traditional.' We have only to acknowledge that the people represented through the work in the exhibitions were not, as was suggested at the time, Primitives or Folk vanishing in the face of progress, trade, and civilization.[43] They were members of the contemporary Native cultures of the Pacific Northwest and the economically disadvantaged, rural population of the lower St Lawrence Valley (the French-speaking *habitant* of Isle d'Orléans and the north shore of the St Lawrence River), but they were cast as the pre-modern ancestors of so-called modern Canadian culture.[44] Classified by elite aesthetic opinion as producers of folk art, Native art, or crafts, they were effectively institutionalized, the social relations defined in the exhibitions played out in turn in the modern museum complex. This was, after all, the moment in which the Art Gallery of Toronto, the National Gallery, and the National Museum were taking shape as modern corporate structures, the moment in which, Kathleen McCarthy points out, such 'urban repositories replaced the informality of market mechanisms with a more co-ordinated approach, gathering cultural capital from all corners of the community, sifting it, systematizing it, categorizing it, and making it available to the public in new ways.'[45]

It is important to recognize as well that such cultural hierarchies have more immediate social, political, and economic implications for those within them. This becomes clear the moment we introduce the discussion of what Johannes Fabian calls the 'chronopolitics' of colonial expansion: the ways in which concepts of time have been harnessed by some to situate others outside an advancing world order and, in so doing, to justify the subordination of those others to colonial rule.[46] This concept illuminates the nature of the relationship between museums, as part of the intellectual apparatus of the modern state, and the government policies and legislation that deal with the social, economic, and political life of what was, in this case, an emergent nation. In the light of Fabian's observations, for instance, it is possible to argue that such exhibitions as 'Art in French Canada' and the 'Exhibition of Canadian West Coast Art, Native and Modern,' which apparently operated only within the politically neutral realm of aesthetics, actually served on another level to reinforce and to naturalize social relations that in turn facilitated governmental action designed to maintain them.

This becomes evident, for example, upon examination of the seemingly benevolent state paternalism behind the federal government policies in the 1920s to create a tourist market for the 'French-Canadian homespun industry' (fig. 8.8).[47] It may have appeared simply as open support of the efforts of the Québec

Department of Agriculture to add to the income of rural Québec households by establishing Écoles ménagères and Cercles des fermières across the province 'to give instruction in household science in general and in the homespun industry in particular.'[48] But such paternalism was also an effective response to a belief held at the provincial level among politicians, clerics, and nationalists in Québec that the threat to family – and thus to social stability – they saw in the changing role of women in urbanized, industrial society could be countered by the revival of domestic industries promoting the woman's place as keeper of 'traditional' Québec values.[49] And where revivalist impulses were replaced by assimilationist legislation, it facilitated the policies and programs of coercive tutelage designed by the federal government in the early twentieth century to 'save' the aboriginal population of Canada by ridding it of its aboriginality. It was all part of the process of aggressive assimilation implemented by the Department of Indian Affairs and by Euro-Canadian institutions in the areas of aboriginal culture, education, religion, and land use. In fact, in 1927, as the Department of Indian Affairs faced increasingly organized efforts on the part of aboriginal groups in Canada to secure rights, lands, and resources, assimilation was advanced by the federal government with new rigour. In the same year that the National Gallery of Canada celebrated the seemingly apolitical 'Canadianization' of Native cultures in the 'Exhibition of Canadian West Coast Art, Native and Modern,' the federal government passed an amendment to the Indian Act effectively prohibiting claim-related activity among the aboriginal population of Canada.[50]

All this, of course, would seem to run counter to the all-embracing aestheticism that characterized so much of the Group's polemic – a polemic that advocated the reintroduction of aesthetic appreciation to modern life as the key to social harmony. But, in fact, it does not. The democratization of aesthetic expression advocated in the Group's stance couched a clearly defined set of social relations that legitimated, even facilitated, their easy existence elsewhere. What the Group promoted in this regard was the status quo; in seeing renewed joy in aesthetic expression as a way of quenching social unrest, the artists moved away from any real critique of the social conditions of modern production to a position of ambivalence. Like so many antimodernists both in Europe and on this side of the Atlantic, the artists were essentially accommodationist, preserving what has been described as 'an eloquent edge of protest'[51] in what was otherwise a deep-seated belief in 'progress.' In other words, theirs was a modernizing antimodernism that sought both social and industrial advancement in a return to the imagined state of aesthetic consciousness that had been lost with overcivilization.[52] They wanted to elevate public taste, and thus create a market for the work of the 'authentic' Canadian artist. In the end, as a result, theirs was a polemic that sought to rally the aesthetic appreciation of society as a whole in the cause of elite aesthetic expression. This was not a demotic position. On the contrary, by working with museums in 1920s to institutionalize such exclusive aesthetic opinion, the artists helped to reformulate the cultural authority of the Anglo-Canadian elite.

Given the Group of Seven's now prominent place in Canada's 'official'[53] culture, this is a stinging indictment, and perhaps I should stop here, content with the impact I suspect it has on what I described earlier as 'Canadians steeped in the mythology of the Group of Seven and its call for a "distinctively Canadian art."' It seems to me, however, that what remains to be considered in the light of this counternarrative are the more immediate implications of the National Gallery's ongoing promotion of the 'official' story of the Group. An essential aspect of this story is the Gallery's intimate alignment with the Group's populist stance, an alignment that was reiterated and renewed in the 1995 exhibition 'Art for a Nation,' which was fashioned as a celebration of both the seventy-fifth anniversary of the Group's formation in 1920 and the National Gallery's unstinting support of what it presented as an oppressed avant-garde struggling in the face of 'vociferous opposition.'[54] The ensuing drama, which was played out in a re-creation of the Group's eight flagship exhibitions at the Art Gallery of Toronto between 1920 and 1931, culminated in curator Hill's treatment of the 1924 controversy surrounding the selection of Canadian works for the British Empire Exhibition at Wembley. It was at that point in the narrative of the exhibition – in the context of what could otherwise be described as the Royal Canadian Academy's fight with the National Gallery to retain control of the selection process for international exhibitions – that Hill cast the National Gallery as the defender of the Group of Seven and the embodiment of popular aesthetic opinion.

In doing so, the Gallery actively represented itself as the champion of the Group of Seven, something that was also evident in the fact that the Gallery's support of the artists was profiled in the show while that of their other patrons was not. In fact, Hill stepped outside the parameters he set for the exhibition by including two works that were not exhibited in the Toronto shows, in order to turn them, it seems, to the National Gallery's advantage. Thus, a wall panel explained the presence of a Harris canvas purchased by the Detroit Institute of Arts from the Group's 'U.S. Tour 1920–21' in terms of its place as a 'precursor' to the purchase of Jackson's *Entrance to Halifax Harbour* by London's Tate Gallery. The Jackson canvas (which was also included in the 1995 show) boldly represented the vindicating gesture the National Gallery saw in this purchase, which was made in 1924 from the controversial Wembley show.[55] Other than these two gallerys, the only purchaser of the artists' work identified by name in the 1995 exhibition was the National Gallery of Canada, which was presented, along with the unnamed patrons, as having bought regularly from the Toronto shows.

Of course, this representation of information had other effects as well, not least of which was the contradiction between the self-congratulatory credit given the National Gallery for its staunch support of the artists and the show's central idea of the Group as a beleaguered avant-garde. As Hill points out in the catalogue, in 1920 and 1921 – the first years of the Group's existence – the National Gallery spent over 40 per cent of its budget for Canadian art on this Toronto-based 'movement,' although he laments what he sees as compromises in purchasing occasioned by the resistance of one of the Montréal trustees, who was 'keenly aware of pressure from artists in that city.'[56] The way the argument runs, the favour shown to the Group by the National Gallery, both in terms of purchases and subsequent exhibitions, was actually the realization of policies established in 1914 'to effect some permanent stimulus to the art of Canada.' According to the Toronto *Globe*, government sanction had followed the agreement of both the National Gallery and the Royal Canadian Academy that 'the most satisfying method of recognizing and encouraging Canadian artists was by the direct purchase of as many of their works as possible,' and by distribution of these works through loan to art bodies and societies 'throughout the Dominion.' 'It is believed,' the *Globe* reported,

> this distribution of works of art will encourage the art of Canada in the following ways: it will directly benefit the artist whose work is purchased; it will benefit the exhibition from which the work of art is purchased in that it will encourage the artist to send his best work there; it will benefit the National Gallery by permitting a wider choice for the artist's representation there; it will stimulate the formation of art societies and schools throughout the Dominion by providing them with the nucleus of an exhibition of the work of Canadian artists, and it will benefit the individual who is able to visit these exhibitions by giving him some knowledge of the art of his country, and so, perhaps, inspire him with the desire to possess it himself.[57]

By actively purchasing and touring the Group's 'distinctly Canadian' work, the circular argument goes, the National Gallery fulfilled its own goal to bring Canadian art to Canadians.[58] Thus Hill could conclude, in an essay devoted to this idea, that in doing so, 'the National Gallery and the Group of Seven and their supporters had played a vital role in the development of a Canadian consciousness.'[59] In other words, by aggressively profiling itself as champion of the Group of Seven, the National Gallery portrayed itself, along with the Group, as a champion of Canadian cultural democracy and as such, of Canadian nationality.

Although self-perpetuated, however, the Gallery's recent account of its importance to the Group's story has not been fashioned out of self-conscious self-interest; it seems to me, rather, that its current advancement reflects the increasingly compelling nature of the apparent 'truth' inscribed in what is by now a state-sanctioned narrative. In fact, the first scholarly study of the artists, which was undertaken in 1970 by the National Gallery in celebration of the Group's fiftieth anniversary, used Housser's description of the Group – 'a Canadian art movement' – as the point of departure for an examination of the artists and their work, including a detailed account of the National Gallery's part in advancing what Dennis Reid (then curator of Canadian historical art) identified as the Group's 'social stance.' In the catalogue for this 1970 exhibition, Reid introduced Housser's phrase in the context of his assessment of current public perception and understanding of the Group – situating the artists 'in the Canadian Cultural pantheon ... with a few hockey stars and a handful of beloved politicians.' Reid's catalogue went a long way toward establishing the National Gallery's share of responsibility for this public perception through his account of the place of the Group in Gallery policies and exhibition programs.[60]

When the Gallery went one step further in the 1995 show by celebrating its role in constructing a nationalized citizenry, it was effectively celebrating its function, given that the Western conception of museums as a formative part of the modern nation state hinges on their role in the process of 'nationing' the population. Using museums and heritage sites in Australia as an example, Tony Bennett argues, through Nicos Poulantzas, that 'the modern state ... establishes a unique relationship between time and space, between history and territory, in organising the unity of the nation'; for where the unity of the nation is conceived as 'the unity of a people who share the same space and time,' museums are key in positioning people as such, as 'the occupants of a territory which has been historicized and the subjects of a history which has been territorialized.'[61] Benedict Anderson's well-known observation puts the result in simple terms. 'If nation-states are widely conceded to be "new" and "historical," the nations to which they give political expression always loom out of an immemorial past, and still more important, glide into a limitless future.'[62] Accepting Bennett's observation that the modern nation-state is engaged in an active process of organizing the nation's time-space co-ordinates through museum and heritage policies and sites, I would argue after him as well that in Canada, as in Australia:

> The single most important development [in the area of museum and heritage policies and sites] ... has consisted in the production of a ... completely autonomized national past. This has entailed the organization of a new discursive space for the time-space co-ordinates of the nation, ones which sever its dependency on those of Europe and allow it to emerge as a free-standing entity rooted in its own past. Moreover, this has been accomplished by precisely the means both Poulanzas and Anderson suggest. The historicization of a territory and the territorialization of a history; the subjection of other histories ... [in the case of Canada, of aboriginal peoples, of non-British immigrant communities, of Canada's European pre-history] into the story of the nation's unfolding unity; the back-projection of the nation's history into the deeper history of the land and of nature so that it seems to "loom out of an immemorial past' ...[63]

In Canada, this autonomized national past for art was initially fashioned out of that historical realignment of artistic expression in the 1920s which the 1995 show described as having provided 'a new lineage for the Group of Seven' in the Aboriginal and folk cultures of British Columbia and Québec respectively. Accordingly, an aboriginal culture was described in the National Gallery's 1927 exhibition as having 'sprung up wholly from the soil and sea within our national boundaries,' setting it firmly in this myth of origination at the beginning of human evolution, where it was represented as culture at the point of its emergence from nature and used to connect the story of European settlement in Canada to the deeper history of the land.[64] Like the folk art of rural Québec, which subsequently operated in an intermediary space between aboriginal cultures and the Group of Seven, the products of the aboriginal thus represented a primitive form of cultural manufacture. The pre-industrial, artisanal production identified with the men and women of rural Québec was only an intermediary step toward the fully realized national form of artistic expression embodied in the fine art of the Group's pre-modern 'Canadian type' – that robust and robustly 'modern' Canadian of the capitalist nation-state who also stood in vigorous opposition to the overcivilization of Europe and to what Lismer called 'the manifest ennui of [the] decadent academicism of European art.'[65]

In other words, the Group of Seven's work was fixed as the locus of nationalization in this autonomized past, where it was constituted as both the end of the process of becoming and the beginning of a national art. This position in the history of Canadian art was sustained for the Group by the National Gallery in the 1995 show by revaluing what Hill clearly recognized as a nationalizing past constructed by the Group and its supporters. This past was instead represented to contemporary audiences as evidence of a national consciousness developing around the Group and the National Gallery in the 1920s.[66] Thus, the National Gallery asked its audience (conceived as a nationalized citizenry) to celebrate the gallery's function in advancing what it represented in the exhibition as the latent nationality characteristic of autonomized, national pasts – the deep-seated national consciousness of time immemorial, of which the Canadian nation state, and thus the gallery itself, were the 'new' and 'historical' expression.

Clearly self-referential, such a celebration also had the effect of revealing the essentially nationalist underpinning of the show. The exhibition title, 'The Group of Seven: Art for a Nation,' was a public proclamation of this, clearly operating not only as a statement of the Group's ideology, but also as a contemporary valuation of its worth, through which the Gallery effectively constructed its audience. If viewers accepted the position the title assigned them as national subjects, the art in the show was 'for them'; it provided common ground around which their sense of national community was reinforced. If they rejected it, or did not recognize themselves in this position, then they were probably one of a number of things – chief among them, certainly, either non-Canadian or unpatriotic.[67] I would argue further that this not-so-subtle nationalist bent is everywhere in evidence in connection with the Group, largely because the Group and those connected with it, including art historians and curators, have made little, if any, distinction between 'national' – of the nation in the sense of affecting or being shared by the nation as a whole – and 'nationalist' – actively engaged in advancing nationality, devoted to one's nation, or adhering to nationalism as a political position. Thus the Group's ardent nationalism and its nationalist art was, and is still, equated with being national – as in 'a national school of art,' 'a Canadian art movement,' or 'a distinctively Canadian art' – even as the tale of the artists' promotion from obscurity to seemingly national acceptance is being recounted.

Consider as well the titles of recent exhibitions and catalogues that deal with or prominently feature Group members' work. In addition to *The Group of Seven: Art for a Nation*, which calls up a nationalistic frame of reference, there are *OH!CANADA*, *Our Home and Native Land*, and *The True North*, which all depend for their impact on the fact that they are drawn from the Canadian national anthem.[68] Given this, it should not be surprising that the Group of Seven is identified by its public today in a manner spoofed in a cartoon published in the Toronto *Globe and Mail* during the Art Gallery of Ontario showing of 'Art for a Nation' (fig. 8.9) – not, say, as a collection of individual artists, or even as a group of Canadian post-impressionists, but first and foremost as a corporate body with a nationalist ideology.[69] At a more essentialistic level, the Group's art is still being advanced as representative of the nation as a whole – as something shared by the nation's citizenry and therefore national – because it supposedly triggers national feeling in each member of its audience. In other words, this art is 'of the nation' because anyone who does not feel a sense of nationality in response to it is not, by definition, part of the nation anyway.

Circular as this thinking is, it also seems that this conflation of national and nationalist is largely the reason the National Gallery could boast, and still boasts, about its disproportionately active purchase and exhibition of the artists' work. It was effecting 'a permanent stimulus to the art of Canada' by direct support of the work of Canadian artists where, clearly, Canadian art was implicitly understood to be nationalist art – and thus compellingly 'Canadian' – in contrast to art that was representative of artistic production in Canada, which needed general stimulation through direct purchase by the National Gallery of Canada. Seen in this light, the pressure that one of the Gallery's Montréal trustees felt from artists in Québec during the initial years of the support given to the Ontario-based Group is understandable. The Quebecers' discontent also serves to underline the fact that this nationalist sentiment was regional in both type and expression; ready evidence of this was actually provided in the organization of the 1995 show as a recreation of the eight flagship exhibitions of the Group at the Art Gallery of Toronto between 1920 and 1931. Beyond the fact that this staggering level of institutional support from what is now the Art Gallery of Ontario undermines the National Gallery's assertion that the artists struggled for recognition, it also underscores the regional nature of the Group's nationalism – something that would have been apparent in the 1995 exhibition except for the fact that the role of the Art Gallery of Ontario in the Group's story was not mentioned in the text of the wall panels.[70]

Perhaps the most striking aspect of the representation of this regional nationalism today is the fact that it is also a colonial nationalism; the public narrative it produces is grounded in the idea of cultural homogeneity as the basis of national culture. In a study of Australia, Jon Stratton and Ien Ang have described colonial nationalism as 'a desire for autonomy and independence without severing ... ties with the imperial power.'[71] They have also examined its centrality in the transformation of the Australian settler colony into the new nation specifically to show how ideas of culture based on the European model of the nation state are transplanted as an understanding of national formation in terms of homogeneous culture.[72] In the case of Canada, I would argue, their discussion also has immediate application if we consider the fact that the colonial nationalism of early twentieth-century Ontario was British in orientation, because this means in turn that the National Gallery is advancing an unethnicized British Canadianism as the basis of national culture today.

This sets the Gallery in what can best be described as a curious position in relation to the current cultural policy of the Canadian state, which has moved away from the European-based idea of the state as the political expression of a homogeneous national culture. In Canada, the state has taken on what Stratton and Ang describe as 'a more interventionist role in defining identity away from the imperial connection with Britain' through the introduction of multiculturalism as state cultural policy.[73] This has marked a shift in the conception of nation – what Benedict Anderson has called the 'imagined community.' 'With the introduction of official multiculturalism,' Stratton and Ang point out, 'the emphasis on a homogeneous imagined community [was moved] from the level of the national to the level of the ethnic: now, [in the multicultural state] the national is conceived as the space within which many (ethnically defined) imagined communities live and interact.'[74]

The National Gallery's 1995 show can be seen as the product of this new imagined community only if we acknowledge that it demonstrates one of the central criticisms of multiculturalism: that its advancement of British Canadianism effectively maintains Anglo-Canadian culture as the unethnicized ground on which other cultures are ethnicized; in other words, it disguises the continued hegemony of Anglo-Canadian culture by rendering it invisible.[75] But ultimately, it is incompatible with the multicultural imagined community even on this level. It presents an autonomized national history that locates and celebrates the process of becoming national as an event in the past. In doing so, it runs counter to the notion of national identity in the multicultural imagined community, where it is conceived as something in the process of becoming – the product of cultural difference located in ethnicity. 'In this new understanding of national identity as a process of continual reinvention through the interaction of a plurality of ethnically defined imagined communities,' Stratton and Ang argue, 'the state takes on a new role as guarantor of historical continuity.'[76] Of course, the incongruous role that the Gallery advanced for itself in the 1995 show can be simply explained as practical evidence that the state is 'convenient shorthand'[77] for a collection of governmental agencies and institutions that is monolithic in neither form nor function. But in doing so, we should not lose sight of the reason for the incompatibility here: the fact that in the story of the Group of Seven and its antimodern stance, the National Gallery of Canada fashioned a myth of origination for itself. It recast the corporatization of the cultural sphere as the democratization of aesthetic opinion, and then used its cultural authority to legitimate itself.

NOTES

The first part of this paper is based upon my 'Prospectors, Bushwackers, Painters: Antimodernism and the Group of Seven,' in *International Journal of Canadian Studies/ Revue Internationale d'études canadiennes* 17 (Spring/printemps, 1998), 193–214.

1 Family letter in possession of Dr Naomi Jackson Groves, Ottawa. I am grateful to David McTavish both for bringing the existence of this letter to my attention and for sharing his research notes on it.
2 Quoted in Dennis Reid, *Le Groupe des sept/The Group of Seven* (Ottawa: National Gallery of Canada, 1970), 34, from notes prepared by Dr Naomi Jackson Groves from family letters in her possession. Jackson made the comment during his first visit to the region, which he spent vacationing with relatives.
3 'The Group of Seven: Art for a Nation' opened in October 1995 at the National Gallery of Canada in Ottawa and subsequently toured to the Art Gallery of Ontario in Toronto, the Vancouver Art Gallery, and the Montreal Museum of Fine Arts, where it closed in December 1996. A 375-page catalogue of the same title was prepared by curator of Canadian art, Charles Hill, and published by the gallery in collaboration with McClelland & Stewart.
4 'Academicians' wall text panel, at 'The Group of Seven: Art for a Nation.' See also Hill, *The Group of Seven: Art for a Nation* (Ottawa and Toronto: National Gallery of Canada and McClelland & Stewart, 1995), 134–51.
5 Established in 1880 with the formation of the Royal Canadian Academy, the National Gallery of Canada was effectively incorporated under its own Board of Directors by an act of Parliament in 1913. This followed the establishment in 1907 of both an Advisory Arts Council and regular government appropriations to purchase works of art, and the appointment of a full-time curator in 1910. The Art Museum of Toronto (now the Art Gallery of Ontario) and Toronto's Royal Ontario Museum were organized in similar fashion during the first two decades of the century. See Jean Sutherland Boggs, *The National Gallery of Canada* (Toronto: Oxford University Press, 1971), 6–17; Lovat Dickson, *The Museum Makers: The Story of the Royal Ontario Museum* (Toronto: Royal Ontario Museum, 1986); and Karen McKenzie and Larry Pfaff, 'The Art Gallery of Ontario: Sixty Years of Exhibitions, 1906–1966,' *RACAR* 7 (1980), 62–5. For discussion of the professionalization and corporatization of the American museum world during this period see Kathleen McCarthy, *Woman's Culture: American Philanthropy and Art, 1830–1930* (Chicago: University of Chicago Press, 1991), 111–16.
6 Ian McKay, 'Introduction: All That Is Solid Melts into Air,' in *The Challenge of Modernity: A Reader on Post-Confederation Canada*, ed. Ian McKay (Toronto: McGraw-Hill Ryerson, 1992), x. According to Reg Whitaker, processes of industrial development that occurred over longer periods in Britain and the United States were telescoped in Canada from the 1890s through the early decades of the twentieth century. See 'Images of the State in Canada,' in *The Canadian State: Political Economy and Political Power*, ed. Leo Panitch (Toronto: University of Toronto Press, 1977), 53.

7 For a history of the now-common use of this phrase in connection with the work of the Group of Seven, see Arthur Lismer, *A Short History of Painting with a Note on Canadian Art* (Toronto: Andrew Bros., 1926), 31, who relates the Group's ideals to 'the development of a distinctive type of painting in Canada'; Frederick Housser, *A Canadian Art Movement: The Story of the Group of Seven* (Toronto: Macmillan Company, 1926), 24, who states that the 'Canadian movement is distinctly a Canadian phenomenon'; Eric Brown, 'Canada's National Painters,' *The Studio* 103 (June 1932), 311, who, as director of the National Gallery, posits the Group of Seven as the source of 'a robust school of painting in a style that is distinctively national'; Reid, *Le Groupe des sept*, 10, who credits Lismer with the phrase 'distinctively Canadian'; Charles Hill, 'The Group of Seven: Art for a Nation,' introductory wall text panel, and *The Group of Seven*, 30, where he credits the artists with fostering 'a distinctive Canadian expression in painting, design, and manufacturing.' See also *Group of Seven*, where Hill refers essentialistically throughout to the development of 'Canadian art' as something 'distinct' from the development of art in Canada.

8 Although William Colgate states that Lawren Harris wrote the foreword to the catalogue of the first Group show, the ideas expressed in it are also those of the other main proselytizers of the 'gospel' of the Group of Seven: J.E.H. MacDonald, Arthur Lismer, and A.Y. Jackson; see Colgate, *Canadian Art: Its Origin & Development* (Toronto: Ryerson Press, 1967), 82, and *Group of 7 Exhibition of Paintings* (Toronto: Art Museum of Toronto, 1920). In fact, the foreword, which became the first collective statement of the Group's position, is less the product of one author than it is an amalgamation of ideas expressed in print by these men, often incorporating their words, their phrases and the structures of their arguments. Of the artists' early writings see, in particular: J.E.H. MacDonald, 'Art and Our Friend in Flanders,' *The Rebel* 2 (February 1918), 182–6; 'Art Crushed to the Earth,' *The Rebel* 2 (January 1918), 150–3; 'A Whack at Dutch Art,' *The Rebel* 2 (March 1918), 256–60; Arthur Lismer, 'Art and the Average Canadian,' *Canadian Courier* 24 (1 February 1919), 13; 'Art Education and Art Appreciation,' *The Rebel* 4 (February 1920), 208–11; and A.Y. Jackson, 'The Vital Necessity of the Fine Arts,' *Canadian Courier* 24 (30 August 1919), 7; 'A Policy for Art Galleries,' *Canadian Forum* 2 (June 1922), 660–2; (Ajax) 'Dutch Art in Canada: The Last Chapter,' *The Rebel* 4 (November 1919), 65–6; (Smoke Lake) 'Figure Versus Landscape,' *The Rebel* 3 (January 1919), 158–9. For a full discussion of the relationship between the artists' early writings and the polemic developed in the Group's exhibition catalogues, see Lynda Jessup, 'Canadian Artists, Railways, the State and "the Business of Becoming a Nation"' (PhD diss., University of Toronto, 1992), 15–98.

9 Lismer, 'Art and the Average Canadian.'

10 National Archives of Canada (hereafter NAC), J.E.H. MacDonald Papers, MG30 DIII, vol. 1, f. A.Y. Jackson – Miscellaneous 1900–[1919], 'Buckeyes,' typescript of unpublished essay [ca. 1919].

11 Jackson, 'Vital Necessity of the Fine Arts.'

12 Ibid.

13 Jessup, 'Canadian Artists,' 14–22. For discussion of late nineteenth-century and early twentieth-century arts-and-crafts ideology in the northeastern United States,

see T.J. Jackson Lears, *No Place of Grace: Antimodernism and the Transformation of American Culture, 1880–1920* (Chicago: University of Chicago Press, 1983), 59–96.

14 See Lears, *No Place of Grace*, xi–xx; Ian McKay, *The Quest for the Folk: Antimodernism and Cultural Selection in Twentieth-Century Nova Scotia* (Kingston and Montreal: McGill-Queen's University Press, 1994), 30–1.

15 Lears, *No Place of Grace*, xv.

16 Peter Donovan, 'Arting Among the Artists,' *Saturday Night* 29 (8 April 1916), 5, quoted in Hill, *Group of Seven*, 52; Housser, *A Canadian Art Movement*, 15; NAC, Arthur Lismer Papers, MG30 D184, vol. 1, f. 'Canadian Art,' 'Lecture in Toronto to the Canadian Club, Dec. 13 1926.'

17 NAC, Arthur Lismer Papers, vol. 1, f. 'Canadian Art,' 'Lecture in Toronto to the Canadian Club, Dec. 13 1926.'

18 Patricia Jasen, *Wild Things: Nature, Culture, and Tourism in Ontario, 1790–1914* (Toronto: University of Toronto Press, 1995), 105. The racial and gendered aspects of this fear of modern civilization – the perceived threat it held for 'civilized' white males of European descent – is developed by Gail Bederman, *Manliness & Civilization: A Cultural History of Gender and Race in the United States 1880–1917* (Chicago: University of Chicago Press, 1995), 77–120.

19 Jasen, *Wild Things*, 132.

20 Carl Berger, 'The True North Strong and Free,' in *Interpreting Canada's Past*, ed. J.M. Bumsted, 2 vols. (Toronto: Oxford University Press, 1986), 2:157–74; Grand Trunk Railway, *Temagami: A Peerless Region for Sportsman, Canoeist, and Camper*, 1905. See also Jasen, *Wild Things*, 105–32; Lynda Jessup, 'Wilderness Imagery in Canadian Advertising and Its Impact on Canadian Painters, 1890–1914' (Phil.M. final paper, University of Toronto, 1983); Douglas Cole, 'Artists, Patrons and Public: An Enquiry into the Success of the Group of Seven,' *Journal of Canadian Studies* 13 (Summer 1978), 69–78; Robert Stacey, 'The Myth – And Truth – of the True North,' *The True North: Canadian Landscape Painting, 1896–1939*, ed. Michael Tooby (London: Lund Humphries with the Barbican Art Gallery, 1992), 37–63.

21 For discussion of these vacation types see Jasen, *Wild Things*, 111.

22 Art Gallery of Ontario Library, 'The Tom Thomson Film, December 1943,' typescript of address by Jackson on the occasion of the first showing in Toronto of the Tom Thomson film, *West Wind*, 3, quoted in Reid, *Le Groupe des sept*, 11.

23 Lears, *No Place of Grace*, xii, 142–9.

24 Hill, *Group of Seven*, 23. The Group members did not confine themselves to landscape painting, but it was predominant in their work and was the genre the public most closely associated with them.

25 Roderick Nash, *Wilderness and the American Mind*, 3rd ed. (New Haven: Yale University Press, 1982), 1.

26 Ibid.

27 [Fred Jacobs,] 'In the Art Galleries,' *Toronto Mail and Empire*, 31 January 1925, 14.

28 NAC, Arthur Lismer Papers, vol. 1, f. 'Canadian Art,' 'Lecture in Toronto to the Canadian Club, Dec. 13 1926.'

29 For expression by Group members of their belief that their painting stimulated the development of Canadian consciousness, spirit, or character see, for example, A.Y.

Jackson, 'Artist-Explorer,' *Canadian Bookman* 9 (July 1927), 216; Arthur Lismer, 'Canadian Art,' *Canadian Theosophist* 5 (15 February 1925), 177–9; Lawren Harris, 'Creative Art and Canada,' *Supplement to the McGill News* (December 1928), 6–11. For their collective expression of this idea see *Group of 7 Exhibition of Paintings* (Toronto: Art Museum of Toronto, 1920); *Exhibition of Paintings by the Group of 7* (Toronto: Art Museum of Toronto, 1921).

30 C.W. Jeffreys, 'MacDonald Sketches,' *The Lamps* 1:2 (December 1911), 12.

31 Reid, *Le Groupe des sept*, 29, n. 11.

32 NAC, Papers of the Royal Canadian Academy of Arts, MG28 I 126, vol. 14, f. 'Scrapbook, Newspaper Clippings (1880–1915),' 'Royal Canadian Academy, Exhibition at Liverpool,' 4 July 1910.

33 Housser, *Canadian Art Movement*, 11.

34 Hill, *Group of Seven*, 19.

35 'Canadian Art at Liverpool,' *Art Chronicle*, 30 July 1910, quoted in Hill, *Group of Seven*, 19. For newspaper accounts of the show, including the *Art Chronicle* review, see NAC, Papers of the Royal Canadian Academy of Arts, vol. 14, f. 'Scrapbook, Newspaper Clippings (1880–1915).'

36 NAC, Papers of the Royal Canadian Academy of Arts, vol. 14, f. 'Scrapbook, Newspaper Clippings (1880–1915)'; NAC, Records of the Canadian Government Exhibition Commission, RG 72, vol. 129, 'Festival of Empire'; John E. Findling, ed., *Historical Dictionary of World's Fairs and Expositions, 1851–1988* (New York: Greenwood Press, 1990), 215–16.

37 Discussion of the British imperial exhibitions is provided in Findling, *Historical Dictionary*; the characterization of the British press response by Hill is from '1922,' wall text panel, at 'The Group of Seven: Art for a Nation.' The degree to which the National Gallery of Canada identified itself with the Group of Seven and sought public vindication of its position in relation to the artists is reflected, for example, in the fact that the Gallery published two books containing reprints of favourable reviews of the show: the 1924 *Press Comments on the Canadian Section of Fine Arts, British Empire Exhibition*, and the 1925 *Press Comments on the Canadian Section of Fine Arts, British Empire Exhibition 1924–25.*

38 The talk was reported widely in the Toronto press. Among the accounts, two described Jackson's references to the exhibitions specifically: 'If Cow Can Stay in Parlor Then Why Can't Bull Moose?' *Toronto Star*, 26 February 1925, 29, and 'Advice to Group of Seven: "Paint the Paintless Barn",' *Toronto Telegram*, 27 February 1925. See also 'Two Views of Canadian Art: Addresses by Mr. Wyly Greer, R.C.A., O.C.A. and A.Y. Jackson, R.C.A., O.C.A.,' in *Empire Club of Canada: Addresses Delivered to the Members during the Year 1925* (Toronto: Macoomb Press, 1926), 105–13; 'Blazing Trails in Art: The Modern Canadian Artists' Point of View,' *Ottawa Citizen*, 17 March 1926.

39 See McKay, 'Introduction: All that Is Solid Melts into Air,' xviii–xxi; L.D. McCann, 'Heartland and Hinterland: A Framework for Regional Analysis,' and Iain Wallace, 'The Canadian Shield: The Development of a Resource Frontier,' in *Heartland and Hinterland: A Geography of Canada*, ed. L.D. McCann, 2nd ed. (Scarborough, Ontario: Prentice-Hall Canada, 1987), 22–33 and 443–4 respectively.

40 The relationships of the artists and the Group with various authoritative cultural institutions are well documented, intimate, and too numerous to mention here. The most recent account is provided in Hill, *Group of Seven*.

41 A catalogue was published in each case. See *Exhibitions of the Group of 7 & Art in French Canada* (Toronto: Art Gallery of Toronto, 1926), which comprises the catalogues of both the 'Exhibition of the Group of Seven,' 2–6, and the 'Exhibition of Paintings, Sculpture and Wood Carvings of French Canada,' 7–12; and *Exhibition of Canadian West Coast Art, Native and Modern* (Ottawa: National Gallery of Canada, 1927). For discussion of the exhibitions and the artists' involvement see Jessup, 'Canadian Artists,' 35–98.

42 '1926 and 1928' wall text panels, at 'The Group of Seven: Art for a Nation.' See also Hill, *Group of Seven*, 32, 176–93.

43 See *Exhibition of Canadian West Coast Art, Native and Modern*, 2; *Exhibitions of the Group of 7 & Art in French Canada*, 8.

44 Jessup, 'Canadian Artists,' 35–98. For discussion of the ways in which the Other is set outside historical time, see James Clifford, 'On Ethnographic Allegory,' in *Writing Culture: The Poetics and Politics of Ethnography*, ed. James Clifford and George E. Marcus (Berkeley: University of California Press, 1986), 98–121; James Clifford, Virginia Dominguez, Trinh T. Minh-Ha, Discussion Group, 'Of Other Peoples: Beyond the Salvage Paradigm,' in *Discussions in Contemporary Culture*, no. 1, ed. Hal Foster (Seattle: Bay Press, 1987), 121–50; James Clifford, *The Predicament of Culture: Twentieth-Century Ethnography, Literature and Art* (Cambridge, Mass.: Harvard University Press, 1988), 189–214, 215–51.

45 McCarthy, *Women's Culture*, 113.

46 Johannes Fabian, *Time and the Other: How Anthropology Makes Its Object* (New York: Columbia University Press, 1983).

47 See, for example, Canada, Department of Trade and Commerce, *The French-Canadian Homespun Industry*, 1928.

48 Ibid., 6.

49 See Susan Mann Trofimenkoff, *The Dream of Nation: A Social and Intellectual History of Québec* (Toronto: Gage Publishing, 1983), 229–40.

50 For discussion of public policy in Canada as it has affected Native peoples, see Noel Dyck and James B. Waldram, 'Anthropology, Public Policy and Natives Peoples: An Introduction to the Issues,' in *Anthropology, Public Policy, and Native Peoples in Canada*, eds. Noel Dyck and James B. Waldram (Kingston and Montreal: McGill-Queen's University Press, 1993), 3–38; E. Brian Titley, *A Narrow Vision: Duncan Campbell Scott and the Administration of Indian Affairs in Canada* (Vancouver: University of British Columbia Press, 1986); Paul Tennant, *Aboriginal People and Politics: The Indian Land Question in British Columbia, 1849–1989* (Vancouver: University of British Columbia Press, 1990); Chief Joe Mathais and Gary R. Yabsley, 'Conspiracy of Legislation: The Suppression of Indian Rights in Canada,' and Shirley Joseph, 'Assimilation Tools: Then and Now,' in *In Celebration of Our Survival: The First Nations of British Columbia*, eds. Doreen Jensen and Cheryl Brooks (Vancouver: University of British Columbia Press, 1991), 34–45 and 65–79 respectively.

51 Lears, *No Place of Grace*, p. xii.

52 For discussion of what he describes as the 'ambivalence' evidenced in much American antimodernism during this period, see Lears, *No Place of Grace*. For reconceptualization of this notion of ambivalence as a modernizing antimodernism with clear political, social, and economic implications see McKay, *Quest of the Folk*.

53 Zöe Wicomb, 'Tracing the Path from National to Official Culture,' in *Critical Fictions: The Politics of Imaginative Writing*, ed. Philomena Mariani (Seattle: Bay Press, 1991), 245.

54 Introductory wall text panel, at 'The Group of Seven: Art for a Nation.' The fact that the exhibition was actually designed from this position of boosterism is declared in the first sentence of the introductory wall text, which sets the tone of the show: 'This exhibition celebrates the seventy-fifth anniversary of the Group of Seven's formation ...'

55 '1921' wall text panel, at 'The Group of Seven: Art for a Nation.' The Harris canvas, entitled *A Side Street*, is now in the collection of the Art Gallery of Windsor, a gift from the Detroit Institute of Arts.

56 Hill, *Group of Seven*, 139.

57 'National Gallery Will Encourage Art. Will Increase Patronage of Canadian Artists,' Toronto *Globe*, 28 May 1914.

58 Hill, *Group of Seven*, 139, and passim; Reid, *Le Groupe des sept*, 11, 168–9.

59 Hill, 'The National Gallery, A National Art, Critical Judgement and the State,' in Michael Tooby, ed., *The True North: Canadian Landscape Painting, 1896–1939* (London: Lund Humphries with the Barbicon Art Gallery, 1991), 81. See also Hill, *Group of Seven*, 287–92.

60 Reid, *Le Groupe des Sept*, 9.

61 Tony Bennett, *The Birth of the Museum: History, Theory, Politics* (New York: Routledge, 1995), 76, 141.

62 Benedict Anderson, *Imagined Communities: Reflections on the Origins and Spread of Nationalism*, rev. ed. (London: Verso, 1991), 11–12; Bennett, *Birth of the Museum*, 148.

63 Bennett, *Birth of the Museum*, 142. See also Martin Prösler, 'Museums and Globalization,' in *Theorizing Museums*, ed. Sharon MacDonald and Gordon Fyfe (Oxford: Blackwell Publications, 1996), 34–7.

64 I am indebted here to Bennett's insightful analysis of the situation of Australia Aboriginal material culture in late nineteenth-century Australian museums. See, in particular, *Birth of the Museum*, 150–1. This perception of aboriginal peoples also accounts for the treatment of what were in reality a number of distinct Northwest Coast aboriginal cultures as one monolithic entity.

65 NAC, Arthur Lismer Papers, vol. 1, f. 'Canadian Art,' 'Lecture in Toronto to the Canadian Club, Dec. 13, 1926.' This narrative was first published as a coherent history in 1926 in Lismer, *A Short History of Painting*, 27–32, the artisanal tradition assigned to Québec having been confined to the (male) apprenticeship system established by the seventeenth-century 'French Canadian regime.' It was also the basis of the National Gallery of Canada's 1938 exhibition, 'A Century of Canadian Art,' which was mounted for the Tate Gallery in London as the first 'oversea' exhibition of Canadian historical painting and sculpture. Writing to High Commissioner for Canada Vincent Massey, National Gallery director Eric Brown made this

clear, stating, 'We are starting the story with one or two West Coast Indian Argelite [*sic*] carvings and a Chilkat Blanket and going from there to Quebec for a group of French Canadian wood-carvings, which will include your "Last Supper." From that background we shall start on the painters and sculptors and carry the story to the present day.' According to Brown, 'the Trustees were greatly taken with the idea [of the exhibition] and think it would be of immense value both as an Empire gesture and an artistic event.' See National Gallery Library and Archives, NGC fonds, 5.4–C, 'Canadian Exhibitions/Foreign, Century of Canadian Art Exhibition 1938,' f. 2, Brown to Massey, 16 June 1938; and Brown to J.B. Manson, Director and Keeper, Tate Gallery, 27 October 1937, respectively. See also *A Century of Canadian Art* (Ottawa: National Gallery of Canada, 1938).

66 '1926 and 1928' wall text panels, at 'The Group of Seven: Art for a Nation.'

67 This may explain why, following a talk at the Art Gallery of Ontario in which I presented some of the foundational ideas for this paper, it was suggested to then curator of Canadian historical art Dennis Reid that I was a communist.

68 *The OH!CANADA Project* was the 1996 Art Gallery of Ontario exhibition held in conjunction with the Toronto run of 'The Group of Seven: Art for a Nation' (in addition to the catalogue, a tabloid of the same title was published to accompany the show). See also Michael Tooby, ed., *Our Home and Native Land: Canada's Sheffield Artists* (Sheffield: Mappin Art Gallery, 1991); Tooby, *True North*. There are no monographic treatments of the Group of Seven's work that do not consider that work primarily in terms of Canadian nationalism; Reid's *Le Groupe des sept* is the only one that does not also advance an overtly nationalistic reading. The National Gallery's publication of Reid's exhibition catalogue, however, effectively reified the Group's nationalistic stance.

69 According to a survey conducted in advance of the recent show, 95.2 per cent of all income groups in the Greater Toronto area had heard of the Group of Seven, in comparison to 86 per cent of middle and upper income groups in London, Ontario; 17.6 per cent across the Canada–United States border in Buffalo, New York; and 8 per cent in Rochester. In contrast, respondents demonstrated relatively little awareness of individual Group members. Jackson was the Group member/associate most frequently mentioned; 29 per cent of respondents in the Greater Toronto area and 12 per cent in London identified him. Respondents in Buffalo and Rochester did not mention Jackson, and only 2 per cent of respondents in either city were able to identify even one member/associate of the Group (those that did were in Buffalo). Although he died before the formation of the Group, Tom Thomson was mentioned as a member/associate of the Group by 43 per cent of respondents in the Greater Toronto area, 30 per cent in London, and 2 per cent in Buffalo.

In this connection it should also be noted that the cartoon identifies seven painters as constituting the Group of Seven when, in fact, the number of members in the Group fluctuated from six to eight and perhaps even nine. My thanks to the Art Gallery of Ontario for making the survey results available to me.

70 As it was, the introductory wall panel to the 1995 exhibition identified the reconstructed series simply as 'the eight exhibitions the artists organized in Toronto from 1920 to 1931.' The Art Gallery of Toronto was not mentioned, either in the eight

wall texts, or in the 109 extended labels. This staggering feat of erasure, which echoes the treatment of those unnamed collectors who purchased the Group members' work, effectively set the stage for a story in which the National Gallery of Canada figured as institutional protagonist. The identification of Toronto as the site of the shows was ineffective in countering this; it simply lacked significance in the narrative, both as the site of the Group's exhibitions and as a marker of the Group's regionalism.

71 Jon Stratton and Ien Ang, 'Multicultural Imagined Communities: Cultural Difference and National Identity in Australia and the USA,' *Continuum* 8 (1994), 131. See also John Eddy and Deryck Schreuder, 'Introduction,' in *The Rise of Colonial Nationalism: Australia, New Zealand, Canada and South Africa First Assert Their Nationalities, 1880–1914*, ed. John Eddy and Deryck Schreuder (Sydney: Allan & Unwin, 1988).

72 Stratton and Ang, 'Multicultural Imagined Communities,' 127–32.

73 Ibid., 132.

74 Ibid.

75 See Homi Bhabha, 'The Third Space: Interview with Homi Bhabha,' in *Identity, Community, Culture, Difference*, ed. Jonathan Rutherford (London: Lawrence and Wishart, 1990), 207–21; Stratton and Ang, 'Multicultural Imagined Communities,' 154. In addition to the difficulty generally posed to the multicultural imagined community both by the politics of aboriginality and by racial – rather than just ethnic – difference, Stratton and Ang point out that the 'multicultural fantasy' in Canada is also 'contentiously restricted to so-called English Canada' (157 n8). What is curious about the 1995 exhibition in this respect is that the advancement of Anglo-Canadian hegemony within the current 'multicultural imagined community' in Canada was actually facilitated in the introductory wall text to the exhibition which stated that the show was a celebration of the seventy-fifth anniversary of the formation of the Group of Seven, while maintaining that 'the Group's goals were nationalist and their prime audience was English Canadian.' Because the show did not address the implications for contemporary, 'multicultural' audiences of celebrating Anglo-Canadianism as the basis of national culture, it effectively forced these viewers to celebrate (and thus reinforce) the cultural hegemony of the ethnic group within which the cultural differences of other ethnic groups in the multicultural imagined community are contained. Thus, even though post–Meech Lake Accord viewers in Canada were aware that current internal conflict in Canada mitigates against this containment of all cultural difference, they were being asked to celebrate an exclusionary, hegemonic 'multicultural nationalism' – one that was exclusive, certainly, of the contentious 'ethnic nationalisms' of First Nations peoples and French-speaking Canada.

76 Stratton and Ang, 'Multicultural Imagined Communities,' 148.

77 Bennett, *Birth of the Museum*, 87.

PART THREE

CHAPTER NINE

Introduction to Part Three: Modernity, Nostalgia, and the Standardization of Time

Kim Sawchuk

And time itself glides on in ceaseless flow,
A rolling stream – and streams can never stay,
Nor lightfoot hours

Ovid, *Metamorphoses*[1]

What time is, of course, nobody knows. Fortunately the lack of a satisfactory definition of time is, for most purposes, no great handicap; all that is necessary is to be able to measure it.

Malcolm M. Thompson, *The Beginning of the Long Dash*[2]

Ever since Western civilization entered the throes of modernization, the nostalgic lament for a lost past has accompanied it like a shadow that held the promise of a better future.

Andreas Huyssen, 'The Search for Tradition'[3]

For many artists and intellectuals living at the cusp of the twentieth century the allegory of an idyllic lost paradise that could be revisited offered the hope of personal and creative redemption. This yearning accompanied a rapid growth in industrialization and urbanization, in the words of Andreas Huyssen, 'like a shadow that held the promise of a better future.'[4] In the following four papers we read of this desire for another place and another time. In each instance the shift that is described is not only to a *place* of serenity, real or imagined, such as the countryside, nature, the land, or back to childhood. It also gestures towards another *temporal* landscape.

Vincent van Gogh describes his journey 'to the slower pace of the less-developed South, with its communities outside of Marseilles still marked by agricultural labor and by the seasons and cycles of nature' as the passage from 'decadence to country purity.' Henry van de Velde, who was associated with the Belgian art nouveau, designs his home, Bloemenwerf, to act both as a zone of comfort and simplicity, and as a space to experiment with artisanal techniques. The Parisian shadow puppet theatres of Henry Somm, George Auriol, and Caran d'Arache (Emmanuel Poiré) fused the folk arts of the Orient by way of modern technologies, offering imaginary transport out of the weariness of urban life and away from the pressures of adulthood. In Sweden painters such as Nils Kreuger, Karl Nordström, and Prince Eugene reclaimed their association with nature, embracing Sweden's 'primitive' landscape and pagan rituals. As Michelle Facos explains, the revival of rituals and festivals, among them Swedish Midsummer, reconnects ritual to landscape and landscape to the passage of the seasons.

The term often associated with this recurrent antimodern sentiment is 'nostalgia.' To understand this contradictory yearning for a future imbued with the past, it helps to know how time itself was being transformed at this particular moment in modernity. Nostalgia for a 'simple' past was felt at the precise historical moment when, in the 1880s, Europe and North America moved from a measurement of time based on the particularity of place. The standardization of time to the pulse of the twenty-four-hour clock was adopted in 1883 by the United States, in 1885 by Europe, and in 1886 by Canada.

T.J. Jackson Lears writes, 'the triumph of clock time was a key component of modernity.'[5] Lears equates the most naïve antimodernist expression with the belief that pre-modern cultures are timeless. The search in this instance, I would argue, was not for inert timelessness outside of history but for alternatives to some of the changes being inaugurated in the name of progress at this time. It is not just that the clock became omnipresent within the period of modernity. Time was standardized, time zones were imposed, and the introduction of new technologies made it possible to cover greater distances quickly – all of this transformed space-time relations.

We take the existence of lines of longitude on maps for granted but one cannot underestimate their significance. Lines of longitude mark distances from east to west, dividing the world into time zones and unifying all the clocks found within a given geographical area. A time without uniform or standardized time zones is a time of unequal hours, a time that is based on the movement of the sun from east to west, mile by mile. Before time zones were established and co-ordinated, communities marked their own time as that point when the sun reached its zenith at noon. The chiming of bells at the church or the town hall symbolically unified all within hearing distance as members of that community. While astronomically correct, the practice of setting clocks to local time lead to a proliferation of time zones at the turn of the century: for example, Wisconsin had thirty-nine time zones, and Michigan had twenty-seven.

Local time caused confusion, but it was not a problem as long as the fastest speed of travel over land was a horse. In North America the aggressive westward expansion of the American frontier at the end of the nineteenth century contributed to the growing need to agree on a system of standardized time for the nation state. As James Carey writes, 'With every degree of longitude one moved westward, the sun reached its zenith four minutes later.'[6] Railroads moved across the continent covering distances at unprecedented rates. The variety of local times caused confusion with scheduling, accidents, and passenger irritation. No one could easily determine when a train would arrive at a particular station, and worse, trains crashed because of shared lines. Legend has it that Sanford Fleming, the 'father' of standardized time in Canada, became an advocate for the co-ordination of time zones when in 1876 a printing error on a train schedule in Ireland caused him to miss a connection with subsequent embarrassment to himself and friends. Throughout North America telegraphy made it possible to synchronize clocks, and hence transmit time from a central place. The Canadian Pacific Railway officially adopted the twenty-four-hour system in 1886, unifying Canada geographically and temporally by signals sent out via the telegraph wire. The telegraph is also significant in the history of communications as it allowed the transmission of messages independent of the transportation routes for stagecoaches or boats. To summarize, in North America the pressure to establish time zones was exacerbated by geography; there is, for example, an eight-hour difference between the most easterly and most westerly coasts of America. Although Britain had long advocated the standardization of time for purposes of Empire and accurate navigation on the high seas, the exigency within Europe was not as profound, given the smaller size of European nation states. The growth of communications technologies, the new speeds attained through transportation systems, and commercial and political expansion all demanded a co-ordination of timekeeping around the world. In this epoch of colonialism (a political and administrative practice to secure the domination of various European nation states) and imperialism (the economic exploitation of these areas), cities, countries, and markets were co-ordinated through refinements in longitudinal determination.

By the 1880s it was deemed 'desirable to adopt a single prime meridian for all nations, in place of the multiplicity of meridians which now exist.'[7] From 1885 onwards, Greenwich observatory, the site of public control of the clocks of Great Britain, was designated the initial prime meridian of longitude to provide a unified and co-ordinated standard of time on a global scale. A 'universal day' would continue to be an average solar day. However, the universal day was 'to begin for all the world at the moment of mean midnight of the initial meridian, coinciding with the beginning of the civil day and date of that meridian.'[8] With the adoption of Greenwich as the point from which all time zones would henceforth be calculated, a new global consciousness was instantiated, a consciousness and coordination of space and time whose ramifications are experienced today even if the mechanisms by which time is calculated are not the same. With the standardization of time, zones were fixed and the globe was divided into lines of longitude. Carey puts it succinctly: 'The development of standard time zones served to overlay the world with a grid of time in the same way the surveyors map laid a grid of space on old cities, the new territories of the west, or the seas. The time grid could thus be read to control and co-ordinate activities within the grid of space.'[9]

In other words, space and time are intimately connected. Separating them analytically as we often do is a reflection of our own spatio-temporal organization. Modern systems of transportation and communication have achieved a separation of time and space from the central, pre-modern prominence of place.[10] Albert Einstein would soon demonstrate theoretically both the intimate connection between space and time and its relative nature. From our purview we now understand that time is simply what the clock says. But a clock can be anything – the drift of a continent, one's stomach at noon, a calendar of religious events, a schedule of instructions. Time is any way of marking the passage of a moment with regularity; speed in this schema is the distance over a measurable unit of time. At the end of the twentieth century the predominance of computer communications has helped to inaugurate a new relationship between space and time on a global scale. Companies racing to develop a new piece of software will rotate the design file forward through time zones to subsidiary teams in Europe or Asia as the case demands, so that work can go on around the clock. This allows those corporate citizens who can afford to participate on a global scale to gain crucial lead-time over their competitors. As a result, time is evolving into an ever-present series of shifting twenty-four-hour days around the globe. The easy movement of information around the globe via computer networks places these global corporations in a perpetual present and a state of hyper-productivity.[11]

Modernity is marked by this increasingly sophisticated micro-management of time and of space, along with a separation from a localized sense of place and a perception of acceleration caused by the collapse of the distance/time ratio.[12] It is by the careful study of these transmutations and the representations of time that we can better understand the organization and meaning of modernity.[13] However modernity is seen, in sociological and political terms, in the rise of secular forms of political power that were culminating at this time in the growth of the nation state and the emergence of capitalist, industrial economies with a system of monatized exchange, there remains considerable debate on the complex meaning of modernity. Modernity marks the decline of traditional social orders and the appearance of a dynamic social and sexual division of labour. Finally, modernity signifies the decline of a religious world-view and an increase in forms of subjectivity and sociality based on individuality, rationality, instrumentality.[14] For Anthony Giddens, as for Max Weber before him, 'who says modernity says organization.' The bureaucratically governed institutions and organizations of modernity are only possible once space and time have been denuded of sacred meanings and are transformed into units to be measured.

Located at the conjuncture of this restructuring of time and space, it is little wonder that the antimodernism of the artists referred to earlier expresses a desire for a falsely idyllic, localized sense of community, one rooted in a concept of belonging to a place with a different – that is pre-modern – temporal order. I say falsely idyllic because pre-modern societies were not without relations of power. As well, the term premodernity covers a multiplicity of social formations that impose a false representational coherence, implying anything from tribal societies based on kinship relations to agrarian cultures under the tutelage of the divine right of kings.

These alterations of the temporal landscape did not begin just at the end of the nineteenth century; rather, there is a history of uneven beginnings. For example, in the late middle ages the European bourgeoisie, the urban merchants and scholars, pioneered the adoption of the concept of a day with hours of uniform duration – a 'time metric' to measure the passage of time and to calculate wages. Until the late fourteenth century, Europeans punctuated their days with hours that varied across the seasons, depending on the length of daylight. As research on time and labour points out, perceptions of time and work differ even within Europe. It is not only a matter of technology but also of customs, culture and political resistance.[15]

This highlights several important points about time and the nostalgic desire for a return to the past. First, the moment of sacred time and the rationalization of time cannot easily be marked as having a definite point of origin, and without a point of origin there is no clear point of return. Second, the history of time cannot be reduced to the technologies that measure it (the sundial and the mechanical or atomic clock); rather, it is contingent upon existing cultural and social practices that are in constant political contestation. Third, history itself does not move like an arrow; there are varying temporal lags and developments and seemingly incompatible temporal orders – even within Europe. Indeed, the linear idea of time (time as an arrow) is a modern idea that invokes a teleological conception of history with a unified unidirectional movement into the future.

It is tempting but erroneous to argue that a force called modernity wiped out all that preceded it, or to overstate the power of a unified space-time grid, or to assume that there has been a total de-sacrilization of time into abstract empty categories. Rituals such as Midsummer live on in Sweden even as they are overridden by calendars that officially date them. Conceptions of time at the turn of the century, as now, remain steeped in moral, aesthetic and sacred symbols. Symbols such as the fir tree or evergreen (whose needles remain to defy seasonal change) continue to signify eternity and life. Ovid's description of time as a river still resonates and can be understood. New rituals are established, even as old ones are obliterated. Cosmological connections remain, even as their origins are forgotten, because time does not move forward in any unidirectional way. Van Gogh's paintings of peasants in fields engaged in seasonally defined work with the industrial landscape hovering overhead wonderfully depict the disjuncture of temporal orders of his period.

Indeed, many of us live under several competing and conflicting temporal orders: profane, biological, physical, geologic and personal time.[16] Differential rates of movement can cause collisions and flows when, for instance, our biological clocks do not move at the same rate as our workday. Our dominant corporeal rhythms do not move with regular twenty-four-hour clock-like precision but rather are attuned to a twenty-five-hour cycle. This innate tendency of our biological schedules to drift later and later is restrained each day as our circadian body clock is reset by the cycle of night and day through a process known as 'entrainment.' This time keeping (the equivalent of continually readjusting a cheap watch, in the words of one researcher) is actually heartier than any well-crafted timepiece. Over a lifetime too much precision would wreak havoc, and on occasion turn the biological cycle upside down. Daylight and darkness, which are powerful cues to reset the body clock's adjustments, are confounded by yet another seemingly benign technology; the electric light can permanently extend the hours of daylight – just ask a chicken in a poultry factory.[17] If indeed we are moving fast forward and out of control then perhaps one of our challenges as subjects within a temporal landscape is to know when to slow down, to stop, or to hasten our movements – what velocity to adopt at any moment in time.

The lurching uneven movements of modernity have changed our lived relations of space-time and their representation. Careful study of their encoding within the space of aesthetic representations such as painting reveal much about the context as well as the contradictions and disjunctures at a given moment in history. And here I would argue for an extension of Mikhail Bakhtin's concept of the 'chronotope.' Bakhtin used the chronotope as a means to analyse genres based on the specificity of the organization of space and time in a novel. A similar reading could be attempted of any aesthetic form if one thinks that 'spatial and temporal relations are constitutive of the work of representation.'[18] The symbolic depiction of time, like Salvador Dali's melting clocks draped over boulders in a surrealistic dreamscape, is one obvious way of discussing the depiction of time. A more profound way of discussing the depiction of time lies in the work of artists such as Paul Cézanne, who forged a new language of representation by abandoning linear perspective, thus making 'spatial dispositions arise from the modulations of colour.'[19] For instance, cubism fractured space and time in the frame of a painting 'by providing images of the same movement from different points in space and multiple views of a single scene in various points in time.'[20] Here, modernism, as an artistic ideology and practice, and modernity, as a social condition, cross paths. In modernism the rise and fall of a fixed-point perspective in painting and the linear narrative in a novel signal changes in space-time apprehension. In our own historical moment, the film *The Matrix* is distinct from earlier science-fiction films; even though it is constrained by a traditional Hollywood plot structure that demands that the boy and girl kiss and live happily ever after, this film incorporates the non-linear sequencing of a video game format to structure its pacing, speed, and narrative logic. But let me return to the not-so-distinct past.

Vincent van Gogh, Henry van de Welde, Nils Krueger, Karl Nördstrom, Caran d'Arache: the works of these antimodern modernists were infused with what all four authors in this section of the present book at various points describe as 'nostalgia' – a desire to be located elsewhere, a desire for worlds with 'a viscous and sticky time that drags itself slowly through space.'[21] Within the experience of modernity and these fundamental transformations of time-consciousness, there is a longing for a past before the clock, before the time zone, a past of seasonal artisanal or agricultural work outside the regularities of wage labour. An antimodernist temporality imagines a rhythm and pacing of life not governed by a clock set in a single location, by a factory whistle, by a seven-day week, or a calendar year with holidays and vacations turned into commercial opportunities for gift-giving. It is the desire for a return to a perceived historical moment in time when the sense of time accommodated the rhythms of the body, the movements of the sun, the rotation of the earth, and the passing of the seasons. It is, in essence, a conception of time with a physical and material connection to a natural order; a time before the railroad, the telegraph, and the time zone; a time when things did not move quite so fast. Bakhtin identified this sensibility as an 'idyllic chronotope' featuring the 'folkloric time' of daily and seasonal cycles with attention to the events of home life.[22] It is a time that seems to stand still but of course doesn't. It is a fantasy that speaks of the transformations taking place, of politics and power. The standardization of time, a hallmark of modernity, ushered in a distinct spatial and temporal organization that has become so fixed in our lives that it seems to be the natural force of time, a history we forget. It is nostalgic to the core.

But here it is worth noting the origins of the words 'nostalgia' and 'sentiment.' According to Webster's dictionary, the origins of nostalgia are Greek, from the words *nostos*, to return home, and *algia*, akin to an old English word meaning 'to survive.'[23] Nostalgia describes a melancholia caused by a protracted absence, a wistful, excessively sentimental, and even abnormal hankering for the return of some real or romanticized period or irrecoverable condition or setting in the past. The word 'sentiment' derives from the French *sentire* (to feel or perceive) and is defined as an emotional idealism or a romantic or nostalgic feeling verging on sentimentality. Sentimentality can apply to anyone, but it especially applies those who are 'unduly, habitually, and promiscuously affected by softer, pleasanter, more feminine emotions.' Usually it suggests a lack of genuine or natural feeling, and implies the emotion is purposely evoked for the thrill, as an affectation.

In *On Longing*, Susan Stewart theorizes nostalgia as a longing for 'face to face communication, for origin, for nature' in a highly mediated age. In general, I agree. However, in Stewart's work nostalgia turns out to be a dreadful thing, a type of 'disease' that obliterates lived experience and offers the false hope of a return to the utopian space of the 'walled unity of the maternal.'[24] According to her, nostalgia is often evoked in miniatures, and while the function of the miniature is to bring historical events to life, it is a sentiment that 'erases their history, to lose us within their presentness.'[25] While all four authors in this section of the present book discuss the nostalgia of the antimodernist sentiment, this discussion must be understood in all its complexity. Nostalgia has been caricaturized as mawkish, maudlin, soppy, mushy and slushy romanticism. Unlike Stewart, I am not convinced that nostalgia obliterates history, condemning one either to the perpetual present, or to an obsession with an idealized past that never existed and that stops one from living in the present. Both of these contradictory states have been associated with the melancholy of the perpetually nostalgic. I wonder whether both nostalgia and the sadness and melancholy associated with it are unintentionally demeaned because of their association with the feminine, which is itself associated with irrationality and sentimentality. Can nostalgia also act as a step towards a remembrance of things past, towards a history that includes the senses, a history of home and hearth?

By refusing nostalgia we are protected from these sentiments, hardened against feeling both the losses in our lives and the changes within our society and culture that are not of our making but that are in the interests of those classes who benefit from the ideology of unrestrained progress. Nostalgia is not necessarily radical but neither is it an inherently conservative valorization of the past or of emotions against rationality. This thinking creates yet another false divide that sets myth against history, the premodern against the modern, the feminine against the masculine, and the emotions against reason. The goal is to understand, in Raymond Williams's terms, thought as felt and feeling as thought. It is for precisely this reason that Williams refuses the term experience and opts for the rather awkward phrase, 'the structures of feeling': the term experience forgets that the past is still in process in the present. Williams eloquently explains: 'We are defining these elements as a "structure": as a set, with specific internal relations, at once interlocking and in tension. Yet we are also defining a social experience that is still in process, often ideas not yet recognized as social but akin to be private, idiosyncratic and even isolating ...'[26] Nostalgia, as I am describing it here, cannot so easily be dismissed pejoratively because it signals a transformation in the structures of feeling of those subjects living within modernity, experiencing but not necessarily cognisant of the major restructurings taking place with the institution of the prime meridian at Greenwich.

In this nostalgic antimodernism, a utopian moment and a state of innocence in the past is imagined before the fall into the clock-time of modernity – theatres of shadows and light played on the putative exoticism of a foreign land and European colonial power re-enacting, in Matt Matsuda's words, 'the space of time past.' However, as Michelle Facos writes, these artists did not naïvely think that they could turn back the clock. Rather, in the words of Amy Ogata, antimodernism was a way 'to negotiate the present by bringing the past into the future.' This sentiment – and aesthetic practice – expresses a complex critique of modernity from within modernity, a critique found within the politics of the day. As the authors in this section remind us, many of these artists and artistic movements were connected to agendas of socialism, anarchism or republicanism – ideologies that called upon a particular remembrance of the past to justify the inevitability and righteousness of their vision of the future. It is in this spirit that we can better comprehend the tension that exists between the perception of a lost past, an uncertain present, and the utopian desire for a better future within the antimodernism of these moderns.

NOTES

1 Ovid, *Metamorphoses*, trans. A.D. Melville (Oxford: Oxford University Press, 1986), XV: 357.

2 Malcolm M. Thompson, *The Beginning of the Long Dash: A History of Timkeeping in Canada* (Toronto: University of Toronto Press, 1978), 169.
3 Andreas Huyssen, 'The Search for Tradition,' in *After the Great Divide: Modernism, Mass Culture, and Postmodernism* (Bloomington: Indiana University Press, 1986), 23.
4 Huyssen, 'The Search for Tradition,' 23.
5 T.J. Jackson Lears, *No Place of Grace: Antimodernism and the Transformation of American Culture, 1880–1920* (Chicago: University of Chicago Press, 1983), 11. Marshall McLuhan also looked at the significance of the triumph of the clock as a means of understanding modernity in *Understanding Media: The Extensions of Man* (New York: McGraw-Hill, 1965), 145–56.
6 James Carey, 'Technology and Ideology: The Case of the Telegraph,' in *Communication as Culture: Essays on Media and Society* (Boston: Unwin Hyman, 1989), 223.
7 Derek Howse, *Greenwich Time and the Discovery of Longitude* (Oxford: Oxford University Press, 1990), 229.
8 Howse, *Greenwich Time*, 229.
9 Carey, 'Technology and Ideology,' 227. James Carey and Doreen Massey's attentiveness to the politics of space, time, and communications is part of the intellectual legacy of Harold Adams Innis. See in particular the essay, 'A Plea for Time,' in his *The Bias of Communication* (Toronto: University of Toronto Press, 1951), 61–91. See also Doreen Massey, *Space, Place, and Gender* (Minneapolis: University of Minnesota Press, 1994).
10 Massey, *Space, Place, and Gender*, 167–72.
11 Heather Menzies, *Fast Forward and Out of Control: How Technology Is Changing Your Life* (Toronto: MacMillan, 1989), 22.
12 Howse, *Greenwich Time*, xiv.
13 Anthony Giddens, 'Foreword,' in *Now Here: Space, Time and Modernity*, ed. Roger Friedland and Deirdre Boden (Berkeley: University of California Press, 1994).
14 Stuart Hall, 'Introduction,' in *Modernity: An Introduction to Modern Societies*, ed. Stuart Hall, David Held, Don Hubert, and Kenneth Thompson (England: The Open University, 1996), 8.
15 Richard Biernacki, 'Time Cents: The Monetization of the Workday in Comparative Perspective,' in Friedland and Boden, *Now Here*, 61–94.
16 Edward Hall, *The Dance of Life: The Other Dimension of Time* (New York: Doubleday, 1983), 13–26.
17 Peter Coveney and Roger Highfield, *The Arrow of Time: A Voyage through Science to Solve Time's Greatest Mystery* (New York: Fawcett Columbine, 1990), 298–313.
18 Julianne Pidduck, 'Intimate Places and Flights of Fancy: Gender, Space and Movement in Contemporary Costume Drama' (PhD diss., Concordia University, Montreal), 67.
19 Charles Taylor, *Sources of Self: The Making of Modern Identity* (Cambridge: Cambridge University Press, 1989), 468.
20 Friedland and Boden, *NowHere*, 2.
21 Mikhail Bakhtin, *The Dialogic Imagination*, trans. Caryl Emerson and Michael Holquist (Austin: University of Texas Press, 1981), 248.
22 Bakhtin, *Dialogic Imagination*, 225.

23 Oxford gives nostalgia's origins as the Greek words *nostros*, to return home, and *algos*, pain.
24 Susan Stewart, *On Longing: Narratives of the Miniature, the Gigantic, the Souvenir, the Collection* (Durham, N.C.: Duke University Press, 1993), 24.
25 Stewart, *On Longing*, 60.
26 Raymond Williams, *Marxism and Literature* (Oxford: Oxford University Press, 1977), 132.

CHAPTER TEN

Artisans and Art Nouveau in Fin-de-siècle Belgium: Primitivism and Nostalgia

Amy Ogata

The international phenomenon that is today called art nouveau was known by many names around 1900. The terms modern style, *nieuwe Kunst*, *Jugendstil*, and *modernismo* have all been used to describe the widely divergent manifestations of public and private architecture and decorative arts and crafts that flourished briefly throughout Europe at that time. While French speakers have always been credited with using the English 'modern style' to refer to art nouveau, the French term appeared frequently in editorial statements of the Belgian cultural periodical *L'Art moderne* in 1884.[1] Calling themselves 'croyants de l'art nouveau,' the editors of the magazine hoped for a complete integration of the arts and equated the new movement with a new vision of society.

The sense of youthful experimentalism inherent in the term 'art' nouveau has never defined any singular artistic style; it encompasses both the plastic arts and engineering, and it is also related to literary symbolism.[2] Yet in the intervening century architectural historians in particular have associated this term with urban buildings, writhing organic lines, and the overt use of iron and glass in the domestic interior.[3] The newness and innovation implicit in the term round out conventional definitions, further reducing art nouveau to a period of art history or a style detached from its historical and social context. In this essay, I argue that a strong current of nostalgia and a persistently anti-urban sentiment are also fundamental aspects of art nouveau in Belgium, particularly in the early work of Henry van de Velde. While van de Velde's significance as an art nouveau designer is firmly established, his notoriety is based principally upon his later career in Germany. Furthermore, the antimodern nature of his work in Belgium has been overlooked in order to situate him within a limited genealogy of Modernism. In examining van de Velde's transformation from artist to artisan and his first architectural project, his own house, Bloemenwerf, I show that a wistful, backward-looking vision of handmade crafts and countryside cottages held the promise of an organic unity between nature and culture that many believed was threatened by modern industrial society. Only by expanding the meaning of the term 'art nouveau' away from narrow conventions of style, and toward its larger cultural significance, can the competing ideologies within art nouveau's discourse of modernity come to light.

By suggesting that aspects of Belgian art nouveau are antimodern, I have relied on the ideas of nostalgia and primitivism as strategies that the artist adopted to reconcile the powerful forces of contemporary life. Rather than looking back to a particular moment in history as a paradigm of human civilization, artists like van de Velde romantizised a generalized idea of the past, as well as an equally constructed notion of the future. While they expressed a deep ambivalence toward industrial modernization, the avant-garde self-consciously appointed themselves leaders of a new and supremely modern vision of the future that promised health, social harmony, and a unique role for the artist. The concept of antimodernism, then, must be situated squarely within the larger context of modernism and not on its 'boundaries.' Indeed, as Marshall Berman has observed, 'to be modern is to live a life of paradox and contradiction ... We might even say that to be fully modern is to be antimodern ...'[4]

The antimodern aspects of Belgian art nouveau were built around the myth of an idealized Simple Life of humble work, rural living, and the presence of art as an intrinsic part of everyday life. Like most myths, the Simple Life was a thick mixture of reality and invention. Indeed, the national heritage of modern Belgium, a region established only with a revolution against the Dutch in 1830, was largely a nineteenth-century invention that was fabricated both to incorporate linguistic and cultural differences into a unified nationality, and also to pacify the social unrest that was becoming increasingly visible.[5] While Belgium possessed a longstanding tradition of a small-scale agriculture and an artisanal economy, it also had a more recent history of industrialization, which predated that of its powerful neighbours France and Germany and threatened such cottage industries as spinning and lace-making. By the time of its fiftieth anniversary of independence in 1880, a complex revision of Belgian cultural history was being reformulated to glorify the artisanal and pre-industrial crafts. From government officials to avant-garde artists, there was a broad-based interest in the decorative art industries and handicrafts of an earlier era.[6]

The most influential circle of turn-of-the-century Belgian artistic culture was Les XX, a group of twenty anti-academic artists who banded together in 1883 to exhibit what their critical supporters called 'l'art nouveau.' After their first show in 1884, Les XX's annual exhibition quickly became one of the most prominent international venues for the work of Belgian artists such as James Ensor, Fernand Khnopff, and Georges Minne, as well as a large annual selection of foreign guests, including Georges Seurat, Paul Gauguin, Aubrey Beardsley, and James MacNeill Whistler.[7]

In the early 1890s, Les XX began to present works of decorative art in the exhibition gallery alongside painting and sculpture. Objects such as Walter Crane's bright and boldly drawn *Toy Books* for children and a vase by Paul Gauguin (fig. 10.1) demonstrate the 'primitivist' tendency of decorative art at the turn of the century. Crane designed his children's books according to the belief that, as he said, 'children, like the ancient Egyptians, appear to see most things in profile and like definite statement in design.'[8] Scholars have shown that in the nineteenth century children were often invoked to represent a utopian 'primitive' state of innocence that was also associated with unindustrialised Asian, African, and peasant cultures.[9] Gauguin equated himself with the exotic, 'savage' primitive, and retreated to the unindustrialised cultures of Brittany and Tahiti because he believed the seemingly primitive ways of these societies were similar to his own visionary insight.[10] Jill Lloyd has suggested that primitivism is a significant aspect of *Jugendstil* theory in Germany, but her idea rests on the assumption of primitivism as non-Western and non-European.[11] Belgian artists, however, demonstrated an affinity for the exoticism of their own vernacular culture, encompassing the peasant, the artisan, and even the innocent child.

Henry van de Velde began his artistic career as a painter and studied at the Antwerp Academy and the Paris studio of Carolus-Duran. Although academically trained, he, like many others at this time, rejected the studio in favour of rural artist colonies in France and Belgium. The subjects of landscape and pastoral village life are consistent in his paintings of the 1880s, but his search for an artistic identity led him to explore a variety of modernist styles.[12] In 1889 he was elected to Les XX and throughout the late 1880s and early 1890s showed images of peasants at the annual exhibition. Works of this period, executed in a variety of post-impressionist styles, include *Farm at Twilight* (1889), painted in a divisionist technique emulating Seurat, and *Peasant with a Straw Hat* (1890), rendered in the manner of van Gogh.

Van de Velde's interest in the image of the hardworking labourer extended well beyond the canvas. In 1891 he lectured at Les XX on the topic of 'The Peasant in Painting.'[13] In this talk, he depicted the peasant as a figure of constance bound to the earth in a continually harmonic relationship of equal humility. He called for a rejection of the theatricality of Jean-François Millet's peasants in favour of Camille Pissarro's more 'authentic' depiction of the agricultural labourer as humble and hardworking. Yet, van de Velde argued, recent changes in the countryside were making the rural landscape increasingly sterile and falsely picturesque. 'Modernity has razed everything,' he stated unequivocally, and he lamented the disappearance of old farms and decaying cottages with thatched roofs, which were being replaced by brand new brick and tile houses. But even if van de Velde mourned a fading image of authentic rural life, it was in the psychological past, rather than the material past, that he found solace and hope for the future. He claimed that only a discovery of 'our soul of yesterday, or the day before ... our unpolluted child's soul' could halt the encroaching banality of modern bourgeois culture. For van de Velde, the rural landscape and the peasant symbolized a natural order and an eternal state of childlike innocence.

The countryside represents an idealised spatial entity linked inevitably with childhood.[14] As Susan Stewart has observed, the longing for lost childhood is a fundamental element in what she calls the 'social disease' of nostalgia.[15] She argues that nostalgia is a sadness without physical object that finds root in the gap between the sign and its signification, and that it attempts to erase the distance between nature and culture and return to a prelapsarian utopia. Others have suggested that nostalgia is the result of an irreversible and unfulfilled sense of linear time, within which the idea of the past becomes an obsession.[16] The desire to recapture something lost, like childhood, is therefore often centred on the idea of an innocent origin – a notion confirmed by the meaning, especially in French, of the word 'primitive' as an early or undeveloped stage.[17]

In the discourse of the antimodern, the primitive peasant and the nostalgic landscape of childhood are related tropes, which, for van de Velde, also included the figure of the artisan.[18] Van de Velde became interested in handicraft in 1892, and the following year he renounced painting and took up decorative design. He believed that decorative art, the art of everyday life, would be available to a larger public than easel painting. His first decorative project, *The Angels' Watch* (fig. 10.2), a large appliqué or 'tapestry' as he called it, was exhibited at Les XX the following year. The embroidery depicts a circle of peasant women dressed in the regional costume of communion, adoring a sacred infant amid the sheltering trees of the Flemish countryside. Like Gauguin's painting *The Vision after the Sermon* (1888, The National Galleries of Scotland, Edinburgh), to which it has often been compared, van de Velde's embroidery portrays the peasant as eternally connected to the land and as the keeper of a mystical folk tradition. The idealised peasant, the pure child, and the rural landscape in which they are set express the various ideals of 'primitive' innocence that are equally emblematic of the nostalgic world van de Velde attempted to realize in his own home.

Les XX voluntarily disbanded in 1893, but many of the same artists continued to exhibit at its successor, the Libre Esthétique. The Libre esthétique was an eclectic salon that showed a greater diversity of objects and much more decorative art. During the 1890s, selections from the English Arts and Crafts Exhibition Society were particularly numerous. While many have suggested that English decorative art had a seminal role in the spread of art nouveau, the antimodern appeal of these objects on the continent has often been overlooked.[19] Charles Robert Ashbee's vigorous, hammered metalwork and William Morris's printed books demonstrated interpretations of handicraft traditions of an earlier, preindustrial era. Belgian critics remarked upon the 'archaic' and 'primitive' quality of the Arts and Crafts objects and credited the English designers with reviving the methods of producing crafts.[20] By the 1890s, Morris epitomized the complicated figure of the enlightened artisan, intellectual, businessman, and socialist. His designs found favour with the continental bourgeoisie who could afford them, yet many free-thinking members of this class also embraced his political theories of an enchanted future, which were based on a romantic vision of the Middle Ages. In turn-of-the-century Belgium, members of the bourgeoisie, especially artists, held prominent positions in leftist political parties. In the circle of the Belgian Workers' Party, the political ideologies of socialism and anarchism and the decorative arts and crafts were intimately linked.[21] Indeed, the model of the artisan or worker provided a counter-identity for artists who sought a new role for art in society.

At the inaugural exhibition of the Libre Esthétique in 1894, the Belgian entrepreneur Gustave Serrurier-Bovy showed an elaborate installation called 'Un cabinet de travail' (*Study*, fig. 10.3). Serrurier-Bovy's completely co-ordinated ensemble took over the space of the entire gallery and turned it into an environment simulating the domestic interior. The only extant photograph of this temporary installation depicts a small room that included a brick hearth as well as a beamed ceiling, papered walls, a panelled frieze of droopy poppies, and sturdy, rectilinear oak furniture. Serrurier-Bovy's ensemble derived its effect from the co-ordinated, deliberately humble style of the furniture and furnishings. A critic from the Brussels daily *Le Soir* remarked that it suited 'followers of the "simple life." We too want to live that life!'[22] Rejecting plush upholstery and historicist motifs of the typical bourgeois interior, Serrurier-Bovy's *Study* embodied a return to the plain, enduring tradition of rural domesticity.

The appealing dream of the Simple Life was powerfully evoked by Edmond Picard, the prominent lawyer, socialist politician, and founding editor of the periodical *L'Art moderne*. In 1894 (the same year as Seurrier-Bovy's *Study* was shown), Picard published *Vie simple*, a collection of impressions and thoughts on the virtues of the Simple Life, which he saw as an alternative to modern urban existence.

> ... in this rustic dwelling, rendered unsteady by the years, guarded by old trees and sleeping waters, I will find my tranquil room with naked walls and my monk's cot. I will go, by fields, by forests, dressed in peasants' clothing, moved by the grave beauty of the immobile land and by the splendor of the moving skies. I will have my hours of contemplation and my hours of manual labor, working the kitchen garden, whitewashing the walls of the farm, turning the fragrant hay ... My food will be that of the artisan, while my mind will remain that of the thinker. No longer will the bitter worry of money, the universal ulcer and burning malady of fortune, gnaw at my side.[23]

Picard's escapist fantasy of retreating into the countryside, where he could live in an old cottage, work hard, assume the appearance of a peasant, and enjoy the meals of a self-sufficient artisan, reveals his anxiety about economic survival in an increasingly competitive world market and his profound distrust of modern industrial society.

At the Libre Esthétique the following year, Serrurier-Bovy showed another installation that he called *Chambre d'artisan (Artisan's Room*, fig. 10.4). This room was similar to that of the previous year. The plain wooden furniture again suggested an unspecified vernacular. A frieze by the artist Émile Berchmans adorned the upper part of the wall, and icons of domesticity – the hearth and window – were again integrated into Serrurier-Bovy's design. The most distinguishable difference between *Study* of 1894 and *Artisan's Room* of 1895 was the profusion of decorative objects in the interior. Heavy ceramic pots, plates, and vases sat on nearly every flat surface. A picture hung on the wall, and books lined the shelf above the mantle. Serrurier-Bovy demonstrated the widely held view that the 'simple life' of the artisan was infused with art through the ornamentation of useful objects. He based his idealized artisan's dwelling on an image of the past as a simpler, happier time. As he explained in a short pamphlet accompanying the *Artisan's Room*, the installation was a study of 'a new artistic idea,' but it also derived from the example of the 'men of yore,' who lived a 'simple and familial life' surrounded by 'window frames, chimneys, porcelain, copper objects, wrought iron, and a thousand other things that attest to their preoccupation with art.'[24]

Serrurier-Bovy and van de Velde maintained a similarly romantic idea of the artisan as one uniquely connected to the natural world, who responded intuitively to materials and obeyed an internal urge to decorate. Like Morris, they also saw the figure of the artisan as a political emblem of left-wing ideology. Van de Velde's utopian view of rural culture also parallels the theories of the exiled Russian anarchist Peter Kropotkin, whose writings van de Velde knew well. Kropotkin's ideal society consisted of loosely associated, decentralized communities or villages located in the countryside. Along with a co-operative system of mutual aid, art was an essential part of the anarchist community Kropotkin envisioned. He credited Ruskin and Morris for their belief that art should be a popular expression visible in all aspects of daily life rather than the luxury of the elite. Not only were artists and workers bound in a common struggle against the bourgeoisie, but, Kropotkin claimed, peasants and artists shared a 'primitive' understanding of the natural world. Van de Velde's own images of village life and the toil of the agricultural labourer were infused with the notion of the peasant as a noble savage. Van de Velde was also associated with the circle around the anarchist theorist Élisée Reclus, who lived and taught in Brussels from the mid-1890s until his death in 1905. Reclus, a renowned geographer, had written the prefaces to Kropotkin's books *Words of a Rebel* (1885) and *Conquest of Bread* (1892). He was invited to the Free University in Brussels in 1892, but deferred the appointment until 1894.[25] By this time, anarchist bombings in France had led nervous university officials, fearful of bringing violence to Brussels, to revoke the invitation. Reclus's supporters incited demonstrations, and eventually an autonomous wing of the university, the Institute of Higher Studies, was created for prominent leftist thinkers.

In 1895 (the same year he designed his house, Bloemenwerf), van de Velde taught a course on the arts of ornamentation at the Institute. In his lectures, published as 'Une prédication d'art' in the radical cultural periodical *La Société nouvelle*, van de Velde argued that when painting and sculpture became autonomous from architecture they degenerated into bourgeois commodities of easel painting and statuary.[26] This, he claimed, was due to the vanity of the artist. Without the vital link to real life, painting and sculpture lost the 'primordial breath of ornamentation.' Van de Velde's notion of ornament was based on his idea that popular art (by which he meant adornment of everyday objects) belonged to the community rather than to any single or private owner. The professional artist, on the other hand, had a vested interest in the notion of 'inspiration' and was tied to the market. Instinct, van de Velde claimed, was the true guide to aesthetic vitality and the 'savage'; the peasant and the fisherman were the keepers of spontaneity, invention, and virility. While he upheld Morris as a model artisan, it was Walter Crane who provided him with a clearly articulated social and aesthetic theory of decorative art. Crane insisted upon art as an essentially social product that could flourish only with the transformation of society towards 'the free federated communes which not improbably will in the future succeed the present jealous nationalities.'[27] Van de Velde acknowledged his debt to Crane's book *The Claims of Decorative Art*, and he specifically cited a chapter in which Crane suggests that man in a 'natural and primitive' condition instinctively decorated the objects of everyday life:

> The handles of dishes and hunting knives and horns, bows, hatchets, nay even man's own skin, all offered opportunities for the early ornamental impulse in carving and painting patterns. The implements in constant use, on which, indeed, rude as they were, life itself depended; the things most familiar, most valuable, constantly before the eyes or in the hands – these were the first things to receive the touch of art.[28]

The belief that primitive man possessed a fundamental and natural desire to ornament himself and his surroundings was widespread at the turn of the century, and this was often considered the very origin of artistic expression. Van de Velde himself claimed that:

> ... instinct guides more certainly than any aesthetic doctrine. The desire for an ornamented life is so intense among the savage that, without hesitation, he takes his baby from the arms of his companion, sitting next to a river, or on the threshold of his hut. In this solemn moment, he is inspired by everything around him: flowers, animals ... [and] cuts the skin of his infant, tattooing patiently, deaf to the cries that his natural commiseration might tempt him to stop, and then, with pride, returns the child to its mother ...[29]

While van de Velde suggested that the urge to decorate was an uncontrollable natural impulse, his own primitivism was clearly of the intellectual and political variety. Adapting the ideas of Kropotkin, Morris, and Crane – that the applied art of the 'primitive' was the essence of expression – he transformed himself from an academically trained painter into an artisan who responded intuitively to the nature of materials. When he decided to build his own house, he explored his own primitivist impulse to create shelter and to decorate in a spirit of craftsmanship, rather than as a trained architect. In his memoirs, van de Velde continually referred to himself as an 'autodidact' in architecture, equated with 'the primitive man who invents and creates his own tools.'[30]

The anti-urban ideology he had expressed in 'On the Peasant in Painting' increasingly took the form of an ideal relationship between art and the rural labourer or artisan. The splendid vitality of popular art derived, according to van de Velde, from a response to an instinctive need to embellish daily life; the innocent state of primitive man was equated with the purity of peasant societies, childhood, and the rural landscape. Theorizing the ideal relationship between art and culture that Serrurier-Bovy's interiors had also demonstrated, van de Velde wrote that:

> the village street is infinitely closer to pure, characteristic Beauty than the streets of cities. For the reason that each house, each object is marked with evidence, sometimes of taste and often of aesthetic sense: but this taste and this artistic sense are only transmitted to peasants, to fishermen ... the sensibility for art, in its unaltered and creative essence will soon be recognizable only among primitive peoples. For them, the ornamentation of life, utensils for the needs of life, constitutes the only means of living life.[31]

The intimate connection between art and life that he revered as 'pure, characteristic Beauty' was an expression of the organic relationship between the everyday life of peasants or fishermen and forces of nature. To replicate this state of grace, he had to go beyond the ornamentation of individual objects, to the symbolic space of the domestic interior itself. Van de Velde's private realm, completely designed by himself and his wife, was a site of reconciliation between the imagined past, the present, and an ideal future. As Vladimir Jankélévitch suggests, only the ability to move within a docile space can cure, or at least temporarily remedy, nostalgia.[32] As long as the departure and arrival can be reversed, the system of longing and returning is kept in balance. Yet, for van de Velde, the desire to overcome a sense of loss amounted to a more complete immersion within the fiction of artisanal integrity and domestic peace.

Bloemenwerf (fig. 10.5) was designed to be part of the natural landscape and to accommodate the simple habits of the countryside in rural Uccle. The name 'Bloemenwerf' came from the farmhouses that van de Velde and his wife, Maria, had seen on their honeymoon trip in Holland. Translated literally, the two words *bloemen* (blossoms) and *werf* (field or harbour) reinforce its visual connection with the surrounding environment. The gables on the front façade were embellished with non-structural half-timbering; the green and grey stripes acted as an emblem of vernacular architecture. Scholars have suggested that the designs of English architects C.F.A. Voysey and M.H. Baillie Scott, reproduced in the influential *Studio Magazine*, provided the model for Bloemenwerf.[33] However, van de Velde's vision was not the product of formal influence; rather, it was conceptually based on the image of the artisan's cottage as a paradigm of integrating art and everyday life in the ideal space of the countryside. Max Elskamp's woodblock image of Bloemenwerf for van de Velde's personal stationery captures the essence of the deliberately naïve forms and the integration of landscape and architecture.

Like Serrurier-Bovy's temporary installations, van de Velde's house was elaborately constructed around a romantic idea of the 'simple' artisan surrounded by art. The two-story central hall was the core of the dwelling and the primary space of family life (fig. 10.6). The plain walls were decorated with a tiny frieze that ran parallel to the picture rail and baseboards, along with the art work of van de Velde's friends and colleagues: a Théo van Rysselberghe portrait of Maria van de Velde, a van Gogh sketch, Japanese prints, and rustic pottery by the Anglo-Belgian artist Alfred-William Finch displayed in a van de Velde vitrine. The dining room further demonstrated van de Velde's careful and aestheticized interpretation of everyday rural life. The sturdy oak table and slender rush-seat chairs were derived from the idea of peasant furniture. He claimed that having a table in one corner of the room was a tradition in the Flemish farmhouse, and he chose 'tissus paysans' for the tablecloths.[34] His own wallpaper lined the walls of this room, and he used William Morris fabric for the armchairs that were next to the hearth. Even Maria van de Velde's loose 'reform' dresses were designed by her husband, and often made of Morris fabric.

Van de Velde's image of the dwelling as a protective, symbolic space where decorative art and architecture were unified according to natural, 'primitive' traditions, implied a mental wholeness that bourgeois industrial society had increasingly fragmented. Like the peasant, the artisan, and the 'savage,' van de Velde's primitivism also included the comfortingly mild, familiar form of childhood as an ideal psychological and aesthetic state. Children not only embodied an idyllic innocence that van de Velde cultivated at Bloemenwerf and associated with the past, but also symbolized the hopes of the future. Within his own work, van de Velde continually attempted to negotiate the present by bringing the past into the future. As I have noted, *The Angels' Watch* depicts the sanctified state of the child, the peasant women, and the Flemish landscape. The legible reference to the landscape and the habits of Flemish peasantry, mapped in abstract planes of colour in the embroidery, are transformed into three dimensions at Bloemenwerf. Van de Velde's attention to the appropriate clothing of the women in *The Angels' Watch* and his evocation of a natural, spiritual link to the countryside correspond in general terms to both the vernacular elements of half-timbering and shutters on the façade and the contrived organization of the dining room at Bloemenwerf.

Like *The Angels' Watch*, Bloemenwerf was designed to evoke protection and innocence uncorrupted by modern industrial society or academic rules. While the presence of a baby is the central subject of the embroidery, the absence of children was conspicuous at Bloemenwerf. The house was planned (but not yet built) in April 1895 when the van de Veldes's first child died a month after its birth. Henry later claimed that this event reinforced his mission to create an environment of 'aesthetic and moral hygiene' for the yet unborn children. Van de Velde's reverence for rural tradition and innocence merged in the space of his own house. His primitivism encompassed the rural landscape and the agricultural worker, as well as the safe, untroubled world of idealized childhood. Yet his nostalgia for these various states of innocence was infused with an ambition to create an indisputably modern way of living. Constructing an ideal realm from the lessons of the past and his hopes for the future, van de Velde relied on antimodern tools to find a modern means of integrating architecture and design into a consummate, if fictional, vision of stability, harmony, and comfort.

In 1902, van de Velde wrote a short obituary on the English illustrator Kate Greenaway. Calling her 'the good fairy,' van de Velde suggested that architects and designers who were 'devoted to the resurrection of pretty houses, the quiet habits of the home, to naive, happy gardens, and to a resurrection of life in simple bright clothing' had borrowed generously from her images.[35] Greenaway's illustrations of the tranquil life of children's games and tea parties in cottages surrounded by neat gardens suggested a calm existence far from the modernized, mechanized world of fin-de-siècle Belgium (fig. 10.7). Like *The Angels' Watch*, Bloemenwerf represented a nostalgic sanctuary of a 'primitive' culture and a space of hopeful resolution. Indeed, van de Velde remarked provocatively, 'who can say that we haven't drawn on the germ of this idea in the books of Kate Greenaway?'

The antimodern romanticization of pre-industrial culture was a fundamental aspect of Belgian art nouveau. Rural architecture and 'primitivist' themes in the decorative arts, along with the ideological position of anarchism and even the safe world of childrens' books were wholesome counterparts to the tropes of a decadent fin de siècle. In exploring some primitivist and nostalgic aspects of architecture and design, I have argued that the antimodern aspects of Henry van de Velde's Bloemenwerf were part of a larger cultural reconsideration of the nature of society, memory, and the role of a 'new art' for the twentieth century. The dream of a simple life of artisans and cottages demonstrates not only the complexity of art nouveau in Belgium, but also the fundamental contradictions inherent in modernity itself.

NOTES

My thanks to Laura Coyle, April Masten, Sally Mills, Gennifer Weisenfeld, Kim Sawchuk, and James Goldwasser for their criticism and suggestions.

1 Roger-Henri Guerrand stated that this was the first use of the term in French, in his *L'art nouveau en Europe* (Paris: Plon, 1965), 66. In the 1884 article, however, the editors compare the new exhibition society, Les XX, to a predecessor, L'Art Libre, by quoting a thirteen-year-old statement of the latter: '"Nous représentons l'art nouveau, avec sa liberté absolue d'allures et de tendences, avec ses caractères de modernité,"' in 'L'art jeune,' *L'art moderne* (9 March 1884), 74.

2 Debora Silverman provides a helpful discussion of the changing definition of art nouveau in turn-of-the-century France, tracing it from its equation with the Eiffel tower and industrial engineering to its reformulation into a style of domestic decoration with implications of interiority. See *Art Nouveau in Fin-de-siècle France: Politics, Psychology and Style* (Berkeley: University of California Press, 1989), 1–9.

3 See, for example, Nikolaus Pevsner, *Pioneers of the Modern Movement, From Morris to Gropius* (London: Faber & Faber, 1936), 114. See also his revised edition, *Pioneers of*

Modern Design (New York: The Museum of Modern Art, 1949, and Harmondsworth: Penguin, 1960), and Sigfried Giedion, *Time, Space and Architecture: The Growth of a New Tradition* (Cambridge, Mass.: Harvard University Press, 1941).

4 Marshall Berman, 'The Experience of Modernity,' in *Design after Modernism*, ed. John Thackara (New York: Thames & Hudson, 1988), 35.

5 The notion of inventing tradition derives from Eric Hobsbawm and Terence Ranger's book, *The Invention of Tradition* (Cambridge: Cambridge University Press, 1983). On the making of Belgian historical and cultural identity, see Aristide Zolberg, 'The Making of Flemings and Walloons: Belgium, 1830–1914,' *Journal of Interdisciplinary History* 5 (Autumn 1974), 170–235; B.S. Chlepner, *Cent ans d'histoire sociale en Belgique* (Brussels: Institut de sociologie, Éditions de l'Université de Bruxelles, 1972); Georges-Henri Dumont, *Histoire de la Belgique* (Verviers: Marabout, 1983).

6 This subject is discussed at length in my dissertation, 'Cottages and Crafts in Fin-de-siècle Belgium: Artisans, Antimodernism and Art Nouveau, 1880–1910' (PhD diss., Princeton University, 1996).

7 See Jane Block, *Les XX and Belgian Avant-Gardism, 1868–1893* (Ann Arbor, Mich: UMI Research Press, 1984).

8 Walter Crane, 'Notes on My Own Books for Children,' *The Imprint* (1913), 81.

9 Elisa Evett, 'The Late Nineteenth-Century European Critical Response to Japanese Art: Primitivist Leanings,' *Art History* 6 (March 1983), 82–106.

10 On the role of photography in this project, see Elizabeth Childs's essay in this volume.

11 Jill Lloyd, *German Expressionism: Primitivism and Modernity* (New Haven and London: Yale University Press, 1991).

12 Susan Canning, *Henry van de Velde (1863–1957), Schilderijen en tekeningen* (Antwerp: Museum voor Schone Kunsten, 1987).

13 Henry van de Velde, 'Du paysan en peinture,' *L'art moderne* (22 February 1891), reprinted in Canning, *Henry van de Velde*.

14 Raymond Williams, *The Country and the City* (New York: Oxford University Press, 1973), 297.

15 Susan Stewart, *On Longing: Narratives of the Miniature, the Gigantic, the Souvenir, the Collection* (Durham, N.C.: Duke University Press, 1993).

16 Vladimir Jankélévitch, *L'irreversible et la nostalgie* (Paris: Flammarion, 1974); Christopher Shaw and Malcolm Chase, eds., *The Imagined Past: History and Nostalgia* (Manchester and New York: Manchester University Press and St Martin's Press, 1989), David Lowenthal, *The Past Is a Foreign Country* (London: Cambridge University Press, 1985).

17 Marianna Torgovnick, *Gone Primitive: Savage Intellects, Modern Lives* (Chicago: University of Chicago Press, 1990), 18–19.

18 Ian McKay's use of 'Innocence' instead of 'antimodernism' demonstrates this notion. See his *The Quest of the Folk: Antimodernism and Cultural Selection in Twentieth-Century Nova Scotia* (Kingston and Montreal: McGill-Queen's University Press, 1994).

19 Robert Schmutzler suggested that the 'English roots' of art nouveau show examples of curvilinear graphic design and book illustration, such as the periodical *The Hobby*

Horse and Walter Crane's *Flora's Feast*. See 'The English Roots of Art Nouveau,' *The Architectural Review* 117 (February 1955), 109–17; and his *Art Nouveau* (New York: Abrams, 1962).

20 'Le Salon de la Libre esthétique, L'art applique,' *L'art moderne* (18 mars 1894), 84–5.

21 Eugenia W. Herbert, *The Artist and Social Reform: France and Belgium, 1885–1898* (New Haven: Yale University Press, 1961); Liske Tibbe, *Art nouveau en socialisme, Henry van de Velde en de Parti ouvrier belge* (Amsterdam: Kunsthistoriese Schriften 5, 1981); Paul Aron, *Les écrivains belges et le socialisme (1880--1913)* (Brussels: Labor, 1985).

22 *Le Soir*, 18 February 1894.

23 Edmond Picard, *Vie simple* (Brussels: Larcier, 1894).

24 Gustave Serrurier-Bovy, *Une chambre d'artisan* (Liège: Bénard, 1895).

25 Reclus was awarded gold medals by the Paris Geographical Society in 1892 and the Royal Geographical Society of London in 1894. He advocated an quiet, intellectual anarchism rather than violence. Marie Fleming discusses Reclus's interrelated theories of geography and anarchism in *The Anarchist Way to Socialism: Élisée Reclus and Nineteenth-Century European Anarchism* (London and Totowa, N.J.: Croom Helm and Rowman & Littlefield, 1979). See also Hem Day, *Élisée Reclus en Belgique: sa vie, son activite 1894–1905* (Paris and Brussels: Pensée et action, 1956), and *Élisée Reclus* (Brussels: Institut des hautes études de Belgique et Société royale belge de géographie, 1985).

26 Henry van de Velde, 'Une prédication d'art,' *La Société nouvelle* 132 (décembre, 1895): 733–44; 139 (juillet 1896), 54–63. This essay is based on lectures for a course on the decorative arts given in Antwerp in 1893.

27 Walter Crane, *The Claims of Decorative Art* (Boston and New York: Houghton Mifflin, 1892), 17.

28 Crane, *Claims of Decorative Art*, 108.

29 Henry van de Velde, 'Une predication d'art,' 736.

30 Van de Velde, *Récit de ma vie* (Brussels: Versa, 1992), 283.

31 Van de Velde, *Apercus en vue d'un synthèse d'art* (Brussels: Monom, [1895–6]), 19–20.

32 Jankélévitch, *L'irréversible*, 299.

33 Françoise Dierkens-Aubry, 'Henry van de Velde et le Bloemenwerf,' *La Maison d'hier et d'aujourd'hui* 41 (mars 1979), 48–59; 'Henry van de Velde,' in Georges-Henri Dumont, *Belgique: des maisons et des hommes* (Brussels: Nouvelles Éditions Vokaer, 1980).

34 Van de Velde, *Récit de ma vie*, 291.

35 Henry van de Velde, 'Kate Greenaway,' *Innendekoration* (French edition) February 1902: 47.

CHAPTER ELEVEN

Van Gogh in the South: Antimodernism and Exoticism in the Arlesian Paintings

Vojtěch Jirat-Wasiutyński

After a two-year stay in Paris, Vincent van Gogh travelled to Arles on 19 February 1888, to start 'this enterprise of a long voyage in the Midi' (469).[1] This was not a sudden decision. As early as the end of 1886, less than a year after arriving in Paris, he had written to H.M. Livens, an English painter whom he had met in Antwerp, that he was 'in *color* seeking life' and that he saw the South as 'the land of the *blue* tones and gay colors' (459a, original English) where he would practice this new painting. He also wrote to his sister in the fall of 1887 that it was his 'intention to go as soon as possible temporarily to the South, where there is even more color, even more sun' (W1). Yet the journey south was about more than the bright colour revealed by the southern sun; van Gogh later remembered it as a flight from Parisian decadence to country purity (595), from the incapacitating modern city, where he had become 'very distressed, quite ill and nearly an alcoholic' (553a), to the revitalising countryside where he hoped to restore his physical and mental health.[2] He believed that the sun and the warmth of the South would make his blood circulate again, purifying his body (B7) and intensifying his sense of life (B17). The trip was to be both an exploration of an exotic locale suited to the development of a new art of colour and a search for a haven in which to regenerate the enervated modern artist.

Van Gogh's retreat from the metropolitan modernity of Paris to a small provincial centre in Provence has been seen as an instance of the primitivism of turn-of-the-century artists, such as the group around Paul Gauguin in Pont-Aven, Brittany, who set up rural colonies. The move to Arles can certainly be understood in terms of that pattern, although van Gogh's Studio of the South lasted a scant two months and Gauguin was the only painter who participated. In this paper I consider van Gogh's sojourn in the South and the paintings produced there as an instance of antimodernism, a broader cultural pattern that may be more helpful to understanding his enterprise. The dominant form of antimodernism, which was widespread among the cultural elites of fin-de-siècle Europe and America, has been defined by Jackson Lears as 'the recoil from an "overcivilized" modern existence to more intense forms of physical or spiritual experience supposedly embodied in medieval or Oriental cultures.'[3]

Artisanal, martial, and spiritual ideals characterized antimodernist discourse; medievalism and orientalism were its common expressions in nineteenth-century Europe. Van Gogh shared many of these ideals and they are reflected in his representation of Arles.

The goal of such a withdrawal from the extremes of metropolitan modernity in order to draw on what were seen as older and emotionally more satisfying cultural norms was not only an escape but also, Lears argues, a discovery of strategies for coping better with new forms of modernity. Thus, while van Gogh rejected many aspects of modernity after leaving Paris, he did not paint a timeless vision of Arles as he would of Saint-Rémy in 1889–90.[4] He depicted the contemporary town of Arles, its immediate surroundings, and the inhabitants: fields, orchards, and vineyards producing for the urban markets of Marseilles and beyond; agricultural labour harvesting wheat on large farms; laundresses by the canals; sand barges on the Rhône; and portraits of a soldier, a postal employee, and a gardener, among others. Van Gogh's vision, however, was selective; he gave preference to painting the agricultural landscape and manual labour around Arles over industrial workers and the bourgeoisie.

Above all, his images transformed the everyday into an intensified experience of 'authentic' life with their exaggerated colour. The new art of colour that van Gogh developed at the end of his stay in Paris in a small group of paintings strongly influenced by Japanese prints, such as *Portrait of Pere Tanguy* (Musée Rodin, Paris) and *Italian Woman* (Musée d'Orsay, Paris), was applied consistently in the South. Arriving in Arles from Paris equipped with an avant-garde post-impressionist technique and style, the Dutch artist reworked the raw material of the South into an exotic image of vitality and authenticity. There is a clear analogy with industrial and commercial exploitation of the provinces and colonies by advanced technologies for metropolitan profit. Van Gogh presented his colourful paintings of Arlesian people and sites portrayed in the bright light of the South of France as counter-images to the drained, over-refined modern life of Paris.

'Un long voyage dans le Midi'

Van Gogh travelled by train from Paris to Arles – an overnight journey of some sixteen hours. Arles lies about eighty kilometres west and slightly north of Marseilles, and is located about thirty kilometres inland from the Mediterranean sea, where the Rhône river divides to form the delta of the Camargue (fig. 11.1). In the nineteenth century, geographers and historians often divided France into North and South, running an imaginary line from Saint-Malo to Geneva. The area to the south, including Provence, was characterized as backward in relation to the economically and socially progressive North.[5] The division of France into North and South was not, in the first place, a matter of climate and environment, although these often functioned as explanatory principles; it was one of development, a division based on material progress resulting from political and educational revolutions for which the North was the model and which was part of a broader division of Europe into North and South. Van Gogh's letters reflect this perception. He commented several times on the lazy and undisciplined attitude of the inhabitants of Arles (for example, 475, 480, 502), in effect applying a stereotype of premodern, precapitalist society to Southerners that was also regularly applied in Orientalism. The North–South divide could also be inverted to support a conservative vision of society based on the rejection of modernity, in which happiness, morality, and sociability would be located in the South, and pauperism and miserable workers in the North.[6]

Thus, van Gogh could envisage his journey south in space – 'this enterprise of making a long voyage in the Midi' (469) – in search of new subjects and a sunny climate, as a journey back in time, down the timeline of progress established by modernization: it was a journey from the fast-paced rhythms of modern city life, represented by Paris with its teeming boulevards, omnipresent commerce, industrial suburbs, and mass entertainment, to the slower pace of the less-developed South, with its communities outside Marseilles still marked by agricultural labour and by the seasons and cycles of nature. In a letter of August 1888 to his brother Theo, the artist juxtaposed *Portrait of Patience Escalier* (fig. 11.2), his image of a Provençal gardener and former cowboy (*bouvier*) in the Camargue that he had just finished painting, with Toulouse-Lautrec's *Poudre de riz* (fig. 11.3), a portrait owned by Theo that showed a Parisian woman preparing to apply her make-up over a rice-powder base. Van Gogh saw the two paintings as an antithetical pair. He used the contrast between rustic vigour and city refinement to underline his preference for the former and to signal a return to the project of painting the countryside that had motivated him in the Netherlands before his discovery of Paris and the Impressionists in 1886–7 (520).

In keeping with his sense of journeying into the past, van Gogh found similarities between the flat landscape near Arles and the historical, premodern landscape of his native Holland depicted in Dutch seventeenth-century painting. Describing some recently completed drawings that he was sending to his brother, he compared the landscapes of the Crau, a stony plain to the east of Arles, and the delta of the Camargue to 'the old Holland from the time of Ruysdael,' albeit noting a 'difference in color and in the limpidity of the atmosphere' (509; see also 502). Trying to find his bearings, van Gogh linked the contemporary Arlesian landscape to the past, to a Dutch landscape obliterated by modern progress but preserved in art.[7] He also used this strategy to give meaning to his Arlesian portraits; it stemmed from an antimodernist desire to build historical bridges to tradition and to find order in society to counteract a sense of rootlessnes (B14).

During 1888 van Gogh's vibrant paintings would celebrate contemporary Arles, with its visible links to the past, as a corrective to the fast-paced, fragmented, and inhuman modernity of Paris and the progressive North. In its antimodernism, his turn to the South would seem to have much in common with a conservative reinterpretation of the North–South divide. But van Gogh was no traditionalist celebrating age-old religion and custom like Frédéric

Mistral and many of the Félibres poets and writers.[8] He believed that, by travelling south, he was travelling back to a simpler life; at the same time, as Zemel has argued, he saw in Arles vital images of an 'alternative modernity.'[9]

Exoticism and a New Art of Colour

The Dutch artist's spatial displacement was complex too: his journey south was also a journey east, an exploration of another Europe on the threshold of the Orient.[10] Van Gogh fantasized a link between the South of France and both North Africa and Japan, interpreting all three spaces as antimodernist cultural sites and locations for developing the new art of colour.[11] Based on his readings of the Goncourt brothers and Pierre Loti and on his study of the imagery of the *ukiyo-e* woodcuts he collected, van Gogh imagined Japan as a small-town, agricultural, artisanal society comparable to rural Provence. He believed that, now that Japanese art was 'en décadence' and the torch of the new art of colour had been passed to the Impressionists, the South of France would be the site of its further development and flowering. 'I would like you to spend some time here,' he wrote to Theo in early June. 'You would feel it after a while, your vision changes, you see with a more Japanese eye, you feel color differently' (500).

Exoticism is a particularly useful concept for understanding van Gogh's cultural geography and its associations, especially if we construct it as open and heterogeneous, intersecting with the multiple discourses of gender, class, race, colonialism, and national identity.[12] In the period of France's second colonial empire, exoticism often overlapped with Orientalism as North Africa and Southeast Asia were conquered and exploited. The more general concept of exoticism can be distinguished from orientalism because of the former's relative indifference to detail and documentary accuracy. Both terms recontextualise that which is being represented in order to give it a new meaning.[13] For nineteenth-century Western Europeans, locations susceptible of being exoticized were those relatively unaffected by enlightenment values and modern economic development. Such locations – lying at the edge of contemporary civilization (both outside and inside the West) and poor by modern economic standards – were seen as picturesque, characterized by a combination of colourful costumes, strange customs, unfamiliar physical environments, and extreme climates and temperaments.[14] They were ripe for exploitation by the disaffected Westerner for whom the tensions between self and other, familiar and unfamiliar were all-important to the maintenance of 'authentic' selfhood under the pressures of rampant modernity.[15]

In 1835, Prosper Merimée compared the South of France to Spain: 'so strange did everything, language, costumes and the appearance of the land, seem to someone coming from the centre of France.' He had just arrived in Avignon and its medieval architecture, topography, climate, and vegetation reminded him of Valencia. Much of life was lived outdoors and the colourful, noisy street scenes appeared exotic to the northerner. The pronounced physiognomy, darker skin, and accented speech of the inhabitants completed his 'illusion of being far away from France.'[16] Although the South of Merimée's 'Voyage dans le midi de la France' began south of the Loire (which corresponds roughly to the Saint-Malo–Geneva line discussed above), it was not until he had reached Provence that he felt he had left France, his home culture, for an exotic one. The geographer Elisée Reclus, writing in 1864, noted that the Mediterranean littoral was geographically separate from the North of France, resembling North Africa in its climate, vegetation, and geology.[17] The location of Provence in the Mediterranean world, which had been the basis for classicism in earlier periods, now translated into exoticism and opened up a new Orientalist link with the cultures of North Africa and the Middle East. During the nineteenth century France asserted control over Algeria, Tunis, and Morocco in North Africa. In the 1830s a group of Saint-Simonians proposed a visionary economic system linking East and West around the Mediterranean Sea as the basis for the development of modern civilization. This provided the ideology for such projects as the Suez Canal, inaugurated in 1869, which linked the Mediterranean with the Red Sea and the Indian Ocean.[18]

By mid-century Marseilles had become the booming urban centre of the South and France's major Mediterranean port. In 1868–9, Puvis de Chavannes painted the murals *Massilia, colonie grecque* and *Marseille, porte de l'Orient* for the grand stairway of the art museum in the Palais Longchamp. The subjects for the two murals, chosen with the advice of the city council and the departmental prefect, affirm the classical foundation of Marseilles and celebrate the city's present and future link to the Orient.[19] Van Gogh's paintings acknowledge this vision of the South as part of a Mediterranean world based on the French presence both in North Africa and further afield in Southeast Asia. In the garishly coloured *Zouave* (fig. 11.4), he celebrated the virility of a contemporary soldier, probably just back from the war in Tonkin, dressed in a uniform clearly reflecting the Algerian origins and colonial foundation of the Zouave regiments.[20]

Southern colour was and remains a cultural construct, whether in the colourful fabrics and ochre-washed houses of Provence or in the travel accounts and paintings produced by and for visitors. The South of France was not colourful by nature, as Signac noted in his comments on van Gogh's paintings in 1894,[21] but van Gogh brought with him a northern vision of the South as exotically sunlit and full of colour, painting Arles and its surroundings with a high-key spectral palette organized around complementary contrasts as a sign of its southernness. As early as his 'Salon of 1846,' Charles Baudelaire posited an aesthetic geography of North and South that split France in two. He saw modern art, which he identified with romanticism and 'modeling in color,' as a product of the mist-filled North where imagination reigned supreme. In contrast, the South, where the sun shone and nature needed no supplementation, was typified by a sculptural vision of classicism based on line and tonal modelling.[22] Writing to the painter John Russell (1858–1931) forty years later, van Gogh identified himself with this northern tradition of modern colour painting, but proposed that its future lay in painting the colourful South. Pointing to the paintings of Monticelli and Delacroix as examples, he argued that, in order to give the viewer 'something passionate and eternal – the rich color and rich sun of the glorious South,' local colour should be ignored and 'the South be represented now by contraste simultané of colors and their derivations and harmonies and not by forms and lines in themselves as the ancients did formerly' (477a).

In late May, three months after arriving in Arles, van Gogh visited Saintes-Maries-de-la-Mer, a small fishing village and pilgrimage site forty kilometres from Arles on the Mediterranean coast.[23] The imagined proximity of Africa reinforced his exoticist view of the South as a world of colour; under the intense blue sky of the Mediterranean world, complementary contrasts proliferated and the soil appeared orange-coloured (B6). In a letter to his brother Theo, he ventured that 'if Gauguin comes here, he and I could perhaps accompany Bernard[24] to Africa when he goes there for his military service' (500).

It was Charles Blanc's essay in *Les Artistes de mon temps* (1876) that connected Delacroix, North Africa (Delacroix had visited Morocco in 1832), and the laws of colour, and laid the foundation for van Gogh's exoticist vision of the South. As early as April/May 1885 (401), van Gogh had studied Blanc's text, and in a letter to his brother Theo he copied key passages on the colour system of primary hues and complementary contrasts, which he characterized as 'laws known to Orientals since time immemorial.' In a passage that van Gogh did not copy but must have read, Blanc explains the application of the colour system using Delacroix's *Les Femmes d'Alger* (1834, Louvre, Paris) and *La noce juive* (1834, Louvre, Paris) as examples; at that time, both these paintings were in the Luxembourg Museum in Paris where van Gogh could have studied them. Blanc interpreted the former as expressing the Oriental luxury of a harem interior through the splendour and intensity of colour, and the latter as portraying the freshness of the outdoors under an African sky by contrasts of light and colour. With this model in mind, van Gogh concluded that anyone painting the South should, like Delacroix, use a palette structured around complementary contrasts.

The Romance of the Country

On the whole, van Gogh avoided painting the historic sites and picturesque views that had come to characterise Arles and its surroundings in prints and travel literature. The dominant representation of the city as an antique site famed for its classical monuments did not engage him.[25] In fact, he turned his back on the older inner city to portray the outskirts and surrounding landscape. Van Gogh lived at the north end of Arles near the fertile agricultural area called Trebon,[26] in the part of town inhabited by small-scale *cultivateurs* and agricultural workers, at first in cheap hotels and then, from September, outside the old city walls on the Place Lamartine. Like the workers, he headed out to work nearby, painting the orchards and fields to the northeast. His pictures follow the seasons: flowering fruit trees in the spring, wheat harvest in the summer, and grape vintage in the fall. Van Gogh emphasized the rural aspect of Provençal labour, devoting only a few paintings to shipping on the Rhône and none to the industrial activity associated with the gasworks and the extensive train yards and repair shops of the Paris-Lyon-Marseilles railway. Clearly this selection did not reflect contemporary reality. Traditional employment in agriculture had dropped from almost half of the working population at the beginning of the century to less than fifteen per cent by the 1880s and work on the river had virtually disappeared. New industries, especially, after 1848, the arrival of the railway with its large workshops, provided some of the replacement work.[27]

Industry and commerce are, nevertheless, not entirely absent from van Gogh's Arlesian oeuvre. Industry is evident in panoramic views such as the drawing *View of Arles from Montmajour* (Oslo, Nasjonalgalleriet) executed in May. Absorbed into the skyline, the smokestacks marking industrial sites stand alongside the Roman arena, the Romanesque church towers, and the Renaissance campanile of the city hall. Dwarfed by land and sky, old and new coexist as part of the urban silhouette. A second series of large views of the countryside from the elevated rocky site of the Abbey of Montmajour, drawn in July, self-consciously maps the region: van Gogh compared one to a 'carte géographique, un plan stratégique' (509). He also readily recognized the picturesque nature of some views and their romantic association with regional history. In one letter he wrote that the landscape near the abbey at sunset was 'as romantic as you can get, like Monticelli,' and noted that 'one would not have been at all surprised to see knights and ladies returning from hawking appear suddenly or to hear the voice of an old Provençal troubadour' (508).[28] This romantic perspective, in which the continued presence of the past and the coexistence of tradition and modernity are fantasized, informs all of van Gogh's depictions of Arles. This is why the small group of paintings in which he featured industry and railyards as a prominent backdrop to manual labour, such as reaping grain or washing laundry, is so revealing. Traditional activities are the focus of the images, yet the contrast of these activities with recent industrial development is a crucial aspect of van Gogh's romanticized antimodernism.

The Harvesters (fig. 11.5) shows the wheat harvest in the fields to the northeast of Arles with the city in the background. Adopting a vertical format, van Gogh deliberately used a steep perspective to produce a primitivizing picture like a nineteenth-century almanac image.[29] Three-quarters of the image is devoted to the wheatfields, leaving one-quarter for the sky and city. The two juxtaposed parts are differentiated by brushwork and especially by colour – a complementary contrast of sunlit yellow for the fields and violet for the shadowed buildings. The fields of wheat are more extensive and closer to the viewer, yet the smoky city on the horizon is easily nature's match. By placing two labouring figures just below the horizon, one of whom is a reaper swinging his scythe, van Gogh draws the viewer's eye into space and tries to link the rural and urban parts of the image. The figures remain firmly part of the fields, with the city safely contained in the distance, yet their manual labour is endowed with a special poignancy because of the industrial backdrop.

Another view, *Summer Evening: Wheatfield with Setting Sun* (fig. 11.6), places the city deeper in pictorial space in a traditional horizontal format based on seventeenth-century Dutch landscape painting. The city looms insistently over the acid-yellow wheatfields. There are no labourers in the ripe wheat, but the workshops continue to belch smoke night and day. A pair of lovers walks out from the city in the early evening as the mistral blows through the ripe wheat (B9). Here the large orb of the setting sun, improbably placed behind the city in the southwest, compresses background and foreground. As in the other view of suburban wheat fields, by dramatizing the tensions between industrialized city and agricultural countryside, the image brings out the romance of the countryside – sunset, mistral, and lovers.

A third image, *Roubine du roi* (fig. 11.7), shows an irrigation canal with washerwomen doing laundry at a washplace. The painting is a study that was never realized as a fully worked-out picture. Again using a steep, up-tilted perspective in a vertical format, van Gogh juxtaposes an image of manual labour with the new gasworks lit by the setting sun. As in the two paintings of wheat fields, dramatic tensions structure the composition. Here the glistening canal curves past the industrial site and joins laundresses in traditional costume to church and setting sun. Van Gogh did not need to paint the vision of medieval knights and ladies evoked in his letter to produce a romantic view of Arles. By depicting costumed Arlesiennes in the industrial belt, he evoked a similar antimodern romance: what we are given to see is not prosaic everyday labour, but the poetic and picturesque contrast of tradition and modernity.

Although these paintings are a statistically insignificant minority compared to the overwhelming majority of purely agricultural images, they are most instructive about van Gogh's antimodernism. In them, he acknowledges the presence of modernity – of capitalist markets and development, of industry and rail transportation – but he places this modernity in an exaggerated, distorted perspective full of tensions created by bold colour and flat, decorative surfaces. In all three canvases he sought to intensify the viewer's experience of older forms of labour in natural settings, fighting to preserve a place for the pre-modern and nature in a modernizing world. Empowered by his exoticist vision, he painted the wheat fields as a large expanse of chrome yellow intensified by contrasts of purple shadow and he loaded the blue canal with sulphurous yellow sunlight. The darker, more concentrated energy of the city reminds us that, in all of van Gogh's agricultural images, the city is the invisible other, motivating the intense antimodern experience of the exotically coloured landscape.

Portraits of the People

Van Gogh's most cherished project in Arles was to paint the human figure, an undertaking that he had last attempted in a sustained manner in Holland in 1884–5. His first portraits were of a Zouave soldier who posed for him in June. These images are charged with exotic adventure and virile prowess.[30] In the bust-length *Zouave* (fig. 11.4), the soldier's red cap looms against a green door creating a combination that reflects the Algerian national colours. The portrait is built around harsh complementary contrasts – a deliberately 'vulgar' and 'loud' painting technique, according to van Gogh (501), used to visualise the exotic context and animal vitality of the figure. He described the soldier as having 'a bull's neck [and] a tiger's eye.' In the age of colonialism, this pre-modern stereotype of a warrior male was associated with exotic cultures and hot climates. Van Gogh admired such a display of virility and even entertained fantasies of joining the French Foreign Legion.

Van Gogh's second sitter was a young woman aged 13 or 14; he titled her portrait *La mousmé* (fig. 11.8). Dressed in brightly coloured and patterned fabric, she sits stiffly upright in a bentwood armchair, her pose echoed by the flowering branch of oleander that she holds in her lap. The awkward sensuality of this bourgeois adolescent should be seen in contrast with the refined decadence of Parisian figures by Degas and Toulouse-Lautrec (for example, *Poudre de riz*, fig. 11.3). As a counterfigure to such metropolitan women, *La mousmé* would seem to be a provincial yet modern figure. She wears modern, fitted clothing rather than the traditional Arlesian costume with *ruban* and *chapelle* to which she was entitled at her age.[31] Her provincial Southern identity is nevertheless clearly indicated by the loud colours. Van Gogh took the title of the portrait, *La mousmé* (a Japanese term for a young girl), from his recent reading of Pierre Loti's novel *Madame Chrysanthème*. He also emphasised the olive complexion of his Arlesian model; her almond-shaped eyes and pouting lips create a racial stereotype based on Western literature and physiognomic handbooks.[32] By using *japonisme* to orientalize the young woman, he masked her contemporaneity with an antimodern type. From both his reading and his study of *ukiyo-e* woodcuts, van Gogh imagined Japan as a pre-modern society in which each occupation had a prescribed place and enjoyed the satisfaction of being socially useful for all. *La mousmé*, the Japanese adolescent, prepares to be man's companion and lover. Van Gogh's portrait casts the young woman of Arles, by a double displacement to Provence which is linked to Japan, in that reassuringly traditional role.[33]

Late in July van Gogh painted two portraits of a third sitter, Joseph Roulin, a mail handler at the Arles train station; he is portrayed in his blue service uniform decorated with gold buttons and braid, wearing a cap inscribed 'Postes' in gold lettering. The three-quarter-length *Portrait of Joseph Roulin* (fig. 11.9) presents an image of great vitality and patriarchal dignity, a larger-than-life figure. Self-assurance and energy are suggested by the animated face, steadfast gaze, and magnificent beard. To evoke his vital presence, van Gogh used a painterly handling and an energetic pose, devices that he admired in Dutch seventeenth-century portraiture, and in particular the works of Frans Hals (B14). The bright colour underscores this vitality and gives the portrait a modern look. Roulin appealed to van Gogh as a powerful physical worker, as a man with large appetites who ate well and drank a fair bit, as the potent father of a family (his wife had just given birth to a daughter) and, tying all these qualities together, as an ardent republican man of the people in the tradition of 1789 (516, 520).

Van Gogh identified with men of the people such as Joseph Roulin. He saw them as heroic figures and wanted to emulate their vigorous approach to life by becoming a painter of the people. He was pleased with his two portraits of Roulin, especially the second head-and-shoulders version which he had painted rapidly and with great assurance. In mid-August he wrote to his brother: 'I have kept the big portrait of the postman, and the head which I included [in the shipment] was done at a *single sitting*. But that's what I'm good at, doing a fellow roughly in one sitting. If I wanted to show off, my boy, I'd always do it, drink with the first comer, paint him, and that not in watercolors but in oils, on the spot in the manner of Daumier' (525). The artist was proud of his skill as a quick, technically competent painter, associating speedy, confident manual labour, patriotism, and drinking with the vitality of working-class men. In Paris he had portrayed himself several times dressed in a blue worker's or peasant's smock – a garb that he adopted when painting outdoors.[34] In Arles, far from the decadent metropolis, van Gogh felt that he was recovering his health and becoming as strong as the workers that he portrayed – well enough 'to live on a piece of bread while you are working all day, and to have enough strength to smoke and to drink your glass in the evening' (520).

The Studio of the South

The ambiguities and tensions of van Gogh's antimodernist project in Provence and its exoticist traits were clearly reflected in the Studio of the South that he established in Arles. In May 1888, van Gogh rented a small house at 2, place Lamartine and on 13 September he moved in. He was tired of living in hotels with no room to store his paintings, and he wanted a place of his own with a studio. This practical decision was, however, heavily invested with antimodernism and its ambiguities. The Studio of the South was conceived, in opposition to the commercial spaces and arrangements of the urban art market, as an artist-run co-operative and exhibition space. Supported by Theo van Gogh, it was, in fact, a supplement to the dealer-critic system.[35] Artists who were tired of the city and in need of renewal, as van Gogh had been, could spend time there in return for a modest contribution. Gauguin agreed to come and others might come later. Van Gogh envisaged their life on a monastic model in which, dedicated to their work, they would lead regulated lives (494a). He even depicted himself as a monk, a Buddhist *bonze*, in *Self-Portrait Dedicated to Paul Gauguin* (fig. 11.10),[36] and considered that, Gauguin, when he arrived, would become the abbot or leader. However, this antimodern monasticism was not to be an ascetic renunciation of the world, but rather a therapeutic model of spiritual and physical rearmament for coping with the modern world. We have here, in the self-portrait, an image of antimodernism revitalizing the modernist project, the artist as monk making possible the artist in the field and in the market place.

Van Gogh's antimodernism regularly took the form of exoticism in the South of France. Indeed, in the *Self-Portrait Dedicated to Paul Gauguin* he portrayed himself as an Eastern monk rather than a Western one. Central to exoticism is the tension between home and the other; although van Gogh cast Arles in the role of exotic other, it was he who was the exotic outsider in Arles, consorting with Danish, Belgian, and American painters and limited to exchanges with those like Roulin who spoke French. The Arlesian studio was to be a shelter and a workshop for the wandering artist 'on a long voyage in the South' or en route to North Africa and the 'tropics.' As a regional artistic centre, it was decorated with paintings depicting antimodern themes in an invented Provençal vernacular. Van Gogh conceived an evolving scheme of decoration for its rooms, using such series as the sunflowers and the Arlesian portraits.[37] Local subjects and motifs were transformed by the artist's *japonisme* and a palette of heightened colour. The whole formed an interior decor that celebrated Southern light, colour and a taste for local materials and popular craft.[38]

The Yellow House, as it came to be known, was both studio-home and exhibition space; it had private and public functions, creative and commercial dimensions. Van Gogh was quite conscious of the multiple aspects of his enterprise. He stated his belief that, if Gauguin joined him in Arles, they would be 'squarely in a position to exploit the South' (494). Later, writing of *Portrait of Patience Escalier* (fig. 11.2), he regretted that Parisians had not developed more of a taste for simple, rural things, and that there was not more 'art in clogs' in the city (520). The Yellow House exhibited art and decoration in a modern style, in which vanguard artists refashioned regional sources into an exotic idiom for metropolitan audiences. Emphasising texture, brushwork, heightened colour, pattern, and design, the 'coarse art' (to use van Gogh's term) decorating the Yellow House exploited the exotic for home use, domesticating an image of the regional South for consumption at the Parisian centre. Couched in a personal technique, the paintings visualized an intense, and therefore 'authentic,' experience recorded by a Dutch artist travelling in the South, and made that experience available to the urban art-lover on exhibition in the artist's Arlesian studio or, more to the point, in a Parisian commercial gallery. Van Gogh used the techniques of modern art to communicate antimodernist themes; thus presented, antimodernist themes worked to transform and revitalise modernity for the artist and his urban audiences.

NOTES

I thank Thea Burns, Anne Dymond, Sharon Hirsch, and Lynda Jessup for reading the manuscript in an earlier version and for stimulating discussion of my interpretation.

1 Translations of Vincent van Gogh's letters have been taken from *The Complete Letters of Vincent van Gogh*, 3 vols. (New York: New York Graphic Society, 1958), and have been verified and corrected where necessary based on *Verzamelde Brieven van Vincent van Gogh*, ed. J. van Gogh-Bonger (Amsterdam: Wereld Bibliotheek, 1952–4). The numbers given in parentheses in the text following quotations refer to specific letters. Numbers alone indicate letters to Vincent's brother Theo van Gogh and a few others; numbers preceded by 'B' indicate letters to Émile Bernard.

2 Exhaustion caused by the pace of life in the modern city and its consequences

(alcoholism, madness, and degeneration) were a major preoccupation in nineteenth-century France; rest in the countryside was usually prescribed as an antidote. For the medicalized discourse see Robert Nye, 'Degeneration and the Medical Model of Cultural Crisis in the French Belle Epoque,' in *Political Symbolism in Modern Europe: Essays in Honour of George L. Mosse*, ed. Seymour Drescher, David Sabean, and Allan Sharlin (New Brunswick, N.J., and London: Transaction Books, 1982), 19–41.

3 T.J. Jackson Lears, *No Place of Grace: Antimodernism and the Transformation of American Culture, 1880–1920* (New York: Pantheon Books, 1981), xv. Griselda Pollock, *Avant-Garde Gambits 1888–1893: Gender and the Color of Art History* (New York: Thames and Hudson, 1992), 52, characterises van Gogh as seeking an 'art of consolation' in the form of a 'sublimated religious art [that] articulates the paradox of a modernist project which is anti-modernity.' On pp. 60–7, she points out that vanguard artists such as van Gogh and Gauguin were engaged in a form of tourism, understood in terms of Dean MacCannell's structural analysis. See *The Tourist: A New Theory of the Leisure Class* (New York: Schocken, 1976): 'The spectacle the tourist seeks is shaped as a compensatory belief in the possibility of simple, direct meaning, namely, that which the European metropolitan experience of modernity so systematically disturbs' (66).

4 Vojtěch Jirat-Wasiutyński, 'Vincent van Gogh's Paintings of Olive Trees and Cypresses from St.-Remy,' *Art Bulletin* 75 (Fall 1993), 647–70. Van Gogh moved to the asylum of Saint-Paul-du-Mausole in April 1889 and left for Paris and Auvers-sur-Oise a year later.

5 Roger Chartier, 'The Two Frances: The History of a Geographical Idea,' in his *Cultural History: Between Practices and Representation*, trans. Lydia G. Cochrane (Cambridge, England: Polity Press, 1988), 172–7.

6 Chartier, 'The Two Frances,' 183.

7 Pollock (*Avant-Garde Gambits*, 91–2) recently argued that, through their models, displaced in time as well as in space, van Gogh's paintings of Provence are encoded with 'a pre-modern rural/urban hierarchy, a patriciate political order that makes social order and its authority appear clear and intelligible, easy to situate oneself in ... its difference from the confusing, modernising, chaotic present of both Holland and Provence in the 1880s engenders a kind of nostalgia.'

8 Pierre Pasquini, 'Le Félibrige et les traditions,' *Ethnologie française* 18 (1988), 257–66. The Félibres were a group of seven poets writing in Provençal who banded together in 1854 to preserve and revive Provençal language and customs in the face of modernization and political centralization in France. Their members included Joseph Roumanille, Frédéric Mistral, and Théodore Aubanel. Van Gogh was aware of the writings of Mistral and had read an account of the Félibres in the local paper. See Roland Dorn, *Decoration: Vincent van Goghs Werkreihe für das Gelbe Haus in Arles* (Hildesheim: Georg Olms, 1990), 115–16; and Jirat-Wasiutyński, 'Van Gogh's Paintings of Olive Trees,' 654.

9 See Carol Zemel, *Van Gogh's Progress: Utopia, Modernity and Late-Nineteenth-Century Art* (Berkeley: University of California Press, 1997); on pp. 93–4 she discusses the

portraits in these terms, and on pp. 2–3, she gives van Gogh a Benjaminian 'angelic stance' looking back nostalgically while battling forward.

10 See Larry Wolff, *Inventing Eastern Europe: The Map of Civilization in the Mind of the Enlightenment* (Stanford: Stanford University Press, 1994). Wolff's book has been particularly helpful to my thinking about the spatial metaphors of European cultural history. He points out that the division of Europe into South and North dominant in the fifteenth and sixteenth centuries was replaced in the eighteenth century by a division into West and East. Edward Soja ('History: Geography: Modernity,' Simon During, ed., *The Cultural Studies Reader* [London and New York: Routledge, 1993]) has theorized a spatial critique of historical method based on Foucault and posited a spatial definition of modernity that has also been generally helpful to my analysis.

11 In similar fashion, in his *Lettres de mon moulin* (addressed to a Parisian audience from a fictional mill near Fontvieille, a few kilometers east of Arles), Alphonse Daudet included a few tales of Algeria and Corsica along with his Provençal stories; by doing so, he acknowledged that, for the Northerner, these places and cultures shared a Southern exoticism. See 'Preface de Catherine Eugène,' in Alphonse Daudet's *Lettres de mon moulin* (1879; reprint, Paris: Pocket, 1990).

12 Lisa Lowe suggests such a construct for Orientalism in her critique of Edward Said's *Orientalism* (New York: Pantheon Books, 1978); see Lisa Lowe, *Critical Terrains: French and British Orientalisms* (Ithaca and London: Cornell University Press, 1991), 1–29

13 Exoticism has been distinguished from Orientalism as a more general, less informed representation of the other in Harriet Guest 'Curiously Marked: Tattooing, Masculinity, and Nationality: Eighteenth-Century British Perceptions of the South Pacific,' in John Barrell, ed., *Painting and the Politics of Culture* (Oxford: Oxford University Press, 1992), 101–34. Peter Mason, *Infelicities: Representations of the Exotic* (Baltimore and London: Johns Hopkins Press, 1998), 1–15, defines exoticism as a 'representational effect' produced by 'decontextualization' and 'recontextualization,' a process that 'can be seen as the opposite of Edward Said's Orientalism.'

14 Vincenette Maigne, 'Exotisme: Évolution en diachronie du mot et de son champ sémantique,' in *Exotisme et création: actes du colloque international, Lyon, 1983* (Lyon: L'Hermès, 1985), 9–16.

15 Roger Célestin, *From Cannibals to Radicals: Figures and Limits of Exoticism* (Minneapolis and London: University of Minnesota Press, 1996), 1–27, posits individual desire and the tension between home and elsewhere as fundamental to exoticism. See Pollock, *Avant-Garde Gambits*, 60, for the relation of exoticism to tourism.

16 Prosper Merimée, *Notes de voyage*, ed. Pierre-Marie Auzas (Paris: Hachette, 1971), 96–7. Bernard Thaon has pointed out that Provence appears to be not so much a geographical area (with shifting boundaries, of course, and surrounded by the South) as an isomorphic space, the threshold of which can be crossed at several points. See Bernard Thaon, 'L'invention de l'école provençale d'architecture dans la seconde moitié du XIXème siècle,' in Centre méridional d'histoire, *Images de la*

Provence: Les représentations iconographiques de la fin du Moyen Âge au milieu du xxème siècle (Publications de l'Université de Provence: Aix, 1992), 25.

17 Elisée Reclus, *Les villes d'hiver de la Méditerranée et les Alpes Maritimes*, Collections Guides Joanne (Paris: Hachette 1864), iii. I thank Anne Dymond for this reference.

18 Philippe Régnier, 'Le mythe oriental des Saint-Simoniens,' in *Les Saint-Simoniens et l'Orient: vers la modernité*, ed. Magali Morsy, Colloque de l'Association pour l'étude du monde musulman 1987 (Aix: Édisud, 1989), 29–52.

19 Geneviève Drocourt, 'Puvis de Chavannes et le décor de l'escalier d'honneur du Palais Longchamp,' in *Puvis de Chavannes et le Musée des beaux-arts de Marseille* (Marseille: Musée des beaux-arts, 1985), 13–50.

20 The colonial link was emphasized in Albert Boime, 'Van Gogh's *Starry Night*: A History of Matter and a Matter of History,' *Arts Magazine* 59 (December 1984), 97–100.

21 Paul Signac 'Journal' quoted in Griselda Pollock, 'On Not Seeing Provence: Van Gogh and the Landscape of Consolation, 1888–89,' in *Framing France: The Representation of Landscape in France, 1870–1914*, ed. Richard Thomson (Manchester: Manchester University Press, 1998), 186; published in John Rewald, 'Extrait du journal inédit de Paul Signac 1894–5,' *Gazette des Beaux-Arts* 36 (1949), 106.

22 Baudelaire quoted in Christopher L. Miller, *Blank Darkness: Africanist Discourse in French* (Chicago and London: University of Chicago Press, 1985), 74–82. Colour, as an avatar of sensuality, was fundamentally associated with the orientalist visualization of North African and Middle Eastern cultures.

23 Ronald Pickvance, *Van Gogh in Arles* (New York: Metropolitan Museum of Art, Harry N. Abrams, Inc. Publishers, 1984), 83, has redated van Gogh's visit to Saintes-Maries-de-la-Mer as 30 May to 3 June. According to legend, the three Marys landed on this site in 45 C.E.; along with Martha, Lazarus, and Maximin, they were credited with converting Roman Provincia to Christianity. Their relics, housed in the church at Saintes-Marie-de-la-Mer, were the object of pilgrimages; gypsies especially venerated the servant, Sarah, and made pilgrimages to her relics on 24–5 May.

24 Émile Bernard (1868–1941), a painter who was working with Gaugin in Port-Aven.

25 See the exhibition catalogues: Dominique Séréna-Allier and Bernard Thaon, *Dominique Roman* (Arles: Museon Arlaten, 1990); and Dominique Séréna-Allier, Pascale Picard-Cajan, et al., *L'Arlesienne: le mythe?* (Arles: Museon Arlaten, 1999).

26 Paul Allard, *Arles et ses terroirs* (Paris: Éditions du Centre national de la recherche scientifique, 1992), 35–6 and the map on p. 28.

27 Allard, *Arles et ses terroirs*, 159–60.

28 For Adolphe Monticelli and the van Gogh brothers' admiration of his work, see Aaron Sheon, *Monticelli: His Contemporaries, His Influence* (Pittsburgh: Carnegie Institute Museum of Art, 1978).

29 Bogomila Welsh-Ovcharov, *Van Gogh and the Birth of Cloisonism* (Toronto: Art Gallery of Ontario, 1981), 128–9.

30 Zemel, *Van Gogh's Progress*, 94–8.

31 See Séréna-Allier, Picard-Cajan, et al., *L'arlésiennne* for the costume. Both Gauguin and van Gogh painted the *arlesienne* in traditional costume in November 1888; see my essay in the same catalogue, 175–90.

32 See most recently Zemel, *Van Gogh's Progress*, 142–7. For an incisive discussion see Ludmilla Jordanova, 'Reading Faces in the Nineteenth Century,' *Art History* 13 (1990), 571–4.

33 Tsukasa Kodera, 'Japan as Primitive Utopia: van Gogh's *Japonisme* Portraits,' *Simiolus* 14 (1984), 189–208. Eun-Hye Chung's trenchant critique of Kodera's unproblematic treatment of van Gogh's *japonisme*, in a graduate seminar at Queen's University helped me to develop this analysis. See Zemel, *Van Gogh's Progress*, 115–17 for the 'geisha-in-training.'

34 Zemel, *Van Gogh's Progress*, 149–54; reminiscences about van Gogh by the painters Paul Signac and Camille Pissarro are excerpted in Bogomila Welsh-Ovcharov, ed., *Van Gogh in Perspective* (Englewood Cliffs, N.J.: Prentice Hall, 1974), 35–6.

35 C. Harrison White and Cynthia A. White, *Canvases and Careers: Institutional Change in the French Painting World* (New York: Wiley, 1965); Nicholas Green, 'Dealing in Temperaments: Economic Transformation in the Artistic Field in France During the Second Half of the Nineteenth Century,' *Art History* 10 (March 1987), 59–78.

36 Vojtěch Jirat-Wasiutyński, H. Travers Newton, Eugene Farrell, and Richard Newman, *Vincent van Gogh's 'Self Portrait Dedicated to Paul Gauguin': An Historical and Technical Study* (Cambridge, Mass.: Center for Conservation and Technical Studies, Harvard University Art Museum, 1984).

37 Dorn, *Decoration*.

38 R. Johnson, 'Vincent van Gogh and the Vernacular: His Southern Accent,' *Arts Magazine* 52 (June 1978), 131–5.

CHAPTER TWELVE

Plays without People: Shadow Puppets of Modernity in Fin-de-siècle Paris

Matt K. Matsuda

Towards the end of the nineteenth century, writer and critic Émile Lagarde penned a little volume on a popular amusement of the time – shadow theatre. He warned, however, 'If, dear readers, you seek amusing scenes and stories and tales to make you laugh, do not open this little book ... it contains, in effect, nothing but history.'[1]

'What! History?' Lagarde continued, 'do these groups of blacked-in men acting before an illuminated screen have a history, as armies, as peoples?' The answer was clear, 'But of course!' After all, he argued, doesn't everything have a history, whether brilliant or obscure, great or small, modest or glorious? Aren't all things historical, 'depuis la plume jusqu'à la machine d'imprimerie, depuis l'homme jusqu'à la patrie, depuis le jouet jusqu'au drapeau?'[2] Lagarde sought to ally the shadow world – the world of a child's pastime – with the multiple narratives of a historical world, understanding shadow theatre as a crossroads for stories of social milieu ('simple or great, modest or glorious'), technological development ('the pen to the printing press') and political evolution ('the man to the nation,' 'the plaything to the flag'). To this we need only add his designation of shadow theatre by its popular name *ombres chinoises* (Chinese shadows) to grasp the vogue for non-Western labelling that influenced his writing. Could there be, following Lagarde, a history of social order, technological progress, politics, and empire in the late nineteenth century read through shadows?

This paper is nominally organized around the immensely popular shadow theatres of artists and illustrators Henry Somm, George Auriol, and Caran d'Ache (Emmanuel Poiré) that found their origins in 1880s Paris at the artistic cabaret Le Chat Noir.[3] Yet what follows is not an artistic biography but rather an extended commentary on Lagarde's theses. I seek to locate shadow theatre by writing *around* the artists and the avant-garde. This paper is properly an examination of meanings that extend beyond the projection screen, a sketch of social milieu, aesthetic perception, and the encompassing – and shifting – boundaries of the metropolitan French nation state and empire at the end of the century.

The artistic culture of fin-de-siècle Montmartre is a much-studied phenomenon; the outrages and innovations of the sick and the ingenious, painters, illustrators, musicians, and poets, from the Incohérents and their deliberately absurd *bals* and expositions, to the 'gutsy humour' of the Society of the Bon Bock, to the 'fundamental skepticism' and surface '*prud'homie*' (smugness) of the Hydropathes. Such loose and overlapping artistic collectives were suspicious or unsure of *la patrie*, shaped and shocked by the losses suffered by France in the 1870–71 Franco-Prussian War, and they operated around 'a kind of disdain for everything.'[4] Their search to renew and redefine 'Frenchness' of 'the Gallic spirit' pushed them to create radical new arts, often from presumably forgotten traditional roots. If there were a manifesto for their disparate temperaments, it might be what Hydropathe leader Émile Goudeau wrote of Rodolphe Salis's legendary artistic cabaret, Le Chat Noir: 'On the façade, a gigantic cat on a gold sun basks between two colossal wrought iron lanterns, all designed by Grasset, next to an inscription indicating the date of establishment followed by this admonition: You who pass by, be modern!'[5]

For the artists who gathered to perform and exhibit at Le Chat Noir, one manifestation of modernity was the revival of shadow puppet theatre, a genre not of academies and grand theatre, but of the street and children's amusements. Formal histories generally trace French shadow theatre to the art of playwright François Dominique Seraphin (1747–1800), who created his first spectacles in the Jardin Lannion at Versailles in 1772. Drawing on scattered folk elements, Seraphin created an enormously popular series of shadow plays which combined the best of the silhouette – a fashionable art at which the French excelled – with the dynamics of guignol and marionette puppetry.[6] Seraphin's work was continued by his sons, but shadow theatre as an art form fell out of popular favour, lacking major innovation and creative figures, until the late nineteenth century. Most contemporary histories follow the line that 'It was left to the Cabaret du Chat Noir to revive this little spectacle and to Caran d'Ache (Emmanuel Poiré) to bring back it back into fashion.' By the end of the century popular shadow theatre guides for home use often promised to help readers establish their own 'complete Chinese shadow theatre, *genre Chat-Noir*.'[7]

The model for this popular attention dates to 1885, when artists and illustrators George Auriol and Henry Somm constructed a small guignol puppet theatre in Le Chat Noir, thus linking the medium of puppetry with the venue of cabaret. Soon after this, the printmaker and illustrator Henri Rivière added a cloth over the framework of the stage to create a screen upon which to project small shadow presentations. Finally, in 1887, he replaced the small stage with a real shadow puppet theatre (see fig. 12.1) by breaking through the main wall of the cabaret, and adding templates (cut-metal zincs), sliding glass panels, and transparent screens. He also acquired a more brilliant oxyhydrogen flame to engineer different gradations of shadows.[8] As the art developed, shadow theatre divided into 'two very distinct categories: satirical or humorous shadow pieces, and lyrical shadow pieces.'[9] The most popular shows were those of Caran d'Ache, who mastered the rendering of monumental groups of silhouetted figures, subtle lighting effects, and grand musical accompaniments. His shows included *L'Épopée* (1888) and *La tentation de Saint Antoine* (1887). Another great success, *Marche à l'étoile* (1890) was produced by Rivière and featured multiple sets.

All these productions drew on a fascination with the 'folk' tradition of the shadow theatre, but it would be wrong to suggest that they retained traditional techniques. Instead, traditional forms were adapted into highly contemporary and technically sophisticated arts, exploiting newly developed photomechanical relief printing processes to create high-contrast silhouettes (used in Hydropathe graphics) and experimenting with the merging of two-dimensional movement aesthetics with music and theatrical effects – techniques soon adapted to the newly created cinema and its spectacles. Technically, shadow presentations were masterpieces of organization, engineering, and commerce; far from street theatre, they were well suited to the paid entertainment world of the cabarets. As Émile Lagarde noted, 'Artistic shadow theatre requires a considerable production, painstaking sets, complicated shadows ... a veritable team of technicians, narrators, accompanists, singers, etc. We will surprise no one by saying that such a theatrical success cost more than five thousand francs to mount.'[10] Speaking of the evolution of the shadow theatre from street amusement to high aesthetic, Lagarde suggested, 'one was the work of an artisan, the other the work of an artist. The first knew popularity, the second attained glory. And it is truly a curious destiny that these little shadows begin by amusing children and end by delighting searchers of the ideal and all admirers of beauty.'[11]

This apotheosis of a child's game into high art seems quite a remarkable legacy. Why were puppets and shadows bearers of the modernity that Goudeau extolled? Part of the response must be sought in the pursuit of a particular aesthetic by the artist and the avant-garde, an aesthetic that is similar to revolutionary ideology: the desire to shatter current regimes by returning, in Rousseauist fashion, to republics of youth and virtue in the theatre. Recall the political context of France's loss to Germany in 1871 and the ensuing search for a sense of renewal. The modernist use of shadow puppets was tied into questions of aesthetic strategies in which class definition and class conflicts were displaced into culture. Some presentations, such as Maurice Donnay's *Ailleurs*, an allegory of Voltaire and colleagues wandering modern France, were straightfoward moral dramas. Backdrops included, 'the ruins of the stock exchange' and the spectacle of great multitudes of labourers building 'their new palace – *La Sociale*.'[12]

Less didactically, shadow puppets represent an attempt to seek the space between classes, between the street and the academy, while simultaneously loathing the *canaille* and eviscerating the maddening material 'civilization' of the upper orders. As Lagarde notes above, shadow theatre trades on an association to artisanal traditions, on the creation of hand-works transmuted into the realm of beauty, and on a vocabulary of sublime simplicity. Other shadow-historians concur. In retelling the origins of modern artistic shadow theatre in Paris, Lemercier de Neuville (1911) recounts tales of poets and writers arguing over their beer about the decadence of Europe and the arts, the decadence of a theatre produced by a 'civilization overly savant and overly ingenious' that would soon die 'of an excess of its own qualities, killed by overly-studied and complicated ideas' – about a world suffering from far too much direction and organization. Out of this, suggests Neuville, Le Chat Noir was created and 'the shadows returned to their place of honor.' Thus began the 'renaissance of shadows,' which could revive the small stage, not by killing off grand theatre, but by teaching it that 'simplicity is the soul of great things and the special character of true feelings.'[13]

Neuville rhapsodizes the stirring mystery of shadows, linking it, as did figures like Alfred Jarry in an ironic turn, to the aesthetic of children and young people who respond easily to 'true and natural poetry, frank and simple gaiety ... modest and without pretension.' Thus the shadow is the finest of actors since 'it never allows its personality to intervene'; without the *cabotinage* (heavy-handedness) of the male or the *coquetterie* of the female, shadow theatre is pure sentiment. 'Shadow theatre will live; it is young, of a new youth, it can await the future.'[14] Shadow theatre was modern; it became an art of renewal by means of a return to a past simplicity that was on the edge of the avant-garde.

Such recognition of the shadow puppet's primal role in defining culture is ancient. Puppetry scholar Steve Tillis reminds us of Plato's Allegory of the Cave: 'Between the fire and the prisoners and above them (is) a road along which a low wall has been built, as the exhibitors of puppet shows have partitions before the men themselves, above which they show the puppets ... human shapes and shapes of animals as well, wrought in stone and wood and every material.'[15] In Plato's allegory, the puppet and the shadow are realities that hide other orders of truth. As a schematic human, the puppet represents and mimics human characteristics while transcending the particulars of individual personality. Shadow-puppets could be the ultimate actors – pure authorship of idea or emotion, particular and abstract, unhindered by a human actor who would interpose his body and personality between the creator's vision and practical realization. Tillis also recounts the Belgian playwright Maurice Maeterlinck's argument that human actors inevitably usurp the power of poetry; describing an actor's finest performance of Hamlet, Maeterlinck wrote 'I saw clearly that he had his own destinies ... the whole masterpiece is a symbol, and the symbol will not support the active presence of men.' Anatole France remarked, 'actors spoil comedy for me ... their personality effaces the work they represent.' By contrast dolls 'are worthy of giving form to the dreams of the poet.'[16]

Puppetry was seen not as the denial of the body of the actor, but rather as its subversion and mimicry; it could grandly conceptualize a performing object of pure art, unmediated by corporeality while retaining the form of the body. As Henri Rivière put it, 'the shadow will not tolerate mediocrity.'[17] To adopt puppetry was to adopt a schematic human, and in the shadow, the schematic puppet. Shadow art was a pure, human idea: an attempt to prize the genius, the dreams, the intellect, the psychology and creativity, the symbolist excellence of the creator, a romanticism tinged with the impossibility of true expression through actors and material images. The lamp of artistic romanticism displayed its glowing genius of inspiration and imagination only through the pure light and darkness cast upon the screen. This kind of theatre was pure art, the 'mysterious collaboration of two great agents of nature, that is to say, the light and the shadow.'[18]

I noted above the mythical and historical strains in the tradition of French shadow puppet theatre. If the mythical approach descends from a line uniting Platonic-style idealism and materialism through the creative artist's romantic mediation of the shadow, the historical approach attempts to grasp the particularities of time and place shaping the renaissance of shadow theatre in the late nineteenth century. Part of that history lies in a particular social milieu of shadow theatre that was located in the entertainments and boulevards of post-Haussmann Paris. In his study of turn-of-the-century cabaret culture, Harold Segel suggests that the great popularity of 'shadows' in puppet shows could be 'best understood seen within the context of the enthusiasm of the avant-garde for minor or marginal theatrical forms associated with popular culture.'[19] This 'enthusiasm' can be seen as a form of modernism that is, in effect, antimodern – extolling the life of the street and favouring notions of the folkloric: the people's form of the handbill, the roadshow, the folk tradition, the travelling show, and the country artisan.

Unsurprisingly, at a time when the French were seeking ideological renewal and confidence in Gallic culture and politics, puppetry was appropriated to that most final of nineteenth-century historical moments, the identification with the nation state. Writers such as Émile Lagarde could easily imagine figures of French puppetry and shadow theatre transformed into a patrimony or heritage – the essence of what defined France as an immortal people and tradition. Presentations of marionette and hand-puppet works, of Polichinelle and Guignol, according to Lagarde manifested 'an absolutely and uniquely French character,' representing 'the man of the people.' The puppets were 'animated by our Gallic lifeblood, the heroes of some eternal Rabelais, always alive, always acting, always following France in its evolutions, always of France, never to die except by her side. May they never die!'[20]

Puppetry was antimodern in that it was traditional – theorized in its vital newness, while seeming to draw its inspiration from folkloric lineages and simple, honest lives and sentiments. From guignol to shadow theatre, from avant-garde to heritage, puppetry traded on a vocabulary of childhood explorations and an ethic of sentiment. Consider the appeal manifested in Paul Eudel's *Les ombres chinoises de mon père* (1886, fig. 12.2), a tribute to the writer's father, a poor customs official at Crotoy who amused and enchanted his family with shadow puppets stencilled from 'a mass of papers which for a long time served no purpose; my father used them to save money.' Eudel's testament, written in the language of childhood and nostalgia, is of a world circumscribed by the simple theatricality of a simple man and his children and the affectionate community. 'Ah! these Chinese shadows! It's unbelievable the ineradicable traces they've left in the minds of the old folks of the countryside.'[21]

The theatre itself is a space of time past, a collector of memories of a world to be longed for. Eudel's description is nostalgic social history in which hardship is virtue: 'We were not rich at home; work was not easy to come by and just barely sufficed to raise the small family ... it was necessary to do everything with nothing.' The small town of Crotoy is presented as a counter-memory to the eminence of glittering Paris, a world in which history takes place elsewhere and in other times. 'Towards 1837, Crotoy was not, as today, one of the most frequented whaling ports of the Somme. It was a poor commune relegated to the edge of the world, sitting on a spot formed of a little soil and a lot of sand.' Its inhabitants were 'sailors, a few artisans, and the rare civil servants.' In its insularity of time, space, and memory, Crotoy becomes the expression of a gentle time, of joy, and of puppets. 'My father would have had no dramatic pretensions. Not seeking any literary success, he achieved his heart's desire with a little crowd of children and sailors, all full of excitement.'[22] In this lay the true heart of the French tradition of shadow puppets.

In Eudel's text, we see not only how the shadow theatre plays out tales of the faraway, but also how it engages the faraway – through the text's maritime setting. Nostalgia becomes a function of past time and extended space. 'What a singular destiny these Chinese shadows had!' exclaims the author, 'After having played from Crotoy to Nantes, they one day ended up going – I don't know why – to astonish the natives of the island of Reunion.'[23]

This figure of the simple Frenchman's shadows amusing the locals in the French overseas possessions is worth noting, for the constitution of shadow-theatre was – unlike many Eurocentric traditions – enthusiastically recognised as anchored in non-European origins. As Lemercier de Neuville put it, 'They are the delicate arts of Orientals. It is they, after all, who invented them. In effect, they were not imported into Europe until the eighteenth century, first in Germany under the name Schattenspiel, and after that into France.'[24] The rise of the shadow theatre from street amusement to cabaret art of the avant-garde and high fashion is the story of a form drawn from its 'primitive' to its 'civilized' presentation. As the avant-garde extolled the virtues of apparent childishness and simplicity in their works, they were constructing an aesthetic based upon adapting presumably non-academic traditional arts and revalorizing them.

Neuville suggested that shadow theatre had long been regarded 'beneath the esteem of the civilised world and long set apart,' precisely because 'the Arabs, those people with the souls of children, delighted themselves in their tents with this spectacle of gestures.' In Europe, 'even children were deprived' of such base amusements and only in the late nineteenth century had the art reappeared *sous un autre nom*, 'enlarged, embellished, transformed into a character of importance.'[25] The Baron Grimm opined, 'this beautiful form was not invented in France, it is absolutely what one would call an imported article, that is, something from abroad,' and he precisely claimed 'the Oriental origin of Chinese shadows.'[26]

The notable feature of the puppet theatre was its so-called Oriental origin. As discussed above, the modern revival of the shadow theatre took place during the 1880s within a general history encompassing a social critique of the dominant bourgeoisie, the expansion of commercial society, and the renewed European age of empire, when Africa and Asia were taken under Western domination. If the French were anxious at home, they could nonetheless assert their *mission civilisatrice* abroad.

Shadow theatre genealogies could be and were articulated directly as functions of imperial conquest and struggles over colonial policy. Émile Lagarde, for example, comments on *les chagazill,* the Arab name for Chinese shadows, and the manner in which 'the French would have considered this spectacle in Algeria at the time of the conquest, and in order not to upset the customs of the natives too brutally, tolerated it, though this was not very agreeable.'[27] What could be disagreeable about tolerating an amusing shadow play? The French were attuned to the threat posed by such masters of the art as Garagrousse[28] – they found him a bit too violently patriotic in opposing the Europeans, and they feared his popular shows that harshly attacked French authority. Such puppeteers and their presentations were closely watched and sometimes forced into exile by French colonial governments who read seditious signs in shows such as 'A Thousand and One Nights,' 'The Seven Sleepers,' or 'a naval combat between the Algerians and the Spanish.' These authorities especially feared programs exhorting 'God alone is God and Mahomet is his prophet.' The introduction of and fascination with shadow theatre in France was directly implicated in knowledge of the nation's imperial and colonial projects.[29] For Parisian audiences, Louis Bombled presented a complete shadow production titled 'The Conquest of Algeria,' and he also dramatized inter-European colonial struggles; after the production of 'La moderne épopée: les Boers' he received a complimentary notice from the Transvaal government for his tragic epic of the Boers at war against the rapacious British.[30]

More subtly, artists and critics connected colonial and non-Western peoples and their arts to discursive practices of mysterious simplicity and elemental qualities. Such simplicity allowed a reading of shadow-theatre as a form with an Oriental heritage framed by arrested temporalities. Some writers made the comparison between old Asiatic origins and medieval European traditions: 'Chinese shadows have always been an important diversion for the peoples of the Orient. In India, Japan, and China, the performers went from village to village ... in the way animal trainers, jugglers, and minstrels went about our feudal France.'[31] By the eighteenth century the shadow arts of the Orient met the European traditions of puppetry and street theatre in the Seraphin's popular Versailles pieces, yet while the art developed into its 'civilized' forms in Europe, it remained distinctly timeless and attached to non-progressive histories in the traditional empires of the East. For example, Neuville studied the popularity of shadow theatre 'in Turkey and in all lands of the Islamic religion, the countries of extreme laziness,' where the shadow artist, requiring no more than a lamp and a screen and acting as a *theatre mobile,* 'could not fail to satisfy the taste of natives so supremely averse to effort, even concerning pleasure.' At this remove, Europe acknowledged the Orient.[32]

But of course the idea of 'des Orientaux' embraces a wide cultural range in the European imagination of the age. Algeria and its colonial status are prominent but the traditions also encompass the traditional Orient (or Middle East) and East Asia – from whence the designation 'ombres chinoises' comes. Magician and conjuror O. Alber-Graves wrote, 'The Chinese, from whom the shadows have taken their name, are literally passionate for this sort of spectacle. It is the same in Japan and in India ... all Orientals, young and old, love the shadows.'[33] In general, instructions for decoration of small home theatres suggest lacquer framing, screens with cherry blossoms and cranes, Asiatic theatrical masks, bamboo fan illustrations, and ink-brush water scenes as embellishments for a proper 'Chinese' presentation.

That the modern shadow theatre developed out of a fascination with these broadly construed 'Asiatic' traditions refers not only to the supposed historical transmission of the practice from the East, but also to an Oriental graphic aesthetic – that of single-dimensionality and bold contrast. The shadow-theatre after all was pursued by artists and artisans who were intrigued by the possibilities of non-European art, particularly in the wake of the mid-nineteenth-century rage for *japonisme.* The artist Henri Rivière (who created the shadow theatre at Le Chat Noir) was especially fascinated by both *ukiyo-e* and woodblock – a form in which images were 'stamped' into reality in brilliant and dazzling reliefs. It is interesting to note that, despite the 'Chinese' convention, the June and July 1886 issues of the artistic *revue Le Chat Noir* discuss the cabaret's *ombres japonaises* shows,[34] and that Incoherent writer-founder Jules Levy had his colleague Paul Bilhaud's poem 'Les Petits Japonais' printed with shadow images in imitation of Japanese woodblock prints.[35] Regarding the mechanical and aesthetic complexities of the Montmartre productions, Paul Jeanne has suggested that 'it was truly necessary to have a "Japanese" virtuosity in order to succeed.'[36]

The influence of *ukiyo-e* on Parisian art can be seen in poster design: both the flattened effect associated with Japanese prints and the use of bold and graded colours and sharp reliefs can be seen, for example, in the work of Henri de Toulouse-Lautrec. Through links with the art world, this Japanese influence also played a role in shaping the aesthetic of shadow theatre; Henri Rivière produced both graphic art and shadow plays. Shadow theatre was deliberately presented as a form drawn from an apparent arts and crafts tradition of simplicity of image and of materials in which the very craft was its art. By reading Japanese prints as art of traditional workmanship, the flat, brilliant images express the experimental and innovative aesthetic of the avant-garde: to 'be modern' through the appropriation of simplicity and tradition. In the years after the Franco-Prussian war, this had a political resonance. Siegfried Bing, the great collector and connoisseur of Japanese art, spoke of the 'artistic models' from East Asia that 'we have appropriated to revitalize our national genius,'[37] while another opinionated aesthete proclaimed, 'Let the Germans keep their oversized goblets, with their dull ornamentation ... We are French'[39] – that is, presumably, a people whose essence was refined, cosmopolitan, and open to the world.

To 'be modern' however meant more than cultivating a highly theorized aesthetic nostalgia or sensibility. *Ukiyo-e* after all – and here we must reiterate certain clichés – was the art of the 'floating world,' a term adopted from Buddhist notions of illusory existence and applied to the commercial, unstable urban Osaka and Edo worlds of merchants and commerce. If the reading of the Japanese image through French eyes betrayed a milieu of tea houses, actors, and kimonoed splendour, the historical logic of the images of Hokusai or Hiroshige so admired by the Incohérents and their ilk were those of a floating world of money, commerce, and fluid urban life in early modern Japan, a world reminisent of the role of the cabaret and of Montmartre within the larger context of Parisian and French society. H.D. Harootunian, writing about Edo (present-day Tokyo), says 'Ukiyo was the term used to describe pleasure and entertainment, "society" and the "world"; it carried a sense of instability.' That instability was refracted in 'the prospect of play – which the great city offered in almost excessive abundance.'[39]

Modernism in shadow theatre was a reflexive sort of antimodernity: a search for the timeless and traditional, but a rejection of civilization in favour of the 'authenticity' of the non-West with its entertainments and forms of childlike play, and a celebration of worlds such as Paris and Montmartre destabilised by transformation.[40] According to the famous analysis by T.J. Clark, such destablizing of the 'modern' has put 'a stress on the material means by which illusions and likenesses were made ... Flatness was modernity as surface: the literal presence of the surface, posters, labels, fashion prints, photos, the workmanlike, the reality of artisan and tools, the technicality of painting.' Clark argued modern life and art in terms of the unstable, malformed, discrepancy, the knowledge 'that things and pictures do not add up.'[41]

Modernism is therefore 'unfinished,' just as a shadow is the absence of light cast from an object. Interposition, flatness, negativity, and surface are the essence of shadow theatre. The shadow is the counterpart to the substantial, the monumental. In an accelerated society, seeing and viewing become matters of seizing the ephemeral and transitory. Thus modern life becomes what Jean-Louis Comolli calls 'the frenzy of the visible.' Haussmanization, a city of greater visibility, commerical activities, expositions in 1867, 1878, 1889, 1900, and the animation of the grands boulevards all render Paris an image to be consumed.[42]

Puppet theatre matched this world. Where theatre was substantial, shadow was insubstantial, its ruse, its magic was its invisibility, its suggestion. The shadow theatre comprised qualities distinctive to aesthetic expression in the late nineteenth century, including those leading to the creation of a new 'seventh' art: the cinema. Shadows in their unreal reality – recall Plato's cave – carried not the representation, but the *illusion* of life, an illusion which was a world of flatness. Neuville commented on 'these shadow plays which give the illusion of life to beings without color.'[43] This was a culture of a new way of seeing, the 'visible' of projected light and movement, of insubstantiality and shadow. Press accounts of the earliest cinema programs indicate a reality more than real. 'We saw ten lifelike animated scenes, absolutely intense: men walking, jumping, streetcars rolling by in such a way that there was an absolute illusion of reality.' The black and white projections of movement, intended for entertainment, could be deeply unsettling, as the Russian Poet Maksim Gorky exclaimed, 'It is terrible to see this movement of shadows, nothing but shadows, specters and ghosts.'[44] The cinema of movement, of crowds, figures, and transport becomes this poet's spectral world, meeting a Baudelairean vision in the unreal reality of 'modern' life under the sign of suggestion and the shadow.

The shadow theatre is deeply implicated in these histories of vision. As noted earlier, nineteenth- and early twentieth-century texts tended to relate the revival of shadow play to great artists; Alber-Graves proposed that, 'One day, a talented designer, Caran d'Ache, had the idea of drawing and cutting out not only shadow figures, but entire groups, masses, crowds. The result was extraordinary, the success stupefying.'[45] Clearly, Alber-Graves encodes his presentation in a theory of art as the inspiration of great creative spirits, yet his passage also provides details about the shows themselves that may have appeared self-evident: they are about groups of people. Unsurprisingly, Caran d'Ache's spectacles both read and are informed by a logic of crowds, of impressive yet anonymous masses of figures.[46]

In prints by Henri de Tolouse-Lautrec or Rivière one notices the use of silhouette effect not for primary figures, but precisely to create a mass, a background, a crowd at once mysterious, undifferentiated, and featureless, as one would experience it as an aspect of Parisian urban modernity (fig. 12.3). The figures are not shaded to capture their depths and contours, but rendered opaque and blank, flat, and without qualities save those of anonymity, of metropolitan flux and change. If the reflection is the light, then the shadow is the figure of the dark, of suggestion, of the power of seeing insubstantiality in a spectacular culture. The shadow and its theatre are located in these spaces of modern culture; shadow theatre comes from the cafés and the artists who created the mythology of Montmartre life by crystallizing – and silhouetting – a primary landscape torn between passages and smallness of spaces, and the spectacle of Haussmann and the boulevards.

The logic of the shadow is that of an art form and a cultural expression – as I noted by beginning with Émile Lagarde – invested in history. The revival of the shadow theatre in the late nineteenth century was the relocating of a folk form into an aesthetic of 'avant-garde' modernism. Yet to say this is only to suggest what is obviously true: that the practitioners of shadow theatre attempted to be self-consciously innovative. My point is that through the shadows, the motivations and intentions of the human actors, with their aesthetic theories and social critiques, were expressions of 'history' in the late nineteenth century, a world of national anxiety, class polemics, empire, and exoticism, a fleeting universe of urban change and transformation. The blackness and flatness of shadows captured the state of the bourgeois century, recalling that Baudelaire had declared Paris fashion the expression of undertakers going to this and that: the life of the boulevards was a celebration of the monotone, the mass of people, shifting and indivisible, in a ceaseless flux of movement.

What shadows captured so well was a highly refined history of class critique, a genealogy of Europe in conquest of the Orient, and a new way of seeing – flat yet distinct, monumental yet insubstantial, contingent. By leading a revival of puppet and shadow theatre, creative artists such as Caran d'Ache, Rivière, and Somm did more than delight and shock the bourgeoisie; they embodied its history, taking a world of change, nostalgia, struggle, and empire, and describing it perfectly in plays without people.

NOTES

The title of this essay is taken from the study and memoir by the classicist and puppeteer, Peter D. Arnott, *Plays without People: Puppetry and Serious Drama* (Bloomington: Indiana University Press, 1964). The themes were first presented as a lecture during the exhibition 'The Spirit of Montmartre: Cabarets, Humor, and the Avant-Garde' held at Jane Voorhees Zimmerli Art Museum, New Brunswick, New Jersey, from 4 March to 31 July 1996. I am greatly indebted both to Philip Dennis Cate and Katherine Tako-Girard and to the Museum, its collections, and its library.

I have provided all the translations from French sources quoted in the course of this essay.

1 Émile Lagarde, *Ombres chinoises, guignol, marionettes* (Paris: Louis Chaux, 1900). Throughout this essay I draw on the premise that the European nineteenth century ends in 1914.
2 Lagarde, *Ombres chinoises*, 5.
3 Phillip Dennis Cate, 'The Spirit of Montmartre,' in *The Spirit of Montmartre: Cabarets, Humor, and the Avant-Garde*, ed. Phillip Dennis Cate and Mary Shaw (New Brunswick, N.J.: Jane Voorhees Zimmerli Art Museum, 1996), 53–69. For a comprehensive view of recent work on puppet theatre, see Geneviève Leleu-Rouvray and Gladys Langevin, *Bibliographie internationale de la marionette* (Munich: K.G. Saur, 1993), esp. pt. XXIX, 'Jeu d'ombres.' On shadow puppetry see, *Shadow and Substance: The Shadow Theatre of Montmartre and Modern Art* (Houston: Contemporary Arts Museum, 1956).
4 Daniel Grojnowski, 'Hydropathes and Company,' in Cate and Shaw, eds., *Spirit of Montmartre*, 104.
5 Émile Goudeau, *Les billets bleus* (Paris: Librairie Illustrée, 1886), 266.
6 O. Alber-Graves, *Les théâtres d'ombres chinoises* (Paris: E. Mazo, 1896).
7 Lagarde, *Ombres chinoises*, 9. On the popularity of the fin-de-siècle shadow theatre see Harold B. Segel, *Turn of the Century Cabaret* (New York: Columbia University Press, 1987), 67–9. Segel notes that in the 1880s and 1890s, in addition to the famous Le Chat Noir, one could attend Le Théâtre des ombres lyriques du Lyon d'or, La Boite de musique, Le Théâtre d'application, Le Cabaret de la lune rousse, and Le Cabaret des quat'z'arts for regular shadow plays.
8 For more on this general history, see Cate and Shaw, *Spirit of Montmartre*. For images of the shadow theatre and other items at Le Chat Noir, see *Catalogue de la*

collection du Chat Noir, Rodolphe Salis (Paris, 1898); a copy of this catalogue is held in the collection of the Zimmerli Museum.

9 Paul Jeanne, *Les théâtres d'ombres à Montmartre, 1887–1923* (Paris: Éd. des Presses Modernes, 1937), 19.

10 Lagarde, *Ombres chinoises*, 41.

11 Ibid., 31.

12 The sets for *Ailleurs* were designed by Henri Rivière. For Rivière's large body of illustrated work, see Georges Toudouze, *Henri Rivière: Peintre et imagier* (Paris: Ed. Henri Floury, 1907).

13 Lemercier de Neuville, *Ombres chinoises* (Paris: Le Bailly, 1911), 9–10.

14 Ibid., 30–1. For other contemporary works and historical information, see *Le théâtre des ombres chinoises nouveau; Seraphin des enfants*, by 'Guignollet' (Paris: Le Bailly, n.d.). To play with a real 'home' shadow theatre, ask for R. Theo, *Les Sillhouettes à la main*, a boxed set of cutouts. All of these items are held in the collection of the Zimmerli Museum.

15 For sources on puppetry in ancient cultures, see Steve Tillis, *Toward an Aesthetics of the Puppet: Puppetry As a Theatrical Art* (New York: Greenwood Press, 1997); see especially the discussions of Plato (14–15).

16 For quotations on puppetry by writers such as Maurice Maeterlinck, Oscar Wilde, and Anatole France, see Tillis, *Toward an Aesthetics of the Puppet*, 188–93. For further information see Francis Penny and Henryk Jurkowski, eds., *A History of European Puppetry from its Origins to the End of the Nineteenth Century* (Lewiston: Edwin Mellen, 1996), especially 'Attracting the Artists,' 380–403; and Centre national des marionettes, *Les Théâtres de marionettes en France* (Lyon: La Manufacture, 1985). Lotte Reiniger, *Shadow Theaters and Shadow Films* (London: B.T. Batsford, 1970), 13, explains the theory that 'a silhouette cannot be distorted.'

17 Jeanne, *Les théâtres d'ombres à Montmartre*, 8.

18 Le mercier de Neuville, *ombres chinoises*, 39.

19 Harold B. Segel, *Turn-of-the-Century Cabaret: Paris, Barcelona, Berlin, Munich, Vienna, Cracow, Moscow, St. Petersburg, Zurich* (New York: Columbia University Press, 1987), 66. See also Jerrold Seigel, *Bohemian Paris: Culture, Politics, and the Boundaries of Bourgeois Life, 1830–1930* (New York: Penguin, 1986), especially 'Publicity and Fantasy: The World of the Cabaret,' 215–43.

20 Lagarde, *ombres chinoises*, 120.

21 Paul Eudel, *Les ombres chinoises de mon père* (Paris: Éditions Rouveyre, 1885), ix. Most of the book is dedicated to playscripts. Interestingly and coincidentally Eudel lived across the street from Le Chat Noir in Paris, and the illustrations for his book were created by Le Chat Noir regulars; see Cate and Shaw, *Spirit of Montmartre*, 55.

22 Eudel, *Les ombres chinoises*, x.

23 Ibid.

24 Lemercier de Neuville, *Ombres chinoises*, 10

24 Ibid.

25 Ibid.

27 Lagarde, *Ombres chinoises*, 120.

28 'Garagrousse' is the name given by Lagarde to the puppeteer now commonly known as 'Kargheuz.'

29 Lagarde, *ombres chinioises*, 120–3.

30 The music, lyrics and images of this shadow opera were published in a folio; see Louis Bombled, G. Montoya, and Jules Mulder, *La moderne épopée: les Boers* (Paris: Flammarion, n.d.). The script includes the British invaders singing such notable lines as 'Hurrah! We're England! Hip! Hip! We must have this land! ... Hurrah! What does justice matter?' A copy of the playscript is held in the collection of the Zimmerli Museum. The published folio includes a letter from an aide to Louis Botha who, impressed by this show, wrote to the creators: 'Working for the Boer people and for the children, it is not possible that right and justice will not triumph.'

31 Lagarde, *Ombres chinoises*, 6.

32 Neuville, *Ombres chinoises*, 9.

33 O. Alber-Graves, *Les petits secrets amusants: ombres avec les mains, plis du papier, etc.* (Paris: Hachette, 1908), 1–2, 10. See also Georges Auvray, *Les marionettes javanaises* (Paris: 1882), 6–7.

34 *Le Chat Noir*, 26 juin and 3 juillet 1886. According to the writer, 'all of Paris comes to the Chat Noir to admire this ravishing inauguration of Japanese shadows.'

35 Phillip Dennis Cate, 'The Spirit of Montmartre,' in Cate and Shaw, *Spirit of Montmartre*, 55, 58.

36 Jeanne, *Les théâtres d'ombres à Montmartre*, 9.

37 S. Bing, 'Programme,' *Le Japon artistique* 1 (1888), 4–5.

38 M. Du Cleuziou, 'Les origines de notre céramique nationale,' *Revue des arts decoratifs* 5 (1884–5), 364–73, as quoted in Debora Silverman, *Art Nouveau in Fin-de-siècle France: Politics, Psychology, and Style* (Berkeley: University of California Press, 1989), 131–2.

39 Harry D. Harootunian, 'Cultural Politics in Tokugawa Japan,' in Sarah E. Thompson and Harry D. Harootunian, *Undercurrents in the Floating World: Censorship and Japanese Prints* (New York: Asia Society Galleries, 1991), 7. For more information on this topic see especially the section of Harootunian's essay titled 'The Tokugawa "Society of Spectacle."'

40 See aspects of Japanese puppet traditions in Jane Marie Law, *Puppets of Nostalgia* (Princeton: Princeton University Press, 1997). Of particular interest is Law's analysis, 'in the shape of a person,' concerning the use of puppets as a form of generalization and of expression and triumph over both terrestrial and celestial forces. For the Japanese Bunraku tradition in the context of Japanese theatrical forms in general, see Samuel Leiter, ed., *Japanese Theatre in the World* (New York: The Japan Foundation, 1997), the catalogue of an exhibition of the same name; the essay by Andrew Gerstle and Sakurai Hiroshi, 'Margins Between the Real and Unreal: Bunraku,' 134–41 is of special interest. Laurie J. Sears, *Shadows of Empire: Colonial Discourse and Javanese Tales* (Durham: Duke University Press, 1996), 30–3 explores puppet metaphysics, including questions of history, myth, and nation building. The force of Asia and the old 'Orient' as a shaper of thinking about puppets and shadows continues in recent scholarship. For current research on shadow theatre and

related subjects, see the bibliography compiled by Geneviève Leleu-Rouvray and Gladys Langevin under the heading 'Théâtre d'ombres' in *Bibliographie internationale de la marionette* (Munich and Paris: K.G. Saur, 1993).

41 T.J. Clark, *The Painting of Modern Life* (New York: Alfred Knopf, 1985); see introduction and chapter 1 on the theory of spectacle. See also 'Modernity and the Virtual Gaze,' in Anne Friedberg, *Window Shopping: Cinema and the Postmodern* (Berkeley: University of California Press, 1993), 20–9.

42 For Comolli's use of the formula 'the frenzy of the visible' see Jean-Louis Comolli, 'Machines of the Visible,' in *The Cinematic Apparatus*, ed. Teresa de Lauretis and Stephen Heath (New York: St. Martin's Press, 1985), 122. Splendid extrapolations of this phrase can be found in Vanessa R. Schwartz, 'Museums and Mass Spectacle: The Musée Grevin as a Monument to Modern Life,' *French Historical Studies* 19 (Spring 1995), 9.

43 Neuville, *Ombres chinoises*, 143.

44 Press accounts, *Les annales*, 28 April 1896; *Gorky*, 4 July 1896, quoted in Emanuelle Toulet, *Cinématographe, invention du siècle* (Paris: Gallimard, 1988), 137.

45 O. Alber-Graves, *Les Petits secrets du prestidigitation* (Paris: Mazo, 1908), 8–9.

46 See the shadow images of 'La Ville moderne' in Georges Fragerolle and Henri Riviere, *Le Juif Errant* (Paris: Enoch and Co., 1898), 39. Collection of the Zimmerli Museum.

CHAPTER THIRTEEN

Primitivism in Sweden: Dormant Desire or Fictional Identity?

Michelle Facos

At the turn of the century, a group of prominent Swedish artists and intellectuals definitively reclassified the term 'primitive' for their compatriots. While they never questioned the fact that Sweden's landscape and population were primitive, the term shifted in the 1890s from a designation with distinctly pejorative connotations to one of high praise. What occasioned this transformation? Was it an instance of 'feel good' propaganda in a small country on the periphery of Europe, or did it represent a more profound understanding and acceptance of Swedish culture and geography? Was this re-evaluation historically and/or culturally grounded, or was it constructed by bourgeois intellectuals to further ideological objectives? Finally, in what way was Sweden construed as primitive?

Gill Perry has observed that in the late nineteenth century, the term primitive was used 'to distinguish contemporary European societies and their cultures from other societies and their cultures that were then considered less civilised,'[1] and this was certainly true in Sweden. Indeed, Swedish artists and intellectuals at the time were preoccupied with primitivism, even though thoughts of Tahiti, Indonesia, or sub-Saharan Africa never entered their consciousness in part because Sweden was not a colonialist power. Instead, they thought of themselves and their own country as primitive. And while primitivism was integral to Sweden's national self-definition, it presented an unresolvable and peculiarly modernist paradox for the artists and intellectuals who fostered it.

The case of Sweden, and of the Nordic countries in general, challenges the normative conception of primitivism, which posits the dualistic existence of a civilised Self and a barbarous Other – *our* Western culture defined in categorical opposition to *their* tribal culture. In turn-of-the-century Sweden, while primitivism was also understood dialectically, it elided these categories of Self and Other. There, Self was indigenous and primitive while Other was non-Nordic and urbane. Thus in the 1890s, when a Swedish artist in Italy was queried about his next destination, he could proudly reply, 'Now I am on the way home – home to the land of the barbarians!'[2]

How could Sweden, the land of Ingmar Bergman, Volvos, legal rights for hetero- and homosexual partnerships, and the rock group Abba, have been construed as primitive by Swedish intellectuals at the end of the nineteenth century? Certainly even then, in some arenas, Sweden was more advanced than France, the litmus test for modern civilization. For example, in 1900 about 25 per cent of France's labour force was unionized; in Sweden it was closer to 75 per cent. As early as 1800, literacy in Sweden was almost 100 per cent, while in France it was less than 30 per cent. In Sweden, a system of free universal education was established in 1842, some forty years earlier than in France,[3] and women could enter Swedish universities beginning in 1870, while in France it was not until the twentieth-century that this became a possibility. From a social standpoint, then, late-nineteenth-century Sweden was anything but uncivilized. But these factors were not indices of primitivism according to Swedish intellectuals, who thought of primitivism in larger geographical, demographic, and spiritual terms. Nonetheless, literacy and universal education are particularly important in the context of the current discussion, since they were essential preconditions for the formation of a consensual, generic, national identity.

By some standards, Sweden was primitive. In addition to being sparsely populated and blessed by large tracts of wilderness, by century's end, Sweden's economy was still overwhelmingly agricultural, while that of France was largely industrial. Modern amenities such as electricity and railway travel were slow to arrive on the European margins, as were the latest continental fashions in dress, interior decor, and leisure activity. Staples of Parisian life such as cafe-concerts, music halls, race tracks, and recreational parks were virtually unknown in Stockholm until the 1890s. And not only was Stockholm far from Paris; its population was much smaller – 300,000 in 1900, compared with more than two and a half million in Paris.[4] Furthermore, since the eighteenth century, and reinforced by the installation of a Napoleonic general as king in 1810, Sweden's ruling classes had looked to Paris as a barometer for judging the status of their own socio-cultural affairs, which they did according to rather superficial and materialistic standards. In their society, where implicit trust in authority predominated, insecurity about the inherent worth of their culture was a trait seemingly ubiquitous among affluent, well-educated Swedes.

Thus to Swedes travelling abroad, compatriots at home seemed provincial, and the predominantly uncultivated Swedish landscape, veritably primordial. Artists were particularly disheartened by the harsh and rugged character of Swedish nature compared to the gentler contours of the open terrain to the south. Richard Bergh (1858–1919), the most theoretical of progressive Swedish artists at the turn of the century, reluctantly observed in the 1880s that 'Sweden was not the land for art' because it lacked visual harmony.[5] Indeed, several dozen Swedish painters spent their formative years during the 1870s and 1880s in Paris, an experience that provided a dialectical structure critical to their perception of Sweden as a primitive land. Like previous generations of Swedish painters, they emulated styles that were current in Paris. They adopted naturalism and impressionism as artistic strategies, and used them to try to tame wild Swedish nature. For instance, while winter was (and is) one of the most distinguishing aspects of Nordic life, Karl Nordström (1855–1923) ignored its most salient feature – darkness – in his painting *Winter Landscape – Djurgården* (fig. 13.1). Painted in Stockholm during the winter of 1889, its subject matter, composition, and technique owed much to such French precedents such as Claude Monet's *The Skate* of 1869 (fig. 13.2). Like Monet, Nordström employed a thick impasto to evoke the deep, glistening snow of a bright winter day, preferring to concentrate on the effects of light and atmosphere rather than on narrative. Ironically, impressionist concentration on transitory moments is more poignant in Nordström's work, since at mid-winter Stockholm experiences only about four hours of broad daylight. The spindly branches projecting in the right foreground suggest Nordström's familiarity not only with French impressionism, but also with Japanese prints, whose compositional innovations he borrowed. At that time, such appropriations confirmed his stature as an urbane and sophisticated young artist.

Nordström's colleague Nils Kreuger (1858–1930) was one of the most gifted of all Swedish impressionists, specializing during the 1880s in the sort of village street scenes typical of Sisley, Pissarro, and Monet in the 1860s and 1870s. In Kreuger's *Autumn, Varberg* of 1888 (fig. 13.3), depicting what would soon be a resort town on Sweden's west coast, he evoked the tranquillity of small-town life in a manner reminiscent of Monet's 1879 *Village Street in Vetheuil* (fig. 13.4). Kreuger, who had worked both in Paris and in the nearby artists' colony in Grèz-sur-Loing, adopted the grey tonalities characteristic of France in order to soften the harsh contrasts that Swedish artists found so distasteful in their native land. Like Nordström, Kreuger deliberately sought vistas close in feeling and structure to those familiar from French naturalism and impressionism, rather than landscapes considered uniquely or typically Nordic.

The initial effect of their Parisian experience on Swedish artists was a negative perception of Sweden as geographically marginal, culturally and intellectually philistine, and aesthetically coarse and unyielding, but by the early 1890s this judgment was reversed, as many of the backward qualities initially despised were now esteemed. This change of heart was motivated by three interrelated factors: an acute sense of being outsiders to Parisian culture; homesickness; and distress at the threat posed to traditional ways of life at home by industrialization and urbanization. The fact that the Swedes associated almost exclusively with the tightly knit band of expatriate Scandinavians living in Paris clearly exacerbated their sense of alienation, as did the escalating anti-Germanic xenophobia promoted by General Boulanger in the 1880s. Furthermore, homesickness, or as it is more poetically expressed in Swedish, homelonging (*hemlängtan*), had a distinctly visceral dimension for Swedes. According to Bergh, the hearts of his Swedish colleagues 'were still up in Nordic nature and their art must, sooner or later, return home to their hearts, to the life-giving spring; since art is an affair of the heart.'[6]

In addition to the geographical evidence of a long, rugged coastline and extensive wilderness tracts, this belief in a biomystical link between a landscape and its inhabitants was the single most important element in Swedish primitivism. Its existence was supported by a long tradition of ethnographic writings, beginning with the first-century Roman historian Tacitus, whose *Germania* described the character and habits of Germanic peoples as inextricably linked to their forest environment. In the sixteenth century, Olaus Magnus recorded his Scandinavian travels in the widely published *Carta marina*. Eighteenth-century German romantic writers such as Johann Gottfried von Herder and Friedrich Wilhelm von Schelling reinforced this notion, followed by the folkish philosopher Wilhelm Heinrich Riehl, whose 1855 tract *The Natural History of the German People* asserted the fusion of landscape and history. Not only was the existence of such a linkage accepted as self-evident by Swedish intellectuals, but also the necessity of acknowledging and maintaining this relationship was considered by them to be essential to the psychic well-being of individuals and the survival of society as a whole. Some artists 'felt' more primitive than others. In a letter, Nordström reminded a friend, 'I am a wild animal – remember that!'[7]

Swedes from all regions and classes were exposed to biomystical ideas beginning in the 1840s, the decade in which a national educational curriculum was instituted. Official school books were peppered with stories and poems about the symbiotic, non-hierarchical relationship between Nordic people and nature. The generation of 1890, which had been thus indoctrinated, produced volumes of poems of which Hugo Gyllander's is typical:

> With the land, I was one. And growing together
> with earth I enjoyed life's simple fullness in long
> breaths; and all the old, sick desires,
> that plague human happiness,
> dimmed like lamps without oil.
> But heat streamed from on high,
> and sap rose from deep tracts
> through my limbs, and I stretched my arms
> toward the sun, like pines, in silent prayer to life-giving warmth.[8]

This feeling of unity with nature struck the artist Prince Eugen (1865–1947) in an epiphanic moment in the forests of southern Sweden. *The Forest* (fig. 13.5), painted in 1892, was his attempt to communicate the experience of self-dissolution among the fir trees. Immersed among the pillars of this silent forest, the viewer is offered no secure vantage point; human presence is effaced in this pantheistic, iconic space. The painted surface becomes a participatory tableau for the dedifferentiated Swedish consciousness to regain its primitive harmony with nature, latently lurking in the collective, intracultural psyche. Paintings such as *The Forest* were based on the premise that authentic expressions of one's innermost being reflected ideas and feelings that were common to all members of a culture – a notion that presupposed a fundamental homogeneity of character and values. These national romantic paintings incorporated levels of meaning specifically targeted to a Swedish audience. For instance, the fir tree has symbolic meaning for Swedes. 'In this heathen landscape,' one twentieth-century scholar writes, 'it represents directness in growth, in will, and in character, and even speaks to those properly attuned to its voice.'[9] In Victor Rydberg's poem 'Listen to the Firs by Your Mother's Cottage,' the trees surrounding his childhood home spoke to him of memories long forgotten. And in his reminiscences of an extended stay in Italy, Richard Bergh wrote wistfully of the familial relationship between Swedes and firs:

> The bells stopped ringing, one by one, and finally I heard only the whispering of the pine trees. It sounded like the whispering in a fir forest. – A fir forest! That tore at my breast. Immediately I was overcome by a longing, an irresistible longing for Sweden, the quiet, white land in the north. I now saw it at once so clearly before me, so still, so clear and beautiful under its clean blanket of snow! Involuntarily, I stretched out my arms. Then my eyes fell on the pines; and my arms fell. Suddenly they seemed so strange to me. Never could I be motivated to take one of these fine trees, pines or cypresses, in my arms ... No, spruce and fir, they are of the same timber as my own family – we are brothers. Them, I can take in my arms. – How I longed at that moment to be able to do just that! – Never – I felt that immediately – could I paint a pine with the same love as a fir ... we have no memories in common, you beautiful trees![10]

Still, one cannot judge a nation's primitiveness based solely on the nostalgic yearnings of a painter on holiday. While Sweden was less cosmopolitan, less industrialised, and more sparsely populated than France – that is, more primitive in an economic and geographic sense – was Sweden culturally more primitive? Did atavistic, pantheistic practices and beliefs survive in turn-of-the-century Sweden? The answer is yes. Relics of the primitive past were plentiful and in plain sight. Nordström was among the national romantic artists who reminded Swedes of the survival of highly visible material remains from their distant past. Until the end of the Viking age in the twelfth century, grave mounds such as that in Nordström's *Grave Mound from Tjörn* (fig. 13.6) were erected to mark the burial sites of important persons, and in Nordström's day, folklore was rife with superstitious tales about these configurations. Sometimes they were thought to be gravemarkers of historical figures or giants; other times they were considered to be the homes of trolls or the sites of buried treasure. In contrast to *Winter Landscape – Djurgården*, Nordström not only chose a specifically Nordic motif, but created a mysterious atmosphere, similar to that of Prince Eugen's painting, that was designed to evoke an emotional rather than a perceptual response in the viewer. Emphasizing the geographically and culturally primitive character of Sweden necessitated a shift in conceptual strategy from clarity and rationalism to mystery and imagination.

Without a doubt, pantheism did constitute an integral element of daily life in rural Sweden, and the populace believed in a rich store of folklore, superstitions, and legends. Every house was thought to possess a resident elf or '*tomte*' who could be helpful or mischievous depending on how well he was treated. The sudden appearance of storm clouds was thought to indicate the nearby existence of a troll for whom Thor was hunting, and dozens of practices were variously followed in order to prevent being caught in the crossfire. One of many documented incidents of traditional superstitious behaviour was recorded in 1891 when a farmer, in order to acclimate his cows, walked them counterclockwise three times around a large stone before leading them to the barn.[11] And as late as 1919, there was a serious newspaper account about a stone field being the primordial result of giants dumping aprons full of boulders onto the landscape.[12] At the turn of the century, pantheistic beliefs and practices seem to have been far more widespread in Sweden than in western Europe.

One possible reason for this is that Christianity came to Sweden rather late – the tenth century – and did not gain a toehold in Uppsala, Sweden's medieval capital, until the end of the eleventh century. Experience proved that attempting to eradicate folk beliefs only strengthened anti-Christian sentiments, motivating missionaries to reluctantly accept the coexistence of pagan attitudes with Christian doctrine. Attempts to assimilate pagan celebrations (such as turning the observance of winter solstice into Christmas and the summer solstice into St John's Day) proved only marginally successful.

For many, the most important holiday in the Swedish calendar is not Christmas, Easter, or the national holiday, but Midsummer. It expresses metahistorical and intracultural bonds that reach deep into Sweden's atavistic, agrarian past. Initially a summer solstice celebration, Midsummer is a uniquely Swedish holiday whose observation elsewhere in Scandinavia is of recent vintage. In the late nineteenth century, midsummer constituted a socially sanctioned, ritualistic suspension of strictures against debauchery and an indulgence in 'primitive' passions; it was said that a couple falling in love at Midsummer would eventually marry. Anders Zorn documented the evening's less controversial festivities in his painting *Midsummer Dance* of 1897 (fig. 13.7). Here peasants execute traditional couple dances to a fiddler's melody in the eternal light of a Nordic summer evening, an event with which even urban bourgeois Swedes would identify. While *Midsummer Dance* evidences the survival of pagan rituals in late nineteenth-century Sweden, it also raises questions for modern viewers. The fact that Lutheran strictures against drinking and dancing all but annihilated Midsummer celebrations by the late nineteenth century and that the village-specific peasant costumes worn by the dancers were only codified during the nineteenth century, necessitates a re-examination of the meaning of this image. What were Zorn's reasons for recording this event, and what motivated the revival of Midsummer celebrations in the first place?

The subject itself was suggested by Prince Eugen, who never painted any sort of peasant celebration himself. In the summer of 1896, the Prince was Zorn's Midsummer guest at his ancestral home in Mora, located in central Sweden. Prince Eugen, as his title would indicate, was an outsider to Swedish peasant culture. Still, he was enchanted by the rituals enacted by the natives of the nearby village of Morkarlby as much as he was baffled by their unusual dialect, which he had tremendous difficulty understanding. The inhabitants of this particular region, Dalarna, had relatively little contact with outsiders over the centuries, and they embodied for the Prince a degree of ethnic authenticity, of primitivism, that he had never before encountered. In the context of the dialectical recognition of Otherness and primitivism, the fact that the Prince, and not Zorn, perceived the significance of this particular Midsummer celebration is noteworthy. Since its creation, *Midsummer Dance* has often been used both in school books and in advertising to promote a positive image of Sweden's cultural primitivism.

It is no accident that the 1890s was the decade when bourgeois intellectuals, including artists, rediscovered their primitive roots. Just as the perception of Sweden as primitive evolved dialectically in relation to experiences in France, so the positive connotation that primitivism assumed was directly related to radical social and economic transformations that were occurring in Sweden at the time. For the first time in history, the balance between agriculture and industry tipped decisively towards industry, precipitating a sharp and steady decline which has continued to the present day. Assembly lines and mechanized production were introduced, facilitating a vast increase in the production of export items such as telephones, toothpicks, paper, and raw lumber,[13] and the development of electrical motors in the mid-1890s paved the way for rapid industrial growth.

Many Swedish intellectuals were alarmed by the implications of such radical transformations. They felt it necessary to formulate a strategy for dealing with these changes in order to prevent socially-debilitating consequences. In Sweden, there was general sympathy for socialist worries about the dangers of fetishizing commodities and rationalizing labour, motivated by the fear that these tendencies would have devastating social and environmental consequences. Pointing to the United States, Swedish feminist Ellen Key warned that political democracy combined with economic capitalism led directly to social tyranny, and this was an eventuality she and her colleagues wished to avoid.[14] This is not to say that the cultural conservatism of bourgeois intellectuals in Sweden was accompanied by a desire to turn back the clock to a fictional and idyllic golden age of Swedish rural life. They were in favour (or at least recognised the inevitability) of industrialization and urbanization, but they insisted on the subordination of these trends to larger issues of individual and societal well-being.

Richard Bergh's painting *Nordic Summer Evening* (1899–1900, fig. 13.8) expressed the quandary of turn-of-the-century Swedish intellectuals: their recognition of indigenous primitivism obviated the possibility of their truly experiencing it. On one level, the subject of this painting is the importance of nature as sustenance for the Swedish soul. Two figures, a man and a woman, stand as equals, physically separate but spiritually united in contemplation of a tranquil, twilight landscape. While this painting is about solidarity, it is also about irreconcilable differences – not between the sexes (on the verge of what a *New York Times* writer termed 'a Strindbergian outburst'[14]) but between people, specifically bourgeois people, and nature. Clearly, the figures are upper class (the king's youngest son, Prince Eugen, modelled for the man) and the decorative carpentry belongs to a typical turn-of-the-century summer villa (Ekholmsnas, on the island of Lidingö, now an Arabian horse farm within Stockholm city limits). The figures stand on the balcony, gently but decisively separated from the vista they contemplate. In this setting, Bergh revealed the ultimate paradox afflicting his nature-loving compatriots – the desire to exist in biomystical unity with nature manifests a level of consciousness precluding such a condition. Indeed, Ellen Key observed that urbanites, particularly affluent ones, were incapable of getting as close to nature as those whose entire development was closely tied to the land.[16] As with the expulsion from the Garden of Eden, once cognisant of separation, reunification is no longer an option. Like selfless *bodhisattvas*, Swedish intellectuals relinquished, willingly or not, the possibility of Enlightenment in a pantheistic sense in order to help others maintain it. Bergh created a pictorial metaphor for the ultimate tragedy of Sweden's turn-of-the-century, bourgeois intellectuals: they could promote primitivism and they might even be acculturated into certain aspects of it, but they could never fully attain it themselves.

Still, the vital importance of activating one's latent biomystical relationship with nature to the greatest extent possible was a clear priority for national romantic intellectuals, and it was particularly important for Sweden's bourgeoisie, the audience to whom these works of art were primarily directed. For it was in the hands of this class that the future of Sweden lay; it was from this group that legislators, educators, and captains of industry came. If one could demonstrate to them the benefit, if not the necessity, of asserting their primitive, Swedish identity, the world envisioned by turn-of-the-century, national romantic intellectuals would be that much closer to realization.

If Bergh's painting manifests the reality confronting Swedish bourgeois intellectuals seeking union with nature, Gustaf Fjaestad's 1898 painting *The Boy Who Sees with His Heart* (fig. 13.9) embodied their dream. The youth, rooted in both earth and water, has his haloed head thrown back in ecstatic immersion in nature. His green complexion is in harmony with his environment and his burning heart attests to his bio-emotional linkage with it. Embedded in a gilded frame of the artist's own design, the image functions as an icon of Swedish nature primitivism.

But *is* there something inherently primitive about the Nordic psyche? The most recent Swedish research in ethnology and the history of ideas suggests that there may well be. One scholar has suggested that, 'Nordic culture differs from Continental Culture, whose roots are deep in classical antiquity, feudalism, and the Catholic Church. "Barbarism" had a different set of legal concepts than "Civilization," a different feeling for nature, different social organization, and differing norms of individual behavior.'[17]

NOTES

1 Gill Perry, 'Primitivism and the Modern,' in Charles Harrison, Francis Frascina, and Gill Perry, *Primitivism, Cubism, Abstraction: The Early Twentieth Century* (New Haven: Yale University Press, 1993), 5.

2 Related in Richard Bergh, 'Svenskt konstnärskynne,' in *Om konst och annat* (Stockholm: Albert Bonniers, 1919), 166.
3 Roger Price, *A Social History of Nineteenth-Century France* (New York: Holmes and Meier, 1987), 321. Beginning in the sixteenth century, the state Lutheran church in Sweden required all adults to undergo an annual literacy test given by parish priests. While the motivation was to encourage Bible reading, the result was an unusually high literacy rate.
4 Franklin D. Scott, *Sweden: The Nation's History*, enlarged edition (Carbondale: Southern Illinois University Press, 1988), 344.
5 Bergh, 'Svenskt konstnärskynne,' 151.
6 Richard Bergh, *Hvad vår kamp gällt* (Stockholm: 1905), 10.
7 Quoted in Torsten Svedfelt, *Karl Nordströms konst* (Stockholm: Nordisk Rotogravyr, 1939), 7.
8 Hygo Gyllander, 'Blodet och språket,' in Hygo Gyllander, *Rytmer* (Stockholm: Albert Bonniers, 1925).
9 Ragnar Josephson, *Nationalism och Humanism* (Stockholm, 1935), 117.
10 Bergh, 'Svenskt konstnärskynne,' 156.
11 Donald Ray Floyd, 'Attitudes Towards Nature in Swedish Folklore' (PhD diss., University of California, Berkeley, 1976), 331.
12 Floyd, 'Attitudes towards Nature,' 413.
13 Jan Hult, 'Industrinationens födelse,' in *90tal. Visioner och vägval*, ed. Hans Mendelius and Sten Rentzog (Stockholm: 1991), 65–7.
14 Ellen Key, *Individualism och socialism* (Stockholm: Albert Bonniers, 1901), 34.
15 Penelope Lively, 'The Sophisticated Traveller: Sweden's Two Aquatic Cities,' *New York Times* 3 March 1991, 45.
16 Key, *Individualism*, 39.
17 Bjorn Tordsson, 'Rotter I "Barbari" och "Romantik,"' in *Friluftshistoria Franihardanda Friluftsliv Till Ekoturism och Miljöpedagogik*, ed. Klas Sandell and Sverker Sorlin (Stockholm: Carlssons, 2000), 51. Historical circumstances largely determine the attractiveness of considering oneself civilized or barbarian, and in the country with the highest per capita computer density, it is interesting to see scholars tenaciously asserting Sweden's primitiveness.

Selected Bibliography

Anderson, Benedict. *Imagined Communities: Reflections on the Origins and Spread of Nationalism*. Revised edition. London: Verso, 1991.

Arnott, Peter. *Plays without People: Puppetry and Serious Drama*. Bloomington: Indiana University Press, 1964.

Barkan, Elazar, and Ronald Bush. *Prehistories of the Future: The Primitivist Project and the Culture of Modernism*. Stanford: Stanford University Press, 1995.

Barthes, Roland. *Mythologies*. Translated by Annette Lavers. Frogmore, St Albans: Paladin, 1973.

– *Image Music Text*. Translated by Stephen Heath. London: Fontana, 1977.

Baudelaire, Charles. *The Painter of Modern Life and Other Essays*. Translated by Jonathan Mayne. New York: Phaidon Press, 1964.

Bederman, Gail. *Manliness and Civilization: A Cultural History of Gender and Race in the United States 1880–1917*. Chicago: University of Chicago Press, 1995.

Bennett, Tony. *The Birth of the Museum: History, Theory, Politics*. New York: Routledge, 1995.

Bériau, Oscar. 'The Handicraft Renaissance in Quebec.' *Canadian Geographical Journal* 7 (September 1933), 143–9.

Berman, Marshall. 'The Experience of Modernity.' In *Design after Modernism*, ed. John Thackara. New York: Thames & Hudson, 1988.

Bhabha, Homi. 'The Other Question: Difference, Discrimination and the Discourse of Colonialism.' In *Literature, Politics and Theory*, edited by Francis Barker et al., 148–72. New York, Methuen, 1986.

Blake, Nigel and Francis Frascina. 'Modern Practices of Art and Modernity.' In *Modernity and Modernism: French Painting in the Nineteenth Century*, edited by Francis Frascina et al., 50–140. New Haven and London: Yale University Press in Association with the Open University, 1993.

Boime, Albert. 'Van Gogh's Starry Night: A History of Matter and a Matter of History.' *Arts Magazine* 59 (December 1984), 86–103.

Bongie, Chris. *Exotic Memories: Literature, Colonialism and the Fin-de-siècle*. Stanford: Stanford University Press, 1991.

Bourdieu, Pierre. *The Field of Cultural Production: Essays on Art and Literature*. Edited by Randal Johnson. New York: Columbia University Press, 1993.

Carr, Emily. *Klee Wyck*. Toronto: Oxford University Press, 1941.

Cate, Phillip Dennis, and Mary Shaw, eds. *The Spirit of Montmartre: Cabarets, Humor, and the Avant-Garde*. New Brunswick, N.J.: Jane Voohees Zimmerli Art Museum, 1996.

Celestin, Roger. *From Cannibals to Radicals: Figures and Limits of Exoticism*. Minneapolis and London: University of Minnesota Press, 1996.

Clark, T.J. *Image of the People: Gustave Courbet and the 1848 Revolution*. London: Thames and Hudson, 1973.

Clifford, James. 'On Ethnographic Allegory.' In *Writing Culture: The Poetics and Politics of Ethnography*, edited by James Clifford and George Marcus, 99–121. Berkeley: University of California Press, 1986.

– *The Predicament of Culture: Twentieth-Century Ethnography, Literature, and Art*. Cambridge, Mass.: Harvard University Press, 1988.

Cromarty, Constance. 'Seigniories – Weaving-Looms and Homespuns: An Article on the Quaint Old French Settlements Along the North Shore of the Lower St. Lawrence.' *The Canadian Magazine* 63 (August 1924), 198–204.

Danielsson, Bengt. *Gauguin in the South Seas*. New York: Doubleday, 1966.

Danto, Arthur. *The Philosophical Disenfranchisement of Art*. New York: Columbia University Press, 1986.

Dickson, Lovat. *The Museum Makers: The Story of the Royal Ontario Museum*. Toronto: Royal Ontario Museum, 1986.

Dyck, Noel, and James Waldram, eds. *Anthropology, Public Policy, and Native Peoples in Canada*. Kingston and Montreal: McGill-Queen's University Press, 1993.

Eddy, John, and Deryck Schreuder, eds. *The Rise of Colonial Nationalism: Australia, New Zealand, Canada and South Africa First Assert Their Nationalities, 1880–1914*. Sydney: Allan & Unwin, 1988.

Elliott, Bridget, and Jo-Anne Wallace. *Women Artists and Writers: Modernist (im)positionings*. London: Routledge, 1994.

Evett, Elisa. 'The Late Nineteenth-Century European Critical Response to Japanese Art: Primitivist Leanings.' *Art History* 6 (March 1983), 82–106.

Fabian, Johannes. *Time and the Other: How Anthropology Makes Its Object*. New York: Columbia University Press, 1983.

Fanon, Frantz. *Black Skin, White Masks*. Translated by Charles Lam Markmann. New York: Grove Press, 1967.

Field, Richard. *Paul Gauguin: The Paintings of the First Voyage to Tahiti*. New York: Garland, 1977.

Francis, Daniel. *The Imaginary Indian: The Image of the Indian in Canadian Culture*. Vancouver: Arsenal Pulp Press, 1992.

Goldie, Terry. *Fear and Temptation, The Image of the Indigene in Canadian, Australian and New Zealand Literatures*. Kingston and Montreal: McGill-Queen's University Press, 1989.

Green, Nicholas. 'Dealing in Temperaments: Economic Transformation of the Artistic Field in France during the Second Half of the Nineteenth Century.' *Art History* 10 (March 1987), 59–78.

Guest, Harriet. 'Curiously Marked: Tattooing, Masculinity and Nationality in

Eighteenth-century British Perceptions of the South Pacific.' In *Painting and the Politics of Culture*, edited by John Barrell, 101–34. Oxford: Oxford University Press, 1992.

Handler, Richard. 'In Search of the Folk Society: Nationalism and Folklore Studies in Quebec.' *Culture* 3 (1983), 103–14.

Hill, Charles. *The Group of Seven: Art for a Nation*. Ottawa and Toronto: National Gallery of Canada and McClelland & Stewart, 1995.

Hiller, Susan, ed. *The Myth of Primitivism: Perspectives on Art*. London and New York: Routledge, 1991.

Jessup, Lynda. 'Canadian Artists, Railways, the State and "The Business of Becoming a Nation."' PhD diss., University of Toronto, 1992.

– 'Prospectors, Bushwackers, Painters: Antimodernism and the Group of Seven.' *International Journal of Canadian Studies/Revue Internationale d'études canadiennes* 17 (Spring/printemps 1998), 193–214.

Jirat-Wasiutyński, Vojtěch. 1993. 'Vincent van Gogh's Paintings of Olive Trees and Cypresses from St.-Remy.' *Art Bulletin* 75 (1973), 647–70.

Johnson, Ron. 'Vincent van Gogh and the Vernacular: His Southern Accent.' *Arts Magazine* 52 (June 1978), 131–5.

Kodera, Tsukasa. 'Japan as Primitivistic Utopia: Van Gogh's Japonisme Portraits.' *Simiolus* 14 (1984), 189–208.

Lagarde, Emile. *Ombres chinoises, guignol, marionettes*. Paris: Louis Chaux, 1900.

Lears, T. Jackson. *No Place of Grace: Antimodernism and the Transformation of American Culture, 1880–1920*. New York: Pantheon Books, 1981.

Lloyd, Jill. *German Expressionism: Primitivism and Modernity*. New Haven and London: Yale University Press, 1991.

Lowe, Lisa. *Critical Terrains: French and British Orientalisms*. Ithaca and London: Cornell University Press, 1991.

Lyman, John. 'Hunting the Primitive in Canada.' *The Montrealer*, 1 January 1938.

Marcus, George E., and Fred R. Myers, eds. *The Traffic in Culture: Reconfiguring Art and Anthropology*. Berkeley: University of California Press, 1995.

Mason, Peter. *Infelicities: Representations of the Exotic*. Baltimore and London: Johns Hopkins University Press, 1998.

MacKenzie, John M. *Orientalism: History, Theory and the Arts*. Manchester: Manchester University Press, 1995.

Mackley, Florence. *Handweaving in Cape Breton*. Sydney: privately published, 1967.

McKay, Ian, ed. *The Challenge of Modernity: A Reader on Post-Confederation Canada*. Toronto: McGraw-Hill Ryerson, 1992.

– *The Quest of the Folk: Antimodernism and Cultural Selection in Twentieth-Century Nova Scotia*. Kingston and Montreal: McGill-Queen's University Press, 1994.

Major, Marjorie. 'History of the Nova Scotia Tartan.' *Nova Scotia Historical Quarterly* 2 (June 1976), 191–214.

Miller, Christopher L. *Blank Darkness: Africanist Discourse in French*. Chicago and London: University of Chicago Press, 1985.

Myers, Fred. 'Representing Culture: The Production of Discourse(s) for Aboriginal Acrylic Paintings.' *Cultural Anthropology* 6 (1991), 26–62.

Naremore, James and Patrick Brantlinger, eds. *Modernity and Mass Culture*. Bloomington and Indianapolis: Indiana University Press, 1991.

Nye, Robert. 'Degeneration and the Medical Model of Cultural Crisis in the French Belle Epoque.' In *Political Symbolism in Modern Europe: Essays in Honor of George L. Mosse*, edited by Seymour Drescher, David Sabean, and Allan Sharlin, 19–41. New Brunswick, N.J.: Transaction Books, 1982.

Pearce, Harvey. *Savagism and Civilization: A Study of the Indian and the American Mind*, revised edition. Berkeley: University of California Press, 1988.

Perry, Gill, Charles Harrison, and Francis Frascina. *Primitivism, Cubism, Abstraction: The Early Twentieth Century*. New Haven: Yale University Press in association with the Open University, 1993.

Pevsner, Nikolaus. *Pioneers of the Modern Movement from William Morris to Walter Gropius*. London: Faber & Faber, 1936.

Phillips, Ruth B. *Trading Identities: Souvenir Arts in Northeastern North America, 1700–1900*. Seattle: University of Washington Press, 1998.

Pollock, Griselda. *Avant-Garde Gambits 1888–1893: Gender and the Color of Art History*. New York: Thames and Hudson, 1992.

Prakash, Gyan, ed. *After Colonialism: Imperial Histories and Postcolonial Displacements*. Princeton: Princeton University Press, 1995.

Price, Sally. *Primitive Art in Civilized Places*. Chicago: University of Chicago Press, 1989.

Reid, Dennis. *Le Groupe des sept/The Group of Seven*. Ottawa: National Gallery of Canada, 1970.

Rhodes, Colin. *Primitivism in Modern Art*. New York: Thames & Hudson, 1994.

Rubin, William, ed. *'Primitivism' in 20th Century Art: Affinity of the Tribal and Modern*. 2 vols. New York: Museum of Modern Art, 1984.

Rushing, William Jackson. *Native American Art and Culture and the New York Avant-Garde*. Ann Arbor: University Microfilms International, 1990.

Rutherford, Jonathan, ed. *Identity, Community, Culture, Difference*. London: Lawrence and Wishart, 1990

Said, Edward. *Orientalism*. New York: Pantheon Press, 1978.

Seigel, Jerrold. *Bohemian Paris: Culture, Politics, and the Boundaries of Bourgeois Life, 1830–1930*. New York: Penguin, 1986.

Shaw, Christopher, and Malcolm Chase, eds. *The Imagined Past: History and Nostalgia*. Manchester and New York: Manchester University Press and St Martin's Press, 1989.

Silverman, Debora. *Art Nouveau in Fin-de-siècle France: Politics, Psychology, and Style*. Berkeley: University of California Press, 1989.

Soja, Edward. 'History: Geography: Modernity.' In *The Cultural Studies Reader*, edited by Simon During, 135–50. London and New York: Routledge, 1993.

Solomon-Godeau, Abigail. 'Going Native.' *Art in America* 77 (July 1989), 119–28.

Sontag, Susan. *On Photography*. Harmondsworth, UK: Penguin, 1978.

Stewart, Susan. *On Longing: Narratives of the Miniature, the Gigantic, the Souvenir, the Collection*. Durham, North Carolina: Duke University Press, 1993.

Stocking, George, ed. *Objects and Others: Essays on Museums and Material Culture*. Madison: University of Wisconsin Press, 1985.

Strain, Ellen. 'Exotic Bodies, Distant Landscapes: Touristic Viewing and Popularized Anthropology in the Nineteenth Century.' *Wide Angle* 18 (April 1996).

Teilhet-Fisk, Jehanne. *Paradise Reviewed: An Interpretation of Gauguin's Polynesian Symbolism*. Ann Arbor: UMI Research Press, 1983.

Tillis, Steve. *Toward an Aesthetics of the Puppet: Puppetry as a Theatrical Art*. New York: Greenwood Press, 1997.

Tooby, Michael, ed. *The True North: Canadian Landscape Painting, 1896–1939*. London: Lund Humphries with the Barbicon Art Gallery, 1991.

Torgovnick, Marianne. *Gone Primitive: Savage Intellects, Modern Lives*. Chicago: University of Chicago Press, 1990.

Trofimenkoff, Susan. *The Dream of Nation: A Social and Intellectual History of Quebec*. Toronto: Gage, 1983.

Warner Marien, Mary, ed. *Photography and Its Critics: A Cultural History 1839–1900*. New York: Cambridge University Press, 1997.

Whisnant, David. *All That Is Native & Fine: The Politics of Culture in an American Region*. Chapel Hill and London: University of North Carolina Press, 1983.

Williams, Raymond. *The Country and the City*. New York: Oxford University Press, 1973; Frogmore, St Albans: Paladin, 1975.

Wolff, Larry. *Inventing Eastern Europe: The Map of Civilization in the Mind of the Enlightenment*. Stanford: Stanford University Press, 1994.

Zemel, Carol. *Van Gogh's Progress: Utopia, Modernity and Late-Nineteenth-Century Art*. Berkeley, Los Angeles and London: University of California Press, 1997.

Contributors

Benedict Anderson, the Aaron L. Binenkorb Professor of International Studies at Cornell University, is author of *Java in a Time of Revolution* (Cornell University Press, 1972); *Imagined Communities: Reflections on the Origin and Spread of Nationalism* (Verso, 1983); *Language and Power: Exploring Political Cultures in Indonesia* (Cornell University Press, 1990); and *The Spectre of Comparisons: Nationlism, Southeast Asia and the World* (Verso, 1998).

Lora Senechal Carney, associate professor in visual and performing arts at the University of Toronto (Scarborough), has published exhibition catalogues on Canadian artist David Milne and on several other artists, as well as chapters in two books on Milne. She is currently completing *Writing Modern Art in Canada*, a study of texts by modern Canadian artists and their critics and of the effects of the Depression and the Second World War on modernism.

Elizabeth C. Childs is associate professor of art history at Washington University in St Louis. Her research interests include exoticism and colonialism, and she has published essays considering the art of Gauguin, Matisse, and Daumier from this perspective. She has edited *Femmes d'esprit: Women in the Caricature of Honoré Daumier* and *Suspended License: Censorship and the Visual Arts* (University of Washington Press, 1997). The present essay derives from her current research for her next book, *In Search of Paradise: Painting and Photography in fin-de-siècle Tahiti* (University of California Press, forthcoming).

Michelle Facos is associate professor of art history at Indiana University. Her publications include numerous articles on turn-of-the-century Scandinavian painting. She is author of *Nationalism and the Nordic Imagination: Swedish Painting in the 1890s* (University of California Press, 1998).

Lynda Jessup is assistant professor of art history at Queen's University in Kingston, Ontario. She has published essays on Canadian art, cultural politics, and museum representation. She is editor, with Shannon Bagg, of *On Aboriginal Representation in the Gallery* (forthcoming).

Vojtěch Jirat-Wasiutyński is professor of art history at Queen's University in Kingston, Ontario. His research interests include symbolism, modernism, and the history of technique. He has published numerous articles on Gauguin, Van Gogh, and Redon. He is co-author, with H. Travers Newton Jr, of *Technique and Meaning in the Paintings of Paul Gauguin, 1873–1889* (Cambridge University Press, 2000). He is currently working on a book tentatively titled *North and South: The Representation of Provence in Nineteenth-Century Art.*

Matt K. Matsuda is associate professor of modern European history at Rutgers University and has published widely on cultural-intellectual and modernity issues. He is the author of *The Memory of the Modern* (Oxford University Press, 1996), a multidisciplinary study of memory and historical consciousness in the late nineteenth and early twentieth centuries. His current work concerns European, and especially French, conceptions of empire, romance, and the Pacific at the turn of the century.

Ian McKay is professor of history at Queen's University in Kingston, Ontario. His research interests include labour history, tourism, and cultural theory. He has recently published essays on the invention of Scottish traditions in Nova Scotia and on the 'Death of Marx' as an invented bourgeois tradition. He is author of *The Quest of the Folk: Antimodernism and Cultural Selection in Twentieth-Century Nova Scotia* (McGill-Queen's University Press, 1994) and is currently writing a book about the uses of history.

Gerta Moray is associate professor of art history at the University of Guelph. Her research areas include Canadian art, European nineteenth-century art, and feminist perspectives on art history. She has published essays on Emily Carr, Joyce Wieland, Suzy Lake, and other Canadian artists. Her book, *Unsettling Encounters: The 'Indian' Pictures of Emily Carr,* will be published in 2001.

Fred R. Myers is professor and chair of the department of anthropology at New York University and co-editor, with George Marcus, of *The Traffic in Culture: Refiguring Art and Anthropology* (University of California Press, 1995). His publications also include *Pintupi Country, Pintupi Self: Sentiment, Place, and Politics among the Western Desert Aborigines* (University of California Press, 1991).

Amy Ogata is assistant professor at the Bard Graduate Center for Studies in the Decorative Arts. Her work deals with modern European architecture and design history, and her book, entitled *Art Nouveau and the Social Vision of Modern Living,* will be published by Cambridge University Press in 2001.

Ruth B. Phillips is Director of the Museum of Anthropology and professor of art history and anthropology at the University of British Columbia. She has worked in the areas of African and Native American art, focusing in recent years on the arts of Northeastern and Great Lakes peoples. Her recent books are

Trading Identities: The Souvenir in Native North American Art from the Northeast, 1700–1900 (University of Washington Press, 1998), and *Native North American Art*, with Janet Catherine Berlo (Oxford University Press, 1998). She is also co-editor, with Christopher B. Steiner, of *Unpacking Culture: Art and Commodity in Colonial and Postcolonial Worlds* (University of California Press, 1999).

Kim Sawchuk is an associate professor in the department of communications at Concordia University, Montreal, Quebec, where she teaches courses in communications theory, research design, and feminism and the media. Her writings on the media arts have appeared in numerous catalogue essays, magazines, and journals. She is co-editor of *When Pain Strikes* (University of Minnesota Press, 1999) and *Wild Science: Reading Feminism, Medicine and the Media* (Routledge, 2000). Her present research projects include a book on C. Wright Mills.

www.ingramcontent.com/pod-product-compliance
Lightning Source LLC
LaVergne TN
LVHW082006060826
844660LV00028B/1247
* 9 7 8 0 8 0 2 0 8 3 5 4 8 *